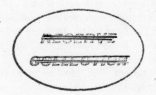

UNWIN UNIVERSITY BOOKS

UNWIN UNIVERSITY BOOKS

5

WELFARE AND COMPETITION

WELFARE AND COMPETITION

The Economics of a
fully employed Economy

TIBOR SCITOVSKY, M.Sc., J.D.

Professor of Economics
Stanford University

LONDON

UNWIN UNIVERSITY BOOKS

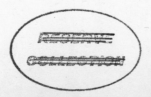

FIRST PUBLISHED IN GREAT BRITAIN IN 1952
SECOND IMPRESSION 1958
THIRD IMPRESSION 1961
REPRINTED IN THIS FORMAT 1963
FIFTH IMPRESSION 1964
SIXTH IMPRESSION 1966

UNWIN UNIVERSITY BOOKS

George Allen and Unwin Ltd.
40 Museum Street, London W.C.1

PRINTED IN GREAT BRITAIN
BY NOVELLO & COMPANY LTD
LONDON

338
.5
SCI

To Anne

PREFACE

THE aim of this book is to bring together price theory and welfare economics. Price theory as currently defined and interpreted comprises an elaborate technique but makes relatively little use of it. This is why so many students of the subject feel that the complexity of its technique is out of all proportion to the main use to which this technique is put: prediction. To predict how a change in costs will affect price, and how a change in price will influence demand, hardly requires a knowledge of indifference-map analysis or of the theory of the firm under pure competition. At the same time, price theory as presented today often fails even to consider the very problems to answer which it was originally developed, and which happen to be among the most essential economic problems of our time. Present-day economists teach the theory of how market prices are determined and how buyers and sellers respond to these prices, but they so often fail to take the further step of examining and appraising the economic organization that results from such behavior.

Many problems of economic policy in this country, the main economic problems of Great Britain and other socialist countries in Europe, as well as the major political issue of the world today—all raise the question of how efficient the market economy is and how its efficiency compares to that of the planned economy. This question and other questions of this type were uppermost in the minds of the classical economists who developed price theory; but the subsequent realization of the limitations of the theory in answering them has gradually led to a change in orientation and to the neglect of welfare economics, the branch of price theory specifically concerned with such questions.

The problem of efficiency, however, is so vital that we cannot ignore it merely because our answers to it are not complete. Welfare economics, despite its limitations, provides a partial answer; and I feel that to provide partial answers to vital problems is at least as important as it is to provide complete answers to lesser questions. This is why, in teaching introductory price theory to seniors and first-year graduate students at Stanford University, I tried to stress the welfare aspects of price theory and to apply each result of price theory to the problem of efficiency in economic organization. This approach proved intellectually satisfying to students and showed the relevance and full usefulness of price theory, but it presented the problem of finding adequate reading material. We possess an ample literature of pure and monopolistic competition at several levels of abstraction and sophistication; but welfare economics, except for a few difficult and highly condensed articles, has never progressed much beyond proving that perfect competition would produce the best of all possible worlds. It was to fill this gap that I tried, in the present volume, to bring together the theory of competition and welfare economics, and to use the latter not merely for stating the conditions of an efficient economic organization but also for appraising the efficiency of our imperfectly competitive economy. This required a more detailed discussion of the meaning and elements of efficiency than is usual. The very detailed exposition of Chapter VIII, for example, may appear tedious; but it seemed essential as a springboard for the further analysis.

I have taken a very long time in writing this book, and so had ample opportunity to ask for and receive the advice of many friends. Chapters II, XII, XIII, XV, XVIII, and the Note to Chapter VII were written almost ten years ago and formed part of an unpublished monograph on the behavior of the firm under monopolistic competition. This was read and criticized by Mrs. Joan Robinson and Professor Abba P. Lerner, and I owe much to their comments. In fact, the welfare orientation of this book is partly due to Mrs. Robinson's criticism that the original monograph merely presented a new tool of analysis, which would have to be applied and proved superior in use if it was to be adopted.

In writing the present version of the book, I have had the benefit of help from my colleagues and students at Stanford. I want especially to thank Professors Paul A. Baran, Melvin W. Reder, and Lorie Tarshis for much useful advice. Of the final draft, fourteen chapters were read by Professor Kenneth E. Boulding; and I want to thank him for his valuable comments. The entire manuscript was read by Professor Bernard F. Haley, and his detailed and painstaking criticism and constructive advice made for a great improvement of every aspect of the entire book. I owe him not only a great debt of gratitude but also an apology for having disturbed his sabbatical leave by pursuing him with manuscript throughout his European trip.

Finally, I want to thank my wife, with whom I discussed every problem that arose in the writing of this book as well as most of its arguments and conclusions, and who also read most of the manuscript. I owe to her a great improvement in the organization, clarity, and logical rigor of the argument. The exposition of Chapters VIII, XI, and XII is largely her work. I also want to thank Miss Hazel M. Scott for an excellent typing job, and Mr. Richard D. Irwin and his staff for their patience and help in preparing the manuscript for publication.

TIBOR SCITOVSKY

STANFORD UNIVERSITY
August, 1951

TABLE OF CONTENTS

PART I. INTRODUCTION

PART II. THE PRICE TAKER'S BEHAVIOR AND PERFECT COMPETITION

PART I

Introduction

CHAPTER I

THE SUBJECT MATTER OF ECONOMICS

ECONOMICS is a social science concerned with the administration of scarce resources. Resources are objects and services that are capable of satisfying human wants either directly, or indirectly by helping to produce other objects and services whose use satisfies human wants. The administration of resources does not always create economic problems. Some resources are so plentiful that they are more than sufficient to satisfy completely all the human wants which depend on them. Air, for example, is such a resource. These resources are called free resources; and there is no need for organizing their use, because any waste or inefficiency in their utilization can be made good from their excess supply and need not abridge the satisfaction of human wants.

By contrast, scarce resources are those that are insufficient to fill completely all the wants they cater to; these wants, therefore, can only be satisfied partially. This raises problems of administration which are the subject matter of economics.[1] To begin with, one problem of administration is to insure the full utilization of scarce resources, because their incomplete utilization would result in a loss of human satisfaction. Second, when scarce resources are fully utilized, there is the further administrative problem of properly allocating these resources among their different uses and to the satisfaction of different wants. For when scarce resources are fully utilized, the fuller satisfaction of any one want can only be achieved at the cost of the lesser satisfaction of some alternative want or wants. Third, yet another problem of administration is the proper distribution among consumers of these resources or of the goods and services produced with their aid.

Most of these problems would present themselves even to an isolated and completely self-sufficient person. Such a person, to fill his needs, would have to rely on his limited capacity to work and would face the

---

[1] The term "administration" is used here in its broadest possible sense and is not restricted to mean only administration by a central authority.

problem of how best to husband his energy and divide his time between leisure and different types of work. This is a problem of administering the scarce resources of his time and energy; but it is his private problem, which he may be left to solve as best he can, because its solution has no repercussions on other people's welfare. Only when several people co-operate for the purpose of satisfying their wants do one man's actions affect other people's welfare. Only in this case does the use and allocation of scarce resources and the distribution of their products raise problems of social organization; and it is only these problems that are of interest to the economist.

People co-operate in the use of their scarce resources even in the most primitive societies, because specialization improves their efficiency and the division of labor increases their total product. The more specialization and division of labor there is among the members of a society, the better use they can make of their limited resources for the satisfaction of human wants. Most economic progress consists in increasing these potentialities; and, from the economist's point of view, almost every innovation and technical invention is merely a new and more efficient method of specializing and dividing up the task of catering to human wants.

The blessings of economic progress, however, are gained at the cost of the increasing complexity of economic organization. The more division of labor there is among the members of a society, the more they lose their economic self-sufficiency and become dependent on each other. Economic interdependence is not a bad thing; but it turns the administration of scarce resources into a social problem. Means must be found whereby different members of society can exchange their respective products, whereby they can be induced to work and to produce different goods in the proportions wanted by society; and when a good embodies the contributions of several people, these must be brought together, their work co-ordinated, and the fruit of their joint effort shared out among them. The organization that this requires may be efficient or inefficient, equitable or unjust; it may function smoothly or be subject to occasional breakdowns. The farther the division of labor is pushed, the more intricate does the economic organization become, and the greater is the likelihood of something going wrong with it. The task of economics is to study economic organization, to appraise its efficiency and equity, and to suggest ways and means whereby its imperfections can be lessened or eliminated.

To appraise the efficiency of economic organization, a standard of perfection is desirable. In the natural sciences such standards are easily established. A perfect locomotive, for example, would be one that transforms all the heat energy of its fuel into traction; and the efficiency of an actual locomotive can be measured by the percentage of energy so transformed. In the social sciences the establishment of standards of perfection is usually very difficult and constitutes one of the main problems. The function of economic institutions is to organize economic life in conformity with the community's wishes; and to find out how well they fulfill this function, one must first ascertain the community's wishes. Sometimes these are expressed through the politically appointed organs of the community. For example, the community's wish to assure a minimum income to the old and to the unemployed may be expressed by a legislative body when it enacts laws providing old-age assistance and unemployment relief. It is even conceivable that all the wishes of the community might be expressed collectively, through its politically appointed organs. This is more or less the case in the communist state. In such a state, appraising the efficiency of economic organization is very simple and consists of little else than ascertaining the extent to which and the speed with which the central production plan has been fulfilled—assuming, of course, that this plan is a true expression of the community's wishes.

In a democratic society, most of the community's wishes are not expressed collectively but must be found out by ascertaining the wishes of each member of the community. In some cases, this is relatively simple. For example, an approximate indication of the community's desire to work is found in the individual actions of its members who accept employment or register with employment exchanges. A comparison of the total number of people who have thus expressed their willingness to work with the number actually employed gives a rough measure of the economic system's efficiency in providing employment.

As a rule, however, to ascertain the community's wishes in a democratic society is a difficult problem; and a large part of this book will be taken up with it. We shall have to ascertain the way in which the market reflects people's preferences between different consumers' goods, between different types of work, and between leisure and the income to be earned by work; for the efficiency of economic organization will to a large extent be judged by its conformity to the community's preferences in these matters.

Having stated the subject matter of economics and the problems that economic organization must solve, we proceed to consider the nature and forms of economic organization. Economic organization consists partly in bringing together different resources in farms, workshops, factories, and other centers of production for the purpose of producing with their aid new, produced resources. These centers of production may be owned by private persons and managed for their personal profit or may be owned by the state and managed by public officials according to rules and directives issued by the state. The two types of production centers exist side by side in most economies; but, depending on which is the dominant type, we distinguish between private enterprise and socialism.

In addition, economic organization also consists in co-ordinating the activities of different centers of production, allocating resources among them, and distributing their products. This, too, may assume two forms. One is trade, which we shall interpret in its broadest possible sense to mean all exchange of goods and services. The other is direct regulation by a system of duties and rights. Trade is a co-ordinating factor, because in the course of trade prices are established, which to a greater or lesser extent reflect the preferences of the trading parties, and which enable both the trading parties and others to act in conformity with these preferences. That the activities of different production centers can be co-ordinated also by direct regulation goes without saying. Trade and direct regulation occur side by side in most economies; moreover, trade itself may be subject to regulation by the state. But, according to whether trade or direct regulation predominates, we distinguish between market and planned economies.

It is customary to associate private enterprise with the market economy and socialism with the planned economy; but this pairing of the two sets of concepts is not the only one possible. Nazi Germany provided an example of planning in a private-enterprise economy; and so did the United States and Great Britain during the Second World War. Of a market economy under socialism there are no practical examples; but it has been demonstrated that the two are not incompatible.[2]

Under private enterprise in a market economy, trade determines most of the relations of firms with each other and with the suppliers of original resources and the consumers of final products. The firm itself, however, may own and control several production centers; and the activities of the several plants and workshops of the firm are co-ordinated through

---

[2] Cf. A. P. Lerner, "Economic Theory and Socialist Economy," *Review of Economic Studies*, Vol. II (October, 1934), pp. 51–61; and Oscar Lange and Fred M. Taylor, *On the Economic Theory of Socialism* (Minneapolis: University of Minnesota Press, 1938); also Lerner's *Economics of Control* (New York: Macmillan Co., 1944). In fact, much of the economic theory of socialism consists in proving that socialism and the market economy are compatible.

direct regulation by the management of the firm, which in such an economy is the authority that makes production decisions.

In a planned economy, most or all relations between the different centers of production are subject to direct regulation and central control by the state; but, for securing the services of labor and distributing final products among consumers, even the planned economy often relies on trade and the market mechanism. Not to rely on the market mechanism at all would necessitate the direct regulation of everybody's economic relations by a system of duties and rights. The state would have to determine who had the duty of performing labor, in what occupation, and for how many hours per day; and it would also have to determine who had the right to consume how much of each commodity.

Such a direct regulation of all economic relations by a system of duties and rights may be conceivable within the family circle or in a primitive tribe; but it would be insupportably rigid and oppressive in a more complex economy. It would require an excessive amount of regulation; and the connection between duties and rights would become so remote as to obscure the fact that the performance of duties is the payment, the *quid pro quo,* for the enjoyment of rights. In consequence, people would soon regard their duties as oppressive, unfair, or unreasonably hard. Moreover, the assignment of duties and the granting of rights can hardly allow for personal differences and preferences and is bound to be rigid and lead to inefficiency and injustice.

Trade is free from many of these shortcomings. It stresses the principle of give-and-take and renders the connection between services performed and benefits received very explicit. As a result, a man who would resent as slavery the state-imposed duty to work may consider himself a free man when working for a wage—even if he is forced to work by economic necessity. The market gives people a freedom of choice in consumption and in the selection of occupation that direct regulation can hardly provide. Furthermore, in the course of trade, market prices are established for the goods and services exchanged; and, provided that certain conditions are fulfilled, these prices express the preferences of the trading parties and their valuation of the resources exchanged. This characteristic of prices enables the market mechanism to register people's preferences and to organize production, allocate resources, and distribute products according to these preferences. In fact, the pricing system provides such a simple means of ascertaining the community's wishes and is so powerful an aid to economic organization that no economy except the most primitive can afford to do without it.

But trade is not superior to direct regulation in every respect. To begin with, the principles of equity and social justice are easily forgotten and ignored when people rely exclusively on the automatism of the market. Moreover, trade is not always efficient as a means of organizing economic life. Its degree of efficiency depends on the nature of markets —the number of people in the market, their sureness of judgment, the degree of equality in their economic power, and so forth; and to insure the efficiency of trade often requires legal safeguards. Hence, even in the market economy, trade is often subject to legal regulation. This may take several forms. Most commonly, it consists of restrictions and corrective measures imposed on private trading. Antitrust legislation and the public regulation of railroad fares and rates are examples of restriction in the interest of the greater efficiency of trade. Minimum-wage legislation, unemployment insurance, and progressive taxation are correctives aimed at modifying the distribution of income as determined by the market. Occasionally, certain economic activities are placed completely outside the market mechanism and their products made available free of charge. Primary and secondary education, police protection, and national defense are the most obvious instances of services provided in this way.

In this book, we shall be concerned mainly with private enterprise in a market economy. It is customary to distinguish between two types of problems in such an economy. One pertains to the degree of employment of scarce resources, and the other has to do with the efficiency and equity of their employment and of their allocation and distribution. Throughout this book, we shall only be concerned with the latter type of problem. In particular, we shall analyze the behavior of firms and the functioning of markets; and we shall try to appraise the efficiency and equity of the economic organization which results from the independent production decisions of private firms whose behavior is co-ordinated by the market mechanism. Before doing so, however, we must say a few words on the problem of employment and on the exact relation that this problem bears to the problems with which we shall be concerned.

We mentioned at the beginning of this chapter that free resources, being more than sufficient to fill all the wants they cater to, exist in excess supply. This means that they remain underemployed. Scarce resources, however, may on occasion also remain underemployed, because, though insufficient to fill all the *wants* they cater to, they may be more than sufficient to fill the *demand* for them. For the wants whose satisfaction depends on scarce resources are filled only to the extent that they are backed up with purchasing power and become effective as demand in the market. Demand, therefore, need not correspond to wants; and the failure of the economic system to register wants properly and make them effective as demand results in the underemployment of scarce resources and a consequent loss of human satisfactions.

When demand is insufficient to call for the full employment of a scarce resource, the only way to increase the satisfaction of wants that depend on this resource is to raise the demand for it. Hence, when a scarce resource becomes underemployed, it no longer matters whether it is used efficiently or not. The only consideration that remains relevant is that of equity. It is not worth while to eliminate inefficiency in the utilization of underemployed resources, because, as long as demand is insufficient to maintain full employment, inefficiency diminishes unemployment and not the satisfaction of wants.[3] Similarly, it does not matter if too large a proportion of underemployed resources is devoted to the satisfaction of one particular want, because this again results in less unemployment and not in the lesser satisfaction of other wants.[4] Efficiency in the use of underemployed scarce resources is as irrelevant as it is in the administration of free resources, and for exactly the same reason. In both cases, there is an unemployed reserve of resources, which is drawn upon to offset losses due to wasteful or improper use. Here, however, the parallelism ends. For the underemployment of free resources is due to the saturation of the wants they cater to and therefore causes no loss; whereas the underemployment of scarce resources is due to imperfection in the economic system and does result in economic loss.

A situation in which there is both underemployment and an inefficient use of scarce resources may be compared to that of a prisoner who serves two sentences concurrently. He would gain by having his longer sentence revoked or revised; but as long as this sentence stands unchanged, he would derive no benefit from proving his innocence of the crime that earned him the shorter sentence, because it would not set him free sooner. Similarly, at a time when the insufficiency of demand causes unemployment, the only way to increase the satisfaction of human wants is to raise demand; for the mere existence of unemployment

---

[3] It should be noted, however, that if an increase in efficiency happened at the same time also to raise effective demand, then it would increase the satisfaction of wants.

[4] In fact, if we regard unemployment not only as the cause of a loss of output and satisfaction but as a bad thing in itself, we might even go further and argue that inefficiency in the administration of underemployed resources is desirable, because, while it does not lower the satisfaction of wants, it lowers unemployment. See, however, pp. 10–11.

proves that the loss of satisfactions due to the insufficiency of demand exceeds and absorbs any loss that may be due to faulty allocation. Hence, if insufficient demand and inefficient administration were equally important, unemployment would disappear. The existence of unemployment is proof that the effect of inefficiency is less important than the effect of insufficient demand.

The problem of unemployment has first claim to the economist's attention. Only in a fully employed economy does allocation become an economic problem. In other words, only when scarce resources are fully employed does the way in which they are employed and allocated among alternative uses become relevant from the economist's point of view. This is why the problems of allocation and distribution dealt with in this book are described as the economic problems of a fully employed economy.

Nevertheless, the usefulness of the following analysis is not confined to those comparatively short periods of high prosperity when all resources are fully employed. For if it seldom happens that all resources are fully employed, it is equally rare that all scarce resources are underemployed. Neither labor nor productive equipment is homogeneous; and the underemployment of labor as a whole or of equipment as a whole seldom means that all kinds of labor or all kinds of equipment are underemployed. As a rule, underemployment in some occupations and of some types of equipment exists side by side with full employment in other occupations and of other types of equipment; and the proper use and allocation of the fully employed resources do create economic problems.

Furthermore, the problems to be discussed in the following chapters are not entirely irrelevant even at a time of general underemployment. For the efficiency or inefficiency of economic organization at any one time inevitably bequeathes a legacy of efficiency or inefficiency to the future. Accordingly, although the efficiency with which employed resources are used and allocated during a period of underemployment is of no immediate relevance, it does become relevant later, when full employment has been restored. For example, technological improvements introduced during a depression often fail to raise output while the depression lasts and only aggravate unemployment. Nevertheless, their introduction at that stage may still be desirable, because it may be the condition of higher output in the subsequent prosperity. Similarly, an employment policy adopted in depression must be judged not only by its immediate effectiveness in raising demand and relieving depression but also by its effects on efficiency. For as soon as the increase in demand has eliminated unemployment, problems of allocation will arise; and the seriousness of these problems may depend on the particular way in which full employment was achieved. While unemployment exists, all cures seem equally good if they are equally effective. But equally effective cures of unemployment may affect the allocation of resources differently; and if they do, they will be differently appraised once full employment has been restored and the proper use and allocation of resources have again become the primary aim of economic policy.[5] Hence, the subject matter of this book, although it is confined to the problems of a fully employed economy, has a bearing even on the choice of employment policies if their long-run effects are taken into consideration.

BIBLIOGRAPHICAL NOTE

For a more detailed and more complete statement of the subject matter of economics, see Oscar Lange, "The Scope and Method of Economics," *Review of Economic Studies,* Vol. XIII (1945–46), pp. 12–32. See also Lionel Robbins, *An Essay on the Nature and Significance of Economic Science* (London: Macmillan & Co., 1932); and R. F. Harrod, "Scope and Method of Economics," *Economic Journal,* Vol. XLVIII (September, 1938), pp. 383–412.

---

[5] For a detailed discussion of this subject, see Melvin W. Reder, *Studies in the Theory of Welfare Economics* (New York: Columbia University Press, 1947), chap. xv.

CHAPTER II

THE MARKET

TRADE between two people comes about when each has something to offer that the other wants and when they can agree on terms of exchange profitable to both of them. As a rule, there is a wide range of possible terms of exchange on which both parties to the deal would be willing to complete it; and it is the subject matter of the theory of markets to determine the exact terms on which, or the limits within which, exchange will actually take place. To find this out is important, because the terms of the contract determine both the efficiency of economic organization and the distribution of the gain from the division of labor.

The actual exchange rate between two exchanging parties (i.e., price) may come about in a variety of ways. It may be the result of isolated bargaining between a buyer and a seller who make repeated offers and counteroffers until they reach agreement. Or it may be the result of competitive bargaining, when several buyers and several sellers bid one against the other and the terms of the different transactions cluster around the level that would "clear the market," that is, the level at which the total offer of all the sellers would equal the total amount that all the buyers taken together want to buy. Or again, price may be set by one of the parties to the transaction, with all trade taking place at the price set by him. This is the kind of situation the consumer faces in practically all of his everyday transactions. A fixed price may also be prescribed by authority. In Soviet Russia, for example, prices are set by the state. In the United States, railroad and bus fares and freight rates in interstate traffic are set by the Interstate Commerce Commission; and during the war the governments of most of the warring countries controlled the prices of a large number of commodities.

1. ISOLATED BARGAINING

The simplest form of trade is isolated bargaining. It occurs between two parties who must either trade with each other or not trade at all, because there are no third persons with whom either of them could trade. The price at which they will close the deal is indeterminate: it may be anywhere within the range of possible prices and is settled by bargaining. It will vary from time to time and depend on the shrewdness, patience, psychological insight, and general bargaining skill of the two parties. The advantage one man gets out of the exchange is limited only by the other man's efforts to get the best terms for himself, a fact that tends to make bargaining between the parties to an isolated exchange bitter and violent and, when the exchanging parties are groups or nations, gives scope to military or political intimidation and pressure.

The earliest example of isolated bargaining and of trade in general is silent trade, in which elaborate precautions are taken to avoid such violence. Silent trade was practiced between neighboring tribes among the Indians of California, the savages of the New Guinea islands, and many other primitive peoples. It is called silent trade because the parties to it never meet and never speak to each other. One party displays in a prearranged spot the wares it wants to exchange and then withdraws to a safe distance, allowing the other party to inspect the wares, place next to them the objects it offers in exchange, and withdraw in its turn. Only then will the first party come forward again to inspect the second party's offer and either accept it and take it away or make a counteroffer by taking away some of the objects it had originally set out. This elaborate ritual eliminates the necessity of the two parties meeting and the danger of their coming to blows.

This danger is inherent not only in the savagery of the primitive tribes which are parties to silent trade but also in the nature of isolated bargaining itself. At a much higher stage of civilization, among the Phoenicians, the ancient Greeks, and even in the early Middle Ages, the temptation to resort to violence was still very strong; and the roles of pirate and trader were easily interchangeable. The terms of exchange between trading groups were often fixed on the basis of arms and numbers rather than on the basis of bargaining and the merits of their respective wares. A trader might plunder his clients if he happened to be on the stronger side and content himself with peaceful trading only if he was the weaker of the two.

Modern examples of isolated exchange are not very different. Collective bargaining between workers and employers on a nationwide scale is isolated bargaining; and it usually is bitter and violent, because so much depends on the two parties' bargaining power. Hence the need for conciliation and arbitration, which fulfill the same function in labor disputes that the physical separation of the parties accomplishes in silent trade. Another modern example of isolated bargaining was Nazi Germany's system of barter trade agreements with her central and eastern European neighbors in the 1930's. In these agreements the terms of trade were largely determined by the weight of Germany's political and military pressure on her smaller and weaker neighbors who, being isolated from the rest of the world by their geographical position, were defenseless against this pressure.

2. COMPETITIVE BARGAINING

The main curb on a person's bargaining power, and the main pacifying influence on trade in general, is competition. A person has competition if the party he wants to trade with has alternative opportunities of exchange. The people who offer these alternative opportunities to his opposite party are his competitors. Competition restricts a person's bargaining power by making the other party less dependent and therefore less keen on striking a bargain with him. Competition may be one-sided, in which case the party who has no competitors has a bargaining advantage over his opponents and is usually able to get a price that gives him the lion's share of the gain from trade. As a rule, however, both parties to a transaction have competitors, which hems in the bargaining power of both. When the two parties start bargaining, each of them knows of some alternative opportunities of exchange open to him, knows what prices have been reached in similar transactions in the past, and expects his opponent to have similar knowledge. It is this last-mentioned factor which limits each party's scope for increasing his share of the gain by bargaining and makes him more modest in his aspirations. Either party can threaten to close the deal with a third person if the other party makes inordinate demands; and both of them know that such threats are meant seriously and can be carried out. Either party can refer to precedent if the other tries to stray too far from the terms of similar past transactions; and precedent has a powerful sway over man's mind. It is the origin of custom and law; and the precedent of past prices is the basis of the notion of a normal or fair price. Competition, therefore, limits both parties' chances of influencing price by bargaining. By doing so, it restricts the scope for bargaining and the range within which the final price will lie; and it renders price more determinate and less dependent on chance and bargaining skill. By reducing the effectiveness of bargaining as a weapon for improving one's position, competition is also a guaranty of the peaceful nature of trade.

These advantages of competition were recognized by the late eighteenth- and early nineteenth-century economists, who regarded competition as a beneficent force, an "invisible hand," which curbed the individual's economic power and brought order into economic affairs without regulation by the state or other authority. They also believed that competition was a natural state of affairs and that the order it brought about was a natural order. The fact that special conditions must be satisfied for competition to come about was not recognized until much later. A detailed discussion of these conditions will be given in Chapter XV; but one of them has to be mentioned already here. For a market to be competitive, it must have several members on both the buyers' and the sellers' side; and to insure the presence of several buyers and sellers in the market, the individual buyer's and seller's scale of operations must be limited to a level that is below the market's total turnover. While there is a natural limit to the scale of operations of persons who sell their personal services or buy for personal consumption, there is no such limit to the size of the firm, which buys for resale and sells what it has bought or produced. The size of the firm must therefore be limited by some special factor or factors, whose presence and adequacy are a condition not only of competitive bargaining but of all other forms of competition as well.

Competitive bargaining is a common form of trade. It is the general rule in communities where economic activity is conducted and organized on a small scale, and in markets where the disparity in numbers between the buyers' and the sellers' side is not too great. It obtains in the Far East and in the Near East and in all agricultural and industrially undeveloped communities in general. Until the Industrial Revolution, it was the rule also in Europe and America, where it still exists in many markets in which business firms deal among themselves. It is generally known that in the Orient even the simplest routine transactions are preceded by bargaining; but it is not always realized that the same was true also in our society as little as one hundred years ago. The art of skillful bargaining was an essential accomplishment of the housewife, who had to bargain in her daily purchases of meat and vegetables just as much as when she bought finery. This is apparent from the English novel of the eighteenth and early nineteenth centuries. Young men would ask a lady friend to help them bargain for a scarf or necktie; and the "cheapening of goods" seemed to be a favorite pastime of ladies, much as window-shopping is today.

3. PERFECT COMPETITION

Since competition restricts the scope for bargaining, the question naturally arises as to how many competitors the two parties would need and what other conditions would have to be fulfilled to render competition perfect in the sense of reducing both parties' bargaining power to nil and making price completely determinate and independent of the chance element of bargaining. In such a situation, neither party would feel that he could influence price; and both would regard price as given to them.

It is not easy to visualize such a situation. Many people in our economy regard price as given to them; but they do so, in most instances, because the price they face is set, either by the other party or by a third person.[1] The difficulty lies in visualizing a price that everybody on both sides of the market regards as given and that is determined by "the impersonal forces of the market." An example may help to resolve this difficulty. Consider a seller who sells his output at a certain price or range of prices but feels that he could also sell at a different price or price range, realizing, of course, that this would lead to a different rate of sales. The realization that higher prices would lead to lower sales restricts the seller's influence on price. Only in the limiting case, however, in which even the smallest raising of his price would stop his sales completely, would the seller feel that he had no influence whatsoever on price.

What conditions must be fulfilled for this limiting case to come about? It is necessary, first of all, that the customers of the seller should be able to withdraw all their custom from him without inconvenience to themselves. This requires the existence of other sellers who offer for sale goods sufficiently similar in nature and sufficiently large in quantity. The problem of the similarity of competing offers will be taken up presently. As to the volume of competing offers, this is sufficiently large if the seller's turnover is small compared to the market's total turnover. Furthermore, if all sellers in the market are to regard price as given to them, each seller's sales must be small compared to the market's total turnover. This requires a large number of competing sellers.

It is not enough, however, that the number of competing sellers should be sufficiently large to enable the customers of any one seller to shift their custom away from him. It is also necessary that all the buyers should know about the existence of alternative offers and that *all* of

---

[1] These cases will be discussed in later sections of this chapter.

them should be prepared to shift *all* their custom in response to even the *smallest* change in price. This second condition is fulfilled only if the buyers are experts in the appraisal of the goods they buy, and only if they are experts in the strictest sense of the term.

Most people's market behavior depends, at least partly, on habit and inertia; and most of us are influenced to some extent by such factors as advertising, suggestion, and the reputation and past performance of the firm we buy from, when we judge the quality of its wares. Habit and inertia, as well as the other factors, would all prevent a person from shifting his custom from one seller to another in response to a small change in price; hence, they must all be absent from the buyer's mind if the sellers facing him are to have no conscious influence on price. Each time he comes to the market, the buyer must have a completely open mind. He must be willing and anxious to consider all alternative offers and able to compare their relative merits; and he must base his decision solely on a rational comparison of prices and quality. It is obvious that no consumer ever exercises such unceasing vigilance and superrationality in his market behavior.[2] In fact, these qualities are only to be found in the professional expert, whose job it is always to make the best purchase, and who is paid to exercise his expert judgment and ability to get the utmost out of every transaction. Only the expert, who is quite sure of his judgment, can be relied upon to make full use of his freedom of choice at every opportunity; for most other people would consider it an intolerable burden to do so.

When the majority of buyers are experts, who insist on inspecting and comparing alternative offers before every purchase, then it is in the sellers' interest to facilitate such comparisons. For example, if a buyer has to choose among five alternatives of which four are easily comparable but the fifth is not, he will concentrate on comparing and choosing among the four and may ignore the fifth altogether. Hence the desire of every seller who faces expert buyers to be near his competitors and render his wares easily comparable to theirs. This explains the standardization of products in the experts' market and the tendency of wholesalers dealing in similar goods to congregate in one building or on one street.

The outstanding examples of experts' markets are the commodity exchanges for wheat, wool, cotton, meat, metals, diamonds, etc. All these markets are highly centralized, and most of them deal in standardized commodities. It is important to realize, however, that standardization in

---

[2] This aspect of the consumer's market behavior will be discussed in sec. 5 of Chap. III and at the beginning of Chap. XV.

such markets is not the result of any natural uniformity of these commodities but a consequence of the buyers' expertness. Different kinds of wheat are hardly more uniform than are different brands of soap flakes; but wheat, unlike soap flakes, is graded and standardized, because the buyers of wheat are experts, who insist on ascertaining the exact quality of the wheat they buy and thereby make it each wheatgrower's interest to facilitate this by standardizing his produce. Needless to say, some commodities are more difficult to standardize than others. For example, there is little, if any, standardization in the market for scrap iron, even though the buyers are experts. That the expertness of buyers does, however, create a strong inducement to standardize is suggested by the example of the wholesale diamond market, where a very high degree of standardization has been achieved, despite the obvious difficulties involved. By contrast, we shall see in Chapter XVIII how the inexpertness of buyers induces sellers to differentiate their products.

The above discussion was concerned with the seller only and showed that, for sellers to regard price as given, there must be many sellers, and the buyers must be experts. The argument, however, is so easily adapted to the buyer's case that we can state without proof that, for buyers to regard price as given, there must be many buyers, and the sellers must be experts.[3] We conclude, therefore, that for price to be regarded as given by *all* members of the market, buyers and sellers alike, the necessary conditions are large numbers and expertness on both the buyers' and the sellers' side.

A person who regards the price of a commodity as given to him and is able, at this price, to buy or sell as much as he likes will be called a price taker. It is apparent that both buyers and sellers can be price takers. The market behavior of a price taker is called pure competition or perfectly competitive behavior.[4] A market in which all the buyers and all the sellers are price takers is called a perfectly competitive market. An economy in which every market is perfectly competitive would be a perfectly competitive economy.

The practical importance of perfect competition is not very great. Few markets in our economy are perfectly competitive, because few markets fulfill the conditions of perfect competition, large numbers, and expert-

---

[3] The proof of this statement follows closely the argument given above and is left to the reader as an exercise.

[4] For consistency's sake, it should be called purely competitive behavior; but, used as an adjective, the expression "perfectly competitive" is less ambiguous and more convenient.

ness on both the buyers' and the sellers' side. The only examples of perfectly competitive markets are the exchanges for staple foodstuffs and raw materials. At the beginning of the nineteenth century, these markets were the only exceptions to the then almost universal rule of competitive bargaining; this fact led many economists of the time to expect competition to become more perfect and the number of perfectly competitive markets to increase with the passage of time. These economists knew that competition depends on the availability of information about competing offers; and they believed that improvements in the means of communication and in methods of standardization would result in increased market information. They failed to realize that, in order that more market information be forthcoming, there must be a demand for it; and that only the expert can make his demand for information felt. They did not anticipate the ever-increasing range and complexity of products, which has rendered the most important buyer, the consumer, less and less of an expert.

From the point of view of economic theory, however, the concept of perfect competition is very important. For it can be shown that perfectly competitive behavior by all members of every market would result in the most efficient organization of production and the best allocation both of productive resources and of consumers' goods and services.[5] Perfect competition, therefore, provides a standard of efficiency by which actual economic institutions and organization can be appraised.

4. PRICE SETTING

The markets in which the consumer deals are not perfectly competitive, because the average consumer lacks and cannot possibly acquire an expert knowledge of all the goods and services he buys. This keeps him from forming an accurate opinion of the relative merits of the alternative opportunities open to him and may prevent his knowing about the existence of all the available alternatives. For both these reasons the consumer is at a disadvantage, which the persons or firms selling to him can exploit. In the same way and for the same reasons the small farmer selling his produce and the individual worker selling his services are also at a disadvantage. They too have a very imperfect knowledge of the alternative opportunities open to them and usually lack the mobility and funds necessary to look around and find out about alternatives. Consequently, they are often at the mercy of the first and nearest buyer or employer with whom they come in contact.

---

[5] See, however, the Note to Chap. VIII.

How can a person or firm selling to inexpert buyers or buying from inexpert sellers exploit his advantage? In a market where the terms of contract are customarily settled by bargaining, the expert merely has a bargaining advantage over his opponent, whose lack of expert knowledge makes him susceptible to persuasion. As pointed out earlier, bargaining is the general rule in communities where economic activity is conducted on a small scale. The small merchant and the small-scale producer or artisan come into economic contact with a few people only and tend to establish personal contact with them, which inevitably leads to bargaining in markets where either the buyers or the sellers are not experts. As long as the economic unit stays small, the expansion of trade and the growth of markets will neither disrupt personal contacts nor eliminate bargaining. For example, the average seller will have only 10 customers regardless of whether the market consists of 5 sellers and 50 buyers or of 5 million sellers and 50 million buyers.

The expert's advantage over the layman assumes an institutional form when increased specialization and increased division of labor disrupt personal contacts. These factors call for mass production and large-scale organization, which widen the disparity in numbers between sellers and buyers, between employers and employees, and increase the number of people with whom the average producer or merchant comes in contact. The large-scale producer or merchant finds that the time and effort involved in bargaining become a burden to him, the cost of which increases as the number of people with whom he has to bargain increases. There comes a point, therefore, beyond which the cost of bargaining exceeds the gain from it. When his market has reached this point, the producer or merchant can increase his profit by refusing to bargain and setting his price on a take-it-or-leave-it basis.

A person who sets his price in this way is a price maker; and his action is price setting. The same factors that induce and enable him to set his price make him take the initiative in determining all the other aspects of his offer as well. His ability to take the initiative in market transactions gives him an apparent advantage over the members of the market who face his set offer and places him in a favored position. The price maker's advantage in the market is called a monopolistic advantage, and his favored position is a monopoly position. Competition among price makers is called monopolistic competition or, sometimes, imperfect competition.

In contrast to the active behavior of the price maker is that of the people who are confronted by his set offer. These are price takers, who, as far as their market behavior is concerned, are in exactly the same position as the members of a perfectly competitive market. In other words, they can buy or sell as much as they want to, but only on set terms, over which they have no control and which they regard as given.[6]

To sum up, the two conditions for price setting are (1) a disparity in numbers between the two sides of the market, which disrupts personal contacts between buyer and seller and renders bargaining uneconomical; and (2) the inexpertness of one side of the market, which, of course, is always the side with the larger numbers. It should be noted that buyers as well as sellers may be price makers and set the terms of their offer, depending on whether the number of buyers or that of sellers is the smaller.

Competition in a monopolistic or imperfectly competitive market is imperfect only on the price makers' side; whereas the price takers, on the other side of the market, are in a perfectly competitive market position. A monopolistic or imperfect market, therefore, is an asymmetrical market, some of whose members are in a perfectly competitive position and others in an imperfectly competitive position, depending on which side of the market they happen to be on. It is to stress this asymmetry and difference in the market position of people on the two sides of this type of market that we use the terms "price setting" and "trade at set prices" in preference to the more usual terminology.

Trade at set prices is the most common form of market relation in our society. We are accustomed to think of it as the normal form of trade in the consumer's market; but it is a relatively recent innovation, which came in the wake of the Industrial Revolution. In England the Quaker merchants set their prices and refrained from bargaining on religious grounds as early as the middle of the seventeenth century; but, according to Daniel De Foe, they did not adhere to this policy very strictly.[7] The definitive introduction of set prices in England probably dates from around 1770, when Josiah Wedgewood, the famous pottery manufacturer, established his first shop in London.[8] In France and the United

---

[6] The terms "price maker" and "price taker" were suggested to me by Professor Abba P. Lerner. The concepts themselves were introduced, I believe, by Professor Ragner Frisch, who uses the terms "price adjuster" and "quantity adjuster." Unfortunately, Professor Frisch's work on this subject, being in Norwegian, was inaccessible to me.

[7] Cf. Isabel Grubb, *Quakerism and Industry before 1800* (London: Williams and Norgate, 1930), pp. 146–47; and Daniel De Foe, *Complete English Tradesman* (2d ed.; London, 1727), pp. 227–28.

[8] Cf. Ralph M. Hower, "The Wedgwoods—Ten Generations of Potters," *Journal of Economic and Business History,* Vol. IV (February, 1932), p. 303.

States, set prices were introduced only in the nineteenth century, and, significantly enough, by the department store—the seller that faces the largest number of customers. The *prix fixe* was adopted in France by the first department stores around 1815; and the innovation is said to have become the generally established pattern in retail trade by 1844. In the United States, A. T. Stewart and Lord & Taylor in New York, Hovey & Company in Boston, and Macy's in Haverhill, Massachusetts, seemed to be the first stores to abolish bargaining and to set prices.[9]

Today, set prices have become the rule in industrial communities in all markets where the consumer buys. They are so thoroughly accepted in our society that bargaining has come to be regarded as not quite respectable or *comme il faut*. The consumer is a price taker in practically all his purchases; he even suspects and often avoids those few shopkeepers who are amenable to bargaining, interpreting this as a sign of dishonest trading. Just as consumers face the prices set by retailers, retailers in their turn—at least the smaller ones among them—face the set prices of producers and wholesalers. The small retailer, therefore, is a price maker when he sells but a price taker when he buys. In contrast to him, the producer and wholesaler not only set the prices at which they sell; but, before the advent of trade unions and farmers' co-operatives, they used to set also the prices at which they hired labor and bought farm products. In the early days of capitalism, therefore, entrepreneurs and businessmen were price makers in all their relations with other social classes.

5. THE TYPES OF COMPETITION AMONG PRICE MAKERS

The advantage that price makers can derive from their strategically favorable market position is limited by competition among the price makers themselves. The extent of this limitation depends, therefore, on the nature and extent of competition. The individual price maker has to meet two forms of competition: the actual competition of his established rivals and the threat of competition from newcomers to his market. The price maker's established rivals offer his customers alternative opportunities of buying or selling, which may force him to offer terms more advantageous to his customers than he would offer in the absence of such competition. Newcomers, attracted by the price maker's profit, threaten to enter his market, through their entry to increase the total

---

[9] For a short account of the origin of set prices in different countries, see Ralph M. Hower, *History of Macy's of New York, 1858–1919* (Cambridge, Mass.: Harvard University Press, 1942), especially chap. iv.

offering in his market, and thus to lower his turnover. Both forms of competition limit the price maker's bargaining advantage and profit; it is in his interest, therefore, to restrain competition from both sources. Of the two, however, the threat of competition from newcomers and restraints on their entry to the market are by far the more important from the price maker's point of view. For restraints on the entry of newcomers may enable an established firm to make a monopoly profit even if competition between him and his established competitors is unrestrained; whereas the entry of newcomers would eliminate monopoly profit, however restrained may be the competitive behavior of the established firms among themselves. Restraints on entry, therefore, are the *sine qua non* of restraints on competitive behavior; and they will serve as the basis of our main classification of competition among price makers.

We shall distinguish between free and restricted competition among price makers, depending on whether the entry of newcomers to their market is free or restricted. Under free competition the individual price maker's monopoly profit tends to zero; for whenever it is positive, it attracts newcomers, whose entry to the market tends to eliminate monopoly profit. Hence, the individual price maker's strategic advantage in the market is largely illusory under free competition. As regards its effects on the organization of production and the allocation of services and goods, free competition is in some, though not all, respects not too dissimilar to perfect competition; in fact, it is regarded by some as the practical reality of which perfect competition is an idealized mathematical abstraction. Free competition was probably most closely approached in New England and the countries of western Europe during the Industrial Revolution; and it still exists in many markets today.

Restricted competition among price makers may assume a variety of forms, depending on whether competition among the established price makers themselves is restrained and, if so, to what extent. When the competitive behavior of the market's established members is unrestrained, and the only restraint is that on entry, we speak of simple restricted competition. When there are restraints also on competition among established competitors, we speak of collective monopoly if these restraints are imposed by agreement, and of oligopoly if the restraints come about spontaneously without agreement. When competition among established price makers is completely absent, either because there is only one price maker in the market or because a complete fusion of interests and unification of market behavior has taken place among former rivals, we speak of single monopoly. All these are different forms of restricted competition among price makers and will be discussed in detail in Part IV of this book.

6. BILATERAL MONOPOLY

We saw above that in trade at set prices, the price maker, taking the initiative in the market, has a strategic advantage over the price takers. When price takers realize the handicap that their market position as price takers involves, they can try to change the form of trade and improve their market position by combination. This reduces the disparity in numbers between the two sides of the market and may thus remove the condition that led to the establishment of set prices. The result is the introduction (or reintroduction) of bargaining, which secures formal symmetry in the market position of buyers and sellers and puts them on an equal footing. When bargaining comes about as a result of combination among price takers, it is usually called collective bargaining or bilateral monopoly.

7. TRADE ON PRESCRIBED TERMS

In general, all forms of trade and all types of competition among price makers are subject to a certain amount of regulation by the state; but when such regulation extends to prescribing the terms of contract, we get a special form of market relationship: trade on terms prescribed by authority. This form of trade may, in the most favorable case, turn all members of the market, buyers and sellers alike, into price takers and so create the ideal conditions of pure or perfect competition, which would come about naturally only in the experts' market. Usually, however, some members of the market can, through political pressure, influence the terms of contract prescribed by authority. When political influence is enjoyed by people on both sides of the market, the terms of contract will be determined by bargaining conducted on the political plane. An example of this is wage determination in cases where arbitration is compulsory and the arbitrator's decision binding. When people on only one side of the market have a say in determining the prescribed terms of contract, trade on these terms is similar to trade on terms set by price makers, except that the latter have a greater control over the terms of trade and hence enjoy a greater advantage when they set prices themselves than when they only have a limited influence over prices prescribed by government officials. The public control of prices, therefore, can be used to supplement or replace competition as a factor limiting the individual price maker's gain from trade. This, for example, is the purpose, in the United States, of the Federal Communications Commission when it sets telephone and telegraph rates.

In conclusion, it may be useful to enumerate the above forms of trade, as shown in the accompanying table.

The three main categories are bargaining, perfect competition, and trade at set terms. Under the first, both parties have a conscious influence over the terms of contract; under the second, neither of them has; under the third, only one of them has a conscious influence. The fourth category, trade at prescribed terms, may resemble any one of the first three, depending on whether political influence is wielded by both parties, neither party, or one party.

Of the different forms of trade and competition enumerated above, many have had their turn in history as the dominant form of market relationship. But, while they may be regarded as stages in a historical development, they also exist side by side in different markets of our economy. Since the economist's main interest lies in appraising the efficiency of economic organization, we shall start with a discussion of perfect competition in order to establish a yardstick for measuring the efficiency of other forms of trade. Part II deals with the perfectly competitive behavior of the individual price taker and with competition in the perfect market, every member of which is a price taker. Since perfect competition is not and never has been a reality, most of the discussion of Part II must be regarded as relating to an abstract and idealized model of our economy, which will be linked up with .reality later on. The analysis of the consumer and his market, however, is reasonably realistic, since he is usually a price taker in our society, and since his behavior is the same whether he faces prices determined by the impersonal forces of the perfect market or prices set by the price makers confronting him. The average worker and the average firm are not price takers in our economy, although there are some workers and some firms that are. Part III is concerned with the market behavior of the individual price maker and with free competition among price makers. The various forms of restricted competition among price makers, bilateral monopoly, bargaining, and trade on prescribed terms are discussed in Part IV.

BIBLIOGRAPHICAL NOTE

The most important work in classifying and distinguishing between different markets and different types of competition has been done by Professor E. H. Chamberlin in his *Theory of Monopolistic Competition* (Cambridge, Mass.; Harvard University Press, 1931); and, following in his wake, by Dr. Robert Triffin in *Monopolistic Competition and General Equilibrium Theory* (Cambridge, Mass.: Harvard University Press, 1940). One important merit of their work is the careful distinction drawn between the nature of markets and the nature of competitive behavior. Thus, for example, Professor Chamberlin distinguishes between the *perfect* market, which denotes a certain market structure, and *pure* competition, which defines a certain type of market behavior. In the present book, I deliberately slur over this distinction and similar ones, in order to stress the importance of institutional factors in determining the nature of competitive behavior. However, this is achieved at the sacrifice of completeness and logical rigor. The student of market structures and the theory of competition should therefore be acquainted with the above works.

Two other systems of market classification which are of interest are the following: Fritz Machlup, "Monopoly and Competition: A Classification," *American Economic Review*, Vol. XXVII (1937), pp. 445–51; and J. S. Bain, "Market Classifications in Modern Price Theory," *Quarterly Journal of Economics*, Vol. LVI (1942), pp. 560–75.

PART II

The Price Taker's Behavior and Perfect Competition

Before starting the detailed discussion of perfect competition and perfectly competitive behavior, we must say a few words about the order in which the discussion will proceed. Our aim in this part, it will be recalled, is to present an admittedly artificial and unrealistic model of economic behavior and economic organization, whose merit and justification are its simplicity and the fact that it is in many (though not all) respects a standard of perfection. The perfection of economic organization depends on its ability to satisfy human wants; we must begin, therefore, by finding out what these wants are. Human beings derive satisfaction out of consuming goods and services. It therefore seems logical to start with a discussion of the consumer. This is the subject matter of the next chapter. Having discussed the consumer's behavior, we proceed in Chapter IV to discuss the concepts of perfection and efficiency with respect to at least one aspect of economic organization: the distribution of consumers' goods and services among consumers.

Human beings, however, are interested not merely in obtaining goods and services for consumption; they also want to obtain them without making too great an effort. Hence, for the best satisfaction of human wants a balance must be struck between the quantity of goods and services made available for consumption and the amount of effort expended in producing them. Accordingly, Chapter V is concerned with the behavior of workers and other people who offer their personal services for sale. In addition, this chapter also deals with efficiency in the subdivision of tasks among these people.

The next two chapters (VI and VII) describe the characteristics and market behavior of the firm, which in a private-enterprise economy is the center of production decisions. For the sake of greater generality, it might have been preferable to discuss, instead of the firm, the individual production center, which—unlike the firm—exists under private enterprise and socialism alike. We have not done this for a variety of reasons; but it might be pointed out that all our results concerning the firm apply also to the individual plant, workshop, farm, or store, since one can always identify the firm with the production center by considering firms that own and control only one production center.

27

In the subsequent chapter (VIII), we discuss the meaning and conditions of efficiency both in the individual firm and in the co-ordination of the activities of different firms. In short, Chapter VIII is concerned with the efficiency of the whole productive system. Here, too, we have concentrated our attention on the private enterprise economy; but the reader is again free to read "production center" whenever he sees the word "firm" and thus to regard our results as the conditions of efficiency in any kind of market economy.

Up to and including Chapter VIII, the analysis is very much simplified; and it is static in the sense that the element of time is ignored. The next two chapters examine what happens when some of the simplifying assumptions are dropped and the time element is introduced. Chapter IX deals with the role of time in the productive process and with the factor capital. In Chapter X the problems of dynamic stability and efficiency are discussed.

CHAPTER III

THE CONSUMER

THE price taker is a firm or person who faces set offers and is free only to choose among the different offers confronting him and to vary the quantities he buys or sells. It is immaterial from his point of view whether these offers are determined by the impersonal forces of the market, set by the other party to the transaction, or prescribed by authority. Whatever the case may be, he has to adapt his behavior to given opportunities of exchange and set terms of contract, which he regards as data.

The most important price taker in our society is the consumer, who faces set offers in practically all his market transactions. He has an income, which he can spend on different goods and services in a variety of ways; and the alternative patterns of expenditure open to him are determined by the variety of offers and the structure of prices facing him. Of the alternatives made available to him by his income and his market opportunities, he will choose the one that best conforms to his preferences. The way in which he actually spends his income, therefore, depends on his personal preferences, on the size of his income, and on his market opportunities. In the following, we shall discuss, first, the way in which the market's offers and the consumer's income determine the latter's market behavior and, second, how *changes* in income and market offers affect his behavior. The consumer's preferences, however, we shall regard as fixed. The economist's task is to analyze how and to what extent economic activity conforms to consumers' preferences; but these he cannot question and must accept as given.[1]

How can we find out what the consumer's preferences are? We can

---

[1] Producers, however, do not always accept consumers' preferences as given but often try to influence them through advertising and other means. This raises the problem as to whether consumers' preferences, dependent as they are on advertising, should really be regarded as the ultimate standard. This problem will be discussed in Chaps. XVIII and XX.

hardly question him on the subject and so establish his scale of preferences. This would be a lengthy and clumsy process even if applied to only one person and is obviously impossible to apply to all members of the community. We can, however, infer the consumer's preferences from his market behavior, on the assumption that this is governed by rational choice and is not merely a matter of habit or accident. When the consumer spends his income in a certain way, we assume that he finds this the best way of spending his income at the existing structure of market prices, because if it were not, he would surely spend his income differently. The theory of consumer's behavior, therefore, is purely descriptive and describes the behavior of the rational consumer. We can neither prescribe how the consumer should behave nor judge his behavior by comparison to an ideal behavior pattern, because we have no such ideal pattern. To establish an ideal behavior pattern would require independent information of the consumer's tastes and preferences; whereas we know these only as they are reflected in his market behavior. This means that the conformity of the consumer's market behavior to his preferences is the assumption we start out with and not something that can be proved or disproved by our analysis. It will be seen later that this renders the theory of consumer's choice fundamentally different from the theory of production.

1. THE INDIFFERENCE MAP

To illustrate the consumer's market behavior, it will be convenient to make use of a diagram in which we can express graphically the consumer's preferences, his income, and his market opportunities. Diagrammatic representation necessarily imposes the restriction of two dimensions, which makes it impossible to illustrate the consumer's choice between more than two commodities. This will make our analysis somewhat unrealistic in the beginning; but the results reached will be seen to have general validity and can easily be extended to the general case of any number of commodities.

Let us call the two commodities ale and bread, and measure pints of ale along the horizontal axis and loaves of bread along the vertical axis (Fig. 1). Any point in this diagram represents a certain amount of ale and a certain amount of bread in the consumer's possession. Since the earning and spending of incomes and the consumption of goods are processes that happen in time, we must also specify the period of time under consideration and shall call this a week. Point *a* in Figure 1, therefore, represents 8 pints of ale and 10 loaves of bread acquired and consumed per week by the consumer.

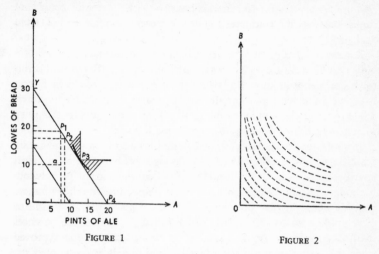

FIGURE 1   FIGURE 2

In a community where there are only two commodities, the consumer must receive his income in one of these commodities; and his weekly income can be expressed by a point on one of the axes. To take a concrete example, assume that the consumer receives a weekly income of 30 loaves of bread, shown by point Y in the diagram. The fact that the consumer receives his income in the form of bread does not mean that he must also consume it in this form. He has access to the market for ale and can buy ale at a fixed price for any part of his income.

The buying of ale for bread at a fixed price can be illustrated in Figure 1 by a movement along a straight line whose slope represents the price of ale in terms of bread. An ale price of, say, $1\frac{1}{2}$ loaves of bread per pint can be expressed by the slope of a line whose intercepts with the two axes stand in the ratio of $1\frac{1}{2}$ to 1. The two parallel lines in Figure 1 are drawn in this way. The ratio of their intercepts with the axes, 15B/10A and 30B/20A, respectively, are both equal to the ratio $1\frac{1}{2}$B/1A. These straight lines are called price lines; and it is apparent that every price can be expressed by an infinite number of parallel price lines.

Of these price lines, only one is of interest to the consumer: the one that goes through the point Y, which represents his income, because different points on this line represent the different combinations of the two commodities that are accessible to him on the basis of his income and the prices of the two commodities. This line, therefore, shows the limitations that the consumer's budget imposes upon him and is called his budget line.

For example, at point p_1 on his budget line, the consumer is buying 8 pints of ale for 12 loaves of bread, which leaves him 18 loaves of bread for his own consumption. By buying an additional pint of ale, he can go to p_2, where he has 9 pints of ale and $16\frac{1}{2}$ loaves of bread, having spent $13\frac{1}{2}$ loaves on ale; and by spending all his income on ale, he can go to p_4, where he has 20 pints of ale but no bread left at all.

In short, the consumer can travel along his budget line and go to any point on it; but the limitations of his budget prevent him from going anywhere above his budget line. He can, of course, go to any point below his budget line, in the area enclosed by the budget line and the two axes; but this would involve throwing away part of his income, which he is most unlikely to do.[2] He usually makes full use of his income, stays on his budget line, and stops at some point on it. The point at which he stops, that is, the proportions in which he consumes the two commodities, we assume to be the most satisfactory to him, since he would not have chosen it otherwise. For example, if the consumer whose income and market opportunities are represented by the budget line in Figure 1 should decide to travel along his budget line to point p_3 and stop there, we assume that p_3 represents the highest level of satisfaction he can reach.

To express graphically the fact that the consumer prefers point p_3 to any other point on or below his budget line, it would be convenient to be able to measure his satisfaction. But, unfortunately, this is impossible, since there is no measure of consumer's satisfaction such as there is of temperature or weight. We can assume, however, that the consumer is able to compare different combinations of commodities and tell whether he would derive the same satisfaction from their consumption, or if not, which would yield him the higher satisfaction. We assume, therefore, that there are other combinations of ale and bread which would give the consumer the same satisfaction as the combination depicted by point p_3. These other combinations can also be shown by points in the diagram; and the curve connecting all these points can be taken as the graphical representation of the level of satisfaction the consumer derives from

---

[2] To get to point *a*, for example, he will travel along his budget line to p_1, the point vertically above *a*, and from there descend to *a* by throwing away 8 loaves of bread.

being on point p_3. This curve is called an indifference curve, because the consumer is indifferent between the various combinations of goods it represents.

What is the shape of this indifference curve? It is obvious, to begin with, that apart from point p_3, where it coincides with the budget line, the entire length of the curve must lie above and to the right of the budget line, since p_3 was assumed to represent a higher level of satisfaction than any other point on or below the budget line. It should also be clear that, in addition to lying above the budget line, the indifference curve will also lie to the left of a vertical straight line drawn upward from p_3, and below a horizontal straight line drawn from p_3 to the right. For going along the vertical line would give the consumer more bread without depriving him of any ale, going along the horizontal line would give him more ale and no less bread, going inside the rectangular wedge enclosed by the two lines would give him more of both ale and bread than he has at point p_3; and all three of these changes would obviously increase his satisfaction. The indifference curve through p_3, therefore, must lie in the area shaded in the diagram. This determines the shape and position of the indifference curve pretty accurately, at least in the immediate vicinity of point p_3. It means that the indifference curve must have a downward slope, be convex to the origin, and, if it is a smooth curve, be tangential to the budget line at point p_3.[3]

That the indifference curve will be downward-sloping and convex to the origin not only in the vicinity of p_3 but throughout its entire length becomes apparent when we consider that indifference curves can be drawn not only through p_3 but through any other point of the diagram as well. In our example the consumer decided on the consumption pattern represented by p_3, because his income and the price of ale were such as to render this his most favorable market behavior. With a different income and a different price of ale, he would probably have chosen a different point; and to every point in the diagram, there corresponds an income and a price the combination of which would induce the consumer to choose that point. His satisfaction at any one point can be represented by an indifference curve going through that point; and in the vicinity of that point the indifference curve will have the same general characteristics we described above: a downward slope and a

---

[3] Throughout this book, we shall always assume that every curve is smooth and without kinks. This will simplify our analysis very much but is not necessary for it. In fact, most propositions in this book could be restated in a way that does not require our curves and functions to be smooth. An example of this will be found on p. 133.

convex shape. The whole diagram, therefore, can be imagined to be covered with small segments of such indifference curves. This is shown in Figure 2 (see p. 31). By connecting the appropriate segments, we obtain a series of indifference curves, all of which are downward-sloping and convex to the origin throughout their entire length.

We have reached this result by inference from the consumer's market behavior; but that indifference curves are downward-sloping and convex from the origin can also be seen from a very elementary analysis of the consumer's psychology. Let us imagine for a moment that we are traveling along an indifference curve. This is an imaginary journey, a mental exercise, because in actual fact the consumer can exchange goods only in the market; and to do so involves moving along the budget line. A movement in any other direction, along any other curve, is purely hypothetical and merely amounts to the consumer's asking himself what it would feel like to vary the quantities of A and B in his possession in that way. To move along an indifference curve means to change one's pattern of consumption in such a way as to leave one's satisfaction unchanged. If something is taken away from the consumer, he must be compensated for his loss by receiving more of something else; if he is given something, another thing must be taken from him in order to keep his satisfaction unchanged. Only very exceptionally would his satisfaction be unaffected by variations in the quantity of one good in his possession, unaccompanied by compensating variations of his possession of another good. Translated into geometrical terms, this means that indifference curves usually have a downward slope, which in a limiting case may approach the horizontal or the vertical.

What curvature indifference curves tend to have can best be shown by reference to a geometrical example. In Figure 3, we assumed that the consumer's satisfaction would be exactly the same at point *a*, where he consumes 5 loaves of bread and 5 pints of ale, as at point *b*, where he has an additional pint of ale but one loaf of bread less. The question is whether his satisfaction would remain the same if he traveled further along a straight line connecting these two points, that is, if he were able to exchange further loaves of bread for an equal number of pints of ale. The answer obviously is no. For the more a person possesses of any given commodity in relation to the quantities of other commodities in his possession, the more completely will his needs of that commodity be filled relatively to his other needs, and the less eager will he be to obtain additional quantities of it at the sacrifice of his other possessions. Hence, the consumer will only sacrifice successively smaller quantities of bread for additional pints of ale; or, to put it in other words, he will exchange further loaves of bread only for successively larger quantities of ale. This will cause his indifference curve to veer to the right and away from the straight line through *a* and *b*. Similarly, if asked to give up ale for bread, the consumer will offer diminishing quantities of ale for successive loaves of bread, which will also cause his indifference curve to veer to the right and away from the straight line through *a* and *b*. In an extreme case the consumer may have so much of one commodity as to derive no satisfaction at all from further additions to his possession of that commodity, and he may be unwilling to give up even the smallest quantity of something else in exchange. At this point the consumer's indifference curve becomes parallel to the axis on which that commodity is measured.

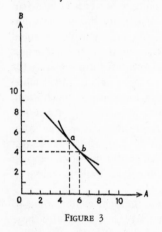

FIGURE 3

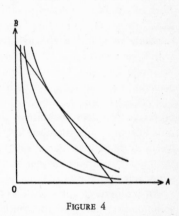

FIGURE 4

The rate at which the consumer can substitute small quantities of one good for small quantities of another good without changing his satisfaction is called his marginal rate of substitution between the two goods and is expressed by the slope of his indifference curve. This rate or slope depends on the quantities of the various goods in his possession, and it changes when these quantities are changed. The consumer's unwillingness to sacrifice one good for successive units of another good except in diminishing quantities is called the law of diminishing marginal rate of substitution and is expressed geometrically by the convexity of the indifference curve.

The curvature of an indifference curve expresses the ease or difficulty with which one commodity can be substituted for another. The more similar two goods are, the less will the marginal rate of substitution between them be affected by changes in the relative quantities of the two goods in the consumer's possession. If two goods are identical, their marginal rate of substitution is completely independent of their relative quantities. This would be true, for example, of the marginal rate of substitution between two brands of butter, identical in quality and fat content. The consumer who regards them as perfect substitutes would be willing to exchange pound for pound one brand for the other, independently of how much he possesses of them already. Geometrically, this would appear as a straight-line indifference curve.

At the opposite extreme are two commodities that cannot be substituted for each other at all. Left and right gloves or left and right shoes are examples of this case. If a consumer derives a certain satisfaction from possessing three pairs of gloves, no addition, however large, to his stock of right-hand gloves could compensate him for the loss of a left-hand glove. An indifference curve between left and right gloves would therefore have an L-shape, its curvature assuming the extreme form of a kink, and its horizontal and vertical arms representing the fact that no increase in the consumer's possession of right or left gloves alone can add to his satisfaction if he has nothing with which to match them.

Needless to say, neither of these extreme cases has any practical importance. One does not think of left and right gloves as separate commodities any more than one regards identical brands of butter as different commodities. As a rule, the consumer distinguishes between commodities that are neither perfect substitutes nor impossible to substitute one for another.

An indifference curve shows not only the different combinations of commodities that yield the consumer equal satisfaction but also those that yield him a lower or a higher satisfaction. For it follows from the definition of the indifference curve that all points below and to the left of it represent lower levels of satisfaction; whereas all points above and to the right of it represent higher levels of satisfaction. Accordingly, when we draw several indifference curves in the same diagram, we can tell that, by passing from one indifference curve to another in the direction away from the origin, we get to higher and higher levels of satisfaction. But this is all we can say about the relation between two indifference curves. We can say that one represents a greater satisfaction than the other; but we cannot say how much greater that satisfaction is, because the statement that it represents a satisfaction, say, twice as great as the other is meaningless. Nor can anything general be said about the relative position of two indifference curves, except that they never inter-sect each other. This is obvious, because their point of intersection would represent a combination of goods that yields simultaneously two dif-ferent levels of satisfaction, which is logically absurd and impossible. This, however, is the only restriction on the relative position of indif-ference curves, which can and does vary from person to person and depends entirely on the consumer's personal tastes and preferences.

Let us now reproduce the diagram with the consumer's budget line and draw into it a whole series of indifference curves, which describe in detail the consumer's preferences as between commodities A and B (Fig. 4, p. 35). This diagram illustrates very clearly how market trans-actions affect the consumer's satisfaction. Traveling along his budget line, the consumer crosses many indifference curves, going first from lower to higher and, beyond a certain point, from higher to lower levels of satisfaction. It is in his interest to stop at the point where his budget line comes in contact with the highest indifference curve. It is apparent from the diagram that this is always the indifference curve which, instead of crossing, merely touches the price line, and that the slopes of budget line and indifference curve are equal at this point.

Recalling that the slope of the indifference curve expresses the con-sumer's marginal rate of substitution between two goods, and that the slope of the budget line shows the rate at which they can be exchanged for each other in the market, we can say that the consumer maximizes his satisfaction at the point where his marginal rate of substitution between two goods is equal to the ratio of their market prices. If we use the symbol MS_{ab} to denote the marginal rate of substitution be-tween goods A and B, and the symbols p_a and p_b to denote the prices of these goods, then the condition for maximizing the consumer's satis-faction can be expressed by the equation:

$$MS_{ab} = \frac{p_a}{p_b}.$$

So far, we have considered only two commodities; but this result, and the analysis on which it is based, can be generalized for any number of commodities. This can be done in either of two ways. First, we could translate our geometry into algebra and show that our above argument holds true and yields the same results also in 3, 4, or n dimensions. Indifference curves would become n-dimensional indifference surfaces in this case, budget lines would become hyperplanes; and we could show that the consumer reaches the highest satisfaction at the point where an indifference surface is tangential to his budget plane, that is, where his marginal rate of substitution between any pair of goods equals the ratio of the market prices of these goods. The second way—and this is the one we shall follow here—is to separate one commodity from the rest and lump together all the others, considering them as the other commodity. This will enable us to deal with any number of commodities in a two-dimensional diagram.

To measure the quantity of a collection of commodities, we shall assume their prices to be fixed and express their quantity in terms of money. In Figure 5, for example, we measure the quantity of a consumer's good, commodity A, on the horizontal axis; and on the vertical axis, we measure money, which here represents the consumer's command over all goods and services *other than* commodity A. This diagram has the advantage that it enables us to express in terms of money both the consumer's income and the price of commodity A. For example, the budget line *ab* in Figure 5 (see p. 41) shows an income of $120 per week and a $15 price of commodity A.

If the consumer goes to point *p* along this budget line and buys 3 units of A for $45, this means not that he saves $75, the rest of his income, but that this sum is partly saved and partly *spent on commodities other than A.* That the consumer goes to point *p* we again take as proof that he reaches his highest satisfaction at that point. This level of satisfaction can be represented by an indifference curve, whose shape and position are derived in exactly the same way as was done above, on page 33. It is tangential to the budget line at *p;* and its slope shows the consumer's marginal rate of substitution between commodity A and money, which latter stands for purchasing power over all other commodities. We shall call this rate the consumer's marginal valuation of commodity A; for —by showing the rate at which he would be indifferent to exchanging A for money or money for A—it expresses the value he attaches to A in terms of money. In Figure 5, for example, the slope of the indifference curve at *p* shows that if he had 3 units of A in his possession and spent $75 on other things, the consumer would value one unit of A as highly as he values $15 of money available for spending on other things. It is obvious that if the consumer's marginal valuation of a good is higher than its market price, he can better his position by buying more of it; and if his marginal valuation of it is lower than its market price, he can gain by buying less of it and spending the money so saved on something else. From this, it follows that the consumer maximizes his satisfaction by buying so much of the commodity as will equate his

THE CONSUMER · 39

marginal valuation of it to its market price. In other words, to maximize his satisfaction, he must buy so much of A that one unit of it gives him the same satisfaction as he would derive from spending its price on other things. In Figure 5, this condition is fulfilled at p, the point of tangency between the budget line and an indifference curve. In symbols, the condition of maximum satisfaction is expressed by the equation

$$MV_a = p_a ,$$

where MV_a denotes the consumer's marginal valuation of good A.

What is true of commodity A is true, of course, of all other commodities as well. When the consumer is a price taker in all the markets where he buys, he so allocates his total expenditure among different goods as to equate his marginal valuation of each good and service to its price. In other words, he spends his income in such a way as to equate the satisfaction derived from a dollar's worth of every commodity he buys to that derived from a dollar's worth of every other commodity he buys. His buying nothing of a particular commodity shows that its marginal value to him is below its price. This becomes apparent when we recall that a consumer can gain by buying less of a commodity whose price is above his marginal valuation of it. He can only do so, however, if he has bought something of it previously. When he has none of it in his possession, he is unable to buy less of it and hence unable to equate its marginal value to him with its price. For example, if the price of a new car is $2,000 and this is above his marginal valuation of a new car, the consumer will feel that he can spend $2,000 more usefully on other things. Such feeling on his part need not mean that he disdains the pleasures of owning a new car; it can also mean that his income is so low that he has not yet filled more urgent needs than his need for a new car—in short, that he cannot afford one.

We can now state our results in their final form. We have shown that the consumer, in his effort to maximize his satisfaction and get the most out of his income, plans his expenditures in a way that makes his marginal valuation of every commodity equal to its price, except for goods of which he buys nothing, whose marginal value to him is below their price. This means that in a market where every consumer is a price taker, the price of every good equals and expresses its marginal valuation by all its consumers.

This is a very important result of our analysis of the consumer's behavior, but let us be quite certain that we know exactly what it means. The simplest way of making our result quite clear is to show what it does not mean. If we had inside information about the consumer's preferences, we could draw his indifference maps; knowing what his income and market prices are, we could draw his budget lines; and we could then say that he maximizes his satisfaction *if* he proceeds to the points of tangency between budget lines and indifference curves and equates marginal values to prices. It is essential to realize that this is not what we have done above. We have no inside information about the consumer's preferences and therefore cannot tell whether or not he maximizes his satisfaction and makes good use of his income. We derived his indifference map, it will be remembered, from his actual market behavior, on the *assumption* that he aims at maximizing his satisfaction and proceeds to the point where marginal values and market prices are equal. This being the assumption on which we based our analysis, we cannot possibly prove or disprove it as the *result* of our analysis. As we stated at the beginning of this chapter, the theory of the consumer's behavior is purely descriptive. It adds nothing to our knowledge of the consumer's behavior and merely rationalizes whatever happens to be his actual market behavior. The usefulness of the theory lies not so much in the new light that it sheds on the consumer's behavior as in the fact that it proves market prices to be an expression of consumers' marginal preferences. This will be discussed in detail in the next chapter.

2. THE INCOME-CONSUMPTION CURVE

So far, we have been concerned with the consumer's market behavior when his income and market prices are given. Our next task is to discuss how he reacts to a change in his income or a change in market prices. We shall do this by deducing the consumer's reaction to income and price changes from his indifference map and by comparing the behavior pattern so derived with the consumer's actual market behavior, as we know it from market experience and statistical demand studies. The consistency of the two behavior patterns will serve as a check on the correctness of our analysis of the consumer.

The main factor influencing the consumer's purchases in the market is his income. We know that when his income rises, he usually spends more and buys more consumers' goods and services; but we also know that of a single commodity he may buy a larger, the same, or even a smaller quantity. Each of these three types of behavior can be shown to be compatible with the general characteristics of the indifference map as we have drawn it.

In a diagram where money is measured along the vertical axis and the consumers' good A along the horizontal axis, different levels of income can be represented by different points on the money axis (Fig. 5). From each of these points a budget line can be drawn. When the price of A is fixed, these successive budget lines will be parallel to each other. As the consumer's income rises, he gets onto higher and higher budget lines; and he travels along each budget line to the point where it is tangential to an indifference curve. By connecting the different points of tangency with each other, we get a curve, called the income-consumption curve, which shows how the consumer apportions his expenditure between good A and other things as his income rises.

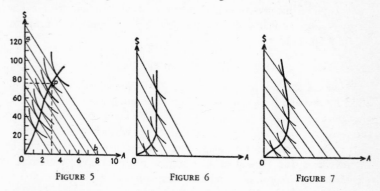

FIGURE 5   FIGURE 6   FIGURE 7

The shape of the income-consumption curve depends on the relative position of successive indifference curves. This can vary within the very wide limits imposed by the requirements that no two indifference curves intersect and that they all slope downward and are convex to the origin. Accordingly, the income-consumption curve can have almost any shape; and we usually distinguish between three types. Commodities for which the demand rises whenever the consumer's income rises have an income-consumption curve with a positive slope throughout its range.[4] This is probably the most important type and describes the consumer's demand for the largest category of goods. It is illustrated in Figure 5.

The second type of income-consumption curve may have a positive slope at first but becomes and stays vertical beyond a certain point. This type illustrates the consumer's demand for necessities, the need for which is biologically determined and limited. As long as the consumer's

---

[4] A slope is positive when the angle it forms with the horizontal axis is between 0 and 90 degrees. A slope is negative when this angle is between 90 and 180 degrees. A positive slope, therefore, is an upward slope; and a negative slope is a downward slope.

need for a necessity is insufficiently filled, a rise in his income will raise his demand for it; but when his consumption of a necessity has reached the saturation point, his demand for it remains unchanged despite a further increase in his income. This is illustrated in Figure 6 (p. 41).

The third type of income-consumption curve shows the consumer's demand for so-called "inferior goods." These are goods bought only or mainly by low-income consumers and replaced by higher-grade substitutes as soon as the consumer can afford them. Among foods, margarine and probably bread are inferior goods; and, in general, low-grade textiles and the cheap variants of most manufactured goods belong to this category. The income-consumption curve of an inferior good has a positive slope at first and then turns back upon itself, as shown in Figure 7 (p. 41).

3. THE PRICE-CONSUMPTION CURVE

While we saw above that a change in the consumer's income may affect his demand for a commodity in almost any way, his response to a change in price shows a certain regularity. We know that in most cases the consumer's demand for a commodity rises when its price falls, and falls when its price rises, although there are exceptional cases in which the reverse is true. How does this compare to the behavior pattern deducible from the consumer's indifference map?

In the same way in which we can draw an income-consumption curve into the consumer's indifference map, we can also draw into it a price-consumption curve, which shows how the consumer's demand for a commodity is affected by changes in the latter's price. When his income is fixed and price changes, the consumer's market opportunities can be represented graphically by drawing budget lines with different slopes from the same income point on the money axis. This is shown in Figure 8. If the consumer travels different distances along the different budget lines, he does so, we assume, because indifference curves are tangential to the different budget lines at different points. By connecting all the points of tangency between budget lines and indifference curves, we can derive the consumer's price-consumption curve. This also is shown in Figure 8.

As drawn in Figure 8, the price-consumption curve shows that the lower the price of A (i.e., the flatter the budget line), the greater the consumer's demand for A. This relation between price and the consumer's demand can be shown more graphically by transferring the price-consumption curve from the indifference map of Figure 8 onto

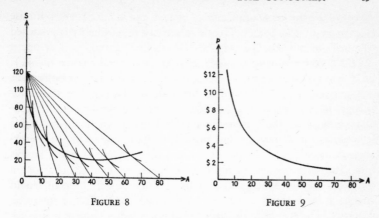

FIGURE 8   FIGURE 9

the price-quantity diagram of Figure 9. Here, the horizontal axis measures the quantity of A as before, but the vertical axis shows the price
of A; and the price-consumption curve of Figure 8 becomes an individual
demand curve with a downward slope.[5] This demand curve corresponds
to the observed relationship between price and consumers' demand; but
we have yet to see whether it is a general rule or whether it is only
the result of the particular way in which the indifference map in Figure
8 was drawn.

The advantage of representing the consumer's response to a change
in price with the aid of the demand curve of Figure 9 is that such individual demand curves can be added together to form a market demand
curve. To perform this addition, all the buyers in the market must face
the same price. In this case the market demand curve is obtained by
adding, for each ordinate (price), the abscissae of the individual demand

---

[5] The identity of the price-consumption curve of Fig. 8 and the demand curve of Fig. 9
is shown by the following table, which gives the numerical data derived from Fig. 8 and
used for drawing the demand curve in Fig. 9:

EXPLANATION	p_1	p_2	p_3	p_4	p_5	p_6	p_7
Slope of price line (ratio of intercepts with the two axes)....................	$\frac{120}{10}$	$\frac{120}{20}$	$\frac{120}{30}$	$\frac{120}{40}$	$\frac{120}{50}$	$\frac{120}{60}$	$\frac{120}{80}$
Price of A in dollars (obtained by carrying out the division indicated in the row above).	12	6	4	3	2.40	2	1.50
Quantity of A demanded (abscissa of the point of tangency in Fig. 8)...........	5	14	24	32	42	50	64

curves of all the buyers in the market (i.e., the quantity demanded by each buyer at that price). This is sometimes called the horizontal addition of the individual curves.

Let us now return to the individual consumer and analyze the way in which a change in price affects his demand for a commodity. For this purpose, it is convenient to break down the effect of the price change into two parts. A price reduction, for example, can be thought of as influencing the consumer's market behavior in two ways. First, it improves his welfare, because it enables him to buy more goods with a given income; and, second, it changes the structure of prices facing him. The improvement in his welfare affects his market behavior in the same way in which a rise in his income would; the consequent change in his demand is therefore called the income effect of the price reduction. The change in the structure of prices induces him to rearrange his consumption pattern; and the resulting change in his demand is the substitution effect of the price reduction. The meaning and usefulness of separating the effect of a price change on demand into these two effects can best be shown with the aid of a diagram.

In Figure 10 the lowering of A's price from p_1 to p_2 has induced the consumer to raise his demand for A from a_1 to a_2; and it is apparent from the diagram that the reduction in price has improved his welfare, since it has enabled him to reach a higher indifference curve. But the same improvement in his welfare could have been brought about also without a price reduction, by a rise in his income sufficient to bring him onto the same indifference curve. This hypothetical rise in the consumer's income expresses what the reduction in the price of A is worth to him in terms of money. It is called the "equivalent variation," because it represents the income variation which would be equivalent to the price change in its effect on the consumer's welfare. In Figure 10 the equivalent variation is shown by the distance m_2m_1 on the vertical axis.

But, although the equivalent variation in income would have the same effect on the consumer's welfare as the change in price, its effect on the consumer's demand would be different. This is apparent from the diagram. A rise in the consumer's income from m_1 to m_2 would raise his demand for A from a_1 to a_3. This change in demand is the income effect of the price reduction, that is, the change in demand due to the consumer's being better off as a result of the price reduction.

The consumer's demand for A, however, changes not only because he is better off but also because the price of A has changed relative to the prices of other goods. We know that the consumer equates his marginal valuation of A to the price of A; and, when the latter falls, he must substitute A for other goods in order to lower A's marginal value to him. This substitution of A for other goods is shown in the diagram by a movement along the indifference curve from l_3 to l_2; and the resultant increase from a_3 to a_2 in the consumer's demand for A is the substitution effect of the price reduction. The sum of the income effect, a_3a_1, and the substitution effect, a_2a_3, constitutes a_2a_1, the total change in the demand for A caused by the price reduction.

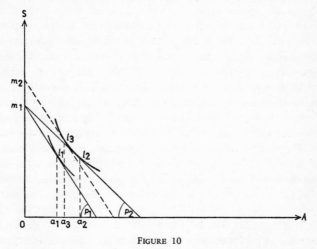

The purpose of separating the effect of a price change on consumer's demand into two parts is that it enables us to say a little more about the nature of this change than we could say otherwise. It is apparent, to begin with, that the substitution effect, which results from a movement along an indifference curve, always pulls in the same direction. The substitution effect of a fall in price tends always to raise demand and that of a rise in price tends always to lower demand for the good whose price has changed. We can also tell that, the closer substitutes there are for the good in question, the greater the substitution effect will be; and that it will be zero if there are no substitutes at all.

As to the income effect, no general statement can be made about its direction. We have shown that a price reduction is equivalent to a rise in income; but a rise in income may raise, lower, or leave unchanged the consumer's demand for a good. Accordingly, the income effect of a price reduction may also raise, lower, or leave unchanged the consumer's demand. In the first case, where a rise in income would raise demand, the income effect and substitution effect of a price change are additive. This was illustrated in Figure 10. In the last case, where a change in income would leave demand unchanged, the income effect is zero; and the only effect of a price change is its substitution effect. In the second case, where a rise in income would lower demand, income effect and substitution effect pull in opposite directions; and the total effect of a price change is the difference between the two. This happens in the case of inferior goods. For example, a fall in the price of bread tends to induce the consumer to substitute bread for other forms of food and so adapt his marginal rate of substitution between bread and other foods to the changed ratio of their market prices. At the same time, however, the fall in the price of bread renders the consumer better off than he was before and enables him to consume his calories in the form of more expensive foods. Whether, on balance, the fall in the price of bread will make him buy more or less bread depends on whether the substitution effect is greater or smaller than the income effect. The factors determining the substitution effect have been discussed above; the magnitude of the income effect depends mainly on the importance of the commodity in question in the consumer's budget. A given fall in the price of a commodity will make the consumer the better off the more he spends on the commodity; and the better off he becomes, the more his demand will be affected by the change. The fall in the price of bread, therefore, will have a large income effect on the demand of a person with a very low income, whose expenditure on bread looms large in his budget. Only in his case is the income effect likely to exceed the substitution effect and cause his demand for bread to fall as the price of bread falls.[6]

This argument shows that a rising demand curve is possible but not very likely. For a rise in price may raise and a fall may lower demand only in the case of inferior goods, which are a special and probably small group. Moreover, even in the case of inferior goods, the consumer's

---

[6] To render the measurement of income and substitution effects independent of the unit of measurement in terms of which the quantity of the commodity in question is being expressed, economists have developed the concepts of income elasticity and elasticity of substitution. Income elasticity is defined as the ratio of the percentage change in the consumer's demand for a commodity to the percentage change in his income that has (or would have) brought about the change in his demand. For the definition of elasticity of substitution, see S. Weintraub, *Price Theory* (New York: Pitman Publishing Corp., 1949), pp. 67–68.

demand will be lowered by a price rise and raised by a price reduction if the income effect of the price change is smaller than the substitution effect. Only if the income effect exceeds the substitution effect will the individual's demand rise (fall) with a rise (fall) in price; and for the market demand curve to be rising, it would be necessary for the majority of the members of the market to behave in this way.

4. COMPLEMENTARITY AND SUBSTITUTABILITY

So far, we have been concerned with the effect of a price change on the consumer's demand for the commodity whose price has changed. But the consumer's demand for any one commodity depends on the price not only of that commodity but of all other commodities as well; and a change in the price of one commodity will affect his demand not only for that commodity but also for other commodities. We have to try, therefore, to answer the question as to how a change in the price of A affects the consumer's demand for commodity B.

Here again, it will be convenient to break down the total effect of the price change into an income and a substitution effect. The income effect is easy to deal with. A reduction in the price of A makes the consumer better off; and the improvement in his welfare has an income effect on his demand for B essentially similar to its income effect on his demand for A. In other words, the income effect on B of a price reduction in A is to raise the consumer's demand for B if this is an ordinary good, to lower it if this is an inferior good, and to leave it unchanged if B is a necessity.

To determine the substitution effect would be simple enough if there were only two commodities. We know that a reduction in the price of A always leads to a substitution of A for other goods; and if B were the only other good, the substitution effect on B of the price reduction in A would necessarily be to lower the consumer's demand for B. When there are more than two commodities, however, this need no longer follow. When a reduction in the price of A prompts the consumer to rearrange his expenditure pattern in favor of A, he may or may not do this at the cost of B; and he may even increase his consumption of B. For example, a reduction in the price of whiskey may cause the consumer to substitute whiskey for beer; but, at the same time, he may also be prompted to substitute soda water for something else. The substitution effect of a reduction in the price of A, therefore, may tend either to lower or to raise the consumer's demand for B, depending on the type of relation that exists between the two commodities. A relation like that between whiskey and beer in the above example is called substitutability; whereas that between whiskey and soda water is called complementarity. If B is complementary to A, a fall in the price of A is likely to raise the consumer's demand for B; although it will lower his demand for B in the unlikely case that B is an inferior good and the income effect is strong enough to swamp the substitution effect. If A and B are substitutes for each other, it becomes more difficult to predict the effect of a change in the price of one on the consumer's demand for the other. For in this case, substitution and income effects pull in the same direction only if B is an inferior good; and only then can we say definitely that a fall in A's price will lower the demand for B. If B is an ordinary good, substitution and income effects pull in opposite directions; and a fall in A's price will lower or raise the consumer's demand for B, depending on whether the substitution effect or the income effect is stronger.

5. THE IMPORTANCE OF TIME AND HABIT

The theory of the consumer's behavior, as presented above, describes the actual market behavior of the rational consumer. It may be objected, however, that the consumer is not as rational as this theory presents him. Surely, it may be argued, consumers' preferences are not as set and definite as an indifference map might suggest. Furthermore, one can hardly imagine one's wife weighing alternative opportunities and equating marginal value to price every time she runs down to the corner grocery store to buy something. She will not do this—not even when she is a professional economist herself—because the saving in money achieved by such superrational shopping would not be worth the expenditure of nervous energy which it would require. In other words, the consumer's rational behavior need not mean the careful weighing of alternatives each time he buys something; and his reliance on habit and past experience may itself be the result of a rational preference for leisure as against the small saving to be achieved by supercareful shopping.

The average consumer has fixed consumption habits, which he has acquired on the basis of past price constellations; and it takes time for a changed price to break an old habit and form a new one. When relative prices change or new opportunities arise, the consumer usually continues in his accustomed grooves for a while, because he needs time to learn about a change, to appraise its significance, and more time still to adapt his behavior to it and face the inconveniences or hazards that changing one's behavior often involves. In other words, people's propensity to form habits and their slowness in adapting themselves to changed circumstances render their economic behavior a function not only of current but also of past prices. The equating of marginal values to prices must be conceived of more as a goal constantly aimed at and approximated than as something actually accomplished at every moment of time.

During stationary periods, when price changes are few and small, the consumer may have enough time to make full adjustment to the market situation; but in times of rapid change, he may never catch up with the changing pattern of prices. The time lag with which the consumer adjusts his market behavior to a changed market situation depends on a variety of factors, among which the consumer's information or lack of information is perhaps the most important. An informed person, knowing the merits of alternative offers, will be quick to profit by a price reduction or to adjust his behavior to a price rise. An uninformed consumer, however, has to rely on habit and past experience to a greater extent and will feel his way slowly and cautiously toward trying out a new brand of a commodity or otherwise adjusting his behavior when prices change. Accordingly, the consumer's reaction time is different with respect to different commodities. He can easily appraise simple commodities; hence, his reaction to a change in their prices, or to a new commodity offered in their market, will be fairly quick. He has less self-confidence in appraising technically or chemically complex commodities and therefore needs more time for adjusting his purchases to a change in the relative prices of such goods. For example, the average consumer is a fairly good judge of clothes and will be quick to profit by a price reduction or to abandon his favorite make if its price rises out of proportion to its quality. In the case of an electric iron, however, or an automobile, or any other complex good about whose technical intricacies he knows little or nothing, the consumer is likely to be strongly attached to a particular brand or manufacturer he already has confidence in; and he will be slow to switch to an untried brand in response to a changed market situation.

Another determining factor of the consumer's reaction time is the durability and divisibility of a good. Buying a new brand of a commodity is always a gamble for the consumer; and the longer the time for which that commodity is meant to be in use, the greater the gamble. For the consumer can seldom judge the quality of an untried brand at the moment when he buys it; and the longer it lasts, the more he will

c

suffer from it if it turns out to be of inferior quality. Hence, the more durable or the less divisible a good, the more time people need to make up their minds to change to another brand in response to a change in price. A simple illustration of the truth of this argument is the popularity of so-called "sample sizes." We will try a new kind of tooth paste much sooner if it is available in small tubes than if it can only be had in large ones.

Yet another and perhaps more important determining factor is the importance of a commodity in the consumer's budget. The greater the proportion of his income that he spends on a given commodity, the more keenly will he feel the effects of a change in its price, and the sooner will the change induce him to adjust his behavior to it. Thus, a rise in the price of meat will soon induce people to consume less meat and eat more fish or fowl or vegetables instead; whereas a similar rise in the price of coffee will be slow to combat the coffee-drinking habit. Another example is the common observation that rich people are always more firmly set in their buying habits than the poor, especially as far as necessities are concerned. This is so because almost any good, and certainly any necessity, looms larger in the poor man's budget than in that of the rich. Hence, the poor are more affected by a change in price and are sooner induced by it to change their buying habits.

These factors and their influence on the speed or time lag with which the consumer's market behavior responds to a change in prices are not relevant to our discussion of perfect competition. They will become important for us only at a much later stage, in Chapter XII, where we shall discuss the stability of the price maker's behavior.

BIBLIOGRAPHICAL NOTE

The modern theory of consumer's choice and market behavior is based upon the work of J. R. Hicks and R. G. D. Allen in "A Reconsideration of the Theory of Value," Parts I and II, *Economica*, N.S., Vol. I (February and May, 1934), pp. 52–76 and 196–219. Later, the theory was restated in somewhat more complete form in J. R. Hicks, *Value and Capital* (Oxford: Clarendon Press, 1939), Part I. The argument of the present chapter follows Professor Hicks's presentation in his book. For a critical view of Hicks's presentation, see I. M. D. Little, "A Reformulation of the Theory of Consumer's Behavior," *Oxford Economic Papers*, N.S., Vol. I (January, 1949), pp. 90–99.

CHAPTER IV

THE CONSUMERS' MARKET AND THE NOTION OF ECONOMIC EFFICIENCY

THE discussion in the last chapter of the individual consumer's market behavior has enabled us neither to help him plan his expenditures nor to sit in judgment over his behavior; but this, it must be remembered, was not the aim of our analysis. In the economist's eyes the consumer is king; and the aim of our analysis was to see not whether consumers conform to an ideal behavior pattern but whether the economic system conforms or can be made to conform to the consumer's wishes. For this purpose, it has been necessary, first of all, to ascertain the way in which the consumer's wishes—whatever they may be—make themselves felt in the market as demand; and this is why, in the last chapter, we developed a method whereby we might infer the consumer's preferences from his behavior. Much of what follows will be concerned with appraising economic institutions and policies by their conformity with consumers' preferences. In the present chapter we shall apply this criterion to the one institution that, in the absence of a discussion of production, can be so appraised already at this stage: the consumers' market through which consumers' goods and services are distributed.

1. THE EFFICIENCY OF DISTRIBUTION

In order to set up the criteria of an ideal distributive system, we shall assume the available quantity of goods and services to be fixed and start out with the simple case of only two people and two commodities. Let us call the two commodities A and B, and the two people Frank and George or, for short, F and G. Both Frank and George consume A and B and buy these commodities for consumption only. In a diagram in which Frank's consumption of A is measured along the horizontal axis and his consumption of B along the vertical axis, any combination of A and B consumed by Frank can be expressed by a point. In a similar diagram drawn for George, points express George's consumption of commodities A and B. Turning George's diagram around by 180 degrees, so that his consumption of A is measured from right to left and his consumption of B is measured vertically downwards, and superimposing this upside-down diagram on Frank's diagram, we get the box diagram shown in Figure 11. The width of this box measures the

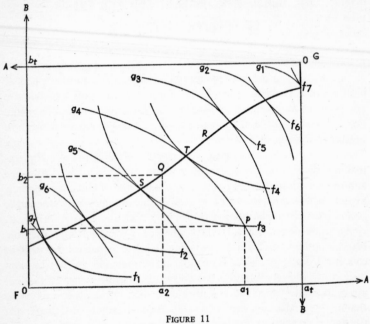

FIGURE 11

fixed quantity of A, a_t, which is available to the two people; the height of the box measures the fixed quantity of B, b_t, available to them; and any point within the box shows a given distribution of A and B between the two people. For example, the mid-point of the box shows an equal distribution of both A and B between F and G. Point P shows that F gets a_1 of A and b_1 of B; whereas G gets the remainder, a_1a_t of A and b_1b_t of B. A movement in the box diagram from one point to another represents an exchange of commodities between the two people. For example, a movement from P to Q is the geometrical representation of a transaction whereby Frank gives George a_1a_2 of commodity A in exchange for b_2b_1 of commodity B.

Whereas the quantities of the goods consumed by the two people are shown by the co-ordinates of a point referred to the two pairs of axes, the satisfaction the two people derive from consuming these quantities can be represented by indifference curves. F's system of indifference curves has the appearance we are accustomed to from the previous chapter; G's indifference curves are similar, except that they are turned around and upside down. Through every point in the box diagram, two indifference curves can be drawn, showing the two people's levels of satisfaction at that point. For example, at point P, F's satisfaction is shown by the indifference curve f_3, G's by the indifference curve g_4. F would be in a better position anywhere above the curve f_3, whereas G's position would be better anywhere below the curve g_4; and it is apparent from the diagram that, starting from point P, both F and G could simultaneously better their positions by moving to any point within the area bounded by the indifference curves f_3 and g_4. For example, moving from P to Q, which represents an exchange of goods between F and G, would raise the satisfaction of both of them. There is nothing surprising, of course, about an exchange of goods making both parties to the exchange better off: this, after all, is the aim of every market transaction. People would not trade if they did not expect thereby to better their position; and the mere fact that trading occurs proves that it is to mutual advantage.

An inspection of Figure 11 will show that from every point in the diagram where two indifference curves cross, it is possible to proceed to a whole range of other points which lie on the concave side of the two intersecting indifference curves and which represent higher levels of satisfaction from both people's point of view. An exchange of goods that involves such a movement, therefore, would benefit both F and G. By contrast, there are other points in the diagram from which no movement is possible that would benefit both parties simultaneously. These are the points where indifference curves only touch each other. Point T, for example, where the indifference curves f_4 and g_4 are tangential to each other, is such a point. Proceeding from T, either F or G could be brought onto a higher level of satisfaction, but only at the cost of reducing the other person's satisfaction. There is a whole range of such points in the figure, where two indifference curves are tangential to each other, and wherefrom no movement beneficial to both parties is possible. In Figure 11, these points have been connected by a curve, which is called the contract curve. Moving along the contract curve from left to right would bring F to successively higher and G to successively lower levels of satisfaction; but at no point on the contract curve is it possible to improve one man's satisfaction without diminishing the other's.

In addition to the points of tangency between indifference curves, there are also other points in the diagram wherefrom no movement is possible that would benefit both parties simultaneously, even though the indifference curves through these points are not tangential. For example, the meeting point of indifference curves f_7 and g_1 on the right-hand vertical axis is such a point. The reason that, starting from this point, we cannot move in such a way as to benefit both people simultaneously is that we cannot go outside the box diagram. If we could prolong the two indifference curves to the right, we would probably find a point that is on the concave side of both curves; but we cannot do this, because going outside the box to the right would mean that G consumes a negative quantity of A, which is impossible and absurd.

Since we must imagine every indifference map densely covered with indifference curves (of which only a few have been drawn in our diagrams), it is apparent that there are many points like the meeting point of the f_7 and g_1 curves; and all these points must lie on the axes, in the sections between the origin and the point where the contract curve reaches the axis. It will be convenient to draw the contract curve so as to include also these points. Accordingly, the contract curve in Figure 11 extends from origin to origin and coincides with the axes along these sections.

We are now ready to set up standards for the distribution of the two goods between the two people and to examine how distribution in our economy measures up to these standards. It is obvious, to begin with, that distribution between two people always involves a clash of interests. What F gets, G cannot get; and this immediately raises a moral problem: Is it equitable for F to get this much when G is getting that much? This is an important problem, but it is not the only one. In addition to being equitable, distribution must also be efficient. We shall therefore have to discuss both the ethical and the efficiency aspects of distribution, and it will be convenient to start with the problem of efficiency.

We saw above how a movement from P to Q in Figure 11 represented a redistribution of A and B between F and G that brought both of them onto a higher indifference curve. Such a redistribution of goods involves no redistribution of satisfactions in the sense of benefiting one man at the expense of another. A change that benefits somebody without hurting anybody can objectively be said to be a change for the better; and it is a change of this kind that the movement from P to Q involves. This idea is the basis of the notion of economic efficiency.

We shall say that any change of economic policy or institutions capable of making some people better off without making anyone worse off is a change that improves economic efficiency. A situation in which it would be impossible to make anyone better off without making someone else worse off, therefore, will be called an economically efficient situation.

We have derived this definition of economic efficiency in connection with our discussion of the distribution of goods and services among consumers; but its applicability is much more general. We shall use the same criterion of economic efficiency to appraise all economic institutions and not only the system of distribution among consumers. In particular, we shall use it later to appraise the efficiency of the labor market, of the firm, and of the productive system in general.

In addition to economic efficiency, we shall also be concerned, at a later stage, with another form of efficiency, called technological efficiency. Technological efficiency, and the difference between it and economic efficiency, will be discussed in detail in Chapter VIII. Suffice it here to say that an economically efficient distribution of consumers' goods is one that distributes a given quantity of goods in best conformity with consumers' preferences; whereas a technologically efficient distributive system is one that performs the physical task of distribution at a minimum cost in terms of manpower, equipment, and other resources.

Returning now to the particular problem at hand, we can say that the distribution of goods between F and G is economically efficient when it is impossible by a mere redistribution of the fixed quantities of A and B to bring either F or G onto a higher indifference curve without pushing the other person onto a lower one. Therefore, to prove that a distributive system is efficient, we have to show that it enables any pair of consumers to get onto their contract curve.

In Chapter III, we showed that when the consumer is a price taker, he always equates his marginal rate of substitution between any two goods he buys to their relative market prices; or, in geometrical terms, he always proceeds to a point in his indifference map where an indifference curve is tangential to his budget line. When all consumers are price takers and they all face the same prices in the market, the budget lines of all consumers have the same slope; and each consumer proceeds to a point in his indifference map where one of his indifference curves has the same slope as the budget lines and indifference curves of all the other consumers. In other words, each consumer adopts a consumption pattern which makes his marginal rate of substitution between any two goods the same as that of any other consumer who also consumes the same two goods.

It is easy to see that such behavior brings any pair of consumers onto their contract curve. Figures 12 and 13 show the consumption patterns of two consumers who have different incomes and different tastes and

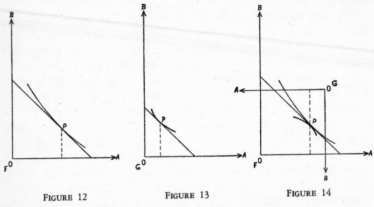

FIGURE 12   FIGURE 13   FIGURE 14

who consume different quantities of the two goods, but both of whom face the same market prices and choose a consumption pattern (p and P, respectively) for which their marginal rates of substitution between the two goods are the same. To represent the possibilities of barter between these two people, the two figures must be superimposed upon each other in such a way that the length and width of the resulting box diagram represent the total quantities of the two goods in their joint possession. This has been done in Figure 14. It is apparent that this will *always* cause the two budget lines and points p and P to coincide, from which it immediately follows that the two indifference curves on which p and P are respectively located are tangential to one another at the point at which p and P coincide. This shows that barter to mutual advantage is impossible between these two people and that they are on their contract curve.

So far, we have been concerned with two people who are both consumers of the two goods considered and are therefore able to equate their marginal rates of substitution to the ratio of market prices. We have yet to show that barter to mutual advantage is also impossible between people who are not both consumers of the two goods. To do this, let us pair off the person whose indifference map and market behavior are shown in Figure 12 with a third person who consumes B but cannot afford to consume A, because his marginal valuation of A is lower than its price. Figure 15 shows the budget line, indifference

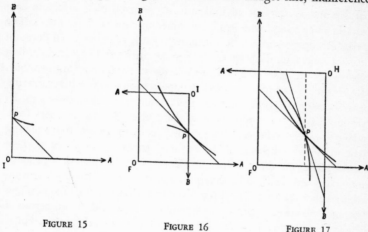

FIGURE 15   FIGURE 16   FIGURE 17

curve, and consumption pattern of such a person. In Figure 16, this diagram is superimposed on that of Figure 12; and it is apparent that, although these two people's marginal rates of substitution between the two goods are not equal, they are nevertheless unable to barter to mutual advantage. This completes our proof of the proposition that when all consumers are price takers and they all face the same market prices, any two consumers will always be on their contract curve.

Although the above argument has been concerned with only two commodities and only two consumers, the conclusion we have derived from it is perfectly general and applies to any number of commodities and any number of consumers. This is so because we proved our proposition not for a specially selected pair of commodities and a particular pair of consumers but for any two commodities and any two consumers chosen at random. In other words, we started out with a large number of commodities and a large number of consumers; and then we showed that, however a pair of commodities and a pair of consumers are selected from among these, we always get the same result. It is clear that a result so reached must apply to all the consumers and all the commodities from among which the selection was made.

Having proved that perfect competition among consumers results in an efficient allocation of consumers' goods and services, we may consider for a moment what happens when competition among consumers is not perfect. Imperfect competition among consumers may assume a variety of forms. First of all, the consumer may be able to bargain and so exert a conscious influence over price. This seldom happens in our society, where the consumer usually faces set prices. The mere fact, however, that the consumer regards prices as given does not in itself render him a price taker. For the price taker, while regarding prices as given, must also be free to decide what and how much to buy. Hence, the second form of market imperfection occurs when rationing or a shortage of goods deprives the consumer of his freedom to determine his rate of purchases. Rationing keeps some consumers from buying as much as they want of rationed goods and hence from equating their marginal valuation of the rationed goods to the prices of these goods. Therefore, different people's marginal valuations of a rationed commodity are likely to be different; and the same is true also of commodities that are in short supply. Even in the absence of rationing and shortages, however, competition among consumers may be imperfect if all consumers, though price takers, do not face the same prices. For if different consumers or groups of consumers pay different prices for the same commodity, their marginal valuations of that commodity will also be different. Price discrimination, therefore, is the third form of market imperfection.

In the following, only the results of this last form of market imperfection will be analyzed. This case is illustrated in Figure 17 (p. 57), where on top of F's indifference map, as shown in Figure 12, we have superimposed the indifference map of consumer H, who pays for commodity A a higher price than F and whose budget line therefore has a steeper slope than F's. Again, the two diagrams are superimposed in such a way that the distribution of the two commodities between F and H is shown by point p. But now, the two budget lines, having different slopes, intersect at this point; and so do the two people's indifference curves that go through this point and are tangential to their respective budget lines. Accordingly, the distribution of the two commodities between F and H is not efficient; and the same could be proved, with the aid of similar diagrams, also in the case of rationing, shortages, or any other form of imperfect competition among consumers.

We have proved, therefore, not only that perfect competition among consumers results in efficient distribution but also that imperfect competition among them results in an inefficient distribution of consumers' goods and services. This is an important result, because competition among consumers is usually perfect in our economy, and because the resulting efficient distribution of consumers' goods and services is one of the elements of an efficient economic system. But lest we exaggerate the importance of having an efficient distribution of consumers' goods and services, let us examine its limitations and see what exactly it amounts to. One look at Figure 11 shows that an efficient distribution of goods is not in itself enough to insure an ideal distribution of goods. For distribution is efficient at any point on the contract curve; and since the contract curve runs diagonally across the whole diagram, efficient distribution appears to be compatible with extreme inequalities in different people's income and welfare. In fact, goods and services can be efficiently distributed for any and every income distribution. Perfect competition among consumers and the consequent efficient distribution of goods and services can be likened to a system of balloting that enables everybody to register his preferences and distributes goods and services according to people's preferences; but such a system is not necessarily democratic because, instead of giving everybody equal votes, it weights people's preferences according to their purchasing power. It follows from this that, for the distribution of consumers' goods and services to be ideal, the distribution of wealth and income—the two sources of purchasing power—would also have to be ideal.

Efficiency, therefore, is only one of two criteria by which economic organization must be appraised. Equity is the other criterion; and it is an equally important one. Unfortunately, the economist cannot set up standards of equity as he sets up standards of efficiency; nor have objective or universally accepted standards of equity been set up by anyone else. This raises the difficult problem as to how the economist can provide the basis for appraising economic organization when he only has one of the two yardsticks by which economic organization must be judged.

Only in one special case is there a simple solution to this problem. If he has to choose between two situations that are exactly equal as far as the distribution of income and wealth is concerned, the economist can pass judgment by the criterion of efficiency alone. This is so because, for any *given* distribution of wealth and income, it is better to have a more efficient economic organization than a less efficient one. But very rarely is the economist's task as simple as this. As a rule, he has to weigh alternatives that differ both in efficiency and in the distribution of wealth and income; and we shall have to discuss the nature of the problem that is raised by such a choice.

Before doing so, however, we must first explain why we regard the distribution of income and wealth as a matter of equity alone.[1] One might define an efficient economic organization as one that maximizes the sum total of human satisfactions. Accordingly, one might argue that taking $100 from a millionaire and giving it to a beggar would not only render income distribution more equitable but would also raise the efficiency of the economic system, since the millionaire's loss of satisfaction would be negligible, the beggar's gain considerable, and the sum of their satisfactions would therefore be increased on balance. This argument appeals to common sense but cannot be proved, because we cannot compare or add one person's satisfaction to another person's. In other words, we have a strong subjective feeling but no objective proof that such a redistribution of income would increase the sum total of satisfactions—as, indeed, we can attach no definite and rigorously defined meaning to the idea of a sum of satisfactions. It seems advisable, therefore, to keep objective and provable statements meticulously apart from arguments based on subjective feeling alone. This is the basis of our distinction between efficiency and equity. We regard all arguments based on subjective judgment as matters of equity and use the term "efficiency" only in connection with statements that can be proved.

2. EQUITY AND EFFICIENCY

When the economist has to appraise the relative merits of two alternative systems of distribution among consumers—or more generally, of two alternative economic policies or forms of economic organization —he usually finds that they differ with respect to both efficiency and equity.[2] Accordingly, he must be prepared to make his appraisal on both efficiency and equity grounds. On occasion, this may be very difficult; for it may happen that one alternative is preferable on efficiency grounds, whereas the other is better on equity grounds.

It will be convenient to analyze the nature of this problem diagrammatically, with the aid of the box diagram in Figure 11. We have discussed the difference between a point on the contract curve and one off

---

[1] We are deliberately ignoring here the effect of income distribution on incentive. That topic will be discussed in sec. 6 of Chap. V.

[2] In this section, we shall be concerned only with the distribution of goods and services among consumers. But the argument is of general validity and applies *pari passu* to the connection and possible conflict between equity and efficiency in all fields of economic organization.

it; and this difference has served as the basis for our definition of economic efficiency. We have shown that, to any given point off the contract curve, such as P in Figure 11, there corresponds a whole range of points on the contract curve, such as the range between S and T, which is preferable to it from the point of view of both persons. It is important to realize, however, that from this it does *not* follow that both would prefer *any* point on the contract curve to *any* point off the contract curve. Compare, for example, points P and R in Figure 11; and think of them as representing the results of two alternative economic systems that would bring these two people to points P and R, respectively. Unlike P and Q, points P and R differ from each other not only in efficiency but also in the two people's relative levels of satisfaction. Distribution is undoubtedly more efficient at R, and F is better off there; but G is less well off at R than at P; and if we were very much concerned with G's welfare, we might well prefer P to R, despite the former's lower efficiency.

It could be argued, of course, that the equity of distribution is a matter of ethics or politics and, as such, is none of the economist's concern. One might say, therefore, that the economist should always favor R as the more efficient measure of the two, leaving equity to be taken care of by whoever is responsible for taking care of it.

This might conceivably be the correct attitude in a socialist economy, or generally in an economy in which the state assumes full control over the regulation of economic affairs and takes full responsibility for maintaining an equitable distribution of income. In such an economy the economist could make policy recommendations on the basis of efficiency considerations alone, because he could rest assured that if his recommendations were followed and resulted in a redistribution of income which was considered undesirable, this would be corrected as a matter of course by the authority responsible for maintaining an equitable distribution of income. In terms of our diagram, if the economist's recommendations should lead to R and the state should consider R an inequitable position, the latter would tax away some of F's gain, from this compensate G for his loss, and so bring the two people to, say, point Q in the diagram, enabling both of them to benefit by the superior efficiency of measure R.

In the free-enterprise economy, however, we cannot take it for granted that changes in economic policy will be accompanied by a state-imposed redistribution of income offsetting any loss of equity which may be caused by such changes. This is so not because the state is unwilling to take action to mitigate inequities in distribution (progressive taxation and social insurance testify to the contrary) but because there is a presumption in such an economy against the state's interfering, except in a general way, with the income distribution brought about by the market mechanism. A change in a country's foreign-trade policy, the raising or lowering of tariffs, a change in farm policy, or any other economic change usually benefits some people and harms others; but it seldom happens in our economy that those harmed are compensated for their loss. In other words, the effects of economic policy on efficiency on the one hand and on income distribution on the other hand cannot—as a rule—be separated, because compensation payments are seldom feasible politically in the free-enterprise economy. From this, it follows that in such an economy all policy decisions must be based on considerations both of efficiency and of equity.

Nevertheless, it is sometimes argued that, even in the free-enterprise economy, economists should concern themselves with efficiency considerations alone. According to this argument, economists should offer the policy maker their expert advice on matters of inefficiency and warn him at the same time that he must also get expert advice on matters of equity and base his decision on both efficiency and equity considerations.

This argument would be valid if there were experts on equity, whose opinions could be pitted against the economist's expert opinion on efficiency. In our society, however, there are no such experts. The economist is as good a judge of equity as anyone else; as a matter of fact, he, as a social scientist, is considered by many a better judge. Also, the economist is in the best position to appraise the relative importance of efficiency and equity considerations. In any case, whether the economist is better or merely no worse than others in judging equity, he cannot neglect it. For if he did, and based his recommendations on efficiency considerations alone, he might unwittingly cause these considerations to be given more weight than is their due. If he ignored considerations of equity although the public regarded him, rightly or wrongly, as the best judge of equity, he would give the impression that he considered efficiency a more important criterion than equity. But even if the public did not regard him as the best judge of equity, he could still not ignore equity considerations; for if he did, there would be danger that his expert advice on efficiency would be given more weight than the public's vague feelings concerning equity. In our society, therefore, the economist must, whether he likes it or not, weigh both efficiency and equity considerations when he tenders his advice on policy decisions. He must make it clear, of course, that his recommendations are based on both criteria; and he must also stress the fact that, on matters of equity, he does not consider himself an expert.

The impossibility in most cases of separating considerations of efficiency from those of equity and the consequent need for considering both together explain one essential difference between economics and, say, engineering. The standards of efficiency are as objective and scientific in economics as they are in engineering; but whereas they are the only standards of the engineer, the economist must weigh, in addition to the objective and scientific standard of efficiency, also the subjective and ethical standard of equity. This is why it is not enough for the economist to be merely a competent technician. Since most of his recommendations are bound to affect the distribution of welfare between individuals and between social classes, he must also have a sense of fairness and economic justice.

Let us now return to our diagram. We are concerned with the problem of how to choose between P and R on the basis both of efficiency and of equity. To emphasize the fact that the choice has to be made on the basis of two entirely separate criteria, we shall make the comparison between P and R in two separate steps, by comparing the two points not to each other but to an intermediate point, Q. There may be a slight difference in equity between P and Q; but this can be neglected, since Q is preferable to P from both people's point of view. This part of the comparison, therefore, can be made on the basis of efficiency considerations alone. Points Q and R are equally efficient, since both lie on the contract curve; but they differ as far as the two people's relative satisfactions are concerned, since F is better off at R, and G is better off at Q. This part of the comparison, therefore, can be made on the basis of equity considerations alone. In choosing between Q and R, one person's gain must be weighed against the other's loss; and according to one's appraisal of their relative needs and deserts, one may regard either Q or R as representing the more equitable distribution of welfare between the two people; or one may regard them as equally equitable.[3] These three possibilities give rise to three different cases, each of which merits closer examination.

Before discussing these three cases in detail, let us summarize them, together with the two simpler ones, in which the comparison between

---

[3] For an example of two different but equally equitable income distributions, consider a community consisting of two people, Frank and George; and assume that their needs, tastes, and deserts are similar. Then, giving an income of $6,000 to Frank and $4,000 to George is as equitable as giving $6,000 to George and $4,000 to Frank.

the alternative situations can be made on the basis of only one criterion. We shall list the two simpler cases first, and the three more complex ones afterwards:

1. One of the simpler cases is that in which two alternative situations are equally efficient, differing only in the distribution of income. An example of this would be the choice between two situations that lead our two consumers to positions R and Q, respectively. In choosing between these two situations, we need not worry about efficiency at all and can make up our minds on the basis of equity considerations alone.

2. Equally simple is the choice between two situations that differ only in efficiency but not in the distribution of income. This case (mentioned on page 59 corresponds to a choice between P and Q. In choosing between these alternatives, we can forget about equity, concentrate on efficiency, and on efficiency grounds give Q preference over P.

3. We now come to the first of the three complex cases, where the choice between two alternatives must be made on the basis of both equity and efficiency considerations, and which therefore correspond to a choice between P and R. The simplest of these is the case in which R is considered to represent a more equitable distribution than Q, because, say, F's needs and deserts are greater than G's. In this case, R is better than Q (and hence also than P) on equity grounds, P is inferior to Q (and hence also to R) on efficiency grounds, and R is therefore preferable to P on both counts.

4. Almost as simple is the next case, in which R and Q (and hence also P) represent welfare distributions of equal degrees of equity. Since P is inferior to Q (and hence also to R) on efficiency grounds, we conclude in this case that R is to be preferred to P, because it results in greater economic efficiency and in a different distribution of welfare which, if no better, is at least no worse than that obtaining at P. This case is similar to case (2), above, because in both of them a choice has to be made between two equally equitable situations. The difference between them is that, whereas in case (2) the alternatives are equally equitable because they involve the same welfare distribution, in case (4) they involve different but equally equitable welfare distributions.

5. The problem of choice becomes difficult only in the last case, in which R is inferior to Q (and hence also to P) on equity grounds. Since P falls short of Q (and hence also of R) as regards economic efficiency, there is a conflict here between considerations of equity and efficiency. R is inferior on equity, P on efficiency grounds; and in choosing between the two positions, the relative importance of the two criteria must be weighed against each other. Either of them may be considered the more important of the two; accordingly, either P or R may be preferred on balance.

Having listed the five possible cases, we may consider examples of at least some of them. An example of the first case is the payment of relief to the needy out of an income tax levied on taxpayers. Such a redistribution of income redistributes welfare without affecting the efficiency with which consumers' goods are distributed. In other words, when competition among consumers is perfect, we can make any pair of consumers move along their contract curve by taking away part of one man's income and giving it to the other man to spend; and this is exactly what happens when sums of money raised by income tax from some people are paid out as relief to some other people. Hence, relief payments financed by income taxation correspond to a movement from *R* to *Q* in Figure 11; and their desirability can be appraised without reference to efficiency considerations. This result is subject to one minor qualification. The administration of relief involves a cost; and in deciding for or against relief, this fact must also be taken into account.

Entirely different is the situation when relief is not paid out in money but made available in some other form. An example of this is the Food Stamp Program, introduced by the United States federal government in 1939, under which unemployed and needy families were enabled to buy certain foods at half the market price,[4] the other half being paid by the government. This program lowered the efficiency of distribution by making the price of foodstuffs different for different people; and the resulting loss of economic efficiency can be expressed in terms of money by the difference between the cost of relief to the taxpayer and its value to the relief recipient.

It will be helpful to illustrate this argument graphically. In Figure 18, where money is measured on the vertical axis and a foodstuff (say, butter) on the horizontal axis, a person's market opportunities before and

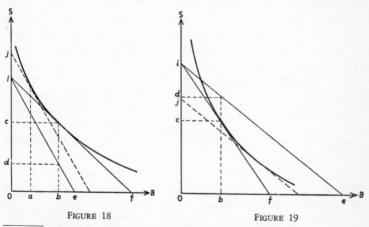

FIGURE 18   FIGURE 19

[4] In actual fact the extent of the price reduction varied; but for the purposes of this example, we shall assume it to have been one half.

after the introduction of the food subsidy are shown by the budget lines *Ie* and *If*, respectively. The slope of the first budget line shows the market price of butter, that of the second shows the price paid by a person entitled to the subsidy. When the Food Stamp Program enables him to buy butter at half price, he will buy *0b* of butter, spending on it *Ic*. Since the full market value of this much butter is *Id*, the cost to the government (or taxpayer) of subsidizing this person's butter consumption is *dc*, the vertical distance between the two budget lines at point *b*. The money value of the subsidy to the subsidized person is expressed by the equivalent variation *IJ*, which shows the amount of additional income that in the absence of the subsidy would bring this person to the same indifference curve which the subsidy enabled him to reach. It is apparent from the diagram that *IJ*, the value of the subsidy to the subsidized person, is smaller than *dc*, the cost of the subsidy to the government. This is so whatever the shape of a particular indifference curve, as long as it has a smooth curvature.[5] The common-sense interpretation of this result is that one can make a man happier by giving him cash and letting him spend it as he thinks best than by forcing him to take all his relief in the form of one commodity. Hence, relief payments in cash are preferable to a food subsidy, because they are economically more efficient, giving the relief recipients either a greater gain at the same cost to the government or the same gain at a lower cost.[6] A choice between the two forms of relief, therefore, corresponds to case (2) and is represented in Figure 11 by a choice between points *Q* and *P*.

Such a choice between an efficient and an inefficient form of relief is easy to make, because it raises no problems of equity and can be made on the basis of efficiency considerations alone. It is conceivable, however, that relief in the form of cash payments should be ruled out by political considerations, in which case the choice would lie between an inefficient form of relief and no relief at all. Geometrically, this is a choice between *P* and *R* in Figure 11; and since relief is presumably more equitable than no relief, this would correspond to case (5) and would have to be decided by weighing the gain in equity against the loss in economic efficiency.

As an example of case (3), consider the choice of raising public reve-

---

[5] Only if the indifference curve had a kink at its point of contact with the budget line would the cost of the subsidy equal its value to the person subsidized.

[6] Needless to say, there are also other considerations than those discussed here. For example, the 1939 Food Stamp Program had the very important additional purpose of disposing of agricultural surpluses. For yet other considerations, see pp. 68–69 and sec. 1 of the Note to Chap. VIII.

nue (for relief or for any other purpose) either by an excise tax (e.g., the cigarette tax) or by income taxation. An excise tax on a particular commodity raises the price of that commodity to the consumer and thereby lowers his satisfaction. This is shown in Figure 19 (p. 65). The imposition of the excise tax shifts the consumer's budget line from *ie* to *if*. If he buys 0*b* units of the taxed commodity, he will have to pay for it *ic*, or *cd* more than he would have had to pay in the absence of the tax. Hence, *cd* is the amount of tax collected from him by the government. The consumer's loss of satisfaction due to the tax is expressed in terms of money by the equivalent variation *ji*. That this will always be greater than *cd*, the amount of tax collected from him by the government, is apparent from the diagram. An excise tax appears, therefore, as a less efficient way of raising public revenue than the income tax, since *ji* obtained from this person by income tax would make him no worse off than the payment of *cd*, a *smaller amount*, in the form of an excise tax. The above argument also implies that the amount, *cd*, levied by an income tax would cause the taxpayer a smaller loss of satisfaction than if it were obtained by an excise tax.

The difference between an excise and an income tax, however, lies not only in their relative efficiency but also in their incidence. A flat-rate income tax taxes everybody in proportion to his income; a progressive income tax taxes away a higher proportion of people's income in the higher income brackets and a lower proportion in the lower brackets. An excise tax is proportional to people's expenditures on the commodity taxed; and its incidence therefore depends on different people's expenditures on this commodity. Since the poor always spend a larger proportion of their income than the rich and therefore spend a larger proportion on any average commodity, an excise tax on an average commodity is regressive in the sense that it takes away a larger part of people's income in the lower than in the higher income brackets. Even more regressive is an excise tax on a necessity, the consumption of which is little affected by the consumer's income, so that a tax on it costs the poor as much or almost as much money as it costs the rich. This is why an excise tax on food or cigarettes is regressive. Assuming, therefore, that a progressive or proportional tax is more equitable than a regressive one, income taxation is preferable to most excise taxes on grounds both of equity and of economic efficiency.

The above examples should suffice to illustrate the nature of the connection between equity and efficiency and of the problems raised by it. Throughout all this, however, it is very important to realize that we defined "economic efficiency" as conformity to consumers' preferences and that economic efficiency is therefore a meaningful concept only as long as we accept the consumer's preferences as a datum and regard him as the best judge of what is good for him.[7] It would be meaningless to apply the criterion of economic efficiency to a measure aimed deliberately at changing the consumer's preferences or influencing his market behavior.

For example, it appears from Figure 18 that a food subsidy will always cause the relief recipient to consume more food than an equivalent payment of cash would. A cash payment of *IJ* added to his income would prompt him to consume $0a$ of butter; the equivalent food subsidy, *dc,* makes him consume $0b$; and the difference between the two, *ab,* will be recognized as the substitution effect of the food subsidy. A food subsidy, therefore, encourages people's food consumption; and it can be used as a public-health measure when the government is more concerned with providing an adequate diet for needy families than with giving them the greatest satisfaction at minimum cost.[8]

In the same way, Figure 19 shows that an excise tax, because of its substitution effect, discourages the consumption of the taxed commodity more than an equivalent income tax would. Hence, an excise tax may be adopted for the sake of the special discouragement it offers, just as a food subsidy may be preferred to relief payments in cash for the premium its puts on food consumption. Thus, although an excise tax on alcoholic beverages is inequitable and inefficient as a means of raising revenue, it is useful as a public-health measure, because it lowers liquor consumption and discourages drunkenness. In other words, the very measure that we condemn as inefficient for its failure to conform to consumers' preferences may be considered useful if we cease to regard the consumer as the supreme authority on what is good for him. There are many instances of an excise tax being used to sway consumers' prefer-

---

[7] Throughout this book, we shall often be concerned with the conformity of economic organization to consumers' or the community's preferences. In all these cases, we shall be concerned with the community not in Hegel's sense of a collective entity which is something more than the sum of its members but with the individual members of the community and with conformity to their individual preferences. It is not intuitively obvious that economic organization can conform to the different preferences of different people all at the same time; nor is this always possible. But an example is distribution between two persons represented by a point on the contract curve in Fig. 11, which does conform simultaneously to the preferences of both people. For further discussion of this subject, see pp. 72–73, 163, and 178.

[8] For a further discussion of the argument of this paragraph and the next, see sec. 1 of the Note to Chap. VIII.

ences and to discourage the consumption of a particular commodity. For example, during World War II the United States government imposed an excise tax on travel, telegrams, and long-distance telephone calls, in an effort to discourage the civilian use of these services and so make them available for the use of the armed forces. These taxes were very well suited for that purpose; but their retention after the war for the purpose of raising revenue was objectionable because, for this purpose, they were inefficient and inequitable.

In the chapters that follow, we shall concentrate on the study of efficiency and make few references to the problem of equity. It must be emphasized, however, that we shall do so not because we believe that efficiency is more important than equity but solely because we can make objective statements about efficiency, whereas everyone must make his own judgment about equity according to his own conscience and ethical norms. It must be understood, therefore, that whenever we say that one situation is more efficient than another, we shall *not* mean that this situation is necessarily better than the other. The more efficient situation may be preferable, but only if it also happens to be more equitable, or no less equitable, or so little less equitable that the loss in equity is more than offset by the gain in efficiency. In other words, the reader must bear in mind constantly that few judgments in this book are welfare judgments. Usually, we shall say not that one situation is better than another but only that it is more efficient and would be better if it were found acceptable also on equity grounds. This is a serious limitation; but it is a limitation not only of this book but of all economic theory, which can never be more than a partial guide to economic policy.

BIBLIOGRAPHICAL NOTE

I know of no good elementary discussion of the basic principles discussed in this chapter. This is undoubtedly due to the fact that there is no general agreement among economists on the important problems of the economist's function in society, the basis on which he should make his recommendations, the extent to which he can make recommendations, and so forth. While there is no agreement, there has been considerable controversy; and the reader is referred to the following articles on the subject: R. F. Harrod, "Scope and Method of Economics," *Economic Journal*, Vol. XLVIII (September, 1938), pp. 383–412; N. Kaldor, "Welfare Propositions in Economics," *Economic Journal*, Vol. XLIX (1939), pp. 549–52; J. R. Hicks, "The Foundations of Welfare Economics," *Economic Journal*, Vol. XLIX (1939), pp. 699–712; I. M. D. Little, *A Critique of Welfare Economics* (Oxford: Clarendon Press, 1950); and my summary of the recent controversy, "The State of Welfare Economics," *American Economic Review*, Vol. XLI (1951) pp. 302–15.

As to detail, the box diagram, as defined in this chapter, was first used, I believe, by Professor A. L. Bowley, in his *Mathematical Groundwork of Economics* (Oxford: Clarendon Press, 1924), chap. i; although the idea probably originated with F. Y. Edgeworth (in his *Mathematical Psychics* [London: C. Kegan Paul & Co., 1881]). The argument that excise taxes are inferior to income taxes was stated already by Dupuit in 1844; but, in the form presented here, the argument first appeared in Miss M. F. W. Joseph's "Excess Burden of Indirect Taxation," *Review of Economic Studies*, Vol. VI (1939), pp. 226–31.

NOTE TO CHAPTER IV: PRODUCTIVE EFFICIENCY AND THE SIZE OF THE NATIONAL PRODUCT

In Chapter IV, we were concerned with the distribution of consumers' goods and services; and, in order to isolate this problem from other problems, we assumed that the quantity of goods and services to be distributed was fixed. We dealt with problems of equity and efficiency, and defined the efficient distribution of consumers' goods and services as a situation in which a fixed quantity of commodities cannot be so redistributed among consumers as to make anyone better off without making someone else worse off. In other words, when distribution among consumers is efficient, only a change in the quantity of goods and services can further improve some people's welfare without diminishing that of others.

The quantity of goods and services produced with given resources depends on how efficient production and the division of labor are. This suggests that statistics on the quantity of goods and services produced might be used as an index of the efficiency of production and the division of labor. Unfortunately, however, national product statistics are occasionally a misleading and never a conclusive index of productive efficiency. For this reason, we shall not rely on them. In the chapters to follow, we shall analyze and express the conditions of efficiency in all fields of economic organization in terms (and with the aid of diagrams) very similar to those used in Chapter IV. Nevertheless, it is helpful to know what meaning can be attached to national product statistics—if for no other reason than that such statistics exist and are the only statistical data we have on productive accomplishment and national well-being. We proceed to analyze, therefore, how, in what sense, and under what conditions these statistics can be used as an index of efficiency. The argument, however, is somewhat difficult; and the reader is invited to skip this Note on first reading and proceed directly to Chapter V.

That neither national product data nor national income statistics can do more than indicate very roughly the efficiency of economic organization should be obvious. They cannot measure national welfare, because we can neither construct a scale for measuring the individual consumer's satisfaction nor compare and add up different people's satisfactions. A rise in national income may be and usually is the net result of a rise in some people's and a fall in some other people's income. In such cases, we cannot tell whether the rise in national income corresponds to a rise in national welfare, since we cannot tell whether, say, a $2,000 rise in Jones's income represents a greater change in welfare than that caused by a $1,000 fall in Smith's income. Hence, the utmost that national income and national product estimates might do is to indicate the efficiency of production and the division of labor. The greater this efficiency, the larger will be the quantity of goods and services available for consumption, and the more closely will the nature of these goods and services conform to consumers' preferences. We can say, therefore, that the efficiency of the productive system determines the material basis of welfare or, in short, potential welfare. For example, a change in economic organization which raises the available quantity of one product without lowering the available quantity of any other product and without raising the amount of productive effort expended can be said to raise potential welfare. For a larger quantity of goods and services *could* be so distributed among consumers as to make some people better off than they were before, without making anyone else worse off. There is no guaranty, of course, that it would be so distributed; for an increase in output may be accompanied, and often is, by a redistribution of income which may make some people worse off than they were before. In such cases, therefore, we can only speak of a rise in *potential* welfare, that is, in the *possibility* of making some people better off than they were before without making others worse off. Hence, any change in economic organization that raises the quantity of at least one product without lowering that of any other product represents an improvement in efficiency and an increase in potential welfare. Such an increase in the quantity of available goods and services will raise national product estimates—which means that, in this case, national product estimates, efficiency, and potential welfare will all rise together.

The above, however, is a relatively simple case. It is not always that a change in economic organization raises (or lowers) the output of some products without lowering (raising) that of any other product. Very often, a change in economic organization raises the output of some products and lowers that of others; and this poses the very difficult problem of how to appraise such a change, how to tell whether it has raised or lowered potential welfare and whether it therefore represents a rise or a fall in the level of efficiency.

To take a concrete example, let us assume a change in output between years 1 and 2 such that whereas in year 1, 100 million units of good A and 100 million units of good B are produced, in year 2 the output of A falls to 99 million, and the output of B rises to 101 million units. Let us also assume that the output of all other commodities remains unchanged. The question is whether this change, which is neither a rise nor a fall in national product but a change in its composition, represents an improvement or a worsening of efficiency and whether it has raised or lowered potential welfare.

It is worth noting that this problem is not unlike the problem of measuring national welfare, which we just dismissed as insoluble. We saw that we cannot appraise a change in national welfare when some people's position improves while that of others gets worse, because we cannot weigh one man's gain against another man's loss. Our present problem of comparing the gain in B output with the loss in A output is similar, except for the important difference that, unlike two people's satisfactions, the value of two commodities can be compared.

Whether a person regards the loss of a given quantity of A and the gain of an equal quantity of B as a net loss or a net gain depends on his tastes, his needs, his total expenditure on consumption, and on the way in which his total expenditure is apportioned among different goods and services. Hence, one might think at first that a given change in the composition of the national product would be appraised differently by different people, depending on their personal differences. If this were so, it would be impossible to evaluate a change in the composition of the national product from the nation's point of view; and it would also be impossible to attach any meaning to the idea of efficiency in production. For production to be efficient, it must conform to consumers' preferences; and it could hardly conform to the different preferences of different people all at the same time. These difficulties are largely resolved, however, when competition among consumers is perfect. For we saw on pages 55–56 that perfect competition among consumers equalizes their marginal preferences.[1] A consumer who is a price taker in every consumers' market equates his marginal valuation of every good he buys to its price. In other words, when he is a price taker, he adopts a consumption pattern which renders the price of each good equal to the market

---

[1] The term "marginal preference" is used as a synonym for "marginal rate of substitution."

value of other goods whose possession would exactly compensate him for the loss of one unit of that good. When every consumer is a price taker in every market and faces the same prices as all other consumers, he equates his marginal valuation of every good to its market price and hence also to its marginal valuation by all its other consumers. Perfect competition among consumers, therefore, insures that the market price of every good expresses its marginal valuation by all its consumers. In other words, while consumers' preferences differ, perfect competition among them causes each consumer so to organize his consumption as to equate his *marginal* preferences to the *marginal* preferences of all other consumers of the same goods. Hence, as long as competition among consumers is perfect, we can rest assured that their *marginal* preferences will be the same at any moment of time.

The uniformity of consumers' marginal preferences solves one of our problems. It is apparent that if all consumers of A and B valued A more highly than B, the loss of one million units of A would outweigh the gain of an equal quantity of B; and the change in the composition of output would be regarded as a net loss. This is simple enough. Unfortunately, however, people's marginal preferences, while uniform, do not remain unchanged over time. To begin with, *marginal* preferences depend on the quantities of goods consumed; and when these change, people's marginal preferences change, too. The problems that this creates, however, are minor and can be ignored for the moment. Second, the community's preferences vary with the tastes of the individual members of the community. It must be borne in mind that we are trying to compare two situations at two different periods of time; and it would hardly be realistic to assume that nobody's tastes change from one period to the other. Third, our problems would not be solved even if individual tastes did remain unchanged; for the community's tastes can change even in that case. The community's tastes are the aggregate of individuals' tastes, as expressed by their effective demand in the market; and this means that each person's tastes are weighted by his total expenditure, which in turn depends on his income. The tastes of the rich pull more weight in the market than the tastes of the poor. Hence, the community's tastes may change not only when individual tastes change but also when the distribution of income—and with it the weighting of different people's tastes—changes. It is hardly necessary to add that a change in the composition of a community's output is almost always accompanied by a change in income distribution.

Whichever of these factors—the change in individual tastes or the change in income distribution—is responsible for the change in the community's preferences, the latter change always creates a problem, whose nature is best illustrated by an example. Let us assume that the community's preferences in year 1 are such that good A is valued more highly than good B, so that the loss of one million units of A is considered a greater loss than the gain derived from the additional availability of B. In other words, the change in the composition of the national product from year 1 to year 2 is considered a net loss of potential welfare. But years 1 and 2 usually differ not only as far as the composition of the national product is concerned but also as regards the community's preferences. If either individual tastes, or the distribution of income, or both, are different in year 2 from what they were in year 1, this will generally change the community's preferences and may change its relative valuation of A and B. If, despite this change, people in year 2 still value A more highly than B and still regard the change in output as a net loss in potential welfare, we can say unequivocally that, by the standards both of year 1 and of year 2, the change in output represents a loss in potential welfare and productive efficiency. It may also happen, however, that people in year 2 should value B more highly than they value A, so that, looking back upon the change in the composition of the national output, they should regard it as a net gain in potential welfare. In such a case, when a given change in the composition of the national product appears as a loss when regarded from the point of view of year 1 and a gain when considered from the second year's point of view, the attempt to measure changes in potential welfare must be abandoned.

The above example should make the nature of our problem amply clear. We are trying to evaluate a change in output by a standard which is itself in the process of changing. We compromise, therefore, by using two standards: the community's preferences as they were before and as they have become after the change. If the change in the standard is not too great, the two appraisals of the change in output are likely to yield results which, if numerically different, are at least the same in sign and show an unequivocal gain or an unequivocal loss in potential welfare.[2] Only if the standard changes very much from one period to the other are the two appraisals likely to show contradictory results; and only in such cases do we have to refrain from evaluating the change in output. Finally, it should be added that our problem becomes greater in degree

---

[2] Since welfare cannot be measured, we need not worry about the numerical ambiguity of our results.

if we want to compare not two but three or more situations; for in this case the comparison must be made not by two but by three or as many standards as there are situations to compare.

Having outlined the theoretical aspects of our problem and its suggested solution, we can now proceed to consider its practical aspect, which consists in inferring the community's preferences from statistical estimates of the national product. We know that in our economy, where competition among consumers is perfect, the price of each commodity expresses its marginal valuation by all its consumers. Hence, the total quantity of consumers' goods valued at the prices that consumers pay for them shows consumers' marginal valuations of the total consumers'-good output. Annual estimates of this figure are available in national product statistics; and it will be convenient to express these symbolically by sums such as the following:

$$\sum_{i=1}^{n} p_i{}^1 q_i{}^1 , \quad \sum_{i=1}^{n} p_i{}^2 q_i{}^2 , \tag{1}$$

where the subscripts denote commodities and the superscripts denote years.

These figures cannot be used as indexes of potential welfare, because they vary with changes not only in output but also in the community's marginal valuation of output; and this in turn changes, as we know, with the quantity of output consumed, with individual tastes, and with the distribution of income. As was stated earlier, our main difficulty stems from the change in the community's preferences due to changes in individual tastes and income distribution; and it might be said right away that we have no statistical information with whose aid we could either appraise the significance of these factors or correct for the changes caused by them. Nevertheless, we need not give up hope of estimating changes in potential welfare. For, although we cannot correct for changes in the community's preferences, we can do so for changes in prices; and statistics of the value of output corrected for price changes will be shown to yield at least approximate estimates of the change in potential welfare.

To eliminate the effect of price changes on a statistical series, the latter must be corrected by a price index. There are two types of price indexes used for this purpose. One is Paasche's index,

$$\frac{\sum p_i{}^2 q_i{}^2}{\sum p_i{}^1 q_i{}^2} ,$$

which shows the weighted average change in prices, using the quantities of the second year as weights. By dividing this index into the second sum of (1), we get the quotient $\sum p_i^1 q_i^2$, which shows what the second year's output would be worth at the first year's prices, and whose comparison with the value of the first year's output shows what statisticians call the change in "real output." The second type of price index is Laspeyres' index,

$$\frac{\sum p_i^2 q_i^1}{\sum p_i^1 q_i^1},$$

which shows the weighted average change in prices, using the quantities of the *first* year as weights. If we multiply this index with the first sum of (1), we get the product $\sum p_i^2 q_i^1$, which shows what the first year's output would be worth at the second year's prices, and whose comparison with the value of the second year's output provides an alternative way of expressing the change in "real output."

Statisticians have had a hard time in choosing between these two ways of measuring the change in "real output"; but it will be seen in the following that both of them are needed. For let us recall that we want two estimates: one to show the change in potential welfare from the point of view of the community's preferences in the first year and the other to show the change in potential welfare from the point of view of the community's preferences in the second year. For the sake of convenience, we shall call the two changes C_1 and C_2, respectively; and we shall see that statistics of the value of output corrected for price changes by Paasche's index number yield an estimate of C_1; whereas the same statistics corrected by Laspeyres' index number yield an estimate of C_2. To show that this is so, let us return to our numerical example and consider the case in which the output of A falls and that of B rises by one million units. We shall illustrate our argument with this example but shall state our results in a general form, in terms of our symbols.

Let us assume that in year 1 the price of A is \$5 and that of B is \$4. This shows that, given the tastes and the income distribution of year 1, and given the quantities of the two commodities consumed in year 1, the consuming public values A more highly than it values B. We might conclude from this that from the point of view of the community's preferences in year 1, the loss of one million units of A, accompanied by the gain of an equal quantity of B, will be regarded as a net loss of potential welfare. To make a tentative numerical estimate of this net loss, let us value the loss of A and the gain of B output at the first year's prices and add the two together, treating the loss as a negative gain. We shall express this estimate by the symbol Est(C_1), which in our example is

$$\text{Est}(C_1) = (- \$5 \text{ million} + \$4 \text{ million}) = (- \$1 \text{ million});$$

that is, the estimated change in potential welfare is a $1 million loss. More generally,

$$\text{Est}(C_1) = \sum p_i{}^1(q_i{}^2 - q_i{}^1) = \sum p_i{}^1 q_i{}^2 - \sum p_i{}^1 q_i{}^1, \qquad (2)$$

which shows that our estimate of C_1 is the difference between the second year's output valued at the first year's prices and the value of the first year's output.

This estimate, however, is not always correct. For it must be remembered that the $5 price of A and the $4 price of B express their *marginal* value to consumers. Each consumer of A can be compensated for the loss of one unit of A by $5; but if he loses, say, 3 units of A, his marginal valuation of it is likely to rise, and he may require something more than $15 (3 × $5) to compensate him for his loss. This means that the loss of one million units of A to all the consumers of A represents a loss that they may value at $5 million *or more*. Conversely, one additional unit of B will be worth $4 to each consumer of B; but when he is given, say, 3 additional units, his marginal valuation of it may fall, and he may value his total gain at something less than $12 (3 × $4). Hence, the availability of one million additional units of B represents a gain to the consumers of B which they may value at $4 million *or less*. It appears, therefore, that in estimating C_1 by expression (2), we are in danger of underestimating losses and overestimating gains, so that, on balance, our estimate of the net change in potential welfare may be an algebraic overestimate of the true change in potential welfare. This may be expressed in symbols as follows:

$$\text{Est}(C_1) \geq C_1.$$

In our particular example, this is not fatal. When Est(C_1) is negative, C_1, which cannot be greater than Est (C_1), will also be negative; and we can be certain that there was a loss in potential welfare, even though it may be greater numerically than that shown by our estimate of C_1. Trouble arises only when Est (C_1) is positive. Had we assumed, for example, that the price of A was $4 and the price of B $5, our computations would have shown a gain:

$$\text{Est}(C_1) = \$5 \text{ million} - \$4 \text{ million} = \$1 \text{ million};$$

and in this case not only could C_1, the *true* change in potential welfare, represent a smaller gain than \$1 million; but we could not even be certain whether C_1 was positive or negative and whether the true change in potential welfare was a gain or a loss.

The uncertainty that arises when Est (C_1) is positive could be eliminated if we knew to what level the changed output of the two commodities had raised people's marginal valuation of A and lowered people's marginal valuation of B. If we knew this, we could make a second estimate of C_1 based on people's *new* marginal valuation of the two commodities; and, since this would tend to be an underestimate, it would, together with the first estimate, show the upper and lower limits within which the true value of C_1 must lie. Such information, however, is not available. We know the prices of the different commodities in the second year, and we know that these prices again express consumers' marginal valuations; but these prices are what they are not only because the output of the different commodities has changed but also because individual tastes and/or the distribution of income may have changed and affected the community's preferences. For example, with unchanged tastes and an unchanged distribution of income, we would expect the price of A to rise and the price of B to fall; but since we have no information on the exact amount by which these prices would change, we can never tell whether the actual change in prices is greater or smaller than this amount. In fact, it is conceivable that the fall in A and the rise in B output should be accompanied by a change in tastes or a redistribution of income which changes the community's preferences to such an extent as to cause the price of A to fall and that of B to rise!

We conclude, therefore, that Est(C_1), defined in expression (2) and based on national product statistics corrected by Paasche's index, is the only estimate of C_1 that is available. We have seen that this estimate is likely to overestimate the true value of C_1 and that therefore only a negative value of Est(C_1) enables us to appraise with certainty the direction in which potential welfare has changed. We can say nothing certain when Est(C_1) is positive.

We can now proceed to estimate C_2, the effect of a change in output on potential welfare, looking at the change from the standpoint of the community's preferences as they are *after* the change. As may be expected, the argument here is very similar to the foregoing; and we get into exactly the same kind of difficulties. Returning once more to our numerical example, let us assume that in the second year the price of A has risen to \$6, and the price of B has fallen to \$3. If we then value the loss of A output and the gain in B output at the second year's prices, we get a tentative estimate of the change in potential welfare from the point of view of the second year's preferences:

$$\text{Est}(C_2) = (-\$6 \text{ million} + \$3 \text{ million}) = (-\$3 \text{ million}),$$

which shows a loss of \$3 million. More generally,

$$\text{Est}(C_2) = \sum p_i^2(q_i^2 - q_i^1) = \sum p_i^2 q_i^2 - \sum p_i^2 q_i^1, \qquad (3)$$

where Est (C_2) is the difference between the value of the second year's output and what the first year's output would be worth at the second year's prices.

Here again, our estimate of C_2 may be incorrect, because the second year's prices express consumers' marginal valuations as they are after, and as a result of, the change in output. For example, the \$3 price of B expresses each consumer's valuation of the last unit of B added to his consumption; but if any consumer is now getting, say, 3 additional units of B, his total gain derived from this is likely to be something more than \$9 (3 × \$3). Hence, the total gain consumers derive from a one-million increase in the output of B may be undervalued when we enter it in our estimate of C_2 at \$3 million. The corresponding argument for A shows that the loss of welfare due to the fall in the output of A may be overvalued at \$6 million. In general, we can say that Est(C_2), as defined in (3), is likely to underestimate gains and overestimate losses, and hence to underestimate the net change in potential welfare. In symbols:

$$\text{Est}(C_2) \leq C_2.$$

This result corresponds to, but is the exact opposite of, the result we reached concerning the relation between C_1 and our statistical estimate of it. Here, it is a positive value of Est(C_2) which definitely indicates a gain in potential welfare; whereas a negative value of Est (C_2) leaves us uncertain whether potential welfare has diminished or increased. It would now be useful to have a second estimate of C_2, based on consumers' marginal valuation *before* the change in output; but, again, it is impossible to make such an estimate, because the first year's prices, although expressing consumers' marginal valuation before the change, may express it for different tastes or a different income distribution and hence for a different scale of community preferences. It appears, therefore, that just as (2) was the only available estimate of C_1, so (3) is the only available estimate of C_2.

What conclusions can we draw from these results? It will be recalled from our discussion of the theoretical problem that the effects on potential welfare of a change in output must be appraised both by the community's preferences as they were before the change and by the community's preferences as they have become after the change. Only if these two appraisals yield similar results can we say definitely that there has been a gain or a loss in potential welfare. When we examined the practical problem of estimating changes in potential welfare statistically, we saw that we can only make approximate estimates, which are likely to be inaccurate, but which have a systematic bias and always err on the same side. In particular, we have shown, first, that statistics of consumers' expenditures, when corrected for price changes by Paasche's index, yield an estimate of C_1, the change in potential welfare from the point of view of the first year's preferences, which is likely to err on the high side. Second, we have shown that the same statistics corrected by Laspeyres' price index yield an estimate of C_2, the change in potential welfare from the point of view of the second year's preferences, which is likely to err on the low side. This means that, looking at the change in output from the standpoint of the first year's preferences, we can usually tell a loss but never a gain; whereas, looking at it from the standpoint of the second year's preferences, we can usually tell a gain but not a loss. Hence, we can never appraise with certainty the change in potential welfare from both points of view, except in the paradoxical case when the two appraisals conflict.[3]

Normally, we would expect both estimates to be either positive or negative; and, in such cases, we can only make one certain and one uncertain statement. When both estimates are positive, we can tell for certain that potential welfare has increased as far as the second year's preferences are concerned; but, from the point of view of the first year's preferences, we can at best say that potential welfare *may* have risen. Conversely, when both estimates are negative, we can tell for certain that potential welfare has fallen from the point of view of the first year's preferences; but, from the point of view of the second year's preferences, we can only say that potential welfare *may* have fallen.

This is as far as we can ever go in interpreting the significance of a change in the national product. We could go beyond this and make a more definite statement only if we had additional information indicating that neither individual tastes nor income distribution has changed between the two dates compared. It is also worth pointing out that the

---

[3] I.e., when Est $(C_1) < 0$ and Est $(C_2) > 0$.

special case in which prices have remained unchanged is no simpler to interpret than the general case. If prices are the same in the two years, our two estimates coincide, and we get the following relation:

$$C_1 \leq \text{Est}(C_1) = \text{Est}(C_2) \leq C_2 .$$

This shows that, if the value of output has increased (i.e., $\text{Est}(C_1) = \text{Est}(C_2) > 0$), we can be certain that potential welfare has risen from the point of view of the second year's preferences; if the value of output has diminished (i.e., $\text{Est}(C_1) = \text{Est}(C_2) < 0$), we can be certain that potential welfare has fallen from the point of view of the first year's preferences; but we are again unable to appraise with certainty the changes in potential welfare from both points of view. The reason for this is that we cannot tell whether the constancy of prices is due to the constancy of tastes and income distribution and to the smallness of the change in the composition of output, or whether prices have remained unchanged because the change in the first two factors happens to have offset exactly the change in the last factor.

So far, we have been concerned with interpreting changes in the output of consumers' goods. The national product, however, consists also of government expenditure and private capital formation. Changes in the composition of these components and in the relative quantities of the different components can be interpreted in exactly the same way in which we interpreted changes in the composition of the consumers'-good output. The only question that remains to be answered is whether the prices of government services and capital goods can be taken to represent their marginal valuation by the public in the same way in which we assumed the prices of consumers' goods to represent their marginal valuation by consumers. As far as government services are concerned, the answer is in the affirmative. The volume of government services is determined by the community's political representatives, who, in most cases, regard the prices of these services as given and presumably equate their marginal valuation of these services to the latter's prices. As to people's marginal valuation of capital goods and its relation to the price of capital goods, this subject cannot be discussed here; it will be taken up in Chapter XVI, and the reader is especially referred to footnote 13 on page 361.

BIBLIOGRAPHICAL NOTE

The meaning of national product estimates has been the subject of much controversy and a voluminous literature. The problem has been attacked both by economists and by statisticians; and it is a curious and regrettable fact that the economists have all but ignored the statisticians' contributions. For the economists' controversy, see J. R. Hicks, "The Valuation of the Social Income," *Economica,* N.S., Vol. VII (1940), pp. 105–24; Simon Kuznets, "On the Valuation of Social Income—Reflections on Professor Hicks' Article," Parts I and II, *Economica,* N.S., Vol. XV (1948), pp. 1–16 and 116–31; J. R. Hicks, "The Valuation of the Social Income—A Comment on Professor Kuznets' Reflections," *Economica,* N.S., Vol. XV, pp. 163–72; I. M. D. Little, "The Valuation of the Social Income," *Economica,* N.S., Vol. XVI (1949), pp. 11–26; and Paul A. Samuelson, "Evaluation of Real National Income," *Oxford Economic Papers,* N.S., Vol. II (1950), pp. 1–29.

As to the contributions of the statisticians, see the excellent summary (and bibliography) in R. Frisch, "Annual Survey of General Economic Theory: The Problem of Index Numbers," *Econometrica,* Vol. IV (1936), pp. 1–38. See also A. A. Konüs, "The Problem of the True Index of the Cost of Living," *Econometrica,* Vol. VII (1939), pp. 10–29.

CHAPTER V

THE WORKER AND THE EFFICIENCY OF THE LABOR MARKET

HAVING completed our discussion of the consumer and the market where he buys consumers' goods, we can proceed to discuss the behavior and problems of the same person but in his capacity as a seller of productive services. For most people have to earn their income—as workers, salaried employees, or professional people, selling their personal services; or as entrepreneurs, managing a firm. In this chapter, we shall be concerned only with the seller of his personal services; and we shall call him, for short, the worker. But the reader is asked to bear in mind that by "workers" we mean not only manual workers but also salaried employees and professional people; and that the analysis of this chapter is applicable also to other individual sellers, such as the small farmer selling produce raised by his own and his family's labor, or the collector selling out his collection of pictures, antiques, etc.[1]

In the present chapter, we shall assume that the individual seller of his personal services is a price taker, who is free to choose his occupation and to vary the quantity of services he sells, but who has to adjust his behavior to market prices and offers, which he regards as given and outside his control. On this assumption, there is a close resemblance between his market behavior and that of the consumer discussed in Chapter III. There is a great difference in realism, however, between the analysis of Chapter III and that of this chapter. For, unlike the consumer, the worker is seldom in the position of a price taker. Very often, he is able to bargain or even to set his own price; and, in this respect, his position may be better than a price taker's. On the other hand, he is not always free to choose his occupation; he is seldom in a position to determine how much of his services to sell (i.e., how many hours to work); and, to this extent, he is in a worse position than a price taker. Hence, to treat

---

[1] People who mix their labor with that of their employees and sell the fruit of their joint effort are considered entrepreneurs. Their behavior and problems are discussed in Chaps. VI and VII and in the Note to Chap. VII.

him as a price taker is frankly unrealistic; but it is necessary for our understanding of perfect competition and as a preparation for the discussion of subsequent chapters. We shall see later how our argument is affected by the fact that as a rule the worker is not a price taker in our society.

Facing a market that sets different prices on different services, the worker has to solve two problems: what to sell and how much to sell. These problems are similar to the consumer's problems of what and how much to buy, except for the following important difference: Whereas the consumer buys a variety of commodities and decides in what proportions to buy them by weighing the relative attractions of a little more of this or a little more of that, the worker cannot, as a rule, make comparisons on the margin and must make an "either-or decision." In other words, he is seldom able to sell different services in varying proportions and must usually choose between alternative professions or occupations. For example, the average worker cannot spend, say, 30 hours a week as a plumber and 10 hours as an electrician but must usually decide which of the two trades to pursue as a full-time occupation. It follows from this that, whereas the consumer makes up his mind as to what and how much to buy in one single decision, the seller must first decide what to sell and afterward make an entirely separate decision concerning the quantity or the terms on which to sell. This separation of the two decisions is inherent in the nature of the worker's problem. Just as he cannot usually divide his time between several occupations, so he is also unable to switch at short notice from one occupation to another. Learning a trade or a profession requires training and experience, which renders the choice of occupation a momentous decision which few people can afford to make more than once or twice in a lifetime. The choice between alternative occupations, therefore, is essentially a long-run decision.

But, once he has chosen a trade or profession and acquired training and experience in it, a worker still has some scope left for exercising his freedom of choice when he seeks employment. For a price taker, who faces given rates of earnings, this consists in choosing either more leisure or a higher income obtained at the cost of more work. This is essentially a short-run decision. It will be convenient, therefore, to discuss separately the short- and long-run problems both of the individual worker's behavior and of its effects on the market where he sells his productive services. Hence the difference in the organization of this chapter from that of the last two, even though the essence of the argument is the same.

1. THE WORKER'S CHOICE BETWEEN WORK AND LEISURE

To illustrate graphically the market behavior of a worker who sells his services at a fixed wage rate, let us draw a diagram in which time is measured along the horizontal axis and income along the vertical axis (Fig. 20). Any point in this diagram represents a combination of money

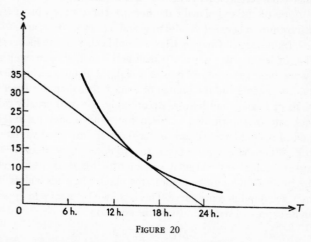

FIGURE 20

income and leisure time in the individual's possession. The fact that he is a price taker and can sell the use of as much of his time as he desires at a fixed price (wage) is expressed by the drawing of a budget line, whose slope represents this price. In Chapter III, we drew the consumer's budget line from the point on the vertical axis representing the consumer's total money income per unit of time; here, we draw the worker's budget line from the point on the horizontal axis representing the total amount of time per day, week, or year at his disposal. The market's willingness to buy any amount of his services at a fixed hourly wage rate enables him to travel along the budget line from the 24-hour point, showing the total time per day at his disposal, to any other point on the budget line. In Figure 20, for example, the slope of the budget line represents a wage of $1.50 per hour; and point p on the budget line shows the position of a person who works 8 hours per day, earns a daily wage of $12, and has 16 hours a day to himself for rest and leisure. If a person who is free to decide how many hours to work goes to point p, we assume that he does so because this combination of money income and leisure time gives him the greatest satisfaction; for, if it did not, he would have gone to some other point on his budget line. The amount of satisfaction enjoyed by the individual when he is at the preferred point of his budget line can be represented by an indifference curve going through this point. The shape and position of this indifference curve, as well as its method of derivation, are completely analogous to those of the consumer's indifference curve discussed in Chapter III.

The slope of the individual's indifference curve shows his marginal rate of substitution between leisure time and money income; and, following the terminology of Chapter III, we should call this rate his marginal valuation of leisure. But when a person decides whether to work more or to work less, we think of him as weighing against each other the attraction of income and the burden of work rather than the alternative attractions of income and leisure. Accordingly, we shall usually call his marginal rate of substitution between time and money his marginal valuation of his productive effort or, for short, his marginal valuation of his work. When he is a price taker, free to decide how much to work, the worker equates his marginal valuation of his work to his rate of earnings by proceeding to the point in the plane where his budget line is tangential to an indifference curve. This is shown by point p in Figure 20 and can be expressed symbolically by the equation:

$$MV_x = p_x .$$

1a. THE INCOME-OFFER CURVE

Having discussed the worker's market behavior in a given situation, we can now proceed to discuss the way in which he reacts to changes in his situation. To begin with, we can draw into the worker's indifference map an income-offer curve, which corresponds to the consumer's income-consumption curve and shows how the worker's market behavior is affected by a change in his initial position (Fig. 21). The amount of time available to him is fixed, of course; but his financial position may change, and the income-offer curve shows how such a change may affect his market behavior. For a worker may have an income independent of and additional to that derived from the sale of his personal services; and, in such a case, his budget line may start out from, say, point a, showing that he has a daily income of $5 additional to that derived from the sale of his services. Conversely, he may have debts to pay, representing a negative additional income, in which case his budget line starts out from a point vertically below the 24-hour point on the horizontal axis. For example, point b in Figure 21 shows the position of a person who faces an hourly wage rate of $1.50, works 10 hours per day, and spends, out of the $15 daily income so derived, $5 on the payment of a debt, leaving him a net daily income of $10.

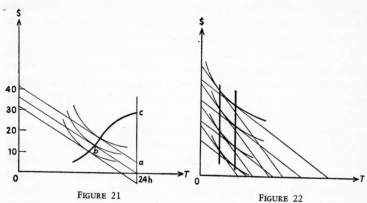

FIGURE 21 FIGURE 22

The income-offer curve drawn in Figure 21 shows the different numbers of hours a person will work as his independent income changes. The curve is drawn in such a way as to represent a diminished desire to work with a rise in the person's income. This is a reasonable assumption to make, since many people want to have more leisure when their income rises, especially if their work is onerous or unpleasant. As a person's independent income rises, it may eventually reach a point at which he will choose to stop working altogether (point c in Fig. 21).

It is improbable that the income-offer curve should ever curve back toward the vertical axis, since leisure is not likely to be regarded as an inferior good, of which people want less when their income rises. It is possible, however, and also very likely, that in many cases the income-offer curve should, beyond a minimum level, become a vertical straight line, indicating that once the person has reached this minimum income, further increases in income will not induce him to work less. Artists, scientists, professional people, and businessmen often regard their work not merely as a means of earning income but as an important and interesting part of their lives. People who feel this way about their work will hardly let their working habits be influenced by changes in their income—a psychology represented by the vertical slope of the income-offer curve. When we discussed the consumer's behavior, we drew this type of income-consumption curve for necessities, the demand for which has a saturation point. In the same way the worker's vertical income-offer curve can be interpreted to mean that his demand for leisure is limited and has a saturation point. This type of psychology, in which a person's demand for leisure and willingness to work are independent of his income, will become very important for our discussion of the entrepreneur's behavior on pages 142–47, below. It will be useful, therefore, to analyze the geometrical representation of this type of psychology.

In our general discussion of indifference maps in Chapter III, we stated that the shape and relative position of indifference curves may vary within wide limits, depending on the individual's tastes and psychology. A particular type of psychology, therefore, can be represented geometrically by a particular type of indifference map; and we want to see what type of indifference map corresponds to the psychology described above. We have seen that an income-offer curve connects points of equal slope on successive indifference curves. For the income-offer curve to be a vertical straight line, the successive indifference curves must have equal slopes at points vertically above each other. For the income-offer curve to be vertical for any price (that is, for any slope of the price lines), it is necessary that successive indifference curves be identical in shape and differ from each other only in their position in the plane, in the sense of being vertical displacements of each other. An indifference map of this type is illustrated in Figure 22 (p. 87), together with two income-offer curves derived from it.

1b. THE PRICE-OFFER CURVE

In the same way in which the seller's response to a change in his income is represented by the shape of his income-offer curve, so his response to a change in his rate of earnings can be illustrated with the aid of a price-offer curve. This is an exact counterpart of the consumer's price-consumption curve,[2] with the only difference that the price lines expressing different prices are drawn not from a point on the money axis but from the point on the horizontal axis representing the seller's total supply of the services or goods he sells, or from any point in the diagram representing his total supply of services plus the independent income (positive or negative) with which he starts out. Figure 23 shows such a price-offer curve, which connects the points of tangency between the different price lines and indifference curves and shows the amount of work a person is willing to perform at different wage rates.

The effect of a price change on a person's offer of his services can be

---

[2] See pp. 42 ff.

broken down into an income effect and a substitution effect in the same way in which we broke down the effect of a price change on the consumer's purchases.[3] This is shown in Figure 24. As the figure indicates, a rise in the worker's rate of earnings from w_1 to w_2 causes him to reduce his hours of work from $l_1 l_0$ to $l_2 l_0$ and brings him onto a higher indifference curve. The increase in his satisfaction can be measured in terms of money by the equivalent variation of income expressed by the distance $m_2 m_1$ in the diagram. Such a rise in a person's independent income, however, would cause him to reduce his hours of work more

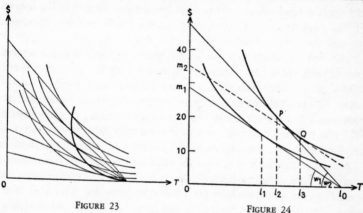

FIGURE 23   FIGURE 24

drastically than would the change in his rate of earnings. Instead of reducing his hours of work by the amount $l_1 l_2$, he would curtail them by the amount $l_1 l_3$. This change in the amount of his services offered is the income effect of the rise in his rate of earnings. As drawn in Figure 24, the income effect is positive. The income effect is zero when the worker has the psychology we attributed to artists, scientists, and so forth, and illustrated in Figure 22; but it can never be negative, since leisure is not an inferior good.

Besides increasing his satisfaction, a rise in a person's rate of earnings also raises the price of leisure for him, which will cause him so to rearrange his expenditure pattern as to consume less leisure at any given level of satisfaction. This corresponds to a movement along an indifference curve and results in the substitution effect, shown in Figure 24 by the distance $l_2 l_3$. In other words, whereas the income effect of a rise in a person's rate of earnings means that, being better off, he can afford to

[3] See pp. 44 ff.

work less and have more leisure, the substitution effect means that, since time has become more expensive to him, he tries to get his enjoyment from other things than leisure. Hence, income effect and substitution effect pull in opposite directions; and either of them may prevail over the other. In other words, a rise in wage rates may cause people to work less as well as to work more; and we cannot tell on theoretical grounds alone which is the more likely. The progressive shortening of the working week during the past one hundred years suggests that people tend to choose shorter working hours when their rate of earnings rises; for, although the individual worker is seldom free to determine the length of his working day in our society, he does influence it collectively through the actions of his union.

The way in which a person's willingness to work depends on his rate of earnings is best illustrated by transferring the price-offer curve onto a price-quantity diagram, where it becomes an individual supply curve. This can be done in exactly the same way in which we derived the consumer's demand curve from his price-consumption curve in Chapter III.[4] The individual supply curve so derived may either rise or fall, depending on the relative importance of income and substitution effects.

A definite statement as to whether a change in someone's rate of earnings will raise or lower his willingness to work can be made only in special cases in which we have good reason to think that the substitution effect alone is important, because special factors render the income effect negligibly small. For example, as mentioned earlier, we would not expect scientists, professional people, or businessmen to shorten their working hours or otherwise relax their productive efforts as a result of a rise in their rate of earnings; for we believe that they have a special kind of preference scale (shown in Fig. 22) which renders the income effect of the rise in their rate of earnings zero or negligibly small.

As another example, consider the effect of the imposition of an income tax or of the raising of income-tax rates. Nothing general can be said on the subject. Income taxes may raise as well as lower people's willingness to work. There is a special case, however, in which income taxation is likely to lower the willingness to work.

The influence of taxation on the willingness to work can be analyzed in the same terms in which we analyzed the effects of a subsidy on the consumer's demand for the subsidized commodity.[5] In fact, a tax on income can, in a sense, be regarded as a subsidy on the commodity leisure.

---

[4] See pp. 42–43.

[5] See p. 68.

When a man has to surrender x per cent of his income to the tax collector, he realizes that this amounts to an x per cent reduction in his rate of earnings—which, as we know, can be regarded as the price he pays for leisure. To illustrate this diagrammatically, consider a person who works a 10-hour day at an hourly wage of $2. This is shown by point P in Figure 24. Assume, next, that a flat-rate income tax of 40 per cent is imposed. This will have the same effect on our worker as a reduction of his hourly wage rate to $1.20, which is represented in Figure 24 by the slope of the price line l_0m_1. It would appear that the tax will lower this person's satisfaction and change his willingness to work by the balance of income and substitution effects, which may be positive or negative. This, indeed, will happen if the proceeds of the tax are used to finance rearmament or war. The situation is quite different, however, when the proceeds of the tax are, in some form or another, returned to the taxpayer himself. The simplest example of this would be a tax out of whose proceeds interest is paid to holders of government bonds who at the same time are also taxpayers. But the situation is essentially the same also when the tax revenues are used to provide social services, free education, highways, public parks, police protection, and the whole machinery of government, all of which contribute to the taxpayer's welfare and satisfaction.

When public expenditures for these purposes have been voted through the orderly processes of democratic government, we can legitimately assume that they constitute at least an adequate *quid pro quo* for the taxes levied; otherwise, they would not have been voted. Some people may, of course, get less and others more than their money's worth; but we shall assume that the diagram in Figure 24 represents the position of a person whose satisfaction remains about the same. Although 40 per cent of his income is taxed away from him, the free services provided by government and paid for out of this tax bring him back onto the same indifference curve where he would be without taxes and without government services. These government services are provided, however, whether or not he is working and paying taxes. This means that they are like an independent income and can be represented in Figure 24 by shifting the budget line l_0m_1 vertically upwards, by a distance sufficient to bring it into contact with the indifference curve ii. The vertical distance, m_2m_1, is called the compensating variation and represents the worth of public services to this person in terms of money.[6]

---

[6] Compensating variation and equivalent variation (defined on p. 44) are two different ways of expressing in terms of money the effect of a price change or similar

The new budget line, Qm_2, contacts the indifference curve at point Q, which is always to the right of P, the point of tangency between the indifference curve and the old budget line.

Hence, the imposition or raising of an income tax, accompanied by additional free public services, always tends to diminish people's willingness to work. The consequent shortening of the working day is shown by the distance l_2l_3, which is the substitution effect of the tax. Our assumption that the individual stays on the same indifference curve is, of course, an oversimplification. He usually gains and sometimes loses on balance as a result of the change. But whenever the burden of the tax is compensated by a gain in public services, the net change in the taxpayer's welfare position is likely to be small; and the consequent income effect on his willingness to work is likely to be small, too.

2. ALLOCATION OF WORK WITHIN ONE OCCUPATION

From the above analysis of the individual seller's behavior, we can now draw conclusions for the market as a whole. In particular, we shall prove that a given amount of employment will be efficiently distributed among a group of workers if competition among them is perfect.

Competition among a group of workers is perfect if they are all price takers and face the same wage rate. If there is a wage rate at which the members of the group want to perform the exact amount of work that is available to them, then this wage, offered to all and regarded as fixed by all, will result in an efficient distribution of employment among the members of the group. To prove that this is so, let us take two members of the group and represent the uniform wage rate they face and their market behavior in indifference maps of the kind shown in Figure 20. We can then superimpose their indifference maps in the same manner in which we superimposed the indifference maps of consumers in Chapter IV. This is shown in Figure 25. The height of the box diagram so obtained shows the two people's combined daily income, its width shows the total quantity of leisure enjoyed by them, and the horizontal distance between the origins of the two people's budget lines shows the total amount of work performed by them. Point p in Figure 25 shows the

---

measure on a person's satisfaction. The equivalent variation is the change in a person's income which would, in the absence of the price change, bring him to the same level of satisfaction as the price change does; whereas the compensating variation is the change in income which would, after the price change, bring him back to the level of satisfaction from which he started out. For the origin and detailed discussion of these concepts, see J. R. Hicks, "The Four Consumer's Surpluses," *Review of Economic Studies*, Vol. XI (Winter, 1943), pp. 31–41.

two people's actual position and the distribution of income, leisure, and. work between them. Since the two indifference curves are tangential to each other at this point, the distribution it represents is efficient, because no redistribution of income, leisure, and work could improve either person's position without worsening the other's.[7] We can prove this result for any two members of a profession; and it is true, therefore, of the whole profession. Hence, we conclude that the total amount of work

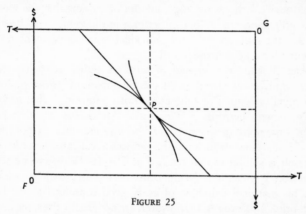

FIGURE 25

performed, leisure enjoyed, and income earned in any profession will be efficiently distributed among the members of that profession *if* they are in a perfectly competitive position, that is, if they are all price takers and face the same wage or salary rate.[8] This implies that discriminatory wage policies are economically inefficient, besides being inequitable, and that the argument in favor of equal pay for equal work is an economic argument in addition to being a moral one. The reader is invited to prove this proposition to himself with the aid of a box diagram obtained by superimposing on each other the indifference maps of two workers who are paid *different* wage rates for the same work.[9]

---

[7] Moreover, this distribution appears to be not only efficient but also fairly equitable, in the sense that any difference between them in income earned and work performed must be due to a difference in tastes, needs, or willingness to work.

[8] If the equal wage rates are time rates, the above conclusion holds true only if all the workers are equally quick and efficient and accomplish the same work in a given length of time. If the members of a profession differ in their speed and efficiency, then equal *piece rates* are needed to bring about an efficient distribution among the members of that profession.

[9] Remember to superimpose the indifference maps in such a way that the two budget lines' points of tangency with an indifference curve coincide.

A further consequence of perfect competition among sellers of productive services is that we can draw a short-run market supply curve of the services offered in each profession, by the horizontal addition of the individual supply curves of the members of that profession. Such addition is performed in exactly the same way in which we added together the demand curves of individual consumers in Chapter III to obtain a market demand curve. The short-run market supply curve of personal services shows the total amount of services that the members of that profession are willing to perform at different rates of earning; and it has the same shape as the individual supply curves whose sum it represents: it may either rise or fall.[10]

Besides showing the amount of service supplied at each price, the market supply curve also shows, for each amount of service performed, the marginal valuation of (the burden of performing) that service by the people who perform it. This follows from the fact that perfect competition among the members of a profession causes each of them to equate his marginal valuation of his services to the latter's market price. This result is similar to that reached in Chapter IV, where we showed that perfect competition among consumers causes each consumer to equate his marginal valuation of every good consumed to the latter's market price. The two results, however, are not exactly the same because, whereas the consumer's marginal valuation of a certain good shows his marginal rate of substitution between this good and other goods, the worker's marginal valuation of his services shows his marginal rate of substitution between income and leisure but not that between the performance of one service and that of another. Accordingly, whereas in Chapter IV we showed that the ratio of the prices of any two consumers' goods expresses the rate at which consumers are willing to substitute one for the other, we have yet to examine the relative burden or cost to society of two different types of services.

3. THE WORKER'S CHOICE OF OCCUPATION

The choice between alternative occupations is a long-run problem for the seller of productive services. As already mentioned, this is not a marginal choice as a rule, not a decision how to combine varying amounts of different types of work, but a choice between one full-time occupation and another.

---

[10] The long-run market supply curve of labor would differ from this to the extent of taking account of changes in the membership of the group brought about by changes in wage rates.

People's choice of occupation is governed by weighing the relative incomes offered in different occupations against their relative attractiveness. A person will not always choose the occupation that promises him the highest income, because he puts a premium on income offered for work he enjoys and discounts income earned in some types of work for the unpleasantness or danger they involve or for the lengthy or difficult training they require. Given a person's preferences and the relative attractiveness to him of two occupations, there exists a ratio in which earnings in the two occupations would have to stand in order to offset differences in their attractiveness and so render this person indifferent between them. For example, a person choosing between a dentist's and a doctor's career may find dentistry more attractive, because his talents lie that way and he likes the dentist's work, or because of the more regular hours it involves and the shorter training it requires. If the incomes to be earned in the two occupations were the same, he would become a dentist; but his enthusiasm for dentistry will be dampened if he expects a dentist's income to be lower than a doctor's.

For example, if he could look forward to an annual income of $10,-000 as a doctor, there will be a minimum annual income in dentistry —say, $8,000—the prospect of which would make him indifferent between the two professions. He would choose dentistry if this promised him anything above $8,000 a year; he would become a physician if as a dentist his income would be likely to be below $8,000; and he would have a hard time making up his mind if a dentist's income were exactly $8,000. Hence, $8,000 a year is his own valuation of the burden of performing a dentist's work, based on the consideration that, by becoming a dentist, he would lose the opportunity of earning $10,000 a year as a physician, and that this $10,000 has to be discounted by 8/10 for the lesser attractiveness to him of a doctor's career.

Conversely, if this person could expect to earn $8,000 as a dentist, his valuation of his services as a physician would, on the same argument, be $10,000; and he would become a doctor only if this would promise him an income anywhere above $10,000.

A person's own valuation of his services in a given occupation, as determined by the alternatives open to him in other occupations, has received a variety of names in economic literature. It has been called his reservation price, because it represents the minimum sum needed to reserve him for that occupation. It has also been called his transfer price or transfer income, because, if his income in that occupation fell below this minimum, he would transfer his services to another occupation. The ratio of a person's transfer price in one occupation to his actual earning power in another occupation shows the relative burden to him of the two types of work. Thus, to the person discussed in the example above, the relative burden of performing a dentist's and a doctor's services was in the ratio of 8 to 10.

So far, we have considered only two alternative occupations; but the problem of choosing among any number of alternatives can always be reduced to this case by elimination. Among all the alternatives open to him, a person can always choose two between which he can easily make up his mind; and, having dismissed one of these as the less desirable of the two, he can proceed to compare the other to a third alternative. Proceeding step by step in this way, he can reduce the number of eligible alternatives to two—the case discussed above. It is obvious that in all the occupations he rejects, this person's expected income must be below his transfer price for those occupations, and that he tries to choose the one occupation in which he expects to earn an income that is above, or at least equal to, his transfer price.

Expectations may be disappointed, of course, and relative earnings in different occupations may change with the passing of time, so that at any time one will find people in occupations they would not have chosen had they foreseen correctly the trend of relative earnings. In other words, the free choice of occupation cannot guarantee that everybody's earnings will always be equal to or above his transfer price; it only establishes a trend in that direction.

4. SPECIALIZATION AMONG WORKERS

A person is a perfect competitor in his choice of occupation if he regards rates of earnings in different occupations as given and is free to enter any occupation. When everybody is in this position and every person can earn, in each occupation, the same income as others for equivalent services performed, competition among sellers in the labor market is perfect as far as choice of occupation is concerned. The consequences of this will be seen to be an almost exact counterpart of the consequences of perfect competition among consumers in the market for consumers' goods.

Given the nature and quantity of the services that the community wants to have performed, there is a set of wage and salary rates that calls forth exactly these services. When competition among the sellers of their services is perfect, each person, facing this set of wage and salary rates, will choose the occupation in which his rate of earnings is equal to or higher than his transfer price. It can now be shown that when all members of the community behave in this way, specialization among them will be efficient. This means that the tasks performed by the members of the community will be so allocated among them as to involve a minimum of sacrifice, because everybody will perform the work he likes most (or dislikes least) and is best fitted for.

To prove this statement, we must show that no exchanging of jobs between any two people could lighten any one person's burden without either raising the other person's burden or lowering the quality or quantity of some of the work performed. Let us call the two people F and G and assume, first, that F's income is lower than G's. Then F must have chosen his own occupation in preference to G's, either because, lacking aptitude for G's occupation, he could not have earned G's income in it or because G's work seemed so disagreeable to him as more than to offset the higher income paid for it. In neither case could the efficiency of specialization be improved by an exchange of jobs between F and G. For in the first case the swapping of jobs would lower the quantity or quality of work performed in G's original occupation; and in the second case it would make F worse off than he was before. The argument is exactly the same—except for the interchange of the two letters—when it is G's income that is smaller than F's.

Assume, next, that F's income is equal to G's. Again, F's choice of occupation suggests either that, having no aptitude for G's occupation, his income would have been lower there, or that he prefers his own job. Again, therefore, the swapping of jobs would, in the first case, lower the quantity or quality of work performed in G's former occupation; whereas, in the second case, F's sacrifice would be increased. In the limiting case that F and G are equally good at and indifferent between the two occupations and have chosen their own more or less as a matter of chance, the swapping of jobs between them would leave unchanged the quantity and quality of work performed and would make them neither worse nor better off than they were before. This exhausts all possibilities and proves our proposition that free entry to and nondiscrimination in different occupations would lead to efficient specialization.

The above result has an important corollary. It can be shown that if conditions are such that at the ruling wages, salaries, and professional earnings, everybody renders the service he likes best and is best fitted for, then these wages, salaries, and earnings express the relative burden to society of rendering these services, given the number of people employed in each occupation. In other words, when there is perfect competition among the sellers in the labor market, the prices paid for different services express the marginal cost of these services from society's point of view.

To prove this proposition, let us recall that the cost of securing a person's services in his occupation is his transfer price, and that the ratio of his transfer price to his expected earning power in his next most eligible occupation shows his own estimate of the relative burden to him of the two jobs. Let us also recall that actual earnings in any given occupation exceed the transfer price of most people in that occupation and equal the transfer price of only a few marginal people. Actual earnings, therefore, express the cost of obtaining the services of these marginal people only; and the ratio of earnings in two occupations expresses their relative burden for these marginal people only. But it is easy to see that these are the only people who matter from society's point of view. For it is they who will change occupations when more people are needed in one and fewer in another occupation; and it is therefore their job preferences and their appraisal of the relative burden of rendering different services which determine the marginal cost to society of obtaining the services of an adequate number of people in any given occupation. Hence, if there is perfect competition among workers, and we find that earnings in F's occupation exceed those in G's, we can take this as proof that getting the services of one more person in F's job would not only cost more money but would also involve a greater or more onerous productive effort than obtaining an additional person's services in G's occupation.

There may be a variety of reasons, of course, why F's earnings are higher than G's. F's job may, in everybody's opinion, be more unpleasant than G's; but it may also be that while some people prefer F's occupation to G's, society's need for the services rendered in F's occupation is greater than these people can supply and requires the services of some additional people who do find F's occupation more onerous. In either case the marginal sacrifice involved in rendering additional services is greater in F's occupation than in G's; and relative earnings express the relative sacrifice of rendering different services *only on the margin.*

5. AN ALTERNATIVE APPROACH

The argument of the last two sections was stated in a form that to the present writer seems to be the simplest. In the following, however, we shall also give an alternative presentation of the argument, which, though clumsier, has certain advantages.

Let us consider four people, F, G, H, and K, all of whom are free to choose between two occupations, which we shall call S and T. Each person's preferences between the two occupations can be expressed in a diagram whose axes measure the number of hours worked in the two occupations. For we can ask each person how many hours of work in occupation T he would regard as equally onerous and requiring the same sacrifice as, say, 8 hours of work in occupation S; and we can register each answer in a diagram by drawing a straight line between the two points that mark the hours of work which he regards as equally onerous. This is illustrated in the diagrams of Figure 26 (p. 100) by the thick lines. They show that F has a great and G has a slight preference for occupation S, that H is indifferent and regards 8 hours of work as equally distasteful in either occupation, and that K prefers occupation T. These lines may be called indifference lines, for the points they connect represent alternatives that are equally onerous and between which, therefore, the person is indifferent as far as the sacrifice involved is concerned.[11]

Of the two occupations, each person will choose the one in which the same sacrifice yields him the higher income. To show which this is, we have to draw price lines into the diagram. The price lines show relative rates of earnings in the two occupations and connect points on the two axes which represent amounts of work whose performance yields the same income. For example, the price lines shown in the diagrams of Figure 26 represent a one-third higher hourly wage rate in occupation T than in S. Successively higher price lines represent successively higher levels of income. Each person, therefore, will go to that end of his indifference line which brings him onto the higher price line. In the example illustrated, F and G will choose occupation S; and H and K will choose occupation T.

It is easy to see that if relative wages were different from what we assumed them to be in the above example, the allocation of the four

---

[11] Strictly speaking, we should draw several indifference lines for each person, one for each successive amount of effort expended; and these indifference lines may but need not be parallel to each other. For example, from the fact that F considers 2 hours of work in occupation T as tiring as 8 hours of work in S, it need not follow that he would also consider one hour of work in T as tiring as 4 hours in S. For simplicity's sake, however, we have made this assumption in the above argument and, on the basis of this assumption, have dispensed with drawing more than one indifference line.

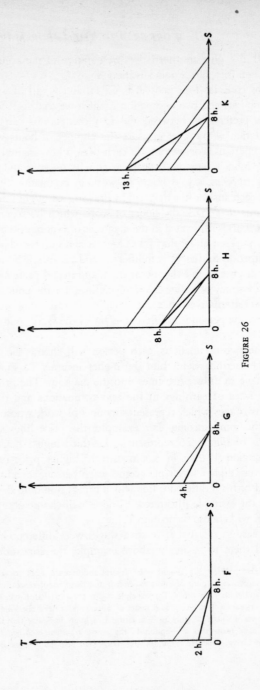

FIGURE 26

people's services between the two occupations would also be different; and that, depending on what relative wages are, the following four alternatives are possible in addition to the one already mentioned: (1) All four people may go into occupation T, (2) all but K may go into T, (3) all but F may go into occupation S, (4) all four may go into S. In other words, when all members of the group are free to choose their occupations, society can influence their choice through the medium of relative wages and by these means can obtain their services in any one of the above-mentioned five combinations.

All five cases are represented in Figure 27 by the two ends and three corners of the solid-line curve, each of which shows the total number of hours of service offered in one of the five alternative cases. This curve has been obtained by joining together the indifference lines of the four people in the order of their increasing steepness; and it is called an opportunity-cost curve. Since each person makes exactly the same sacrifice in all the five cases, the opportunity-cost curve may be regarded as a group indifference curve, different points of which show the different combinations of the two services that the group as a whole can render at a given sacrifice. Moving along the opportunity-cost curve from left to right amounts to transferring one person after another from occupation T into S and thus sacrificing successive amounts of service T for the sake of obtaining additional quantities of service S.

When the group consists not of four but of a large number of people, the opportunity-cost curve becomes a smooth curve; and its slope at any point shows the marginal cost of S in terms of T, which, of course, is identical with the rate at which the marginal person is willing to exchange work in T for work in S. Such a curve is shown in Figure 28.

If we now draw price lines into Figures 27 and 28, showing the ratio of earnings in the two occupations, we can illustrate the way in which this ratio determines the quantities of the two services offered by members of the group. For we have seen that, when people are free to choose their occupation, they choose the one in which a given sacrifice yields them the highest income. If every member of the group behaves this way, the total income of the group taken as a whole will also be maximized. But the income of the group is highest at the point where the opportunity-cost curve comes in contact with the highest price line; this point, therefore, determines the allocation of the members of the group between the two occupations.

For example, in Figure 27 (p. 102), point *q* is such a point; and it illustrates the case that was discussed on page 99. In Figure 28 the income

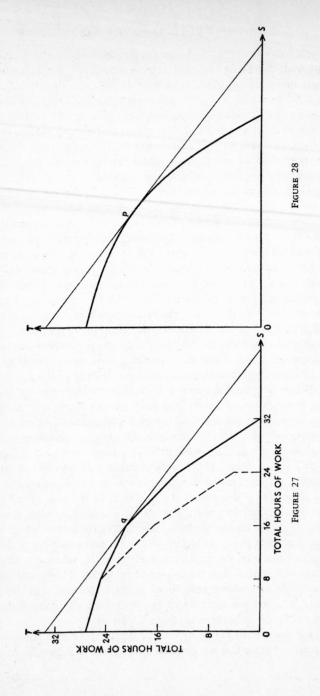

TOTAL HOURS OF WORK

TOTAL HOURS OF WORK

FIGURE 27

FIGURE 28

of the group is highest at point p, where the opportunity-cost curve is tangential to and has the same slope as a price line. This shows that when everybody is free to choose his occupation, people will be allocated to different occupations in such a way as to equate the marginal person's preferences—and hence also the marginal cost of one service in terms of the other—to the ratio of earnings in the two occupations.

This last result is the same as that obtained above on pages 96–97. In fact, until now, the whole analysis of this section has been no more than a restatement in somewhat different form of the arguments and results of the preceding two sections. Now, however, we can go a little beyond the results already reached. For, so far, we have only shown that when people are perfect competitors in their choice of occupation, specialization will be efficient; and we can now show how restrictions of entry lower the efficiency of specialization.

Let us assume that entry to occupation S is restricted and that, say, G finds himself barred from entering S—either as a result of racial or sex discrimination or simply because the training needed for acquiring the skill necessary in S is expensive and G cannot afford it. Whatever the reason that bars G from occupation S, it will always reduce the quantities of services S and T made available to society, unless the latter's preferences are such that G's services in S would not be needed (and he would not be attracted to that occupation) in any event.

This is illustrated in Figure 27 by the broken line, which was drawn, like the opportunity-cost curve, by piecing together the indifference lines of Figure 26, but with G's indifference line omitted. Part of this curve coincides with, part of it lies below, the opportunity-cost curve. For, depending on what society's preferences are, the barring of G from occupation S may or may not interfere with efficient specialization among the members of the group. It is obvious, for example, that if society had no need of service S and wanted all members of the group to exert themselves in occupation T, the barring of G from S would have no practical significance, because it would bar G from an occupation that he would not enter even if he could. In this case, therefore, the barring of G from occupation S would make no difference to the quantity of services rendered by the group. It is less obvious, but no less true, that the same would hold if society needed only 8 hours of service S; for also in this case G would not choose occupation S even if he were free to do so. This is also shown by Figure 27.

But assume, next, that society wants 16 hours of service S and as much of service T as the diversion of two people to occupation S leaves available. How much this will be depends on which two of the four people go into occupation S; and Figure 27 shows that here the restriction of entry does make a difference and results in a net loss of 4 hours of service T. In particular, we saw on page 99 that if entry were free, G would be among the two people in occupation S; and this would leave H and K to render 21 hours of service in occupation T. But if G is barred from S, he must change places with H, which will lower the amount of service T rendered to a total of only 17 hours. The difference, 4 hours of service T, is a net loss to society; and although this could be made good by a greater expenditure of effort, that would change only the form but not the amount of the loss.

We can draw two general conclusions from the above argument. First of all, it appears that the opportunity-cost curve does not represent all possible combinations of the amounts of the two services that can be rendered with a given sacrifice but only the highest or most efficient combinations, which come about when specialization is efficient. In other words, the opportunity-cost curve shows, for each quantity of one service, the highest quantity of the other service obtainable with a given sacrifice. All less efficient combinations lie below the opportunity-cost curve. The second general conclusion we can draw is that restraints on people's freedom to choose their occupations lower the efficiency of specialization whenever the restraints are effective and keep at least one person from the occupation he would have chosen in the absence of restraints. In other words, such restraints inflict a loss on society either by lowering the amount of services rendered with a given sacrifice or by requiring a greater sacrifice for obtaining a given amount of services.[12]

So far, we have considered only the effects of the outright barring of a person from an occupation. It is easy to see, however, that the payment of discriminatory wages or salaries also interferes with efficient specialization if such discrimination causes anyone to choose an occupation different from that he would have chosen in the absence of discrimination. This means that guaranties of free entry and nondiscrimination, the provision of free education and training, the levying of progressive inheritance taxes, and all other measures aimed at creating more equal opportunities for all insure not only greater equity but also greater efficiency.

---

[12] See p. 426, however, for a case in which restraints on entry do not force the system off the opportunity-cost curve, although they do lead to inefficiency.

6. THE DISTRIBUTION OF INCOME PAID
FOR PERSONAL SERVICES

We are now in a position to discuss the distribution of income among the sellers of personal services, both in its relation to the efficient distribution of consumers' goods among consumers and from the point of view of efficient specialization among workers. We saw in the last chapter that, for the distribution of consumers' goods and services to be efficient, all consumers must be price takers; and they must all pay the same prices for the same goods. These conditions are, by and large, fulfilled in our economy; and we concluded, therefore, that the distribution of goods in our economy is efficient. But, in the argument of the last chapter, we left out of account a very important consumers' good: leisure. We must now make good this omission.

If leisure is to be included among the consumers' goods that are efficiently distributed, one might be inclined to argue that the price of leisure would have to be the same for everybody. We saw, however, at the beginning of this chapter that the price of leisure is the wage or salary that a person must sacrifice in order to have leisure. Are we to conclude, therefore, that the distribution of leisure among workers is efficient only if all wage rates, salary rates, and other rates of earning are equal?

This conclusion is perfectly valid as far as the distribution of leisure among members of the same occupation is concerned. In fact, we have shown on page 93 that equal pay for equal work is a condition of the efficient distribution of leisure, income, and jobs within any given profession or occupation. But what about earnings in different occupations? We have shown above that, for specialization to be efficient, relative earnings in different occupations must correspond to the occupational preferences of the marginal person; and only by accident would these preferences be such as to call for the same rates of earning in different occupations. Does this mean that there is a conflict between efficient specialization among workers and the efficient distribution of leisure?

It does not. For let us remember that leisure is a consumer's good of a very special type. It means freedom from the burden of work; and the satisfaction it yields is the enjoyment of not working. Looking at it in this way, one realizes immediately that freedom from different types of work cannot be regarded as one and the same commodity, since one's enjoyment of leisure depends very much on what type of work is one's alternative to leisure. There is no reason, therefore, why freedom from different types of work should have the same price; accordingly, there is no incompatibility between the efficient distribution of leisure and efficient specialization among workers.

Incidentally, the above argument also shows the kind of pitfalls one might fall into by regarding leisure as a commodity. It is much safer, as well as more natural, to look at the face of the medal and concentrate our attention on work and the burden it involves, rather than on freedom from work and the satisfaction this yields. We can, if we like, think of work as a negative commodity, of its burden as a disutility or negative satisfaction, and of the earnings received for work as a negative price. This approach has the advantage of bringing into focus the parallelism between a person's choice of consumers' goods and services and his decision concerning the type and amount of work he wants to perform. The efficiency of specialization and job allocation then appears as an exact counterpart of the efficient distribution of consumers' goods and services; and, in the same way in which the prices paid for goods and services consumed express consumers' marginal preferences, so the prices received for productive services performed express the marginal worker's job preferences. The parallelism is not quite complete; for, while the relative prices of two consumers' goods express the marginal rates of substitution of *all* consumers of the two goods, relative earnings in two occupations express the preferences of the *marginal* worker or workers only. This slight difference is due to the fact that, while the consumer's choice of consumers' goods is a marginal choice, the worker's choice of occupation is not.

Special interest is lent to the prices received for productive services by the fact that they determine the distribution of income among workers. Since efficient specialization and job allocation require a certain set of prices for productive services, they also require a certain income distribution among workers. We might call this an efficient income distribution, because it provides efficient specialization and job allocation; that is, it provides the productive system with the desired quantities of the different types of productive services at a minimum cost to society in terms of human effort and burden of work. We shall say, therefore, that an income distribution is efficient if it provides people with the correct incentive to perform the kind and amount of work society wants from them.

What the different rates of earnings are when income distribution is efficient we saw above, when we discussed the efficiency of specialization and job allocation; but it may well be worth repeating here. We showed, to begin with, that earnings in different occupations must equal the transfer price of the marginal person in each occupation. Whether his services are really the most useful in his actual occupation and whether society is making the best use of his services is another subject, which will be discussed at a later stage. But, given the fact that, for good reasons or bad, society wants his services in his actual occupation, it seems obvious that he must receive the minimum income necessary to retain him in his occupation. All other, intramarginal people must be paid an income that exceeds their transfer price and equals the transfer price of the marginal person in their occupation. The amount by which an intramarginal person's income exceeds his transfer price is called his rent (sometimes also called his quasi rent). The rent received by an intramarginal person is not necessary to retain him in his occupation; [13] but it is necessary to insure the efficient allocation of work and leisure within his occupation. We can say, therefore, that an efficient distribution of income among workers is one that pays everybody his transfer price and his rent.[14]

It should be mentioned here that there is no connection between an efficient and an equitable income distribution. An efficient income distribution is one that provides the right incentive for the efficient allocation of tasks; an equitable income distribution is one that leads to an ethically acceptable and satisfying distribution of consumers' goods and services. An efficient income distribution need not necessarily be equitable, although it may be and, as a matter of fact, often is. For differences in income which can be explained by differences in ability are usually accepted as equitable. Few people begrudge a person his high income if it is due to his possession of a special skill or talent which happens to be in great demand—provided that his income is no greater than necessary to call forth the supply to fill that demand. It must be remembered, however, that the problem of equity is raised mainly by the distribution of income between social classes; whereas, in this section, we were concerned with the distribution of income only among the sellers of personal services.

---

[13] Specialization would be efficient if everybody were paid no more than his transfer price.

[14] For a detail discussion of rent, see Joan Robinson, *The Economics of Imperfect Competition* (London: Macmillan & Co., 1933), chap. viii.

BIBLIOGRAPHICAL NOTE

Much of the analysis of the individual worker's behavior is just an adaptation of the theory of consumer's choice as developed by Professor J. R. Hicks (see *Value and Capital* [Oxford: Clarendon Press, 1939], chap. ii). A more detailed discussion of the worker's special problems is contained in K. E. Boulding, *Economic Analysis* (rev. ed.; New York: Harper & Bros., 1948), chap. xxxiii. The problem of efficiency in the labor market is discussed in A. Bergson, *The Structure of Soviet Wages* (Cambridge, Mass.: Harvard University Press, 1946), chap. ii.

See also J. R. Hicks, *The Theory of Wages* (London: Macmillan & Co., 1932), chap. v; and Lionel Robbins, "On the Elasticity of Demand for Income in Terms of Effort," *Economica,* Vol. X (1930), pp. 123–29.

CHAPTER VI

THE FIRM

THE firm is a person, partnership, or corporation selling goods or services that incorporate goods or services bought from others. Manufacturers and farmers sell an output produced with the aid of the services of their employees and with materials and equipment bought from other firms; merchants sell goods bought from producers or other merchants. A firm, therefore, is both a seller and a buyer; and we must discuss its behavior both in the markets where it sells and in the markets where it buys. The goods and services sold by a firm are its products, which may be final products sold to the consumer or intermediate products sold to other firms. The goods and services bought by a firm are its factors of production, whether they are original factors bought from the individual sellers of productive services or produced factors bought from other firms, from whose point of view they are intermediate products. Thus, the same commodity is a consumer's good when bought for the buyer's personal use but a factor of production when bought for resale—either in unchanged form or incorporated in a final product in combination with other factors of production. When we speak of production, we usually mean manufacturing or farming; and when we speak of the factors of production, we usually think of fuel, raw materials, semimanufactures, and the services of the workers, managers, and equipment of a factory or farm. In a wider sense, however, a retailer is also a producer; and the product he buys for resale is, from his point of view, a factor of production, which, together with his personal services and the services of his establishment, enters into the finished consumer's good. For a consumer's good consists not only in the parcel that the consumer takes home from his shopping tour but also in the convenience of being able to buy that parcel in a conveniently located, nicely decorated store, under pleasant circumstances, and from a pretty salesgirl. Manufacturing and farming are, of course, the main forms of production; but the principles that govern the market behavior of the firm are the same whether it is a farm, a factory, a mine, or a department store.

In this and the following four chapters we shall assume that the firm behaves like a price taker in the market, just as we assumed that consumers and workers behave like price takers. We pointed out earlier that while it is perfectly realistic to treat the consumer as a price taker, it is not nearly so realistic to make this assumption about the worker. The same is also true of the firm. In our society, there is hardly a firm that would be a price taker in *all* the markets where it buys and sells, although many firms are price takers in *some* of the markets in which they deal. In the markets where firms sell their products, only the small farmer selling his produce to mills, packing houses, canneries, or large wholesale merchants is likely to deal on terms set by the buyer. Most other firms either set their own terms or are able to bargain when they sell their products; and, in either case, they are not in the perfectly competitive position which characterizes the price taker's behavior.

In the markets where it buys the factors of production, the firm sometimes is and sometimes is not in the perfectly competitive position of a price taker. Most firms are price takers with respect to some factors of production, usually their less important ones; and some of the smaller firms may buy all their factors of production at prices set by the sellers. The latter is probably true of the small retailer, who buys his merchandise at the price set by the manufacturer or wholesaler. But in many transactions between firms, price is settled by bargaining; and the same is true of price determination also in the labor market. Sometimes, the firm even sets the price at which it buys factors of production, as in the markets where wholesalers and processors buy the small farmer's produce and in markets for labor where the workers are unorganized. Nevertheless, we shall discuss the behavior of the firm as a price taker in considerable detail, partly because of the theoretical importance of perfectly competitive behavior, and partly as an introduction to our discussion of the firm as a price maker or bargainer.

In the last three chapters, we discussed the behavior of the consumer and the individual seller on the assumption that they aim at maximizing their satisfaction. The exact nature and implications of this assumption were discussed in sufficient detail to need no repetition here; but we want to remind the reader of one feature of this assumption: it is incapable of proof or disproof and amounts to little more than a rationalization of whatever the individual's market behavior happens to be.

About the firm, we shall make the much more tangible and definite assumption that it aims at maximizing its profit. Profit, unlike satisfaction, is a measurable quantity. It is expressed in terms of money; and its magnitude can be ascertained from the firm's Profit and Loss account. Hence, by saying that the firm aims at maximizing profit, we make a statement about the firm's behavior which may be true or false and which can be proved true or false. In fact, there has been a growing consciousness among economists in recent years that they may have been too rash in assuming that firms always aim at maximizing profit. The actual behavior of firms often seems to be at variance with what one would expect their behavior to be on the assumption that they aim at maximizing profit; and this seeming incompatibility between the firm's actual market behavior and the economist's theory of his behavior has led to a growing demand for a new and more realistic theory of the firm.

So far, however, no such new theory has been developed; and none will be presented here. Empirical studies of businessmen's behavior suggest the need for modifying or qualifying the assumption of profit maximization here and there, rather than scrapping it altogether. Accordingly, in what follows, we shall retain the assumption that the firm aims at maximizing its profit. But we shall regard this assumption as a working hypothesis rather than as a universal rule. We shall try to list all the exceptions to it; and we shall pay special attention to the different interpretations and implications of this assumption and to the problem of reconciling the theory of the firm based on this assumption with the latter's actual market behavior.

Considering the fact that, unlike our assumption about the consumer's and the worker's market behavior, the assumption of profit maximization is not a mere truism and rationalization of whatever the firm may be doing, we can hardly expect it to hold true equally of all firms and under all circumstances. At best, it is true of the majority of firms. Furthermore, the same aim of maximizing profit need not always lead different firms to pursue the same policy; therefore, differences in the policies of different firms need not imply differences also in their aims. Two people, both aiming at maximum profits, need not necessarily act the same way when confronted with the same situation. They may evaluate the situation differently; and even when they do not, they may act differently. To begin with, we must bear in mind that the manager of a firm must act on the basis of what he expects future conditions to be; and different people may, of course, have different expectations. Second, even if they have the same expectations, one person may attach less confidence to his expectations than another and may therefore exercise more caution in acting upon them. Third, one person may be more efficient or have more drive than another; or he may be more eager to maximize his profit, which explains why different people, even if they entertain the same expectations with the same degree of confidence, may still act differently.

The above differences may be due to differences in temperament and ability; and to the extent that they are, they must be accepted as given. Human differences must be allowed for in economic behavior as in everything else; and in an uncertain world, there is no unique and best way of maximizing profit, just as there is no best way of choosing a wife or bringing up children.

To some extent, however, the above differences are due not merely to human and temperamental differences but to economic causes. There are indications, for example, that large firms, whose profits are large, tend to be much more cautious in their policies than small firms. It is also established that the keenness with which the entrepreneur tries to maximize profit depends on his incentive. He usually tries harder if it is a matter of turning losses into profits than if it is a matter of rendering already large profits larger still.

Whenever differences in the policies of different firms are due not to differences in ability and temperament but to factors such as those cited above, it is well to make them explicit. Accordingly, we shall say that a person aims at maximum profit only if he tries to maximize profit to the best of his ability.

The firm in our society is either a corporation or an individual proprietorship or partnership. The owners of individual proprietorships and partnerships aim at maximizing their satisfaction; but it will be shown in the Note to Chapter VII that they usually achieve this aim by maximizing the firm's profit. As for the owners of a corporation—its stockholders—it is reasonable to assume that they are interested in seeing the corporation's profit maximized; but they do not always exercise control over the corporation's policy. They do so when, as often happens, the managers of the corporation hold the majority of its shares, in which case there is little difference between a corporation and a partnership. But when this is not the case and the separation between the functions of ownership and management is fairly complete, conflicts between the owners' interests and the management's policy may arise. Shareholders are primarily interested in dividends; whereas managers often prefer paying small dividends or none at all and ploughing back profits in order to strengthen and expand the firm and so to increase the importance, security, or lucrativeness of their own personal position. Such conflict of interests, however, centers mainly around the disposal of profit. On the desirability of making profit as large as possible, shareholders ar. l management generally agree. An important exception to this rule will be discussed in Chapter IX; but it may be pointed out already here that such exceptions do little harm to the assumption of profit maximization. The producer has to deal in several markets simultaneously; and if he does not aim at maximizing profit in one market, his behavior in other markets may still be governed by the principle of profit maximization. In fact, it will appear as we go along that most exceptions to the rule of profit maximization are likely to affect the firm's market behavior in some markets or in one market only.

1. THE PRODUCTION FUNCTION

The firm's output depends on (is a function of) the quantities of the factors of production utilized. This dependence can be expressed in mathematical form; and the function symbolizing it is called the firm's production function. The shape of the production function—that is, the particular way in which output depends on the input of factors—can be illustrated graphically with the aid of a production indifference map, which is the exact counterpart of the consumer's indifference map.

The production function represents the scope and limitations of production as determined by technical conditions, which the economist cannot change and must accept as given. These technical conditions of production may be rigid, or they may be flexible. They are rigid if they prescribe exactly the quantity of each productive factor needed to produce a given output; and in such a case the firm's production policy raises few economic problems. For example, if the making of a suit of clothes of given size would require exactly 3 yards of cloth, one yard of lining, one reel of thread, 2 dozen buttons, and 12 hours of labor, all that would have to be determined is the tailor's rate of output. Once he has decided how many suits of clothes to make, his demand for the factors of production would be automatically given.

In most cases, however, the technical conditions of production allow a certain freedom of choice. There usually are some factors of production which are required in exact quantities per unit of output; and the demand for these is uniquely determined when the firm's rate of output is decided. These are called limitational factors. Most factors of pro-

E

duction, however, can be combined in varying proportions to produce a given output, because the methods of production can be varied. Such factors are called substitutional factors. For example, the number of buttons on a suit may be rigidly determined by fashion; but tailors usually have some scope for saving material at the cost of more careful and slower cutting or, conversely, of saving some of the cutter's labor

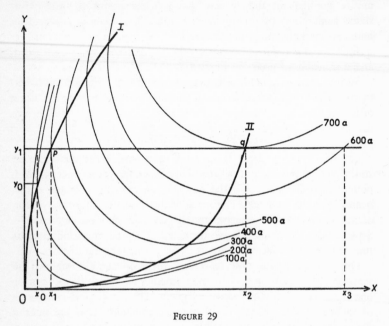

FIGURE 29

time at the cost of greater material wastage. Similarly, the manufacture of automobiles requires both steel and aluminum; but there is considerable leeway for substituting one for the other; and such substitution is likely to take place whenever there is a significant shift in the relative prices of the two metals. In other words, when technical conditions are flexible and allow some latitude in the combination of factors, the method of production chosen depends on economic as well as technical considerations. This is obvious enough and seems mere common sense; but it will be worth our while to illustrate the principle graphically and express it in more exact terms. The advantages of graphical illustration, however, must again be paid for by the limitation of two dimensions. Hence, we shall have to restrict ourselves to the firm that employs only two factors of production and leave to a later stage (pp. 125–26) the generalization of our results to any number of factors.

In the diagram of Figure 29, where quantities of the factors of production X and Y are measured along the two axes,[1] we can draw production indifference curves, usually called isoquants,[2] showing the different combinations of factors which can produce given quantities of the finished product, A. For example, the isoquant labeled 100*a* shows all the combinations of factors X and Y which will produce 100 units of the finished product; the isoquant 200*a* shows the different quantities of the two factors which will produce 200 units of the product, and so forth.

What is the shape of the producer's isoquants? There are two ways in which we could determine it. First of all, we could infer the shape of isoquants from the producer's behavior in the markets where he buys the factors of production, assuming that his behavior is rational and prompted by the desire to maximize profit. This would correspond closely to the way in which we derived the consumer's indifference map and would amount to little more than a repetition of the argument presented in Chapter III. Second, we can also derive the shape of isoquants directly, from a few elementary assumptions about the nature of the production function. In what follows, it will be convenient to depart from the method followed in Chapter III and to adopt the second line of approach.

Our first assumption has been stated already. We assume that the same output can be produced in more than one way and with more than one combination of factors but that there is a limit to the possibility of substituting one factor for another. Accordingly, the isoquants in Figure 29 have been drawn with a downward slope through part of their range to indicate the fact that, when less of one factor is used, more of the other is needed for producing the same output. This corresponds to the downward slope of the consumer's indifference curve. The slope of the isoquant in this range expresses the rate at which one factor can be substituted for the other without changing output. This is called the marginal rate of technical substitution between the two factors and corresponds exactly to the consumer's marginal rate of substitution between two products. Since two factors cannot be perfect

---

[1] Throughout this book, we shall denote products by letters taken from the beginning, factors by letters taken from the end of the alphabet, and persons and firms by the letters F, G, . . . , K.

[2] *Isos* is Greek for "equal."

substitutes for each other (if they were, they would not be called separate factors), the isoquants in this range are convex toward the origin, because the more is used of one factor relative to the other, the more difficult it becomes to substitute yet further quantities of it for the other factor. For example, the tailor who tries to save material at the cost of more careful cutting is likely to find that the further he pushes this policy, the larger becomes the amount of his cutter's labor time needed to save successive quantities of material.

In fact, the substitution of one factor for another will not only become more difficult as it is pushed further and further; there usually is an absolute limit to it, beyond which further substitution becomes impossible. At this point the isoquant becomes parallel to one of the axes, representing the fact that beyond this point an increased use of one factor will not increase output at all, even when the quantity of the other factor is not reduced further but kept constant. Hence, the points where the isoquants become parallel to the axes show the limits within which substitution is possible.

The question now arises: What is the shape of an isoquant beyond the limits of substitution? We could assume that it stays parallel to the axes, showing that additional quantities of one factor alone are useless and leave output unchanged. We could also assume, however, that beyond the limits of substitution, additional quantities of one factor alone are not only useless but cumbersome. In this case, if output is to be kept constant, the encumbrance caused by using too much of one factor would have to be offset by using a little more also of the other factor. Graphically, this case is represented by the isoquants veering away from the axes beyond the limiting points and curving back upon themselves. This is shown in Figure 29. It makes no difference to our results which of the two alternative assumptions we adopt; but, for the sake of simplifying the argument, we shall adopt the second.

The implications of this assumption become apparent when we consider the relation of successive isoquants to each other. Take, for example, the case of a manufacturer whose two factors of production are labor and equipment and who, in the short run at least, can vary only the number of his workers, because his equipment is fixed in quantity. If we denote the fixed quantity of his equipment by y_1 and measure the number of workers employed along the X axis, we can represent changes in his rate of activity by a movement along the horizontal line drawn through y_1 (Fig. 29). As we move along this line from y_1 to the right, we come to higher and higher isoquants; and this shows that an increased input of labor will, with given equipment, raise output. But it will raise output only up to a point. In Figure 29 the highest isoquant which can be reached by traveling along this line represents an output of 700 units, which is reached when the quantity of labor is x_2. This represents the highest number of workers that can be usefully employed with the capital equipment y_1. If more than x_2 workers are employed, they interfere with the smooth functioning of the factory, cause overcrowding, get into each other's way, and thereby reduce total output. For example, x_3 workers would produce a total output of 600 units only.

Needless to say, the producer will never operate in the region beyond x_2 if he can help it. He will always try to keep out of the range where one of the factors is redundant and stay within the range of substitutability. In fact, it will be useful to draw the border line between these two regions, by connecting the points on successive isoquants where these are parallel to one of the axes. In Figure 29, this is shown by the curves marked I and II. Factor Y is redundant above curve I; factor X is redundant to the right of curve II; and the region bounded by the two curves represents the range of substitutability between the two factors.

But although the producer will always try to remain within the region of substitutability, he is not always able to do this, because he is seldom free to vary at will the quantities and proportions in which his factors of production are employed. It may happen, therefore, that the firm cannot help employing one of its productive factors in redundant quantity. Assume, for example, that the producer whose capital equipment is y_1 cannot get or does not want to employ more workers than x_0. In this case, he is clearly employing too much capital equipment, because he could raise his output from 100 to 200 units by *lowering* the quantity of his equipment from y_1 to y_0. In other words, y_1 represents a factory designed to be operated by a number of workers between x_1 and x_2; and, although x_0 workers can operate it, they do so under a handicap. They would be more efficient and could produce a higher output if employed in a smaller factory, such as that represented by y_0. For y_1 stands not only for more capital equipment than y_0 but also for equipment organized in a different way. A large factory contains not only more machinery than a small factory but machinery of a different type; and once a manufacturer has installed machinery for large-scale production, he has to use it even when his output is small.

To show how output varies with varying quantities of one factor, while the other factor is kept unchanged, it is convenient to draw a new diagram, such as is shown in Figure 30, where along the horizontal axis we measure, as before, the quantity of the variable factor, X; but, along the vertical axis, we measure the quantity of output, which in the production indifference map was represented by the isoquants. Curves drawn in this diagram show, for each quantity of factor Y, the dependence of output on the quantity of X utilized. For example, the curve labeled y_1 shows the relationship between output and factor X when the quantity of Y is fixed at y_1. Similarly, the curve labeled y_2 shows the

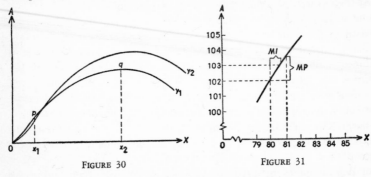

FIGURE 30   FIGURE 31

dependence of output on the quantity of X when the quantity of Y is fixed at y_2. These curves are called productivity curves; and their relation to movement along a horizontal straight line in the isoquant map is evident. They do not give additional information about the firm's production function but present the information already contained in Figure 29 in a different form.[3]

Movement along a productivity curve shows the transformation of factor X into product A; and the slope of the curve shows the marginal rate of transformation of factor into product. This rate is also called the marginal productivity, or the marginal physical productivity, of the factor; and the additional quantity of product due to the utilization of one additional unit of the factor is called the marginal product, or the marginal physical product, of the factor. The marginal product of factor X is abbreviated as MP_x or, sometimes, to show the identity also of the product, as $MP_x{}^a$. It is convenient to have a name also for the additional

[3] The relation of the diagrams of Figs. 29 and 30 may become clearer to the reader if he imagines a three-dimensional representation of the production function showing the dependence of output A on the utilization of factors X and Y. The production indifference map of Fig. 29 is a contour map showing the intersections of this three-dimensional figure with planes parallel to the X-Y plane; whereas Fig. 30 shows the intersections of the same figure with planes parallel to the X-A plane.

quantity of the factor needed to produce an additional unit of a product. This quantity is called the marginal input of the factor. The marginal input of factor X needed to produce an additional unit of product A will be abbreviated as MI_x or MI_x^a. For example, in the case of the productivity curve in Figure 31, the marginal rate of transformation of factor X into product A is $1 : 1\frac{1}{2}$. At that point, therefore, the marginal product of factor X, that is the additional product of an additional unit of X, is $1\frac{1}{2}$ units of product A. In symbols: $MP_x^a = 1\frac{1}{2}$. At the same point the marginal input of factor X is two thirds of one unit of X. In symbols: $MI_x^a = \frac{2}{3}$. It is apparent from this example that marginal product and marginal input are reciprocals of each other; that is, $MI_x \equiv 1/MP_x$. Geometrically, the marginal product varies directly, and the marginal input varies inversely, with the slope of the productivity curve.

A simple and important relation exists also between the marginal inputs and marginal products of two factors on the one hand and their marginal rate of technical substitution on the other hand. The marginal rate of technical substitution between factors X and Y, MTS_{xy}^a, expresses the rate at which Y can be substituted for X in the production of A without changing the quantity of output. This rate can also be expressed as the ratio of MI_y^a to MI_x^a. For example, if the marginal inputs of factors X and Y are 3 and 4, respectively, then adding 4 units of Y will raise the output of A by one unit, taking away 3 units of X will lower output by one unit; and a simultaneous adding of 4 units of Y and subtracting of 3 units of X leaves the total output of A unchanged and corresponds to a movement along an isoquant. In symbols,

$$\frac{4}{3} = \frac{MI_y^a}{MI_x^a} \equiv MTS_{xy}^a .$$

From this, it also follows that

$$\frac{MP_x^a}{MP_y^a} \equiv MTS_{xy}^a ,$$

considering that the marginal input of a factor is the reciprocal of its marginal product.

Let us now return to Figure 30 and see what shape the productivity curve y_1 has. Its position and slope are most easily determined at points p and q, whose relation to the corresponding points in Figure 29 is simplest to establish. It appears from Figure 29 that output is highest at point q, from which it follows that the productivity curve will have its highest point at *q,* rising up to there and descending beyond it. Since the slope of the productivity curve shows the marginal productivity of factor X, this means that the marginal productivity of X will be positive up to point *q.* At point *q,* it will be zero; and beyond point *q,* it will be negative. In other words, the increased utilization of factor X will raise the output of product A until point *q* is reached; it will leave the output of A unchanged at point *q;* and it will lower the output of A beyond point *q.*

To determine the slope of the productivity curve y_1 at point *p,* we must first make our third and last assumption about the nature of the firm's production function. We shall assume that the firm can always increase its output in a given proportion by increasing the quantity of *all* its factors of production in the same proportion. This assumption, whose validity will be discussed in detail at a later stage (see Chap. IX), is so important that it has a special name: the assumption of proportional returns. Proportional returns mean that the firm could raise its output by 1, 10, or 100 per cent, by adding 1, 10, or 100 per cent to its labor force, to its administrative staff, to its plant capacity, and to the input of fuel, materials, and all the other factors of production. Needless to say, only seldom will it be necessary to increase the quantity of *every* factor of production in the same proportion in which output is to be raised; accordingly, this will rarely be the most economical way of increasing output. We assume, however, that it is one way of doing it.

Returning now to point *p* in Figure 29, we assume that a one per cent addition to the input of factors X and Y at point *p* would also raise output by one per cent. But at this point the isoquant is parallel to the Y axis, indicating the fact that at this point an additional input of factor Y, unaccompanied by a simultaneous increase in factor X, would not increase output at all. In other words, at point *p* the marginal productivity of factor Y is zero. From this, it follows that the one per cent increase in output must be imputed entirely to the one per cent addition to the input of X; and the additional use of Y must be regarded as gratuitous. In other words, at point *p* the increased input of X results in a proportional increase in output.

This result enables us to draw the productivity curve y_1 at point *p.* The level of output is shown by the isoquant going through *p* in Figure 29; and the slope of the productivity curve at this point must be the same as that of a straight line going through the origin, because the slope of such a line indicates a proportional change in the quantities measured along the two axes.

From here on, it is easy to complete the drawing of the productivity curve y_1. Assuming, as we always do, that the curve is smooth, we must make it concave from below between points p and q. As to the range to the left of p, there the productivity curve must always have a slope that is steeper than that of a straight line through the origin. This represents the fact that in this range, increases in the input of X result in more than proportional increases in output; for in this range the marginal productivity of Y is negative.

The isoquants and productivity curves together describe the firm's production function. They express not only the technical but also the human characteristics of the conditions under which the firm operates. For example, two firms producing an identical product will have different production functions if the efficiency of their managers or the technical knowledge of their engineers is different. In other words, the production function expresses the firm's productive possibilities as they actually are, and not as they would be under ideal conditions, with the most efficient management and the most up-to-date technology.

So far, we have been concerned with the firm that produces one commodity. But many firms produce several commodities. This raises the question as to what the production functions of such firms look like. Here, however, our geometry is no longer sufficient. We could, indeed, construct a diagram measuring along its two axes the quantities of two products and draw into this diagram indifference curves which show the different combinations of the two products that can be produced with given quantities of the factors of production. Such a procedure would be perfectly feasible if the firm employed only one factor of production; for in this case, successive indifference curves would represent successive quantities of this single productive factor. But what if, as is usually the case, the firm employs more than one factor of production? In this case, it would no longer be enough to draw one family of indifference curves, representing successively larger quantities of the factors; for we would have to draw a different family of indifference curves for each combination of the different factors.

It is true, of course, that we need not consider every combination of the different factors because, for every output, there is one combination of factors which is preferable to all other combinations. But what this optimum combination is depends on the prices of the factors. It seems advisable, therefore, to postpone the discussion of the many-product firm until we have analyzed the market behavior of the firm. This is the subject matter of the next chapter.

(For Bibliographical Note, see the end of Chap. VII.)

CHAPTER VII

THE FIRM (CONTINUED): THE MARKET BEHAVIOR OF THE FIRM

IN OUR discussion of the production function, we argued that technological considerations seldom prescribe exactly the quantities of factors required for producing a given output but allow some leeway and scope for variation. The nature and limitations of this leeway and of the firm's freedom of choice between different combinations of factors and different rates of output were illustrated graphically by our isoquants and productivity curves. The question we now have to answer is how the firm makes use of its freedom of choice to maximize profit. This clearly depends on market conditions. Facing given prices in product and factor markets, and having its freedom of action circumscribed by its production function, the firm must make three decisions. It must decide (1) how to produce; (2) how much to produce; and, if it produces several products, (3) what combination of products to produce. The three decisions are not independent of each other, and all of them are determined by the same principle of profit maximization. It is only for the sake of convenience that they are discussed separately in the following pages.

1. THE COMBINATION OF PRODUCTIVE FACTORS

To maximize his profit, the entrepreneur must allocate any given cost expenditure in such a way as to get the maximum output; or, what amounts to the same thing, he must produce any given output at a minimum cost.

The geometry of showing the most economical way of combining the factors of production is exactly the same as that used in Chapter III for illustrating the consumer's market behavior. When the firm is a price taker in the factor markets, its market opportunities of buying the factors of production can be expressed geometrically by price lines. Such price lines are shown in Figure 32, together with the firm's isoquants. These price lines are called isocosts, because each one of them expresses the various combinations of the two factors which can be bought at the same cost. In other words, traveling along an isocost amounts to incurring the same cost of production in different ways. To achieve his aim of maximizing profit, the entrepreneur must go to a point of tangency between an isoquant and an isocost, because it is at such points that a given isocost comes in contact with the highest isoquant (maximum output at given cost) and a given isoquant comes in contact with the lowest isocost (given output at minimum cost).

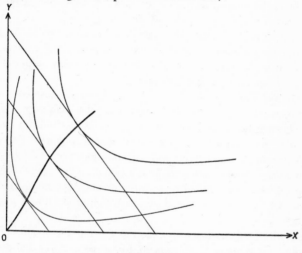

FIGURE 32

In other words, the conditions of minimizing cost are, first, that the slope of isocost and isoquant be the same and, second, that the isoquant be convex to the origin in the neighborhood of that point. The second condition is fulfilled when the firm produces within the range of substitutability, bounded by the curves *I* and *II* in Figure 29 (p. 114). The first condition is fulfilled when production is so organized that the marginal rate of technical substitution between the two factors (the slope of the isoquant) equals the ratio of their market prices (the slope of the isocost). In symbols, this condition can be expressed by the equation

$$MTS_{xy} = \frac{p_x}{p_y}.$$

Since $MTS_{xy} = MI_y/MI_x$,[1] the same condition can also be expressed by the equation

$$\frac{MI_y}{MI_x} = \frac{p_x}{p_y},$$

which can also be written as

$$p_x MI_x = p_y MI_y . \tag{2}$$

In equation (2), $p_x MI_x$ is the market cost of the marginal input of X, or the marginal cost of an additional unit of output when this is produced by the increased utilization of factor X only. Similarly, $p_y MI_y$ is the market cost of the marginal input of Y, or the marginal cost of an additional unit of output when this is obtained by the increased utilization of factor Y only. Equation (2), therefore, expresses the condition that marginal cost must be the same whether output is raised by the increased utilization of X or of Y.

When the above condition is fulfilled, marginal cost will be the same also when output is raised by increasing the quantities of both X and Y. Furthermore, the above condition applies not only to increases but also to reductions in the quantities of output and of the factors utilized. Hence, we can express this condition more generally by saying that for costs to be at a minimum, production must be organized and the factors of production combined in such a manner that marginal cost is the same whatever the particular way in which production is increased or diminished.

The truth of this statement is easiest to prove indirectly, by considering a situation in which the factors are combined in a way that does not fulfill this condition but renders

$$p_x MI_x > p_y MI_y .$$

It is apparent that this cannot be a minimum cost situation, because a saving in cost could be achieved by substituting factor Y for factor X in a way that would leave output unchanged. For example, the utilization of X could be reduced by MI_x and the resulting loss of one unit of output made good by using MI_y more of Y. The saving on X is the market value of MI_x, which is $p_x MI_x$; whereas the cost of the additional use of Y is the market value of MI_y, which is $p_y MI_y$. Since $p_x MI_x > p_y MI_y$ by assumption, this substitution of Y for X would result in a net saving of $p_x MI_x - p_y MI_y$. Such a saving on production costs is always possible whenever

---

[1] See p. 119.

$p_xMI_x \neq p_yMI_y$. This proves that costs are at a minimum only when the value of the two marginal inputs is equal.

The above result can be generalized for any number of factors. We can say generally that the firm's cost of production is at a minimum when it so combines the factors of production that the market cost of the marginal input of every factor is the same, that is, when the firm's marginal cost is the same, whatever the way in which it varies output. In symbols the condition of minimum cost is expressed by the following chain of equations:

$$MC = p_xMI_x = p_yMI_y = \cdots = p_zMI_z , \qquad (3)$$

where MC is marginal cost and the letters $x, y, \ldots z$ stand for the different factors of production employed by the firm.

It will be convenient for what follows to express the above conclusions also in a slightly different form. Remembering that marginal input and marginal product are reciprocals of each other,[2] equations (3) can also be written in the equivalent form:

$$MC = \frac{p_x}{MP_x} = \frac{p_y}{MP_y} = \cdots = \frac{p_z}{MP_z} ,$$

or

$$MC \cdot MP_x = p_x , \quad MC \cdot MP_y = p_y , \quad \cdots \quad MC \cdot MP_z = p_z . \qquad (4)$$

These equations state that, to minimize his costs, the producer must equate the price of each factor to the additional cost of its marginal product.

What is the meaning of this rule? By employing an additional unit of factor X, either the producer can add to his output MP_x, the marginal product of X, whose value to him is the price it will fetch in the market; or, if he does not want to raise his output, he can reduce the quantity of other factors employed and so save on the cost of these other factors. For example, by using an additional unit of X, he can economize on factor Y MI_y/MP_x, the amount of Y which would produce the marginal product of X. His saving on Y, therefore, is the market value of this amount of Y, which is p_yMI_y/MP_x. But

$$p_yMI_yMP_x = MC \cdot MP_x ,$$

as a glance at equations (3) will show. It appears, therefore, that $MC \cdot MP_x$ expresses in terms of money what an additional unit of X is worth to the producer.

---

[2] See p. 119.

On the analogy of the marginal value of a consumer's good to the consumer, we shall call $MC \cdot MP$ the marginal value of the factor to the producer; but to distinguish between the two kinds of marginal value, we shall use the notation PMV (producer's marginal value). Hence, PMV_x, the marginal value of X to the producer, is defined by the identity

$$PMV_x \equiv MC \cdot MP_x . \tag{5}$$

We can now restate the condition of minimizing the producer's costs of production by saying that he must buy of each factor the quantity that equates its marginal value to him to its price. In symbols:

$$p_x = PMV_x , \quad p_y = PMV_y , \quad \cdots \quad p_z = PMV_z . \tag{6}$$

These equations repeat equations (4) in a slightly different form; but in this form the condition of minimizing the producer's costs is exactly analogous to the condition of maximizing the consumer's satisfaction.

Needless to say, the producer is not able to fulfill these minimum-cost conditions at every moment of time, because he cannot change his method of production in response to every change in factor prices. When he builds his plant and buys his equipment, he plans to combine plant, equipment, labor, materials, and other factors in the most economical proportions; but, once his plant is built and his equipment installed, he is committed for a while, at least as far as the quantity of these factors is concerned. Changing prices, therefore, may render uneconomical a combination of factors which seemed the most economical when decided upon. But even when the quantity of some factors is irrevocably fixed by past decisions, there usually are other factors whose proportions can still be varied; and the most economical combination of these factors is again given by the above minimum-cost condition.

2. THE DETERMINATION OF THE FIRM'S OUTPUT

Having derived the minimum-cost condition, which determines the most profitable combination of factors and the most profitable method of production that the firm can use, we can proceed to discuss the next problem: how large an output the firm should produce and sell. As a price taker, the firm faces a set price for its product and must decide on the rate of output and sales which will maximize its profit. The firm's profit is the difference between its total revenue and total costs, both of which depend on its rate of output. To show this dependence graphically, let us draw a diagram (Fig. 33) in which we measure the quantity of the firm's output produced and sold per unit of time on the horizontal axis, and the firm's total revenue and total cost per unit of time on the vertical axis.

The market's set price, at which the firm can sell its product, is represented in Figure 33 by a straight line going through the origin. The slope of this line expresses the price that the firm gets for its product; and the line itself expresses the firm's market opportunities, showing its total revenue at each rate of sales. In short, it is a price line of the same kind that we discussed in previous chapters.

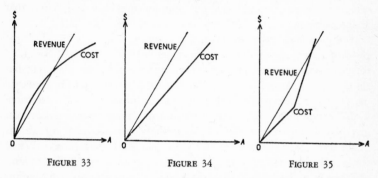

FIGURE 33   FIGURE 34   FIGURE 35

Facing the price line or total-revenue line is the firm's cost curve, which shows total cost for each rate of output. The *slope* of the cost curve shows, for each output, the rate at which cost increases with an increase in output. This rate is called marginal cost and is defined as the change in total cost due to a one-unit change in output. Since the firm's cost is the sum of the cost of its factors of production, the cost curve can be derived from the production indifference map. Having shown that the firm minimizes its cost at any point of tangency between an isoquant and an isocost, we can connect the points of tangency between successive isoquants and parallel isocosts and so obtain a curve called the firm's expansion path (Fig. 32, on p. 123). This corresponds to the consumer's income-consumption curve and shows, for each level output, the most economical combination of the two factors. Since each isocost expresses a given cost expenditure, and each isoquant represents a given output, one can read off the expansion path what is the lowest cost of producing each level of output. If we then plot this information in a diagram such as is shown in Figure 33, we obtain a new curve, which is the firm's total-cost curve.

What is the shape of this total-cost curve, as derived from the expansion path? It would be easy to determine if the expansion path in

Figure 32 were a straight line going through the origin. For movement along such a line represents a proportional change in the quantities of both factors utilized. When factor prices are constant, a proportional change in the utilization of factors causes production costs to change in the same proportion; and it results, according to the assumption of proportional returns, in a change in output also in the same proportion. Consequently, the cost curve corresponding to such an expansion path would also be a straight line through the origin, because only such a line represents a proportional change in production cost and output. A straight-line cost curve of this type is shown in Figure 34 (p. 127).

The expansion path, however, is not always a straight line through the origin, because a proportional increase in the utilization of both factors need not be the cheapest way of raising output. Hence, whenever the slope of the expansion path diverges from that of a straight line through the origin, traveling along the expansion path raises output more than in proportion to cost (increasing returns) or, in other words, raises cost less than in proportion to output. Accordingly, the corresponding section of the total-cost curve must have a slope that is less steep than that of a straight line through the origin. Such a cost curve is shown in Figure 33.[3]

When both the price line and the total-cost curve are drawn in the diagram, the vertical distance between them shows the firm's total net profit when the price line is higher than the total-cost curve or the firm's total net loss when the price line is lower than the total-cost curve. This vertical distance generally varies with the rate of output; and to maximize its profit, the firm must produce and sell that rate of output at which the price line is above the total-cost curve and the vertical distance between the two is greatest.

It is apparent that for profit (the vertical distance between the two curves) to be a maximum at a finite rate of output, the firm's total-cost curve must have a particular shape. It is also apparent from an inspection of Figures 33 and 34 that neither of the total-cost curves we derived from the expansion path has such a shape. Whether the cost curve is a straight line, or whether it is concave from below, the principle of profit maximization would lead, depending on the slope of the price line, either to an indefinite expansion of output or to no output at all; but it could

---

[3] It will be remembered that we assumed on p. 120 that a given percentage increase in output can *always* be achieved by increasing the quantity of all factors by the same percentage, although sometimes the firm can do better than this. In other words, we assumed that it is always possible to increase output *at least* in proportion to the increase in costs.

never lead to a finite, positive output. The principle of profit maximization would determine a finite output only if the cost curve had either of the shapes shown in Figures 35 (p. 127) and 36 (p. 132). That is, for the firm's output to be finite, its cost curve must have at least one segment which is convex from below and lies under the price line, because only in such a segment will there be a determinate rate of output which maximizes profit. The kink in Figure 35 must be regarded as an extreme case of convexity.

What conclusions can we draw from this result? Here, for the first time, our two methods of determining the shape of our curves seem to be in conflict. In Chapter III, we inferred the shape of indifference curves from the consumer's market behavior; but we turned around afterward to examine what exactly such a shape implies, and we saw that the consumer's psychology implied by this shape is not unreasonable. In our analysis of the firm in the last chapter and in this one, we adopted the alternative line of attack. We derived the shape of isoquants and productivity curves from a few simple assumptions about the firm's productive possibilities and then proceeded to investigate what market behavior could be expected on the basis of these assumptions. We have already seen that, as far as the firm's choice of factors is concerned, the shape we attributed to isoquants does not conflict with the firm's observed behavior in factor markets. It now seems, however, that the shape of the firm's total-cost curve, as we derived it from the firm's isoquant map, is in conflict with the observation that firms produce a finite rate of output. This suggests that there is something wrong with our assumptions.

Something may be wrong with the assumption that the firm aims at maximizing profit, or with the assumption that the firm is a price taker in both product and factor markets, or with the assumption of proportional returns, on which the derivation of the cost curves in Figures 33 and 34 was based. This problem is very important; but its detailed discussion must be deferred to Chapter IX. In the meantime, we shall sidestep the issue by concentrating on the firm's short-run problem.

When we derived the cost curves shown in Figures 33 and 34, we assumed implicitly that the firm is able to vary the input of all (both) its factors of production. This may be true in the long run;[4] but in day-to-day and even in month-to-month decisions the firm always regards some of its factors as fixed in quantity. An important fixed factor of this kind is the plant and equipment of the firm; indeed, the economist's short

---

[4] See, however, Chap. IX.

period is defined as the length of time for whose duration the entrepreneur regards his plant and equipment as fixed.[5]

In the short period, therefore, during which the producer regards some of his factors as fixed in quantity, he cannot usually combine all his factors in the most economical way; consequently, he does not move along the expansion path when he varies his rate of output. In the special case in which he has only two factors of production, one fixed and the other variable, the producer's short-period behavior can be represented by movement along a productivity curve, which is drawn for a given quantity of the fixed factor. The curve y_1 in Figure 30 (p. 118) is an example of such a productivity curve. This curve shows, for each level of output, the quantity of the variable factor X required to produce that level of output, given the fixed input y_1 of the fixed factor Y. By multiplying the quantity of the variable factor by its price, that is, by measuring along the horizontal axis the cost instead of the physical quantity of the variable factor X, the productivity curve can be transformed into a cost curve, which shows the total variable cost of each level of output. If we then shift this curve rightward, by a distance representing the fixed cost of the fixed factor, it will show the total cost of producing each level of output. This is shown in Figure 36, in which the productivity curve y_1 of Figure 30 has been shifted and the axes of the diagram have been interchanged, so that output is measured along the horizontal axis and cost along the vertical axis.

In Figure 36 the ordinate of the horizontal line shows the cost of the fixed factor $(p_y y_1)$; and the ordinates of the curve show, for each level of output, the sum of fixed and variable costs, that is, the firm's total cost of production. The slope of the curve shows, for each level of output, the cost of the marginal input of the variable factor, $p_x MI_x$, which is the marginal cost of the product. The curvature of this curve expresses the fact that when one factor is held constant in quantity, it becomes increasingly difficult after a certain point to increase output by the increased utilization of the other factor only; and there is an absolute limit to the output that can be produced with one factor held fixed. This result was deduced on pages 119–21, where we derived the shape of the productivity curve.

So far, we have considered two factors only; but the above argument can easily be extended to the case in which the firm uses three factors or more. When some factors are fixed in quantity, they will, if at all essential to production, set an absolute limit to the rate of output which

---

[5] See p. 283 in Chap. XII for an exact definition of the short period.

can be produced with however great a utilization of the variable factors of production. For example, when the plant, storage space, amount of machinery, and other equipment of a firm are fixed, output can be raised by the increased utilization of labor, fuel, and materials, but only up to a certain point; and the raising of output may become increasingly difficult even before this point is reached.

This can be illustrated graphically for the case of two variable factors, X and Y, and any number of fixed factors, with the aid of the producer's indifference maps shown in Figures 29 and 32. For this purpose, however, we must give a new meaning to our indifference maps. So far, we have thought of a point on the indifference map as showing the quantities of all (both) factors utilized, and of an isoquant as showing the various combinations of all (both) factors needed to produce a given output. Now, we shall reinterpret an isoquant as showing the different combinations of the *variable* factors X and Y needed to produce a given output, *given the fixed quantities of the fixed factors,* which are not shown in the diagram. The most economical combinations of the variable factors are again represented by the points of tangency between isoquants and isocosts; and the minimum-cost condition is also the same: marginal cost must be the same whether output is varied by varying one variable factor or the other. A movement along the expansion path now shows a changed utilization of the *variable* factors and the resulting change in output, while the fixed factors are kept unchanged in quantity. Now, therefore, a movement along the expansion path no longer represents an increase in output that is proportional or more than proportional to the increased utilization of factors X and Y.[6] For now, the fixed quantity of the fixed factors limits output and renders it increasingly difficult to raise output by the increased utilization of the variable factors alone. Hence, if we now read off the expansion path the total variable cost of each level of output, we shall find that, beyond a certain point, output increases less than in proportion to variable costs, and that sooner or later a further point is reached beyond which it becomes impossible to raise output at all. Accordingly, if we plot this information in a diagram in which output and costs are measured along the two axes, we shall obtain a cost curve whose shape is similar to that of the curve in Figure 36. It is true that this cost curve shows the connection between output and variable costs only; but this is easily remedied and the curve turned into a total-cost curve by shifting it upward along the cost axis by a distance that represents the cost of the fixed factors of production. This has been done in Figure 36.

---

[6] See p. 128.

In the short run, therefore, when some factors are fixed to the firm, its cost curve will always have a shape such as is shown in Figures 35 and 36; and when this is the case, there will exist a finite output for which profit—the vertical distance between price line and cost curve—is a maximum.

Let us now discuss in detail the conditions for maximum profit. Assume, to begin with, that the seller produces and sells the output a_2 (Fig. 36). He is making a net profit at this point, shown by the vertical dis-

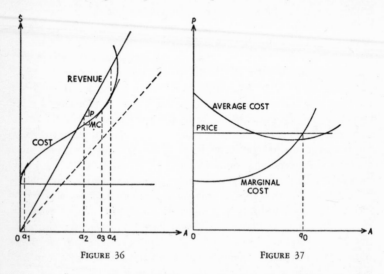

FIGURE 36   FIGURE 37

tance between cost curve and price line; but it is obvious from the diagram that he could raise his profit by raising sales. By selling one more unit, he would raise his total revenue by the price and his total cost by the marginal cost of the additional unit. In the diagram, price and marginal cost are shown by the distances marked p and MC, respectively. The addition to his total net profit is the difference between these two distances, that is, the difference between price and marginal cost. This addition to profit is positive and provides an inducement to raise output as long as the price line is steeper than the cost curve, that is, as long as price is higher than marginal cost. At a_4, where the two slopes become parallel, that is, where marginal cost becomes equal to price, a further increase in output will no longer add to profit; and the inducement to further expansion disappears. Beyond this point the cost curve becomes steeper than the price line, and marginal cost exceeds price. In this range, therefore, expansion would lower profit; and there is an inducement to restrict output.

This argument shows the first two conditions of maximum profit. One is that marginal cost must be equal to price; or, expressed geometrically, the slope of the cost curve must equal that of the price line. In itself, however, this condition insures only an extreme position, which may be one either of maximum or of minimum profit. For example, the same condition is also fulfilled at a_1, where it is apparent that profit is at a minimum, since it is loss that is maximized. Hence, for the extreme point to be one of maximum profit, it is also necessary that, in the neighborhood of this point, marginal cost should be rising or, geometrically, that the cost curve be convex from below. These two conditions can also be expressed by saying that profit is highest at the rate of output above which marginal cost exceeds and below which marginal cost falls short of price. This formulation is clumsier but more general, because it applies also to such special cases as that shown in Figure 35.

These conditions, in either formulation, determine the rate of output at which profit is maximized; but they leave undetermined the problem of whether, at this point, profit is positive or negative. For example, if the price were that given by the slope of the broken line in Figure 36, the above conditions would call for the output a_3, at which the firm incurs a loss, but at which its loss is smallest. It appears, therefore, that these two conditions determine the point either of maximum profit or of minimum loss.

To render profit positive, a third condition must also be fulfilled: total revenue must exceed total costs. This last condition, however, is not relevant in the short run and bears only on the firm's long-run decision whether to enter or stay in the market and produce at all. Once an entrepreneur has decided to operate in a market, he may want to continue producing even if he is temporarily incurring a loss; and in this case, he will try to produce the output that minimizes his loss. The first two conditions, therefore, are sufficient to determine the firm's rate of output as long as the firm is operating at all, and independently of whether it is making a profit or a loss.

Summing up the above argument, we have shown that to earn the maximum positive profit, the firm must produce and sell that rate of output (1) whose marginal cost equals price, (2) in whose neighborhood marginal cost is rising, and (3) at which total revenue exceeds total cost. The first condition assures that profit is at an extreme value; the second is necessary for this extreme value to be one of maximum profit; and the two together determine the firm's rate of output. The third is the condition of profit being positive and determines the long-run problem of whether or not the firm should produce at all.

The firm's short-run behavior in the market where it sells its product and the three conditions of maximum profit can also be illustrated in a diagram in which the horizontal axis measures the rate of output and the vertical axis measures revenue and cost *per unit of output* (Fig. 37, p. 132). This is the familiar price-quantity diagram. The price line in this diagram is a horizontal straight line, whose ordinate shows price and also, at the same time, the firm's average revenue per unit of output. Cost conditions can be represented in this diagram by two curves: the marginal-cost curve, whose ordinates show marginal cost for each rate of output; and the average-cost curve, whose ordinates show average cost for each rate of output. Total cost cannot be expressed directly in this diagram; but it is shown by the area under the marginal-cost curve up to any point of it or by the area of the rectangle subtended by any point of the average-cost curve. The area under the price line, up to any point, represents total gross revenue. Geometrically, the ordinates of the marginal-cost curve show the slope of the total-cost curve of Figure 36; whereas the ordinates of the average-cost curve show the slope of straight lines which can be drawn in Figure 36 from different points on the cost curve to the origin. The main advantage of this type of diagram is that it shows very graphically both the conditions of maximum profit and the rate of output determined by these conditions. Price and marginal cost are equal at the point of intersection of price line and marginal-cost curve (q_0 in Fig. 37); rising marginal cost is shown by a rising marginal-cost curve; and total revenue exceeds total cost wherever average revenue, shown by the price line, is above the average-cost curve. All three conditions are fulfilled at point q_0 in Figure 37, which therefore represents the output that maximizes the firm's net profit.

3. THE COMBINATION OF PRODUCTS

We now come to the problem of the firm that produces several commodities and has to decide in what proportions to produce them. Strictly speaking, we have solved this problem already. For it follows from the argument of the preceding section that if the firm can produce commodities A and B, whose market prices are $6 and $4, respectively, it will maximize profit by pushing production to the point where A's marginal cost of production is $6 and B's is $4. It will be useful, however, to present this result also in a slightly different form and illustrate it with the aid of a diagram.

In Figure 38, we have drawn two co-ordinate axes along which we measure the quantities of the two commodities A and B. In this diagram, we can draw a family of parallel price lines, whose slope expresses the ratio of the market prices of the two commodities, and each of which shows the different combinations of the two commodities that would sell in the market for the same sum of money. For example, the price line labeled $120 in Figure 38 shows the combinations of A and B whose market value is $120. Sometimes these price lines are called iso-revenue lines.

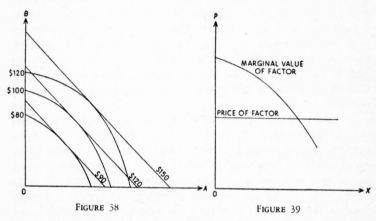

FIGURE 38   FIGURE 39

Next, we can draw into the same diagram a family of curves that con-nect the different combinations of goods A and B which the firm can produce at a given cost. For example, the curve labeled $100 shows all the combinations of A and B which the firm can produce with a total expenditure of $100 on their joint production. This curve is called a product-transformation curve, because traveling along it would amount to keeping production costs unchanged and transforming one product into the other, that is, increasing the output of one at the expense of the other. The slope of the transformation curve at any one point shows the marginal rate of transformation between the two products, which is equal to the ratio of their marginal costs. In symbols:

$$MT_{ab} = \frac{MC_a}{MC_b}.$$

(7)

To illustrate this proposition, assume that the output of products A and B is such that their marginal costs of production are $6 and $4, respectively. This means that producing an additional unit of A would add $6 to total costs; and to save this sum on the production of B would require lowering B's output by $1\frac{1}{2}$ units. Hence, the marginal rate of transformation between A and B is $1\frac{1}{2} : 1$, which equals the ratio of their marginal costs, $6 to $4.

The definition of transformation curves resembles that of isoquants, but there is a very fundamental difference between them. Isoquants, as defined in Chapter VI, represent given levels of physical output; they describe the nature of the firm's production function; and their shape, therefore, is independent of market prices. By contrast the transformation curves defined above represent given levels of cost expenditure; and their shape and position depend on factor prices and the firm's behavior in factor markets as much as they depend on its production function. This is the reason why we have not drawn transformation curves in Chapter VI, where we were concerned with the firm's production function alone.[7]

The shape and curvature of transformation curves depend on the way in which and the extent to which the production of the two commodities is interconnected. If they are joint products of the same productive process, if one is the by-product of the other, or if the production of one is in any way facilitated by the production of the other, then the transformation curves are concave from the origin, as shown in Figure 38. Furthermore, the more closely the production of the two commodities is interconnected, the more curved the transformation curves will be.

The transformation curves are concave to the origin even if the production of the two products is entirely independent. This follows from equation (7), above, if the marginal cost of each product is rising with its output. Only if the production of one commodity is hampered rather than facilitated by the same firm producing also the other commodity can it happen that the transformation curves become *convex* to the origin.[8]

---

[7] It should be mentioned, however, that had we tried to draw isoquants for a firm that produces more than one commodity, we would have run into exactly the same difficulties that at the end of Chap. VI (p. 121) made us postpone the attempt to draw transformation curves. One could draw isoquants for the multiproduct firm, but they would have to be defined in very much the same way in which we defined transformation curves above. They would show the various combinations of factors which produce a given *value* of output.

[8] The proof of this statement is too cumbersome to be included here. That it is correct,

Let us now confront transformation curves and price lines with each other. To maximize its profit, the firm must get the maximum income for a given cost expenditure or, what amounts to the same thing, a given income for the least cost expenditure. Geometrically, these conditions are fulfilled at points where a given transformation curve touches the highest price line or a given price line touches the lowest transformation curve. These points show the most profitable combinations of products A and B for different levels of output; and of these the producer will choose that point which represents his most profitable level of output, which in turn is determined by the principles discussed in the preceding section. It is apparent that all such points lie on one of the axes if the transformation curves are convex to the origin. In this case, therefore, the firm produces either one or the other product but not both at the same time. Only if the transformation curves are concave to the origin will both products be produced simultaneously. In this case, which is shown in Figure 38, the above conditions of maximum profit are fulfilled by those combinations of the two products for which a price line is tangential to a transformation curve. At all such points of tangency the marginal rate of transformation between two products equals their relative market prices; or, in other words, the ratio of their marginal costs equals the ratio of their market prices. As was pointed out above, this condition is always fulfilled when the producer equates the marginal cost of each of his products to its price.

4. THE FIRM'S OFFER OF PRODUCTS

So far in this chapter, we have been concerned with the problem of how the firm behaves in a given situation. We showed that, given its production function and given the market prices of its factors and products, the firm will choose a certain combination of factors, a certain rate of output, and a certain combination of products in preference to all other alternatives, because this choice will yield the highest profit obtainable under the circumstances. We are interested, however, not only in how the firm behaves in a given situation but also in how its behavior changes in response to a change in the market situation. In particular, we shall discuss how the firm's offer of products and demand for factors change in response to changes in the market prices of its products and factors.[9]

---

however, will become evident to the reader if he bears in mind that in this case the marginal cost of each commodity is an increasing function of the output of *both* commodities.

[9] The reader will notice the lack of parallelism between our analysis of the individual

The way in which a change in the price of a product calls forth a change in its quantity sold by the firm is easiest to show when the firm produces only one product. We have seen above that in order to maximize profit, the firm produces and sells its product in the quantity that equates marginal cost to price. A change in price, therefore, will disrupt the equality between price and marginal cost and call forth a change in output that re-establishes this equality. The nature and magnitude of this change in output can be read off the firm's marginal-cost curve (Fig. 37), which shows the dependence of marginal cost on output. This means that the producer's marginal-cost curve also shows the way in which his output depends on price and can therefore be regarded as his supply curve.[10] The supply curves (marginal-cost curves) of different producers of the same good can then be added together to form a market supply curve, in exactly the same way in which we added together the demand curves of individual consumers to form a market demand curve. Since marginal cost must always rise in the neighborhood of the equilibrium point, the supply curve, both of the individual firm and of the market as a whole, must also be rising.

The situation is slightly more complex when the firm produces and sells more than one product. In this case, if the production of the firm's several products is interconnected, the marginal cost of one product depends on the output not only of this but of all the other products of the firm as well; and a change in the price of one product is likely to change the firm's output not only of this one product but of its other products, too.

Let us consider, for example, a firm that produces two products, A and B. When the price of A rises, the firm adjusts its output of both A and B; and it will be convenient to break down these adjustments into several steps. First of all, the producer will increase his output of A to the point where the latter's marginal cost equals its new, higher price. The extent of this increase may be shown on a marginal-cost curve of

---

consumer and worker on the one hand and our analysis of the firm on the other hand. Whereas in the consumer's and worker's case, we were interested in their reactions to changes both in income and in prices, here we are only interested in the firm's response to price changes. The reason for this difference is that, unlike the consumer, the firm does not operate with a fixed budget. The firm's problem is not how to allocate a fixed cost expenditure for the purchase of different factors and to the production of different products, because its total cost expenditure is itself one of the variables that the firm must determine. See, however, Chap. IX for a discussion of the firm's response to a change in its capital funds.

[10] Let us bear in mind, however, that if marginal cost is below average cost, the entrepreneur may decide to close down his firm and not to produce at all.

A *drawn on the assumption that the output of the producer's other product remains unchanged.* But the higher output of A is likely to change
the marginal cost also of B; and, since the price of B is unchanged, the
producer will find it profitable so to adjust his output of B as to bring its
marginal cost back to equality with its price. The change in the output of
B, however, will in its turn change the marginal cost of A and so render
profitable a second adjustment in the output of A. We shall show later[11]
that this second adjustment is always similar in sign and additional to
the primary change in the output of A. The second adjustment, therefore, is an increase; and this further increase in the output of A will
again change the marginal cost and hence the output of B, which in its
turn will again have repercussions on A, and so forth. Equilibrium is re-
established when the marginal costs of both A and B are again simultaneously equal to their respective prices.

Taking account of all effects of the price change, we can say that a
rise in the price of A will always raise and a fall will always lower its
output. This follows from the fact that successive adjustments of output
always have the same sign. To show the total effect of a change in the
price of A on its output, we can draw a new kind of marginal-cost curve,
which shows the marginal cost of A as a function of its output *when the
output of the firm's other products is so adjusted as to keep their marginal costs unchanged.* This marginal-cost curve (which is not shown
here) can then be regarded as the firm's supply curve of A.

5. TECHNICAL COMPLEMENTARITY AND SUBSTITUTABILITY

We mentioned in the above argument that when a rise in the price of
a product raises its output, this change in output is likely to affect also
the marginal cost and output of the firm's other products. In particular,
the marginal costs of these other products may be either lowered or
raised; and their output, therefore, may either rise or fall.

It is customary to define the relation between the firm's several products according to which of these two alternatives happens. When a rise
in the price of A lowers the firm's output of B and raises its output of C,
we say that A and B are technical substitutes of each other and that A
and C are technical complements. For example, if a rise in the price of
butter causes dairies not only to sell more butter but also to sell less milk
and more buttermilk, then milk and butter are technical substitutes;
and butter and buttermilk are technical complements.

We are now in a position to prove the statement made above that

[11] See p. 140.

successive adjustments of output always have the same sign. Assume, for example, that A and B are technical complements. This means that an initial increase in the output of A (called forth by a rise in its price) will lower the marginal cost and thus raise the output of B. But the rise in B output will in turn lower the marginal cost and thus *further raise* the output of A, because complementarity is a reciprocal relationship; and if B is a technical complement of A, then A must be a technical complement of B. This proves the proposition for this one case; and we leave it to the reader to prove it also for the case in which the two products are technical substitutes.

So far, we have been concerned with the effect of a change in the price of a product on the output of products. It is hardly necessary to add that a change in the price of a product will affect also the firm's demand for its factors. In particular, a rise in product prices will usually raise the demand for factors. Sometimes this is expressed by saying that the firm's products and factors are usually technical complements of each other.

6. THE FIRM'S DEMAND FOR FACTORS

Of greater interest than the relationship between the firm's demand for a factor and the price of a product is the dependence of its demand for a factor on the price of that factor. We have seen that in order to minimize its costs, the firm buys that quantity of each factor which renders its marginal value to the firm equal to its price. A change in the price of a factor, therefore, will induce the producer so to change his purchases of that factor as to render its marginal value to him equal to its new price. It is apparent that if we had a marginal-value curve, showing how the marginal value of a factor varied with its rate of utilization, we could regard this as the firm's demand curve for that factor in exactly the same way in which we regarded the marginal-cost curve as the firm's supply curve of a product. The problem is how to draw such a marginal-value curve.

Let us begin with the unrealistic but simple case in which the firm uses only one variable factor of production. The dependence of output on the quantity used of this one variable factor was illustrated by the productivity curves in Figure 30 (p. 118). It will be remembered how we derived from one of these productivity curves the firm's total-cost curve and later also its marginal-cost curve.[12] In exactly the same way, we can use a productivity curve also for deriving the firm's total-value and marginal-

---

[12] See pp. 130 and 134.

value curves. By multiplying the quantity of output by the price of the product, that is, by measuring on the vertical axis the value instead of the quantity of output, a productivity curve can be transformed into a value-productivity curve, which shows the total value of output for each quantity of the variable factor utilized. The slope of the value-productivity curve shows for each quantity of the factor the market value of its marginal product, $p_a MP_x°$. This, however, equals PMV_x, the marginal value of the factor to the producer whenever he is a price taker in the product market and, in his effort to maximize profit, equates the marginal cost of his product to its price: $MC_a = p_a$.[13]

If we now draw a price-quantity diagram, we can draw into it a marginal-value curve, which is derived from the above value-productivity curve in exactly the same way in which we derived the marginal-cost curve from the total-cost curve (Fig. 39, p. 135). The ordinates of the marginal-value curve show the marginal value of the factor for each quantity of factor utilized. This curve, which has a downward slope in the relevant range, is the firm's demand curve for the factor.

To proceed from here to deriving the firm's demand curve for one of its several variable factors involves the same kind of argument we used for deriving the firm's supply curve for one of its several products. The marginal-value curve shown in Figure 39 is drawn on the assumption that the quantity of the other factor or factors used by the firm is fixed. But when the firm employs several variable factors, a change in the price of one is likely to affect the firm's utilization not only of this one factor but of all its other variable factors as well.

To analyze the nature of these adjustments, it will again be convenient to break them down into successive steps. For example, a fall in the price of factor X will first of all raise the firm's employment of X by the amount shown by the marginal-value curve in Figure 39. This increase in the employment of X, however, will change the marginal value of the firm's other variable factors; and, since the prices of these are unchanged, the producer will find it profitable to change the utilization of these factors so as to bring back their marginal value to equality with their prices. The changed utilization of these factors in turn affects the marginal value of X and calls for a second adjustment of its utilization. The total effect of a change in the price of X on the utilization of X can be shown on a new marginal-value curve, which is drawn on the assumption that the utilization of the firm's other variable factors is so adjusted as to keep their marginal values unchanged. This curve is not shown

---

[13] See pp. 132–33.

here, but its shape will be exactly the same as that of the marginal-value curve in Figure 39.

As to the effect of the fall in the price of X on the producer's demand for his other variable factors, it may raise or lower his demand, depending on whether they are technical complements or substitutes of X. The fall in the price of a factor will also affect the producer's output of his products; and, since the relation between factors and products is usually one of technical complementarity, the reduction of a factor price will usually raise the output of products.

BIBLIOGRAPHICAL NOTE

For a detailed discussion of the theory of the firm under perfect competition, see Erich Schneider, *Theorie der Produktion* (Wien: Julius Springer, 1934); and Sune Carlson, *A Study on the Pure Theory of Production* (London: P. S. King & Sons, 1939). Compare also chapters vi–viii of J. R. Hicks' *Value and Capital* (Oxford: Clarendon Press, 1939), which deal in detail with the subject of technical complementarity and substitutability. The mathematical reader should consult the excellent article on this subject by Jacob Mosak, "Interrelations of Production, Price, and Derived Demand," *Journal of Political Economy,* Vol. XLVI (1938), pp. 761–87.

NOTE TO CHAPTER VII: THE ENTREPRENEUR

We have been concerned in the foregoing with the behavior of the firm, which we assumed to aim at maximum profit. This, with qualifications, seemed the most reasonable assumption to make about corporations, which are the dominant type of firm in our society. But unincorporated businesses, which are owned and managed by the same person, are also firms; and the question now arises whether these, too, can be assumed to aim at maximizing their profit.

The owner of a firm who is his own manager or entrepreneur is not in a significantly different position from the seller of his personal services, whose behavior we discussed in Chapter V. The only difference between them is that whereas the latter offers his own services for sale, the entrepreneur sells a good or service that incorporates both his own services and those of others. For the services of others, he pays a cost, which must be subtracted from his market receipts to show his net income. This net income he must then weigh against the attractions of leisure in a way similar to that in which the individual worker weighs the relative advantages of income and leisure when he decides how much to work. It seems reasonable, therefore, to assume that the entrepreneur, like the worker, aims at maximum satisfaction; and that in order to achieve this aim, he, like the worker, has to decide on his optimum rate of operations.

The question remains, however, whether, in what sense, and under what conditions the maximization of the entrepreneur's satisfaction coincides with the maximization of his profit.

Let us illustrate the entrepreneur's market behavior in an indifference map, similar to the one we drew for the worker in Chapter V (p. 85). Figure 40 represents such an indifference map. Here, money income and

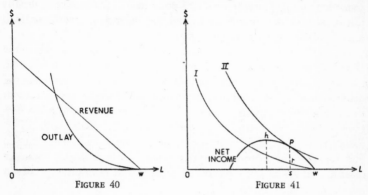

FIGURE 40   FIGURE 41

expenditure are measured along the vertical axis; and on the horizontal axis, we measure leftward from point *w* entrepreneurial activity expressed not in terms of hours, as in Chapter V, but in terms of the entrepreneur's rate of output, which we assume to bear a fixed relation to entrepreneurial activity. From left to right on the horizontal axis, we measure freedom from entrepreneurial activities and worries.

The set price at which the entrepreneur sells his output can be expressed by the slope of a price line drawn through point *w*, which at the same time also shows the entrepreneur's total revenue. It will be noticed that this price line is very similar to that drawn in Figure 36, from which it differs only in being its mirror image. This is due to the fact that in Figure 40 the rate of output is measured from right to left. The entrepreneur's total outlay on labor, materials, and other factors of production is shown by a total-outlay curve, which starts at or above point *w* and rises from right to left with increasing output. The vertical distance between price line and total-outlay curve shows, for each level of output, the entrepreneur's total net income from operating his firm. Taking these distances as ordinates, we can draw into the same or a similar diagram the entrepreneur's net-income curve. This is shown in Figure 41.

The entrepreneur's net-income curve corresponds very closely to the worker's or consumer's budget line. He can go along it to any point; and whatever point he stops at we assume to be his point of maximum satisfaction, because otherwise he would not have stopped there. To indicate graphically the point on the net-income curve at which the entrepreneur reaches his highest satisfaction, we can draw an indifference curve tangential to the net-income curve at this point. In Figure 41, this is illustrated at point p. The entrepreneur's profit may or may not be highest at this point; and our problem is to find out under what conditions (i.e., for what shape of the indifference map) it is.

A glance at Figure 41 shows that point p is not the point where the entrepreneur's net income is highest. We must bear in mind, however, the fact that the entrepreneur's net income and the firm's profit are not the same thing. The profit of a corporation is its gross revenue minus all cost items, which include the salaries of the management. When a firm is managed by its owner, the latter's net income includes both his remuneration for management and his profit as owner of the firm. To find out, therefore, where the entrepreneur's profit is at its highest, we must first of all separate the cost of management from profit proper in the entrepreneur's income.

In order to carry out this separation, we shall assume that the entrepreneur could, if he chose to do so, close down his business and become an employee in a competitor's business. Hence, to make it worth his while to stay in business for himself, the operation of his firm must yield him a certain minimum satisfaction. This minimum satisfaction can be represented in Figure 41 by the indifference curve which goes through point w. If his satisfaction were to fall below this level, he would stop being an entrepreneur in business for himself and become an employee. That part of his income which brings the entrepreneur to this level of satisfaction is called the wages of management and is considered part of the entrepreneur's cost of production. In other words, this is the salary the entrepreneur pays to himself for managerial services rendered. This part of the entrepreneur's income enters into his cost of production, together with his outlays on other factors.[1] Only that part of his income which brings his satisfaction above indifference curve I can be regarded as profit proper. In Figure 41, therefore, of ps, the entrepreneur's total net income at point s, only pr is profit; and rs is the wages of management.

---

[1] The total-outlay curve of Fig. 40, therefore, is not a total-cost curve. To obtain the entrepreneur's total-cost curve geometrically, we would have to sum for each abscissa the ordinate of the total-outlay curve of Fig. 40 and the ordinate of indifference curve I in Fig. 41.

This division of the entrepreneur's total net income into wages of management and profit proper resembles somewhat the division of a worker's income into his transfer price and rent. There is, however, an important difference between the two sets of concepts. For whereas the worker's transfer price is the minimum income which will keep him in his occupation, the entrepreneur's wages of management are the minimum income which will keep him in business for himself as an independent entrepreneur. If the entrepreneur's income fell below this minimum, he might very well stay in the same field, but as a salaried manager in someone else's firm.

For example, a small publisher might feel that if his net income should fall below $20,000, he would rather sell or wind up his firm and seek a position with one of the large publishing houses as a salaried employee. At the same time, he might also feel that his income would have to fall to as low as, say, $7,000 before he would think of leaving the publishing business altogether. Hence, if this person's actual income happened to be $30,000 per annum, we should say that his profit was $10,000, his wages of management $20,000, and his transfer price $7,000. In this example, therefore, the wages of management exceed the entrepreneur's transfer price.

It could also happen, however, that the transfer price should exceed the wages of management. This would mean that the entrepreneur would sooner try his luck in another occupation than become someone else's employee in his present field. For example, our publisher might have started as a realtor and might feel that he would return to the real-estate business if his income as a publisher fell below, say, $22,000. In this case, therefore, the publisher's transfer price is $22,000 and exceeds his wages of management.

Whereas a person's transfer price reflects the attractiveness to him of his next best alternative occupation, the wages of management reflect the attractiveness to an entrepreneur of working as an employee in his present field. We have seen that a person's transfer price depends partly on the income he could earn in another occupation and partly on his preferences as between the two occupations. In exactly the same way the wages of management depend partly on the salary an entrepreneur could earn in his present field and partly on his preferences between being and not being an independent businessman. If he is indifferent, his wages of management will equal the salary he could earn as an employee. But he might so enjoy being independent as to prefer running his own business even if it yielded him a lower income than he could earn as a salaried employee; or he might prefer the security of a salaried position and need the inducement of a higher income to manage his own business. Accordingly, his wages of management may be lower or higher than what he could earn as an employee.

Profit appears, therefore, as that part of the entrepreneur's income which accrues to him in his capacity as owner of the firm. It is a surplus income, whose accrual is not necessary for retaining the entrepreneur's services in his firm.

We are now in a position to answer the question: Under what conditions does the maximizing of profit lead to the maximization of the entrepreneur's satisfaction? Profit is the vertical distance between the net-income curve and indifference curve *I*. Hence, profit is greatest at the rate of output where the slopes of these two curves are parallel. The entrepreneur's satisfaction, on the other hand, is greatest at the rate of output where the net-income curve is tangential to (has the same slope as) indifference curve *II*. It is clear that the two rates of output need not coincide, and Figure 41 is so drawn that they do not coincide. For we used indifference curve *I* to determine maximum profit, indifference curve *II* to determine maximum satisfaction; and, as long as we make no special assumption about the individual's psychology or behavior, there is no definite relation between the shape and position of the various indifference curves in his indifference map. It is also clear, however, that the entrepreneur's profit and satisfaction could be maximized simultaneously, by the same rate of output, if he had a special type of psychology and, corresponding to it, a special type of indifference map, different from that drawn in Figure 41.

The geometrical nature of this special type of indifference map will be immediately obvious to the reader. The net-income curve will be tangential to an indifference curve at the same rate of output at which its slope equals that of indifference curve *I* if the two indifference curves have the same slope at that rate of output. In order that this condition may be satisfied for any and every kind of net-income curve, *all* indifference curves must have the same slope for *each* abscissa. In other words, the several indifference curves of the entrepreneur's indifference map must be vertical displacements of each other.

This is a familiar type of indifference map, which was discussed in detail in Chapter V (see p. 88). It represents the psychology of a person whose working habits are not influenced by changes in his income, because he regards his work not as an unpleasant task which he performs only for the sake of earning his living but as an essential part of his life and a source of satisfaction. We conclude, therefore, that *if* he has this type of psychology, the entrepreneur will maximize his satisfaction by maximizing his profit.

There is reason to believe that entrepreneurs often have this type of psychology, especially when the spirit of competition and emulation is strong among them. Some—perhaps many—entrepreneurs, however, are bound to have a different psychology; and it is well to bear in mind that they do not aim at maximizing profit. The reader is invited to prove to himself diagrammatically that the producer's output is always *less* than that which maximizes profit if his psychology is such that he is induced by a rise in his income to relax his efforts and take life easy.

BIBLIOGRAPHICAL NOTE

For a detailed discussion of the entrepreneur's psychology, see T. de Scitovszky, "A Note on Profit Maximisation and Its Implications," *Review of Economic Studies,* Vol. XI (Winter, 1943), pp. 57–60.

CHAPTER VIII

THE EFFICIENCY OF PRODUCTION

AFTER our descriptive analysis in the last two chapters of the firm's market behavior, we can now proceed to appraise the efficiency both of the individual firm and of the productive system as a whole. The word "efficiency" in this connection can mean two things. The usual meaning attributed to the term is the achievement of the greatest possible output with given means or the achievement of a given output with the smallest means. This form of efficiency may be called technological efficiency. In earlier chapters of this book, however, we appraised economic institutions by their conformity to the community's wishes and termed this their economic efficiency. It is apparent that both these interpretations of efficiency provide valid criteria by which to judge the performance of the firm and the productive system. Although they will be seen to be closely related, it nevertheless seems preferable to deal with them separately. In the following pages, therefore, we shall appraise the efficiency of production by each of these two criteria in turn.

1. THE TECHNOLOGICAL EFFICIENCY OF THE FIRM

The firm is technologically efficient if it produces the greatest output with given resources or—what amounts to the same thing—a given output with the least input of resources. Technological efficiency is in the firm's own interest, since it is a condition of maximum profit. This is true regardless of the firm's market position, that is, regardless of what prices are and whether the firm is in a perfectly or imperfectly competitive position. Competition influences the firm's technological efficiency only to the extent that it may spur the management to greater efforts at maximizing profit and hence also to greater efficiency. But if the firm can be assumed to aim at maximum profit, it can also be assumed to aim at technological efficiency.

The appraisal of the firm's technological efficiency lies largely outside the scope of economics. For technological efficiency is a matter of technical methods and administration; and as regards the former, at least, the economist can neither give advice nor supply a standard of efficiency but must accept the engineer's opinion. As to the administrative problems of the firm, most of these do lie within the economist's competence. In particular, the allocation of tasks and resources among the different plants and workshops of the firm and the co-ordination of their activities are economic problems. But since these problems of allocation and co-ordination among the different production centers of the firm are the same in kind as the problems of allocation and co-ordination among the different firms of an industry, we shall not discuss them separately. We shall only analyze the problems of allocation and co-ordination among the firms of an industry; but the reader is asked to bear in mind that the conditions of efficiency in the industry apply *pari passu* also to the firm.

2. THE TECHNOLOGICAL EFFICIENCY OF THE INDUSTRY

The output of an industry, produced with a given input of resources, depends not only on the technological efficiency of the firms composing it but also on the allocation of the industry's total resources and output among these firms. For firms differ in the technical characteristics of their productive equipment and the human characteristics of their technical and administrative management; and these differences must be taken into account when the resources and output of a group of firms are allocated among the members of this group. The efficient organization of an industry involves the concentration of its output in its most efficient members; and the industry's efficiency in this sense is different from and additional to the efficiency of its members.

However, the efficient organization of an industry means more than the efficient allocation of its resources and output. For the way in which an industry is organized has an influence also on the size, number, and efficiency of the firms that constitute the industry. Hence, for the organization of an industry to be efficient, it must promote efficiency also in the individual firms. Accordingly, we shall discuss the technological efficiency of the industry under two subheadings. We shall deal, first, with the efficient allocation of resources and output within the industry and, second, with the average technological efficiency of the members of the industry.

2a. EFFICIENT ALLOCATION WITHIN THE INDUSTRY

By efficient allocation within an industry, we mean an allocation of factors and output among its members which results in the production of a given output at a minimum expenditure of productive factors, or the production of a maximum output with a given quantity of productive factors. To produce an industry's output with a minimum input of a given factor, output must be so allocated among the members of the industry that the marginal input of that factor is the same in every firm. For assume that firm F's marginal input of factor X is greater than firm G's:

$$MI_x^f > MI_x^g .$$

In this case the same output can be produced at a saving of $MI_x^f - MI_x^g$ of factor X by making G produce one more and F one less unit of output; and a further saving in factor X can be achieved by a further reallocation of output between the two firms until their marginal inputs of X have become equal. This argument can be repeated for all other factors of production used by the industry. Hence, to produce a given output with a minimum input of every factor of production, the marginal input of each factor must be the same in every firm belonging to the industry. Accordingly, for an industry's production to be efficiently organized, the following equations must hold:

$$\left. \begin{aligned} MI_x^f &= MI_x^g = \cdots = MI_x^h , \\ MI_y^f &= MI_y^g = \cdots = MI_y^h , \\ & \cdot \quad \cdot \quad \cdot \quad \cdot \quad \cdot \quad \cdot , \\ MI_z^f &= MI_z^g = \cdots = MI_z^h , \end{aligned} \right\} \quad (1)$$

where the superscripts denote the members of the industry and the subscripts denote the factors of production used in the industry.

To see under what conditions these equations are satisfied, let us first investigate the effects of perfect competition among the members of an industry in the market where they sell their product. When several firms produce the identical commodity and sell it at the same market price, which they all regard as given, each firm will produce that rate of output which equates its marginal cost to market price and hence also to the marginal cost of all the other firms in the industry. When the marginal costs of the firms constituting the industry are equal, the industry's total output will be divided among them in such a way as to insure production at minimum money cost. For, it will be remembered, the marginal cost of the firm is rising in the neighborhood of the point where it equals market price. Hence, if one firm produced one unit less and another firm one unit more, the first firm's saving in cost would be smaller and the second firm's additional cost would be larger than the price of a unit of output; and the net result would be an unchanged total output produced at a higher total cost. This proves the proposition that a total output sold by sellers equating marginal cost to market price is produced at minimum money cost to the industry.

This argument can be illustrated geometrically in two price-quantity diagrams showing market price and the marginal-cost curves of any two members of an industry. If both firms regard the market price as given and aim at maximizing profits, they will produce the output a_1 and A_1, respectively (see Fig. 42). This is the cheapest way of producing their

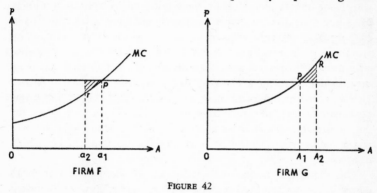

FIGURE 42

total combined output $(a_1 + A_1)$. For, if F's output were reduced from a_1 to a_2, he would save in cost the amount represented by the area a_1pra_2; if G's output were raised by the same amount from A_1 to A_2, his cost would be increased by the area A_1A_2RP; and the net change in the two firms' combined costs would be an increase, shown by the sum of the two shaded areas. Hence, the two firms' combined total cost is at a minimum when their marginal costs are equal. Since this can be proved for any pair of firms in the industry, it is also true for the industry as a whole. The equality of the several firms' marginal costs is the condition of the industry's total money cost of production being minimized; and this condition is always fulfilled when all members of the industry are price takers and face the same price in the market where they sell their product. It appears, therefore, that perfect competition among producers in product markets is a condition whose fulfillment would insure the efficient allocation of each industry's output among its members and cause the output of every good and service to be produced with the least expenditure of effort.

But is this condition enough? In other words, does the minimization of the industry's cost of production really insure the best utilization of its resources? To produce a given output with the smallest input of factors, production must be concentrated in the industry's (technically) most efficient firms. Perfect competition among firms in product markets causes production to be concentrated in the firms with the lowest costs of production (lowest cost curves); but one firm's cost of production and marginal-cost curve may be lower than another's not only because it is more efficient but also because it buys its productive factors at a lower price. For example, a producer may be exceptionally good at bargaining with labor unions and so obtain the services of his workers at a lower wage rate than his competitors; or he may get some of his materials or equipment at specially reduced prices due to the larger scale of his purchases or his friendly relations with the producer of that material or equipment. Whenever low money costs are explained in some such way, they do not represent a low cost also in terms of productive factors. Hence, whenever the members of an industry differ in their bargaining position in factor markets and pay different prices for the same factor, the output allocation which minimizes the industry's cost of production will not minimize the quantity of productive factors required by the industry.

This shows that perfect competition among the members of an industry in the product market alone is not enough to insure the efficient allocation of the industry's output. To achieve efficiency, it is also necessary that the members of the industry pay the same price for each factor. This second condition is fulfilled when the members of the industry are perfect competitors also in the markets where they buy the factors of production. That these are sufficient conditions of the efficient allocation of the industry's output can easily be shown. For, as we have seen, perfect competition in the product market equalizes the marginal cost of the members of the industry. This is expressed symbolically by the equations

$$MC^f = MC^g = \cdots = MC^h . \tag{2}$$

Perfect competition among firms in factor markets implies that the factor prices, $p_x, p_y, \ldots p_z$, are the same for every firm; and it causes each firm to equate the marginal cost of its product to the value of the marginal input of each of its factors.[1] This is expressed symbolically by the equations

---

[1] See p. 125.

$$MC^f = p_x MI_x^f = p_y MI_y^f = \cdots = p_z MI_z^f ,$$
$$MC^g = p_x MI_x^g = p_y MI_y^g = \cdots = p_z MI_z^g ,$$
$$\cdot \quad \cdot \quad \cdot \quad \cdot \quad \cdot \quad \cdot \quad \cdot \quad \cdot \quad ,$$
$$MC^h = p_x MI_x^h = p_y MI_y^h = \cdots = p_z MI_z^h . \tag{3}$$

The fulfillment of the above two sets of equations insures that equations (1) are fulfilled, too. This proves that perfect competition among firms in both product and factor markets is a sufficient condition for the efficient allocation of resources and output among the members of the industry.

That perfect competition among firms *in factor markets alone* is not enough to insure the efficient organization of the industry is also apparent from the above three sets of equations, since equations (1) do not follow from equations (3) alone. It will be worth our while, however, to enlarge a little upon this point. For this purpose, we shall restate the conditions of efficient resource allocation in terms of the marginal products of factors, as follows:

$$MP_x^f = MP_x^g = \cdots = MP_x^h ,$$
$$MP_y^f = MP_y^g = \cdots = MP_y^h ,$$
$$\cdot \quad \cdot \quad \cdot \quad \cdot \quad \cdot \quad \cdot \quad ,$$
$$MP_z^f = MP_z^g = \cdots = MP_z^h . \tag{1.a}$$

When one recalls that the marginal product of a factor is the reciprocal of its marginal input, then it becomes obvious that equations (1.a) are equivalent to equations (1); and an argument along the lines of that given on page 150 will show that the equality of the marginal product of a factor in the several firms of an industry is the condition for the industry's output to be maximized with a given supply of that factor.

Let us now see what happens when all members of the industry are price takers in the market for factor X. Facing the price p_x, which they all regard as given, each producer buys so much of X that his marginal valuation of X equals its price and hence also its marginal valuation by all the other producers. This is expressed symbolically by the equations:

$$p_x = PMV_x^f = PMV_x^g = \cdots = PMV_x^h$$

or

$$p_x = MC^f MP_x^f = MC^g MP_x^g = \cdots = MC^h MP_x^h , \tag{3.a}$$

and is shown geometrically for the case of two firms in Figure 43. The two firms' marginal-value curves for X correspond closely to their marginal-cost curves drawn in Figure 42. Firms F and G, facing the price p_x, buy the quantities x_1 and X_1, respectively, of factor X. This division between them of their total supply of X $(x_1 + X_1)$ maximizes the total value to them of this supply of X.[2]

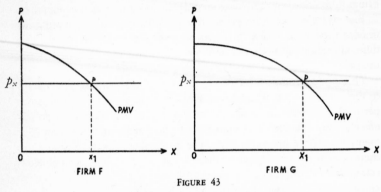

FIRM F · FIRM G

FIGURE 43

We can now generalize this statement for any number of firms and any number of factors. We can state to begin with that equations (3.a), above, are the condition for the industry's total supply of factor X, so to be distributed among its members as to have the highest value to the industry taken as a whole. Furthermore, if the members of the industry are price takers in all factor markets, each of them equates his marginal valuation of *every* factor to its price and hence to its marginal valuation by all the other members:

$$p_x = MC^f MP_x^f = MC^g MP_x^g = \cdots = MC^h MP_x^h ,$$
$$p_y = MC^f MP_y^f = MC^g MP_y^g = \cdots = MC^h MP_y^h ,$$
$$\cdot \quad \cdot \quad \cdot \quad \cdot \quad \cdot \quad \cdot \quad \cdot \quad \cdot \quad ,$$
$$p_z = MC^f MP_z^f = MC^g MP_z^g = \cdots = MC^h MP_z^h ,$$

$$\left.\right\} \quad (3.b)$$

and these equations are the condition for the industry's total supply of *all* factors to be so distributed among its members as to maximize the total value of this supply of factors to the industry taken as a whole.

---

[2] The proof of the above statement is left to the reader as an exercise. It follows closely the proof, given on pp. 150–51, that when the marginal costs of two members of the industry are equal, their combined output is produced at minimum cost.

The value of a factor from the producer's point of view is the value to him of its contribution to output. Hence, an allocation of factors which maximizes their value to producers is one that results in the output that has the greatest value to producers. We can say, therefore, that perfect competition in factor markets among the members of an industry results in that allocation of the industry's total supply of factors which brings about the output whose value to the industry is greatest.

But the output whose value to the industry is greatest is not necessarily the largest output. This becomes obvious when one remembers that different firms may sell the identical product at different prices, in which case a smaller output concentrated in the hands of firms that can sell it at a higher price may be more valuable than a larger output concentrated in the hands of firms that can only sell it at a lower price. Accordingly, perfect competition in factor markets alone is not enough to insure the efficient allocation of an industry's total resources and output among its members. A further condition is that the members of the industry sell their product at the same price; and this is insured when they are perfect competitors also in the product market. Indeed, the conditions (1.a) of efficient allocation within the industry are fulfilled when both (3.b) and (2) hold.

2b. THE AVERAGE TECHNOLOGICAL EFFICIENCY OF THE INDUSTRY'S MEMBERS

The above discussion has shown the meaning and conditions of the efficient allocation of an industry's resources and output. But, as we indicated at the beginning of this chapter, the efficient organization of an industry means much more than just this. So far, we have taken for granted the number of firms in the industry and their technical and administrative efficiency; and these factors may undoubtedly be taken for granted in the short run. In the long run, however, they also are variable; and efficient organization involves, in addition to efficient resource and output allocation, production in the optimum number of firms and the elimination either of inefficiency within the individual firms or of the inefficient firms themselves. It will be shown that efficiency in this latter sense is brought about by the free entry of newcomers to the industry.

In Chapter V, we showed that perfect competition among persons selling their services involves freedom of specialization. In other words, perfect competition among the sellers of personal services means that they are free to enter any occupation and to compete in it on equal terms with others. Since the term "occupation" covers all gainful employment, whether as a wage earner or as an independent businessman, free entry to different occupations implies that everyone is free not only to become an employee in any industry but also to establish himself as an entrepreneur in any field.[3]

The inducement for a newcomer to enter an industry as an entrepreneur is the gain made in that industry by the entrepreneurs already established. This raises the question as to how large this gain must be to attract newcomers. It will be remembered that in the Note to Chapter VII, we divided the entrepreneur's income into two parts. One was the wages of management, which represent the minimum income needed to keep the entrepreneur in business; the other was his profit, defined as the income earned over and above this minimum. Hence, profit is the surplus that makes the opening of a new firm worth while; and, as long as profits are positive, there is an inducement for newcomers to enter an industry.[4] This becomes obvious when we remember that in actual practice the newcomers to an industry or trade are almost always former managers or other employees of already established firms, whose usual motive in making themselves independent is the hope of earning a higher income managing their own business than they earned as salaried employees of others.

The entry of newcomers to an industry has two effects on already established firms. First, it increases supply in the market where the industry's product is sold and so lowers the price of the product. Second, it increases demand in factor markets and so raises costs of production. Both effects are illustrated in Figure 44, where arrows show the direction in which the entry of newcomers shifts the price line and the firm's average- and marginal-cost curves. It is apparent that both these changes will lower the individual firm's profit; and the lowering of profits is likely to continue until profits disappear completely, because only this will eliminate the inducement for further newcomers to enter the industry. Figure 45 shows the situation of a firm whose profit is zero.

But the question now arises whether Figure 45 illustrates the position of *every* firm in the industry at the time when the inducement for newcomers to enter ceases. After all, the earnings of different firms differ from each other; and there seems to be no obvious reason why the profit of every firm should be eliminated at the same moment. Under perfect

---

[3] The exact meaning of the free entry of entrepreneurs to an industry and the nature of obstacles to their entry will be discussed in detail in Chap. IX and XV.

[4] See, however, Chap. IX.

competition, when all firms face the same prices in every factor and product market, differences in the earnings of different firms can only be due to two causes. One is that entrepreneurs differ in their efficiency, in their methods of management, and in the keenness and energy with which they aim at maximizing profit. Such differences, however, in the managerial worth of different entrepreneurs account for differences in

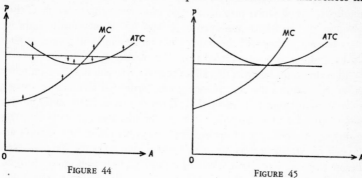

FIGURE 44   FIGURE 45

their wages of management and not in their profits.[5] The other cause, which accounts for differences in profits, is that equally efficient entrepreneurs may use different methods of production—for example, because they established their firms at different times. Older firms may use methods of production which, though the best when adopted, have ceased to be the most economical as a result of changes in technology or relative factor prices; and it is apparent that the profits of these firms will be lower than the profits of those whose methods of production are the most up to date and the best suited to present factor prices.

A newcomer to an industry is not yet committed to any particular method of production and can choose the best and most economical method currently available. Newcomers, therefore, will base their profit expectations on the actual profits made by the most profitable of the established firms. Accordingly, they will continue to enter the industry as long as the best method of production yields a profit; and their entry will tend to eliminate the profit obtainable with the best method of production. It appears, therefore, that Figure 45 illustrates the position of firms using the best and most up-to-date method of production. This implies that all other firms must be incurring losses. Their losses will

---

[5] Except to the extent that entrepeneurs differ also in their appraisal of the advantages of being independent. To simplify the argument, we have ignored this factor, which is a minor one and does not affect our main conclusions.

make them use better methods of production and otherwise improve their efficiency to the extent that they are able to do so with their existing equipment. To the extent that their equipment commits them to out-of-date methods, they will usually write their losses off on their equipment but continue operating it until it falls due for replacement; and only at that stage will they try to modernize their equipment and production methods. If and when they succeed in improving their efficiency, their position also will be represented by Figure 45. If they fail to improve their efficiency, they will continue to incur losses and will sooner or later go bankrupt and be eliminated from the industry.

In addition to the firms that suffer losses, there will also be eliminated from the industry the entrepreneurs who, although incurring no losses, have earnings that fall below their transfer prices. Every entrepreneur whose transfer price exceeds his wages of management falls into this category. As the entry of newcomers lowers his profit, his earnings approach his wages of management; and he may leave the industry even before the complete elimination of his profit, as soon as his total earnings (wages of management plus profit) fall below his transfer price.

The industry as a whole is in equilibrium when no member of the industry makes a profit, which could attract newcomers to enter the industry, and when all those who incur losses and those whose earnings have fallen below their transfer prices have left the industry. We call this equilibrium, because it is a situation in which no one has an inducement either to enter or to leave the industry. But this situation is at the same time also that in which the industry's average technological efficiency is highest.

We saw that such efficiency is brought about in three different ways. First of all, the entry of newcomers inflicts losses upon firms that use uneconomical methods of production and may sooner or later cause these firms to improve their methods of production. Second, if these firms are unable to improve their productive methods, they are eliminated; and the industry's average technical efficiency is improved in either case. Third, we saw that the entry of newcomers and the consequent lowering of profits eliminates from the industry the entrepreneurs whose transfer prices exceed their wages of management. Some of these entrepreneurs are people who have preferences for other fields; and some of them are people whose managerial worth in this industry is relatively low, because their ability and training fit them better for other fields. It is apparent that the elimination of the latter raises the industry's average managerial efficiency. As to the elimination of the former type of entrepreneur, this need not raise and may even lower the average managerial talent available to the industry; but it leads to more efficient specialization and to a more satisfactory distribution of talent as between different industries. This, however, is a matter not of technological but of economic efficiency. In fact, this effect of the free entry of firms corresponds exactly to the effect of free entry of workers to different occupations and insures economically efficient specialization among entrepreneurs.[6]

It hardly needs to be added that if all firms and all industries are technologically efficient, the productive system will be technologically efficient, too.

3. THE ECONOMIC EFFICIENCY OF THE FIRM

Having completed our discussion of efficiency in its technological sense, we can now proceed to discuss the *economic* efficiency of production. This, it will be recalled, means conformity to the community's wishes; and it is a matter of correctly combining the factors of production, producing the different products in the right proportions, and choosing the most desirable rate of output. In the following, we shall first appraise the economic efficiency of the firm's behavior and afterward consider the economic efficiency of the productive system as a whole.

This procedure is a little different from the one we followed in the case of the individual consumer and seller. In Chapters IV and V, we appraised the efficiency of distribution among consumers and of specialization and job allocation among workers; but we never appraised the economic efficiency of the individual person's behavior. The reason for this should be obvious. Since economic efficiency means conformity to people's wishes, the individual's behavior is economically efficient when it conforms to his own wishes. But it would have been absurd for us to appraise the degree of conformity between the individual's wishes and his behavior because, by inferring the individual's wishes from his market behavior, *we assumed* that his wishes and behavior are in perfect conformity. This is why we never applied the criterion of efficiency to the individual's behavior and applied it only to economic organization among individuals—distribution among consumers and specialization and job allocation among workers.

---

[6] The free entry of new firms to the industry brings about efficiency in yet another sense. It causes every member of the industry to produce at the point of lowest average total cost. This, however, has to do with the economically efficient combination of the firm's fixed and variable factors of production and will be discussed later (p. 170).

The position of the individual firm is entirely different. It is true that the firm's behavior conforms to the wishes of its owner or owners in much the same way in which a person's behavior conforms to his wishes; but the firm, in addition to being a source of profit to its owners, is an economic organization which affects the welfare also of other members of society—its customers and the suppliers of its productive factors— and it is from their point of view that we shall now appraise the economic efficiency of the firm. In particular, we shall discuss whether and under what conditions the firm's choice of factors, products, and rate of output is desirable from society's point of view. To simplify our discussion, we shall first consider a firm that produces only final consumers' goods and employs only original factors of production. Only after establishing our results for this special type of firm will we be able to extend them to all other firms as well.

3a. The Efficient Combination of Products

Let us begin with the problem of the firm's combination of products. The firm aims at maximizing its profit; and to achieve this aim, it produces its different products in such proportions as to maximize the market value of its total output for any given cost expenditure. From society's point of view, however, it is desirable that the firm should produce the output that is most highly valued by the consuming public. Hence, the firm's combination of products will be economically efficient only when maximizing the value of its output happens at the same time to maximize also consumers' satisfaction. When is this the case?

We saw in Chapter VII that when the producer is a perfect competitor (price taker) in product markets, he maximizes the value of his output by producing that combination of products which equates his marginal rate of transformation between any two products to the ratio of their market prices. In symbols, the producer combines his products in such proportions as to achieve the equality:

$$MT_{ab} = \frac{p_a}{p_b}.$$

On the other side of product markets, the consumers, when they too are price takers, equate their marginal valuation of each product they consume to its market price. In other words, each consumer equates his marginal rate of substitution between any pair of products he consumes to the ratio of their market prices. In symbols:

$$MV_a = p_a, \quad MV_b = p_b;$$

or

$$MS_{ab} = \frac{p_a}{p_b}.$$

It follows from this that when both the producers and the consumers are price takers in product markets, each producer's marginal rate of transformation between any two goods he produces will equal the marginal rate of substitution between the same two goods of any consumer of those two goods. In symbols:

$$MT_{ab} = MS_{ab}. \tag{4}$$

It can now be shown that when equation (4) is satisfied, the producer's effort to maximize the market value of the output produced with a given cost expenditure will at the same time also result in the output most highly valued by the consuming public.

We shall prove this proposition diagrammatically in Figure 46. Let us take a firm that produces quantities a_1 and b_1 of the goods A and B, and a consumer who consumes α_1 and β_1 of the same two goods; and let us superimpose the consumer's indifference map upon the firm's product-transformation map in such a way that the co-ordinate axes of the two

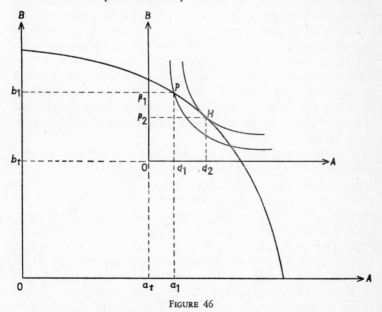

FIGURE 46

diagrams are parallel and the point representing the firm's output coincides with the point showing the individual's consumption.[7] In this diagram, $0a_t$, the horizontal distance between the vertical axes, and $0b_t$, the vertical distance between the horizontal axes, represent that part of the firm's output of products A and B which it sells to all its customers other than the one whose indifference map is shown. A movement, therefore, along that part of the transformation curve which falls within the indifference map represents a change in the firm's output that affects only this one person's consumption, while the firm's sales to all its other customers are kept constant.

Figure 46 is so constructed that point *P* shows both the firm's actual output and the consumer's actual consumption. It appears that at this point the firm's transformation curve and the consumer's indifference curve have different slopes, showing that the consumer would be willing to give up more units of B to obtain additional units of A than the firm has to sacrifice to produce these units of A. This proves that production is not organized efficiently at point *P,* because a simple shifting of some of the firm's resources from the production of B to that of A could make at least one consumer better off than he was before, without making anyone else worse off, and without increasing the firm's cost of production. It also appears from Figure 46 that the most efficient combination of the firm's products from the consumer's point of view would be that corresponding to point *H,* where the firm's transformation curve reaches the consumer's highest indifference curve, and where the consumer obtains α_2 of A and β_2 of B. If both curves are smooth, they will be tangential at this point; and we can express the condition of efficiency by saying that the firm's marginal rate of transformation between the two goods must equal the consumer's marginal rate of substitution between the same two goods.

We have shown, however, that this equality, which was expressed symbolically in equation (4), comes about whenever both producers and consumers are price takers in the product markets. Hence, we have proved our proposition that in his effort to maximize his profit, the producer will combine his products in the socially most desirable proportions whenever both he and his customers are price takers in the markets where he sells his products. It will be noticed that although we proved this for only one producer, one consumer, and one pair of products, these were chosen at random from among any number of producers, consumers, and products. Our result, therefore, is a general

[7] See Fig. 38 and pp. 135–36 for a description of the product-transformation map.

result, which holds good for all producers and products as long as both the producers and the consumers are price takers in all product markets.[8]

There are two important points to note about this result. First of all, it appears that perfect competition among consumers (and the resulting efficient distribution of consumers' goods) is a prerequisite of economic efficiency in the firm. This, indeed, is natural. For an efficient combination of the firm's products means that they are produced in the proportions in which the firm's customers want them to be produced. But for this to be possible, it is necessary that the producer receive information about his customers' preferences. In a market economy the producer receives his information in the form of market prices; and these must therefore reflect consumers' preferences. Furthermore, for the firm's behavior to conform to the different tastes of its different customers all at the same time, their preferences must be rendered equal, at least on the margin. We have seen in Chapter IV that perfect competition among consumers insures both conditions. It equates everybody's marginal preferences (rates of substitution) to relative market prices as well as to everybody else's marginal preferences, which is why perfect competition among consumers is a prerequisite of the efficient combination of the firm's products.

In the second place, it should be noted that, in itself, our result has only limited significance. For what we have proved so far is that when both consumers and producers are price takers in product markets, the profit motive causes each producer to allocate a *given cost expenditure* among his different products in accordance with consumers' preferences. To maximize social welfare, however, it is a *given productive effort* which must be allocated among different products in the way that best conforms to consumers' preferences; and we have not yet proved under what conditions a given cost expenditure corresponds to a given productive effort. We shall see in the next section that this correspondence is insured if the combination of factors is also economically efficient.

3b. The Efficient Combination of Factors

We saw in Chapter VII that the firm tries, for any given level of output, so to combine its factors of production as to minimize its total money cost of production. From society's point of view, however, efficiency requires that the firm combine its factors in the way that minimizes cost in terms of productive effort. We must investigate, therefore, the conditions under which money cost corresponds to productive effort;

---

[8] See p. 57 for a proof of this statement.

and a minimum money cost represents a minimum cost in terms of effort.

When the producer is a perfect competitor (price taker) in factor markets, he minimizes his cost of production by equating the marginal rate of technical substitution between his factors to the ratio of their market prices. This was shown in Chapter VII. On the other side of factor markets, when entry is free to all occupations and this results in efficient specialization among workers, the ratio of the prices of their services expresses the relative cost of obtaining these services from society's point of view. This was shown in Chapter V. Hence, when producers aim at minimizing their costs of production, and when competition is perfect on both sides of all factor markets, each producer's marginal rate of technical substitution between any pair of productive services he uses will be equal to the relative cost to society of rendering those services. When this is the case, money costs correspond to costs in the sense of productive effort; and the firm's combination of factors will not only minimize its money costs but will be efficient in the sense of minimizing costs of production also in terms of productive effort.

The proof of this statement will not be given here, because it follows word for word the proof given in the preceding section. This is so because the equality between the producer's marginal rate of technical substitution between two services and the relative cost to society of rendering them corresponds exactly to the equality—stated in equation (4), above—between the consumer's marginal rate of substitution and the producer's marginal rate of transformation between two products. Even the diagrammatic proof is the same; and the reader can derive it by taking the opportunity-cost curve of Fig. 28 (p. 102) and superimposing on it the isoquant map of a producer. Simpler still, the reader can use the diagram of Figure 46 by regarding the indifference map as a producer's indifference (isoquant) map and the transformation curve as an opportunity-cost curve.

We must again draw attention to the main features of our results. First of all, it should be noted that the free entry of workers into different occupations is a prerequisite of the firm's efficiency in utilizing their services. This is the counterpart of our earlier result that perfect competition among consumers is a prerequisite of the firm's efficiency in the combination of its products. Second, the efficient combination of the firm's factors is meaningful and valuable independently of the firm's efficiency in other respects *if the firm produces only one product.* For such a firm aims at minimizing the money cost of a given (physical) *quantity* of output; and when this implies the minimizing also of productive effort, that is a socially valuable accomplishment. In contrast, a producer of several products minimizes the cost of producing a given *value* of output; and to produce this with a minimum productive effort is socially valuable only if a given value of output represents a given level of consumers' satisfaction. It appears, therefore, that as far as many-product firms are concerned, the efficient combination of factors insures the production of a given consumers' satisfaction at a minimum cost in terms of effort only when the combination of the firm's products is also efficient.

3c. THE EFFICIENT RATE OF PRODUCTION

There is one further aspect of the firm's production policy which should conform to society's wishes: its rate of activity. This, again, is determined by the firm's aim to maximize profit; but from society's point of view the firm's rate of production should be such as to balance correctly the satisfaction derived from its output and the burden of effort needed to produce this output. We have to see, therefore, under what conditions the firm's scale of operations conforms to society's wishes in this sense.

When the producer of product A is a perfect competitor in the market for A, he produces that rate of output which equates the marginal cost of A to its price:

$$p_a = MC_a . \tag{5}$$

When the same producer is a perfect competitor also in the markets where he buys the factors of production, X, Y, . . . Z, he equates the market value of the marginal input of each factor to the marginal cost of his product:

$$MC_a = p_x MI_x = p_y MI_y = \cdots = p_z MI_z . \tag{6}$$

Hence, when the producer is a perfect competitor in both product and factor markets, he produces that rate of output which equates the price of his product to the market value of the marginal input of each of his factors:

$$p_a = p_x MI_x = p_y MI_y = \cdots = p_z MI_z . \tag{7}$$

Recalling from Chapter VI that $1/MI \equiv MP$, we can also express the above result by saying that when the producer is a perfect competitor in both product and factor markets, he equates the price of every factor to the market value of its marginal product:

$$p_a MP_x = p_x , \quad p_a MP_y = p_y , \quad \cdots p_a MP_z = p_z . \tag{8}$$

How does this behavior on the part of the firm agree with society's desire to balance the effort put into and the advantage derived from the firm's output? The advantage to consumers of having one unit of product A is expressed by their marginal valuation of it; and when competition among consumers is perfect, they equate their marginal valuation of A to its price. In symbols:

$$MV_a = p_a . \tag{9}$$

The burden of the effort involved in supplying one unit of a factor (service)[9] is expressed by its marginal value to the people who supply it; and when these people are perfect competitors in factor markets, so that job allocation among them is efficient, each of them equates his marginal valuation of the service he sells to its price:

$$MV_x = p_x , \quad MV_y = p_y , \quad \cdots, \quad MV_z = p_z . \tag{10}$$

Hence, when both consumers and sellers of productive factors are perfect competitors, the prices both of consumers' goods and of productive factors express their marginal valuation by society.

When competition is perfect on both sides of both product and factor markets, all the above equations hold simultaneously; and they can be linked together into either of the two following sets of equations:

$$\left. \begin{aligned} MV_a &= p_a = p_x MI_x = MV_x MI_x , \\ MV_a &= p_a = p_y MI_y = MV_y MI_y , \\ &\quad . \quad . \quad . \quad . \quad . \quad . \quad . \quad ., \\ MV_a &= p_a = p_z MI_z = MV_z MI_z , \end{aligned} \right\} \tag{11}$$

or

$$\left. \begin{aligned} MV_x &= p_x = p_a MP_x = MV_a MP_x , \\ MV_y &= p_y = p_a MP_y = MV_a MP_y , \\ &\quad . \quad . \quad . \quad . \quad . \quad . \quad . \quad ., \\ MV_z &= p_z = p_a MP_z = MV_a MP_z . \end{aligned} \right\} \tag{12}$$

Equations (11) state that the consumer's marginal valuation of one unit of A equals the individual seller's marginal valuation of that quantity of his services which is required to produce one unit of A. This

---

[9] It should be remembered that, in this section, we are dealing with the firm that uses only original factors, i.e., personal services.

implies that every person who both consumes A and contributes to its production attaches the same value to consuming one unit of A as he does to the effort of producing it. Equations (12) put the identical result in a slightly different form by stating that the individual seller's marginal valuation of one unit of his productive effort equals the consumer's marginal valuation of the outcome (marginal product) of this productive effort.

We can now show that when the above equations hold, the firm's choice of its rate of output will maximize not only its profit but also the satisfactions of the people who are affected by its operations: its customers and the sellers of the productive factors it utilizes. To prove this, assume for a moment that the above equations are not fulfilled. For example, if people valued the firm's marginal contribution to the supply of consumers' goods more highly than they valued the productive effort needed to make this contribution, it would be in their interest that the firm produce more. Conversely, if they attached less value to the firm's marginal contribution than to the effort required to produce it, their satisfaction would be increased if the firm curtailed its operations. Hence, the firm produces the optimum rate of output and makes the greatest contribution to the welfare of its customers and the sellers of its factors when their marginal valuation of its output equals their marginal valuation of the effort required to produce this output.

The above argument proves that the principle of profit maximization leads the firm to produce the optimum rate of output, from society's point of view, (1) if there is perfect competition among its customers, (2) if the firm itself is a perfect competitor in the market where it faces its customers, (3) if the firm is a perfect competitor also in the markets where it buys its factors of production, and (4) if there is perfect competition among the suppliers of the factors utilized by the firm. These four conditions were expressed by equations (5), (6), (9), and (10); and they formed the links in the chains of equations (11) and (12). If any one of them is not fulfilled, equations (11) and (12) may not hold; and the maximizing of profit may not lead to the firm's optimum output.

3*d*. THE GENERAL CASE

It will be recalled that for simplicity's sake the preceding discussion was limited to a rather special type of firm which uses only original factors of production and produces only finished consumers' goods. Many firms, however, are engaged in producing intermediate products or produce both intermediate and finished products; and most firms use, in addition to original factors, also produced factors—fuel, materials, parts, and equipment—manufactured by other firms. We must proceed, therefore, to extend the results reached for our special type of firm to all other firms as well.

The Combination of Products. We showed above (pp. 160–62) that when the firm is a perfect competitor in product markets, its combination of products will be efficient, provided that the prices of its products express their marginal valuation by its customers. This condition is fulfilled when all the firm's products are consumers' goods and when there is perfect competition among consumers. But the question now arises: What happens when some or all of the firm's products are intermediate products? The price of an intermediate product obviously cannot express its marginal valuation by consumers, since they have no use for it. It can, however, express consumers' marginal valuation of the contribution that this intermediate product makes to the production of a consumer's good. For one producer's intermediate product becomes another producer's produced factor; and, under perfect competition, this other producer will equate the price of the produced factor to his customers' marginal valuation of its marginal product. This follows from equations (8) and (9), above. Hence, the price of every product expresses consumers' marginal valuation either of its immediate usefulness in consumption or of its ultimate usefulness in the production of a consumer's good, *provided that there is perfect competition on both sides of every market through which that product goes on its way to the final consumer.* When this last condition is fulfilled, the firm's choice and combination of products will be efficient whether these are consumer's goods or intermediate products.

The Combination of Factors. As to the efficiency of the firm's combination of factors, it was shown that this required not only that the producer be a price taker in all factor markets but also that the suppliers of factors be perfect competitors so that factor prices express the marginal worker's relative valuation of the effort involved in supplying different types of services. In the case of produced factors the effort involved in supplying them is that of the original factors required to produce them; and it can be shown that under perfectly competitive conditions the price of a produced factor equals the marginal valuation of the original factors required to produce one unit of the produced factor. For one firm's produced factors are another firm's intermediate products; and when this other firm is a perfect competitor in both product and factor markets and faces sellers of factors who are perfect competitors themselves, it will equate the price of its intermediate product to the individual seller's marginal valuation of (the marginal input of) his services required to produce that intermediate product. This follows from equations (7) and (10), above. Hence, the price of every factor—original or produced—expresses the individual seller's marginal valuation of his effort embodied either directly or indirectly in one unit of that factor, *provided that there is perfect competition on both sides of every market through which his services, and produced factors embodying his services, go on their way to the firm in question.* When this condition is fulfilled, the firm's combination of factors will be efficient independently of whether these are original or produced factors.

The above argument generalizes the result concerning the efficient combination of factors reached earlier for the special firm which employs only original factors. When we reached that result, we assumed implicitly that the firm is able to vary the quantities in which it combines its several factors. This was a legitimate assumption to make in discussing a firm that employs only original factors. But it can hardly be made when we are concerned with firms that employ also produced factors, since at least the plant and equipment of the firm are factors whose quantities are fixed in the short run. The above argument, therefore, gives the conditions of economic efficiency only as far as the combination of the firm's variable factors is concerned. But what about the proportions in which fixed and variable factors are combined with each other?

At the time when the producer sets up his firm and decides what plant and equipment to use, he combines, or at least aims to combine, *all* his factors—fixed and variable—in the proportions that minimize his cost of production. At the outset, therefore, the producer does combine his factors in the most efficient way, provided that perfect competition on both sides of all markets through which his factors have to go insures correspondence between his money costs and the social costs of production. But once his plant is erected and equipment installed, he can no longer vary the quantities of these fixed factors in response to changing conditions, at least not in the short run, although changing conditions will still make him vary his rate of output and with it also the quantity of variable factors which he combines with the fixed quantity of his fixed factors. Hence, there is no guaranty in the short run of the efficient combination of the firm's fixed and variable factors. In the long run, however, there is at least a tendency toward efficiency in this

sense. We saw in section 2*b* of this chapter (pp. 155 ff.) that the free
entry of firms, by eliminating profits, tends to cause each firm to produce at the point of its lowest average total cost. This was illustrated
in Figure 45, above. At the time, we postponed the discussion of this
form of efficiency, because it had nothing to do with technological efficiency. But it is apparent that producing the output whose average
total cost is lowest amounts to combining variable with fixed factors
in the proportions that minimize costs. Hence, if competitive conditions
in factor markets are such as to insure correspondence between money
costs and costs in terms of productive effort, then the free entry of newcomers tends, in the long run, to insure the efficient combination also
of fixed and variable factors. In other words, perfect competition tends,
in the long run, to bring about the optimum number of optimum-
sized firms.[10]

The Rate of Output. We proved in the preceding pages that under
perfect competition (1) the price of an intermediate product expresses
consumers' marginal valuation of its contribution to the production of
consumers' goods; and (2) the price of a produced factor expresses
people's marginal valuation of their marginal effort embodied in that
factor. From this, we can conclude immediately that under these conditions the firm will, by aiming at maximum profit, produce the rate of
output most desirable from society's point of view, provided that it is
a perfect competitor in both factor and product markets. This follows
from the recognition that a firm utilizing intermediate factors and producing intermediate products is in exactly the same position as a firm
using only original factors and producing only final consumers' goods,
as long as there is perfect competition on both sides of every market that
links such a firm to the final consumer on the one hand and to the seller
of original productive services on the other.

It will be useful at this stage to stop for a moment and take stock
of our results concerning the economic efficiency of the firm. We have
shown that the firm's behavior may or may not be in the best interests
of society in three different senses: in the combination of its products,
in the combination of its factors, and in the choice of its rate of output
and degree of utilization of its factors. We have called the conformity
of the firm's behavior to society's preferences the firm's economic efficiency. We have shown that the firm's economic efficiency depends
not only on its own market behavior and on the market conditions under

---

[10] This topic will be discussed in detail in sec. 5*b* of Chap. XVI.

which it operates but also on the market behavior of its customers and on that of the people and firms from whom it buys its factors of production. In particular, we have shown that the economic efficiency of the individual firm is conditional on the efficiency of the consumers' market, on the efficiency of the markets for productive services, and on the economic efficiency of all other firms with which it is linked in the process of buying and selling.

4. THE ECONOMIC EFFICIENCY OF THE INDUSTRY

Having completed our discussion of the economic efficiency of the individual firm, we are left with two more forms of efficiency to discuss: the economic efficiency of allocation within an industry and the economic efficiency of allocation among different industries. The analysis of these forms of efficiency will be relatively simple, because we shall be able to lean heavily on the results reached in the preceding section. For under certain conditions a group of firms behaves like a single firm; and when this is the case, the same conditions that insure the efficiency of the single firm also insure the efficiency of the group. Hence, the conditions of economic efficiency in the single firm, and the conditions that make a group of firms behave like a single firm, together constitute the conditions of the economic efficiency of the group taken as a whole.

The allocation of an industry's output among the firms composing it has been discussed already from the point of view of technological efficiency (pp. 149–55). This, it will be recalled, had to do with so allocating given quantities of resources among the members of an industry as to maximize the industry's total output; and it called for the concentration of the industry's resources and output in its most efficient firms. But firms may differ not only in their efficiency but also in the type of resources they use and in the proportions in which they combine their several resources. Accordingly, the allocation of an industry's output among its members determines not only how efficiently given resources are utilized but also what resources are used by the industry and in what proportions they are combined.

For example, sugar can be manufactured either from sugar cane or from sugar beet; and the division of the sugar industry's total output between its two sectors that process cane and beet, respectively, determines the proportions in which sugar cane and sugar beet are utilized in the manufacture of sugar. These proportions are a matter of economic efficiency and must be appraised by the same standard by which we appraised the economic efficiency of the combination of factors by the individual firm. But whether or not the industry's total output is optimally divided between its two sectors, there is also the further problem of whether the output of each sector is optimally divided among the members of that sector. This is a matter of technological efficiency. It appears, therefore, that the allocation of the industry's output among its members must be appraised by the standards both of technological and of economic efficiency.

When does an industry utilize its different resources in economically efficient proportions? We saw that the combination of the individual firm's several factors is economically efficient when the firm minimizes its money cost of production and both the firm and the sellers of its factors are perfect competitors in factor markets. The same conditions would also render the industry's combination of factors economically efficient; but we have no reason to assume that an industry composed of several independent firms "aims" at minimizing its (the industry's) money cost of production. While it is reasonable to assume that each member of the industry aims at minimizing its own cost of production, it need not necessarily follow from this that the cost of producing the industry's total output is also minimized. For the industry's total cost of production to be minimized, a further condition must be fulfilled. This condition was stated on page 150. We showed there that to minimize the money cost of an industry's total output, the latter must be so allocated among the industry's members as to render the marginal costs of all firms equal. We also showed that this comes about when the members of the industry are perfect competitors in the market where they sell their product. It appears, therefore, that an industry's resources will be combined in economically efficient proportions if in addition to perfect competition on both sides of factor markets, there is perfect competition among the members of the industry also in the market where they sell their product.

It should be noted that when these conditions are fulfilled, allocation within the industry will be efficient not only economically but also technologically. In other words, not only will the industry's output be produced with that combination of resources which minimizes the productive effort involved; but, in addition, this combination of resources will be so allocated as to maximize the output produced with its aid.

5. THE ECONOMIC EFFICIENCY OF ALLOCATION BETWEEN INDUSTRIES

The allocation of the total resources of the economy among different industries must be appraised by the same standard by which we appraised the economic efficiency of the individual firm's allocation of its resources among its several products. We showed above that the combination of the firm's products is economically efficient when the firm maximizes the value of its output and both the firm and its customers are perfect competitors in product markets. The same conditions would insure the economic efficiency also of the whole productive system; but we cannot, of course, assume that the productive system "aims" at maximizing the value of its output. What we can do instead is to state the conditions under which the independent actions of independent firms cause the value of total output to be maximized. As a matter of fact, we have already stated these conditions. We saw on page 154 that when a fixed quantity of resources is so allocated among a group of producers that every producer's marginal valuation of each factor is the same, then the value of the total output produced with those resources is maximized. We also saw that this condition is fulfilled when competition among the members of the group is perfect in all the markets where they buy their factors. It is true that when we stated this result, we were concerned with the members of only one industry; but it is easy to see that the same result holds true for any group of firms and hence also for all the firms constituting the entire productive system. We conclude, therefore, that the allocation of society's resources to different industries and to the production of different products is economically efficient when, in addition to perfect competition on both sides of all product markets, there is perfect competition among producers also in all factor markets.

The above argument is an exact counterpart of the argument of the preceding section; but it will be useful to elucidate it a little further by restating it in a somewhat different form. The problem of allocating factors among firms is very similar to that of distributing goods among consumers. We illustrated the nature of the latter problem with the aid of two consumers' indifference maps superimposed one upon the other; and, in exactly the same way, it is helpful to illustrate the problem of resource allocation with the aid of the isoquant maps (production indifference maps) of two firms superimposed one upon the other. This is shown in Figure 47. The width and height of the box diagram so obtained show the total quantities of factors X and Y used by the two firms together, any point within the box diagram shows a given allocation of the two factors between the two firms, and the isoquants going through this point show the quantities of the two firms' respective products that can be produced with this allocation of factors. Still following

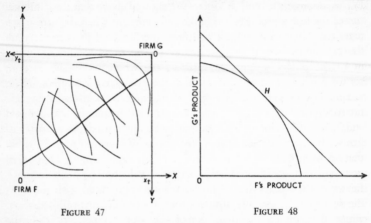

FIGURE 47   FIGURE 48

the analogy of distribution among consumers, we can next draw into Figure 47 a contract curve, which connects all the points of tangency between isoquants as well as those points on the axes where two isoquants, although not tangential, nevertheless represent highest combinations of the two firms' products. For a detailed definition of the contract curve the reader is referred to pages 53–54 in Chapter IV.

It is apparent that, from society's point of view, it is preferable that the two firms should be on the contract curve rather than off it, because until the contract curve has been reached, a mere reallocation of given resources can raise the output of one firm without diminishing that of the other. Being on the contract curve, therefore, is one requirement of an efficient allocation of resources between the two firms.

When is this requirement fulfilled? Relying once more on the analogy with distribution among consumers, we can state at once that perfect competition among firms in factor markets is a sufficient condition for any two firms to be on their contract curve with respect to any two factors. For the producer who is a price taker in all factor markets tries to combine any two factors he uses in the proportions that equate his marginal rate of technical substitution between them to the ratio of their prices and hence also to the marginal rate of technical substitution of all the other producers who use the same two factors and buy them at the same prices. It follows from this that if we take at random any two factors and any two producers who use these factors, and then proceed to superimpose the two producers' isoquant maps in the manner in which we superimposed consumers' indifference maps in Chapter IV, we shall find that the two producers are always on their contract curve. For a more detailed statement of this argument, and for its extension to the case in which one of the producers employs only one of the two factors, the reader is referred to the parallel argument given in Chapter IV (pp. 55–57) concerning the efficient distribution of consumers' goods.

Let us now represent the different combinations of the two firms' products which can be produced with the fixed quantities of factors X and Y on a new diagram whose axes measure the quantities of the two firms' products. This is illustrated in Figure 48. It is easy to see that to every point in the box diagram of Figure 47 there corresponds a point in Figure 48, since through every point of the box diagram there can be drawn a pair of isoquants which represent some combination of the two firms' products. It is also apparent that all the points in Figure 48 which correspond to points in the box diagram must lie within a bounded area, since fixed quantities of X and Y can only yield finite quantities of the two firms' products. The boundary of this area is a curve, different points of which represent the highest combinations of the two firms' products obtainable with the aid of the fixed quantities of X and Y. This curve is shown in Figure 48. But since in Figure 47 the highest combinations of the two firms' products are represented by points on the contract curve, the boundary curve of Figure 48 must correspond to the contract curve of Figure 47. In terms of Figure 48, therefore, the first requirement of efficient resource allocation between the two firms is that they produce a combination of products which is represented by a point on the boundary curve and not under it. We saw that this requirement is fulfilled when the firms are perfect competitors in factor markets.

It should be noted that the boundary curve is a transformation curve, similar to the transformation curves shown in Figures 38 and 46. The only difference between them is that whereas the transformation curves of Figures 38 and 46 showed the highest combinations of products which one and the same firm can produce at a fixed cost, the boundary curve in Figure 48 shows the highest combinations of products which two firms can produce with a fixed quantity of resources. The slope of the boundary curve shows the marginal rate of transformation between the two firms' products, which is equal to the ratio of their marginal costs and expresses the rate at which the output of one firm must be sacrificed if more of the other firm's output is to be produced.

The second requirement of an efficient allocation of resources between the two firms will now also be clear. It has to do with producing on the optimum point of the boundary curve; and it is closely analogous to the requirement of an efficient allocation of a single firm's resources between its several products, which we discussed on pages 160–63 and illustrated in Figure 46, above. The two firms must produce at that point of the boundary curve where the marginal rate of transformation between their respective products equals the consumer's marginal rate of substitution between these products; for, at this point, it is impossible by a mere reallocation of resources to make any consumer better off without making some other consumer worse off.

It is easy to see that this requirement is fulfilled when both the two firms and their customers are perfect competitors (price takers) in the markets for their products. When consumers are perfect competitors, they equate their marginal rates of substitution between the two products to the ratio of the prices of these products. When the two firms are also perfect competitors, each of them equates the marginal cost of its product to the latter's price; and this equates the marginal rate of transformation between the two firms' products to the ratio of their prices and hence also to consumers' marginal rates of substitution between them. In symbols, this is expressed by the following equations:

$$MT_{ab} = \frac{MC_a}{MC_b} = \frac{p_a}{p_b} = MS_{ab} \, .$$

Geometrically, it is represented by the point of tangency between the boundary curve (transformation curve) and a consumer's indifference curve, such as is shown by point H in Figure 46.

This completes our detailed restatement of the conditions of efficient allocation between industries. Our argument was concerned with resource allocation between two firms only; but since it was concerned with two firms chosen at random, our results apply *pari passu* also to resource allocation between the industries to which the two firms belong.

Furthermore, our argument applies to any pair of firms, whether they belong to different industries or to the same industry. In the special case in which the two firms belong to the same industry, their products are interchangeable and fetch the same price in the market. In this case, if the two firms are price takers both in factor markets and in the product market, they will produce at that point of the boundary curve where its slope has a 45-degree angle. It is easy to see that this is the point where the combined output of the two firms is at a maximum. In this special case, therefore, we have merely shown once again what we have proved already in an earlier section: namely, that when competition among the members of an industry is perfect in both factor and product markets, given resources will be so allocated among them as to maximize their total combined output.

6. THE GENERAL EFFICIENCY OF THE PERFECTLY COMPETITIVE ECONOMY

We can now review our analysis of the various forms and aspects of efficiency and shall do this by reversing our former procedure and discussing not the conditions of a certain type of efficiency but the effects of a certain type of behavior. In particular, we shall discuss the effects on the economy of perfectly competitive behavior on the part of all its members.

For, it will be noted, we have now completed our discussion of perfect competition. To begin with, we have discussed the behavior as price takers of three members of the economy: the consumer, the individual seller of productive services, and the firm. Following our analysis of the individual price taker's behavior, we discussed four types of group behavior: (1) perfect competition among consumers, (2) perfect competition among the sellers of productive services, (3) perfect competition among firms in factor markets, and (4) perfect competition among firms in product markets. It will be noted that this analysis takes care of both sides of all the four types of markets which occur in our economy: (1) markets where consumers buy from firms, (2) markets where consumers buy from individual sellers, (3) markets where firms buy from individual sellers, and (4) markets where firms buy from other firms. Hence, we are now ready to review the perfectly competitive economy, in which every market is perfectly competitive in the sense that all its members on both the buyers' and the sellers' side are price takers.

To begin with, we discussed in Chapter IV perfect competition among consumers and saw that this has three consequences. First, it insures the efficient distribution of a given quantity of consumers' goods and services. The meaning and limitation of distributive efficiency were discussed in detail in Chapter IV; but I want to stress one of its features here: it

G

is useful and meaningful even when every other part of the economy is inefficient. The second consequence of perfect competition among consumers is the equality of different consumers' preferences on the margin. That is, although each consumer's tastes and needs may differ from those of every other consumer, his marginal preference between a little more of this and a little more of that is made equal to the marginal preferences of all other consumers of the same goods when there is perfect competition among them. This is of no advantage in itself; but it is the prerequisite, the *sine qua non,* of efficiency in production. Economic efficiency of production, which means conformity to consumers' preferences, would be impossible if consumers' preferences were not uniform, at least on the margin. Production in this case could still conform to the wishes of an economic dictator but hardly to the conflicting preferences of many consumers. The third result of perfect competition among consumers is that the uniform marginal preferences of consumers are reflected in the market prices of consumers' goods and services. This provides producers with information that is essential if production is to be organized according to consumers' wishes.

Next, in Chapter V, we discussed the nature of perfect competition among workers. This was seen to result, first of all, in efficient job allocation and, second in efficient specialization—both of them meaningful concepts even in the absence of efficiency elsewhere in the economy. Third, perfect competition among the members of an occupation was also shown to cause the rate of earnings in that occupation to reflect people's marginal valuation of the burden of work in that occupation. As we have seen, this provides information needed for determining the optimum rate of output and optimum utilization of personal services. Last, free entry to different occupations was shown to cause relative rates of earnings in different occupations to reflect the relative cost from society's point of view of the burden of effort involved in rendering different services. This provides information needed by producers for organizing production in a way that minimizes its cost in terms of productive effort.

In the present chapter, we have been concerned with the efficiency of production; and we have distinguished between the technological efficiency of producing the greatest quantity of a certain product with given amounts of resources and the economic efficiency of producing in accordance with society's preferences.

Technological efficiency, as we defined it, is very near to what the man in the street means by productive efficiency. It has to do with the engineer's and the administrator's efficiency; and, as such, it would not be the economist's concern, except for the fact that an industry's technological efficiency depends on competition and resource allocation within the industry. For we have shown that perfect competition among the members of an industry in both product and factor markets leads to efficient resource allocation; and the free entry of newcomers to the industry insures the highest average technical and administrative efficiency of which that industry is capable. This we have called the technological efficiency of the industry. It will be noted also that the technological efficiency of an industry is independent of efficiency elsewhere in the economy.

Not so the *economic* efficiency of production. This consists in production conforming to the community's preferences; and it therefore depends (1) on the existence of harmony between different people's preferences and (2) on the communication of people's preferences to those in charge of production. Both requirements are fulfilled when competition is perfect among consumers and the sellers of personal services, which therefore enables the individual firm as well as the whole productive system to achieve economic efficiency, provided that firms also are in a perfectly competitive position.

This completes the list of advantages of universal perfect competition we have discussed so far. To enumerate them in yet another way, we have shown that universal perfect competition would make it possible (*a*) to secure productive services at a minimum sacrifice to those who render them (efficient specialization and job allocation); (*b*) to utilize these services for the production of goods in the most economical way (economically efficient combination of factors by the firm and resource allocation within the industry); (*c*) to encourage technological efficiency and concentrate production in the most efficient firms (technological efficiency of the industry); (*d*) to utilize resources to the degree that best conforms to society's preferences (efficient rate of output); (*e*) to produce different goods and services in the proportions that best serve consumers' welfare (economically efficient combination of products by the firm and resource allocation between different industries); and finally (*f*) to distribute these goods and services in best conformity with consumers' preferences (efficient distribution among consumers).

Let it be stressed again, however, that all this has to do with efficiency alone and that considerations of efficiency cannot, in themselves, serve as a guide to economic policy. Economic organization must always be judged and compared by the double criteria of efficiency and equity; and universal perfect competition is a model of perfection only as far as efficiency is concerned.

The effect of perfect competition on income distribution was discussed in Chapters V, VII, and VIII. We saw that perfect competition among workers means equal incomes for equal services performed and that freedom of entry enables everybody to earn at least his transfer price, by causing incomes in every occupation to equal the marginal person's transfer price. This is true of employees, professional workers, and businessmen alike; and it implies that relative earnings in different occupations correspond to the marginal person's appraisal of the relative burdensomeness of these occupations. In addition, we saw that perfect competition among firms in factor and product markets insures that people's rates of income also equal the market value of their marginal contribution to final output (pp. 140–41 and 165–66).

All this goes some of the way but not nearly the whole way toward fulfilling the requirements of equity. Remuneration that is the same for equal services and varies with the burdensomeness of different services as well as with the value of their contribution to output conforms more or less to most people's ideas of social justice. But social justice also requires that incomes should, at least partly, be governed by need; and this requirement is *not* fulfilled by our perfectly competitive model of the economy. Furthermore, and this is the main point, the above discussion of perfect competition is incomplete and inadequate for dealing with this subject. For so far, all we have said and were able to say about income distribution concerned only incomes earned for personal services rendered; whereas the main problem of equity in our economy is the division of total income into earned and unearned incomes. This problem will be taken up in the next chapter.

BIBLIOGRAPHICAL NOTE

That perfect competition would lead to an efficient organization of production most economists have known more or less vaguely and proved more or less rigorously ever since Adam Smith. This is apparent from any of the standard *Principles,* such as, for example, Alfred Marshall's *Principles of Economics* (London: Macmillan & Co., 1890; 8th ed., 1920). Few works, however, have discussed the meaning and conditions of efficiency in economics in detail. Of these the most important are Vilfredo Pareto, *Cours d'Economie Politique* (Lausanne, 1897); A. C. Pigou, *The Economics of Welfare* (London: Macmillan & Co., 1920; 4th ed., 1932); and Enrico Barone, "The Ministry of Production in the Collectivist State," in F. A. Hayek (ed.), *Collectivist Economic Planning* (London: George Routledge & Sons, 1935).

For more recent detailed statements of the formal conditions of efficiency, see

R. F. Kahn, "Some Notes on Ideal Output," *Economic Journal*, Vol. XLV (1935), pp. 1–35; Abba P. Lerner, *The Economics of Control* (New York: Macmillan Co., 1944), chaps. vi and ix; Melvin W. Reder, *Studies in the Theory of Welfare Economics* (New York: Columbia University Press, 1947), chaps. ii–iii; and Abram Bergson, "Socialist Economics," in Howard S. Ellis (ed.), *A Survey of Contemporary Economics* (Philadelphia: Blakiston Co., 1948).

A somewhat different but very interesting approach to this subject, which is now in the making, is that of linear programming. See T. C. Koopmans (ed.), *Activity Analysis of Production and Allocation* (Cowles Commission Monograph 13) (New York: John Wiley & Sons, 1951).

NOTE TO CHAPTER VIII: THE DISTINCTION BETWEEN SOCIAL AND PRIVATE MARGINAL VALUE AND PRODUCT

In every community where there is division of labor, the fulfillment of one person's wants depends on other people's actions. One person's wants are filled the more completely, the greater is the amount of services performed by others, and the smaller the amount of products diverted to the satisfaction of the wants of others. Most of our discussion of efficiency in this chapter and previous ones was concerned with problems raised by the interdependence of different people's satisfactions and actions. So far, however, we have always assumed that a person's satisfaction depends solely on the quantity and nature of the consumers' goods he buys and of the services he sells; and that other people's actions influence his well-being only through these factors, by affecting his market opportunities and the prices at which he can buy goods and sell his services.

Very often, however, one person's actions influence another person's well-being also through more direct channels and without the intermediary of the market. For example, a person who maintains a well-kept garden provides satisfaction not only for himself and his family but also for passers-by. Conversely, a person who buys himself a powerful radio provides enjoyment for himself but often causes misery for his neighbors. A slightly different case, and one that is especially important in our society, is that in which the conspicuous consumption of one person causes a loss of satisfaction to his friends, neighbors, or colleagues, either because it makes them envy him and thus causes them misery or because it makes them feel that for reasons of prestige they have to live up to the standards he sets and thus forces them into a mode of living they have no taste for and would not have adopted otherwise. The converse of this case is that in which a person derives satisfaction not only from his own consumption but also from the knowledge that others, too, enjoy an adequate standard of living.

One can find many examples of such repercussions of one man's consumption on other people's welfare. We have neglected them so far for simplicity's sake; but we must now see how their existence qualifies the results we have reached in preceding chapters.

We discussed the meaning of efficiency in economics and stated the conditions under which economic organization is efficient. One of these conditions was, it will be recalled, that consumers' preferences be reflected in the market prices of consumers' goods and thus be made known to producers. We showed in Chapter IV that this condition is fulfilled whenever competition among consumers is perfect, because in such a case the price of each consumers' good equals and expresses its marginal valuation by all its consumers. When we derived this result, however, we also stated its limitations. We likened the consumers' market to a system of balloting, where each consumer casts a vote to state his preferences, but where each person's vote is weighted by his expenditures. Hence, in a society in which incomes and expenditures are unequally distributed, the prices of consumers' goods express the unequally weighted preferences of consumers. This was one of the reasons why we stressed the fact that economic organization must be judged not only by its efficiency but also by its equity.

We have now found yet another shortcoming of consumers'-good prices as an index of consumers' preferences. Not only do they give more weight to the preferences of the rich than to those of the poor, but they express consumers' preferences only with respect to the goods each consumer buys himself and give no weight whatever to consumers' preferences concerning other people's consumption pattern. For example, the prices of radios and gardening express the marginal values which the owners of radios and gardens attach to the enjoyment each of them derives from his own radio and his own garden; and they are unaffected by the fact that most people enjoy not only their own but also other people's gardens and that many people, while enjoying their own, dislike hearing their neighbors' radios. The prices of radios and gardening, therefore, are an incomplete expression of society's preferences; accordingly, they are an imperfect guide to the allocation of resources. It is to express this fact that it is customary to distinguish between social and private value.

1. SOCIAL VERSUS PRIVATE MARGINAL VALUE

The price that reflects the marginal valuation of a commodity by each person who buys it is called its private marginal value. This may differ from its social marginal value, which is the hypothetical price that would express its marginal valuation if everybody whose welfare is affected by its consumption could express his preferences through the market mechanism. Unfortunately, however, it is impossible to ascertain this price, owing to the absence of machinery through which others than buyers could express their preferences. The best we can do is to imagine how the existence of such machinery would affect the price of a particular commodity and on this basis tell whether its social marginal value exceeds or falls short of its actual market price. It is easy to see, for example, that if every owner of a garden could make passers-by pay for the enjoyment they derive from looking at it, the demand for gardens, and hence the price of the services that go into the making of gardens, would be raised. Conversely, if every owner of a radio would have to compensate his neighbors for all the disturbance he causes them, the demand for and price of radios would be lower than it is now. We conclude, therefore, that the social marginal value of gardens exceeds, whereas that of radios falls short of, their private marginal value.

In general, we can usually tell which way the social marginal value of a commodity differs from its private marginal value as expressed by its price; but we cannot tell by how much it differs. Hence, we can tell roughly how a perfectly competitive system should be corrected in order to render it more efficient, although we are unable to construct a more satisfactory model of an efficient economy. To be exact, it is not at all difficult to state the *formal* conditions of maximum efficiency in an economy in which each person's satisfaction depends not only on his own but also on other people's consumption. All that has to be done is to substitute the term "social marginal value" for "marginal value"—and, as will be seen presently, the terms "social marginal cost" for "marginal cost" and "social marginal product" for "marginal product"— in all formal statements of the marginal conditions of efficiency.

There seems to be no way, however, of translating these *formal* conditions of efficiency into *institutional* conditions. In other words, we cannot tell what type of economic organization and what type of economic behavior would insure efficiency in an economy in which one person's satisfaction is affected by other people's consumption. This is why we retain perfect competition as the best model of an efficient economy, even though it would be a perfect model only if the welfare of each consumer depended on his own consumption alone.

We argued above that whenever the social marginal value of a consumers' good differs from its private marginal value, even perfect competition would fail to lead to an efficient organization of the economy, and that in such cases the efficiency of even a perfectly competitive economy could be improved by a suitable corrective interference with the market mechanism. There are many examples in our economy of corrective interference of this sort; and it is convenient to distinguish three forms of such interference: (1) rules and regulations designed to keep one person's consumption from interfering with other people's welfare; (2) the artificial distortion of prices aimed at making them more nearly equal to social marginal value; and (3) the provision of certain goods and services outside of the market mechanism. We shall discuss examples of each of these three cases.

1. The first case is perhaps the most important. A simple example of it is the prohibition in certain apartment houses of playing radios at night or with open windows; and further examples are speed limits and other rules of the road. In a wider sense, all laws and customs belong in this category, since they all circumscribe individual freedom in order to protect other people's (i.e., society's) welfare.

2. The simplest method of distorting market prices is the levying of excise taxes and the paying of subsidies. These were discussed in Chapter IV. We showed there that excise taxes are an inefficient means of raising revenue and subsidies an inefficient way of giving relief; but we reached these results by considering the effects of excise taxes and subsidies only on the people directly affected by them. Furthermore, we cited some arguments in favor of certain subsidies and excise taxes.

We are now in a position to elaborate these arguments a little further. We stated, for example, that an excise tax on intoxicating beverages should be regarded not as an inefficient way of raising revenue but as a public-health measure, aimed at discouraging drunkenness. This statement can be given two interpretations. One is that the community at large knows better than the individual consumer what is good for him and that, therefore, his loss of satisfaction caused by the collection of public revenue in the form of an excise tax on liquor is not a true loss at all, because it is a loss only by the drunkard's false standards. This is a possible interpretation but a somewhat dangerous one. For if we begin questioning the consumer's ability to decide what is good for him, we embark on a road on which it is difficult to stop; and we may end up by throwing overboard the whole concept of consumers' sovereignty. For this reason the second interpretation seems preferable.

The second interpretation is that each consumer is the best judge of his own welfare; but if his consumption affects other people's welfare, it should be restrained in the interests of these other people. One person's consumption of alcohol affects the health of his family and descendants and may, in addition, be a nuisance to his neighbors. Hence, while an excise tax on alcoholic drinks lowers the drinker's welfare, it is likely at the same time to raise the welfare of his family and neighbors and may thus, on balance, cause more gain than loss.[1] The excise tax achieves this result in two ways: It discourages consumption by raising the price paid by the consumer over and above the cost of producing alcoholic beverages; and it discourages production by lowering the price received by the producer below the price paid by the consumer and expressive of his private marginal valuation of alcoholic drinks.

It is easy to see that a subsidy, which may be regarded as a negative excise tax, has effects that are the exact reverse of those of an excise tax, and that the arguments in favor of subsidies are exactly analogous to those in favor of excise taxes. For example, a subsidy on hospital or other medical services would raise both the supply of and the demand for such services. The argument in favor of it is either that the individual does not realize fully the advantages of medical care and therefore needs special encouragement to demand more of it; or that although the individual knows best how to maximize his own welfare, his health benefits also the rest of the community and future generations; and it is for their sake that he must be induced to make better use of medical services.

3. An example of the third case, in which a service is provided free and outside of the market mechanism, is the provision of free medical service in the Scandinavian countries and in Great Britain. The difference between this case and that of a subsidized service or commodity is very slight; in fact, one might regard free medical service as medical service with a 100 per cent subsidy. Accordingly, the arguments in favor of subsidizing a service or providing it free are also the same.

In addition to the arguments we discussed above, we must mention here two further arguments in favor of either subsidizing or providing free certain goods and services. The first is rather different from our main argument. We saw earlier that the market distributes consumers' goods in conformity both with consumers' preferences and with the distribution of income among consumers. But inequalities in the distribution of a particular commodity that are due to the inequality of income distribution can be mitigated by a subsidy or eliminated by the free provision of that commodity. One of these measures may be adopted, there-

---

[1] Needless to say, we cannot measure welfare and have no objective way of comparing one man's gain to another man's loss. The above calculation, therefore, is highly subjective; but this fact does not render it invalid.

fore, when equity considerations apply with especial force to a particular commodity and when society wants to make its distribution partly or wholly independent of the unequal distribution of income. This certainly is one explanation of free medical service in the above-mentioned countries and of free education in this country.

The other argument is similar to and closely connected with the main argument of this Note. We saw that certain goods and services, besides providing satisfaction to their consumers, also affect, though indirectly and to a lesser extent, the welfare of other people. An extreme type of such goods and services is one that affects the welfare of a group equally —so much so that one cannot distinguish between direct and indirect effects, or between consumers and "other people also affected." Obvious examples are the services provided by the police and the military. We consider public safety and military security indivisible and feel that they cannot be sold, like bread, in different quantities to different consumers, because the military security provided to one member of a community automatically benefits, more or less equally, all other members of the community as well. While the community's demand for bread is the sum of the individual demands of its members, we think of the demand for public safety and military security as a collective demand and not as the sum of individual demands. This is why we do not rely on the market to register the urgency of demand for these services and prefer the machinery of political action to ascertain, and that of government to satisfy, society's demand for them.

It should be remembered, however, that the difference between this case and that of medical service is one of degree only. In fact, military security and personal safety have not always been regarded as matters for public concern and collective action. Feudalism may be looked upon as a first step toward the "collectivization" of military security; and there are many instances in both European and American history in which personal safety was each man's private affair.

2. SOCIAL VERSUS PRIVATE MARGINAL PRODUCT

So far, we have been concerned with cases in which one person's consumption has repercussions also on other people's welfare. Closely parallel to these cases are those in which it is the activity of a firm that affects directly and without the intermediary of the market either the activities of other firms or the welfare of other people. For example, the establishment of the first factory or industry in an industrially undeveloped country or region usually facilitates the establishment of other factories or industries by rendering the population more mechanically minded and more interested in factory employment, thus creating a labor market by which subsequent firms and industries can benefit. In other words, the first factory or industry produces not only its output, which it can sell in the market, but in addition produces also advantages for the next firm or industry to be established—although the nature of these advantages is not such that its beneficiaries could be made to pay for them. Society, however, benefits by them; and their value, therefore, should be added to the value of the firm's marketable product when an estimate of its marginal contribution to social welfare is made. In such a case, therefore, the firm's or industry's social marginal product exceeds its private marginal product.

To cite another case, the working of a factory may pollute the air in its vicinity with soot, smoke, or offensive smells. The unpleasantness that this causes to inhabitants of the neighborhood must, from society's point of view, be considered part of the firm's total product; and since this part has a nuisance value, it must be *deducted* from the value of the firm's output sold in the market. In this case, therefore, the firm's social marginal product is lower than its private marginal product.[2]

Whenever the social product of a firm or industry differs from its private product, the market mechanism cannot, even under perfect competition, bring about an efficient allocation and utilization of resources. Hence the demand in such cases for government intervention of some sort. The corrective measures commonly used are similar to those discussed in the previous section. For example, zoning regulations are aimed at keeping the noise, dirt, and smell of factories out of residential districts. Subsidies and other forms of protection have been used to aid the industrialization of almost every country, on the ground that the social usefulness of the first industries to be established exceeded their private profitability. On the same grounds and for the same reason the state sometimes takes upon itself the task of building factories and industries that would be unprofitable for private enterprise to establish.

BIBLIOGRAPHICAL NOTE

On the distinction between social and private value and product, see A. C. Pigou, *The Economics of Welfare* (London: Macmillan & Co., 1920; 4th ed., 1932),

---

[2] Occasionally, this idea is expressed in a slightly different form. The unpleasantness caused by the operation of the factory is regarded as a cost, additional to the private cost which the firm pays for the use of its factors of production; and then one can say that the social cost of the firm's product exceeds its private cost. It is obvious that the difference between this statement and the one made in the text is purely one of terminology.

especially Part II, chaps. ii, iii, iv, ix, and x. For a short but excellent discussion of cases in which the social usefulness of industry exceeds its private profitability, see P. N. Rosenstein-Rodan, "Problems of Industrialization of Eastern and South-Eastern Europe," *Economic Journal,* Vol. LIII (1943), pp. 202–11.

On the general subject of efficiency in economics and on the conditions of efficiency, when discrepancies between social and private value and product occur, see A. Burk (A. Bergson), "A Reformulation of Certain Aspects of Welfare Economics," *Quarterly Journal of Economics,* Vol. LII (1938), pp. 310–34. For an altogether more general approach, to the subject not only of this note but of economic welfare in general, see Kenneth J. Arrow, *Social Choice and Individual Values* (Cowles Commission Monograph 12) (New York: John Wiley & Sons, 1951).

CHAPTER IX

CAPITAL

THE last chapter brought to a conclusion our discussion of economic efficiency as exemplified by a model of universal perfect competition. In constructing this model, however, we left several unanswered problems and loose ends; and it will be the task of this chapter and the next to answer these problems and tie up the loose ends.

One of the problems we left unsolved is the question of how the size of the individual firm is determined. The importance of this problem appeared already in Chapter II (page 15). We argued there that in order that competition may exist, the number of firms must be large; and that large numbers, in turn, depend on the existence of a limit to the size of the individual firm. In Chapter VII, however, where the problem of size first came up for detailed discussion, we found no solution to the problem. On the contrary, we came to the surprising conclusion that, under perfect competition and on the assumptions of profit maximization and proportional returns, the size of the firm is indeterminate and unlimited. At the time, we noted the unsatisfactory nature of this conclusion; but we evaded the issue by concentrating our attention on short-run problems. In discussing these, we were able to regard the size of the firm as given, because we felt justified in assuming that in the short run the plant and equipment of the firm are fixed in quantity. This, however, still left us with the long-run problems of how the size of the firm is determined and what limits its scale of operations.

Another of our unsolved problems is that of the distribution of income between labor and capital. We stated earlier (p. 180) that on the assumptions so far made, this problem cannot be dealt with; and it will be well to prove this statement. Let us recall that we assumed free entry to every market, and that the only factors of production considered so far have been the personal services of employees, the managerial services of entrepreneurs,[1] and the various produced factors, such as fuel, ma-

---

[1] Professional and other "self-employed" people are best regarded as entrepreneurs.

terials, equipment, and so forth. We saw that the free entry of new-comers tends to eliminate the individual firm's profit and to cause its receipts to be completely exhausted by the payments made for the use of the above factors. These payments consist of the salaries and wages of employees, the "wages of management" earned by the entrepreneur, and the payments made to other firms for produced factors bought. These other firms, in turn, were also assumed to make no profit and to exhaust all their receipts in paying their employees and managers for personal services rendered and in paying still other firms for produced factors bought. If we add together separately first the receipts and then the payments made by all the firms in the economy, the value of produced factors (or intermediate products) occurs on both the receipts and the payments side and therefore cancels out. There remain on the receipts side the value of goods and services sold to final consumers, and on the payments side the total earnings of employees and entrepreneurs for personal services rendered; and these two sides will be equal. It appears, therefore, that on the assumptions hitherto made, all the income of society would be resolved into the wages and salaries of employees and the wages of management; and no income would accrue to the owners of capital. In other words, so far in our analysis, we have assumed away the problem of how income is distributed between labor and capital.

These two problems—what limits the size of the firm, and what determines the distribution of income between labor and capital—are the subject matter of the present chapter. But, to answer these problems, we must drop a simplifying assumption implicit in all our previous analysis: our complete neglect of the element of time.

Considerations of time enter into economic analysis in two ways: First, production takes place in time; second, buyers and sellers take time to adjust their market behavior to changing economic conditions. The analysis of the firm and the productive system which takes account of the time-consuming nature of production is called capital theory. This will be discussed in the present chapter and will be seen to provide answers to the two problems raised above. As to the time element involved in the market's response to changes in conditions, the problems this creates are the problems of dynamic economics; and they will be introduced in the next chapter.

1. ENTREPRENEURSHIP AS A FACTOR LIMITING THE SIZE OF THE FIRM

It will be remembered that the analysis of Chapter VI was based on the assumption of proportional returns, according to which the firm can double its output by doubling the input of all its factors of production. When the firm is a price taker and faces fixed prices in both factor and product markets, this assumption implies that by doubling its purchases and sales, the firm can also double its profit. This is so because, to double his purchases, the price taker must double his expenditures; and, by doubling his sales, he can double his receipts; and when receipts and expenditures are both doubled, profit, the difference between them, will be doubled, too. Hence, if the entrepreneur makes a profit to begin with and aims at maximizing this profit, he will tend to expand output and the size of his firm indefinitely; and there would be nothing to stop his expansionist policy except for the limitations imposed upon him by his competitors and their expansionist policies.

Such a situation, however, is bound to be thoroughly unstable. It is conceivable that equally efficient and equally powerful competitors should keep each other in check; but such a balance would be very delicate and easily upset by any chance event. The slightest advantage of one firm over the others would enable it to make better use than they of the normal ups and downs of trade, first for increasing its initial advantage, and ultimately for expanding at their expense. However, as soon as one firm becomes significantly larger than its competitors, the basis for perfect competition disappears.[2] Hence, if it were true that there is no limit to the size of the individual firm, perfect competition would be an unstable situation, which, even if brought about somehow, would rapidly lead to its own destruction.

In itself, this result need not alarm us unduly. After all, perfect competition is not a description of an actual economy but merely an artificial model of an efficient economic system. The trouble is, however, that the above argument applies to competition in general. Competition of any kind, perfect or monopolistic, depends on the presence of some limit to the size of the firm. The nature and very existence of competition in a market depend largely on the number of firms in that market; and the number of firms, in its turn, depends on the size of the individual firm relative to that of the market. Firms, governed by the profit motive, have a natural tendency to grow; and if there were no limit to the size of the firm, we would have to conclude that all competition would be self-destructive and doomed to disappear. Before accepting such a conclusion, however, we must be careful to investigate all the factors that may set a limit to the size or rate of growth of the firm and thus insure the maintenance and stability of competition.

[2] See Chap. XV for a discussion of the number and relative size of firms as factors determining the nature of competition.

In their search for a factor that would limit the size of the firm, some economists have called into question the validity of the assumption of proportional returns and argued that an absolute limit is set to the size of the firm by the human limitations of the entrepreneur. As the firm grows, it becomes more unwieldy and more difficult to direct, which interferes with the efficiency of its functioning. Hence, so the argument runs, the firm's output cannot be expanded indefinitely by a correspondingly expanded input of its factors of production; for mere size, beyond a certain point, leads to inefficiency, which prevents output from rising in proportion to cost or, in other words, causes cost to rise more than in proportion to output.

Another way of presenting this same argument is to think of entrepreneurship itself as a factor of production. Under perfect competition the firm can obtain the services of all the other productive resources in the market at a fixed price and without limit. Entrepreneurship is the only factor of production which the firm can obtain only in limited quantities, because one firm, by definition, can have only one entrepreneur. It is true that one of the entrepreneur's functions, management, is largely a matter of routine and as such is easily delegated to hired subordinates; but his other function, co-ordination, is essentially a one-man task which can neither be delegated to subordinates nor be divided among a board of directors. One might argue, therefore, that although the increased use of all factors of production *would* yield proportional returns, it is impossible to increase the quantity of all factors, because at least one, the entrepreneur's co-ordinating ability, is always fixed in quantity to the firm.

To examine the validity of this argument, we must first of all ask ourselves what the entrepreneur's co-ordinating functions are. In general, they lie in two fields, production and marketing. Marketing, however, requires planning and co-ordination only from the price maker, who takes the initiative and plays the active role in the market. The price taker, who faces set offers and plays a purely passive role in the market, has no problems of how to plan and co-ordinate the buying of his factors and the selling of his products. His only problem, therefore, is the planning and co-ordination of production.

The co-ordination of the different operations performed in a factory is essential to its efficiency; and the difficulties of co-ordination do render production on too large a scale inefficient. But this factor limits the size only of the technical unit, that is, the manufacturing plant or factory; and this is not the same and must not be confused with the economic unit, the firm, which need not be an operational unit at all and may be identified only by common ownership and a common market policy. The same firm may own several manufacturing plants, give them complete independence in all technical and administrative matters, and yet remain a single firm. Bearing this fact in mind, one realizes immediately that the difficulties of co-ordinating production can hardly limit the size of the firm. In practice, of course, the several plants of a firm are often closely co-ordinated; but this merely proves that the advantages of co-ordination and co-operation often prevail over the disadvantages of too-large administrative units. When the advantages do *not* prevail, and the diseconomies of co-ordinating production on too vast a scale have the upper hand, then these diseconomies limit not the size of the firm but only the size of the manufacturing plant and the degree of co-ordination among the different plants of the firm.

We conclude, therefore, that under perfectly competitive conditions, the entrepreneur's human limitations cannot limit the size of the firm, because none of the entrepreneur's tasks is such that it could not be delegated and divided among several production managers. The situation is somewhat different under conditions of monopolistic competition when the entrepreneur is a price maker and faces the problem of co-ordinating not only production but also his market policies; but this situation will be discussed at a later stage.[3]

2. CAPITAL AS A FACTOR LIMITING THE SIZE OF THE FIRM

Having dismissed entrepreneurship as a possible explanation of the limit to the size of the firm, we shall seek this limit in another factor, the limited availability of capital. So far in our discussion of the firm and the organization of production, we have neglected the element of time. We compared the flow of the firm's receipts to the flow of its expenditures and showed how the firm behaves when it tries to maximize the difference between these two flows, the flow of its profit. We assumed that the firm's costs of production are paid out of its receipts for products sold, and that costs and receipts rise and fall together with the firm's output. Accordingly, we found no budgetary limitation to the firm's expenditures such as there is to the consumer's, because the firm's receipts—unlike the consumer's income—rise automatically with and as a result of its increased cost expenditures.

Throughout the analysis of Chapters VI, VII, and VIII, we ignored the fact that production takes time and that the expenses of production

---

[3] See pp. 326–31 in Chap. XV.

are incurred sooner than the revenue for products sold is received. When we take account of this difference in timing, however, it becomes apparent that the firm must have a fund of money with which to bridge the gap between the time when it pays for its factors of production and the time when it receives payment for the sale of output produced with their aid. This fund of money, needed to enable the firm to pay its factors of production before it has sold their product, is called the firm's capital fund. The possession of a capital fund is as essential to the operation of the firm as is its labor force, its plant and equipment, or any other of its factors of production. Hence, if the availability of capital funds were limited, this might limit the firm's size and scale of operations in much the same way in which the consumer's budget limits his scale of expenditures.

But is the amount of capital funds available to the individual firm really limited? It would not be if the firm could borrow money with the same ease with which it hires workers, and if we could assume perfect competition among borrowers in the capital market just as we assumed perfect competition among employers in the labor market. If these conditions were met, the interest payable on borrowed capital would no more limit the size of the firm than does the wage payable on hired labor; and we would merely add capital funds to our list of productive factors whose input must be doubled when the firm wants to double its profit.

Capital, however, cannot be treated like other factors of production in every respect. To begin with, in our society the ownership of the firm's capital is closely linked with the control and ownership of the firm itself; and we cannot imagine the entrepreneur borrowing *all* his capital funds in the same way in which he hires all his labor. Second, to obtain the use of capital funds, the borrower must not only pay interest but also offer security, because lending inevitably involves a risk. These two considerations set capital funds entirely apart from other factors of production and will be shown always to limit both the amount of capital the firm is *willing* to borrow and the amount it is *able* to borrow.

2a. THE WILLINGNESS TO BORROW

The capital of the firm consists of the accumulated funds of its owner and of funds obtained either from a bank as a loan or from private investors in exchange for securities sold to them. That the individual's own funds are limited in quantity is obvious enough; but we shall show that his willingness to supplement his own funds with borrowed funds for the purpose of expansion is also limited.

First of all, there is a sociological limitation. The management of every firm involves a certain risk of loss, which the entrepreneur must take into account. If, for the sake of the profit to be earned, he risks his own funds and happens to lose them, that is his own affair. But to lose other people's funds is a more serious matter. It involves bankruptcy proceedings and is an ineradicable blot on a businessman's reputation. In order to avoid this, businessmen usually refrain from borrowing more than the amount they consider a safe proportion of the total funds invested in their firm.

A second limit to the entrepreneur's willingness to borrow is set by the fixed cost that borrowing involves. When he borrows in order to expand his plant or build additional plants, he must borrow on long term. When he borrows on long term, he pledges himself to pay a fixed annual sum of money for the use of the funds borrowed. This fixed annual sum is the interest payment on the loan; usually, it is expressed as a percentage of the loan and called the interest rate on the loan. The interest payment on the loan is a fixed cost item, which stays the same and must be met whatever the receipts and rate of operation of the firm. In this, it differs from most other cost items, which usually rise and fall with the firm's rate of operations.

The necessity of meeting a fixed cost item out of receipts that are uncertain and that fluctuate with changing tastes and economic conditions has a disadvantage for the entrepreneur, the nature of which is best illustrated with the aid of an example. Imagine a firm whose gross receipts average $1 million a year and fluctuate around this average by 20 per cent, sometimes falling as low as $800,000 and rising as high as $1.2 million. If the firm's annual costs averaged $800,000, rising and falling with receipts by about 20 per cent (i.e., fluctuating between $640,000 and $960,000), then its net annual profit would rise and fall between $160,000 and $240,000 showing 20 per cent fluctuations around the average of $200,000. If, on the other hand, the firm's costs were fixed at $800,000 per annum, its profit, although still averaging $200,000, would fluctuate around this average by 100 per cent, from zero to $400,000.

These are two extreme cases. As a rule, the firm has some fixed and some variable cost items; and its total costs are neither completely fixed nor as variable as receipts. The degree of variability of total costs depends on the relative importance of fixed and variable cost items. The more important the fixed cost items are, the less variable will total costs be, and the more violently will profit fluctuate with given fluctuations in gross receipts. Entrepreneurs, like most people, prefer a stable flow of income and are therefore reluctant to saddle themselves with too many fixed cost charges. One of the main fixed cost items of the producer is the interest cost of his borrowed capital; the smaller this is, the more stable will be his net profit. Here, then, is a further argument against too much expansion on borrowed capital. The incentive to expand is, of course, the expectation of additional profit; but when expansion has to be financed with borrowed capital, the expectation of higher profit must be balanced against the greater instability of the flow of profit over time. Hence, there usually comes a point beyond which the loss of stability offsets the advantages of additional profit, and beyond which expansion on borrowed capital will not be pushed.

Needless to say, this is only a general tendency rather than an unbroken rule. For example, if an entrepreneur expects a general rise in the prices both of his products and of his factors of production, he will find it profitable to fix in advance as large a part of his cost expenditures as is feasible. Hence the great increase in the demand for loans and the general expansion of plant and equipment in inflationary periods. Apart from such times, however, entrepreneurs usually find it prudent not to let their borrowed capital exceed a certain proportion of their own funds; and whenever they adopt such a rule of thumb, they limit the expansion of their firm to the rate of accumulation of their own funds.

But, while the entrepreneur's preference for a stable flow of profit limits the amount of capital he will borrow on fixed interest, he may be able and willing to raise capital funds by the issuance of stock. We know, in fact, that the incorporation of private firms is a convenient and popular way of raising capital for expansion. The original owner of the firm retains part of the stock issued upon incorporation in payment for his contribution to the firm's assets; the rest of the stock is sold to investors, and the funds so raised are used for expansion. Similarly, corporations often raise funds for expansion by the issuance of additional stock.

Raising funds in this form has the important advantage that it does not involve the burden of a fixed interest cost, since shares in a company's stock entitle the owner only to dividends whose payment and magnitude depend on the profit made. But, while the ownership of stock secures no fixed income and only gives title to sharing the company's good or bad fortune, it confers a share in the control of the company's policy; and this sets a limit to the entrepreneur's willingness to acquire additional capital even in this form. For the owner of a private firm does not want to lose his control over policy when he decides to incorporate his firm. He wants to remain the manager of his firm with a controlling voice in all policy decisions; and, to insure such control, he must retain a certain minimum portion of the company's stock. There is a limit, therefore, to the amount of stock he can sell in the market and the amount of funds he can raise by selling stock *without risking the loss of control.*

The same considerations will also keep the controlling stockholders of a corporation from raising funds by the issuance of additional stock beyond the point where this would endanger their controlling position.

They are interested in maintaining their controlling position partly because the exercise of control in itself yields a certain satisfaction, and partly because a controlling voice enables them to secure managerial positions and pay themselves salaries that they might be unable to obtain otherwise. Both these considerations set a limit beyond which controlling stockholders will not want to raise funds by the sale of additional stock to outsiders. The funds so raised might enable the firm to expand and so raise its profit; nevertheless, such expansion is likely to be vetoed by the controlling stockholders if it may involve their losing control.

Let us stop at this stage for a moment and review the implications of the above arguments for the assumption we made in Chapter VI that the firm aims at maximum profit. So far, we have adhered to this assumption rather closely. In particular, we assumed that the proportions in which the firm employs its productive factors, the proportions in which it produces its several products, and the determination of its rate of output are all governed by the quest for maximum profit. It is true that we allowed for differences in the methods, intensity, and ruthlessness with which different entrepreneurs apply themselves to the task of maximizing profit; and we found in the Note to Chapter VII that, to aim at maximum profit, the entrepreneur must have a special type of psychology, which, however prevalent it may be, can hardly be universal. This, then, was the first breach we made in the assumption of profit maximization; but it was a small breach. It allowed for different interpretations of profit maximization and for the existence of entrepreneurs who stop short of maximum profits side by side with entrepreneurs who do not. This breach, however, was more or less closed later on when we showed in Chapter VIII that the free entry of new firms to a market tends to keep the established members of that market on their toes by penalizing inefficiency and preference for a leisurely life.

A further and more serious breach in the assumption of profit maximization was made in this section. Having seen that under perfectly competitive conditions the quest for profit would lead to an indefinite expansion of the firm, we sought for something that would curb the entrepreneur's desire to maximize profit and thus limit the size or rate of growth of the firm. We have found three such curbs. They are the entrepreneur's fear of bankruptcy, his unwillingness to fix in advance too high a proportion of his total cost expenditures, and his fear of losing control over his firm's policy and the distribution of its gains. None of these considerations keep the entrepreneur from pursuing the policy that will maximize his profit except in one single respect: they limit the expansion of his firm on borrowed capital and restrict the rate at which the firm's total capital grows to the rate at which the entrepreneur is able to increase his own investment. In other words, these considerations keep within limits the expansion of the firm and the profits to be gained by expansion; but within the limitations so imposed, they leave the entrepreneur free to maximize the profits obtainable from a firm of given size.

2b. The Willingness to Lend

So far, we have been concerned with the willingness of those in control of the firm to borrow; and we have seen that their willingness to expand on borrowed funds is limited. Another and additional limit to expansion is the producer's limited *ability* to borrow. This we shall find convenient to discuss from the lender's point of view, as his limited willingness to lend.

Capital funds are lent by the owners of accumulated savings, whom we shall call investors. Investors have a choice between lending their funds and keeping them in the safe and readily available form of cash or bank balances. Since lending involves the risk of not being paid back and the inconvenience of not having one's funds readily available, the investor must be offered a remuneration to induce him to lend and accept the risk and inconvenience that lending involves. This remuneration is the interest on the loan.

The individual investor's problem is very similar to the consumer's. He faces a securities market, which offers him a variety of securities, each of which promises a given (or probable) yield and involves a certain amount of risk and illiquidity. The investor aims at maximizing the average yield earned on his total accumulated savings, subject to the limitations imposed upon him by whatever preference for safety and liquidity he may have. His concern with safety and liquidity makes him hold part of his funds in the liquid form of cash and bank balances; and even the part invested he usually apportions among several different securities so as to spread his risks.

Assuming that he acts rationally, we regard the actual distribution of the investor's funds among cash, bank balances, and securities of different types as the one that best satisfies his preferences. In particular, we regard his actual investment in each security as having been pushed to the point where his marginal valuation of the risk involved equals the yield of that security.

From here onward the formal theory of the investor's behavior parallels that of the consumer's behavior; and the conditions of the efficient distribution of securities among investors are exactly the same as the conditions of the efficient distribution of consumers' goods among consumers. If all investors face the same security prices and regard these as given to them, they all equate their marginal valuations of the riskiness of each security to its yield; and such behavior on their part results in an efficient distribution of securities among the investing public. The main difference between the consumer and his market, on the one hand, and the investor and the securities market, on the other hand, is that whereas the consumer apportions a *flow* of income among *flows* of different consumers' goods and this results in a given distribution of the *flow* of the community's output of consumers' goods, the investor's decision apportions an accumulated *stock* of funds among different securities and results in a given distribution of the community's *stock* of securities.[4]

We mentioned above that each individual investor limits his purchases of a given security for fear of keeping all his eggs in one basket and in order to spread his risks. In view of the large number of investors, however, this would hardly limit the entrepreneur's ability to borrow. The effective limit to borrowing is imposed by the investor's insistence on security. Every loan involves the risk of not being repaid; and in order that the investor may be induced to bear this risk, he must be offered not only an interest payment but also security. To satisfy the investor's demand for security, the firm may have to disclose the purpose for which it borrows and submit to the investor's standards of prudence; in addition, it usually must pledge the security of its assets. Since the firm's

---

[4] We neglect current saving and the current issuance of new securities, because these flows are small as compared to the stocks of accumulated funds and securities already in existence.

assets are limited, its ability to borrow is also limited and depends on the value of its assets.

There is a fundamental difference, therefore, between the producer's position in the market where he borrows capital funds and in the markets where he buys materials and equipment and hires the services of labor. He can hire workers and buy materials and equipment at market prices, with no questions asked; and he could obtain the market's total supply on the same terms on which it is available to others. The same is not true of the market for capital funds. The producer may be able to borrow on the same terms as anyone else but only up to a certain point; and the amount he can borrow is limited not by the limited supply of available funds but by the limited amount of security he can offer.

We can now investigate how this consideration limits the size or rate of growth of the individual firm. Each firm has the security of its assets, on whose basis it can borrow for expansion. When the sums so borrowed are invested by the firm and the investment has proved a success, additional assets are created, which can again be used as security for further borrowing. Nevertheless, the firm cannot go on borrowing indefinitely, because lenders always insist on a comfortable margin of safety and do not lend the full amount that the assets pledged as security are worth. Accordingly, the funds that the producer is able to borrow are limited to a certain proportion (or multiple) of his own funds invested in his enterprise.

It appears, therefore, that the investor's limited willingness to lend limits the size of the individual firm in exactly same way in which the producer's limited willingness to borrow limits it. Both factors keep the firm's borrowed funds from exceeding a certain ratio to the owner's own funds. This limits the size of the firm at any moment of time and limits its rate of growth to the rate at which the owner accumulates his own capital funds.

The above arguments, it will be noted, have also provided an answer to the question posed on page 130 of Chapter VII. There, having found no limit to the size of the firm on the assumptions of perfect competition, profit maximization, and proportional returns, we asked ourselves which of these three assumptions was illegitimate. We have now found that the first two were. For it appeared that there is at least one market, that for capital funds, in which the entrepreneur's demand is *not* motivated solely by his desire to maximize profit, and in which he *cannot,* under any circumstances, be assumed to be in a perfectly competitive position, able to obtain virtually unlimited supplies at the market's given price.

3. CAPITAL AS A FACTOR OF PRODUCTION

We now come to our second problem, that of income distribution between labor and capital. We showed at the beginning of this chapter that, on the assumptions of Chapter VIII, all income would accrue to those who render personal services. This result, it will be recalled, hinged on the assumption that the profit of the firm tends to be eliminated by the additional competition offered by newcomers to its market. It follows from this that a firm or group of firms can always prevent the competitive elimination of its profits if it can restrain the entry of newcomers to its market. The profits so secured are called monopoly profits. The nature of monopoly profits, the nature and cause of competitive restraints, and the effect of these restraints on economic efficiency will be discussed in Parts III and IV of this book. But the question arises whether restraints on competition are the only explanation and monopoly profits the only form of income received for services other than personal. In other words, would a perfectly competitive system eliminate all such incomes and leave room only for the earnings of workers and managers?

Using a very different terminology and theoretical framework, this is what Marx affirms in *Das Kapital*. He explains the existence of profit, the capitalist's income, by the latter's "economic power" (we should call it monopoly power); and he argues that if the economic power of capitalists were broken, they would receive no income, because all the income of society would accrue to workers and managers for personal services rendered. The argument of the previous section, however, makes it apparent that there exists an alternative explanation of the capitalist's income; in fact, capital theory was originally developed to provide such an alternative explanation.

We have seen that the time-consuming nature of production renders capital funds necessary to the operation of the firm. The theory of capital regards these capital funds as a factor of production, similar and additional to the factors of production already considered. According to capital theory, the scarcity of capital funds limits both the number and the size of firms and thus prevents the competitive elimination of profits even in a perfectly competitive economy. The profits so maintained accrue to the owners of capital funds in the form of interest and dividend payments, in return for the services they render by making their capital funds available to the entrepreneur. From the entrepreneur's point of view, therefore, interest and dividend payments are the cost he pays for the use of the factor capital, just as wages are the cost he pays for the use of the factor labor. In short, all that capital theory does is to add capital funds to the list of productive factors, and interest and dividend payments to the list of cost items.

This necessitates but a slight revision of the results we reached in Chapter VIII. We argued there that new firms are always attracted to a market when its established members make profits and that the free entry of newcomers tends, in turn, to eliminate these profits. If we now consider that to found a new firm requires a capital fund, and that interest must be paid for the use of capital funds, then it appears that the profits of established firms will attract newcomers only if these profits represent a yield on invested capital which is more than enough to repay the interest cost on that capital. Hence, the entry of newcomers will not eliminate profits completely but only limit them to the level where they are just enough to repay the interest cost on the capital invested. Under these conditions, therefore, the total income of society can be resolved into the salaries and wages of employees paid for personal services rendered, the wages of management earned by entrepreneurs, and the interest and dividends paid for the use of capital funds to investors, among whom there are also entrepreneurs who use their own capital funds.

So far, we have regarded interest and dividends as part of profit. But since they are payments for the use of the factor capital, interest and dividends could equally well be regarded as costs that have to be deducted from receipts to arrive at the entrepreneur's profit. On this definition of profit the results of Chapter VIII do not have to be revised at all; for it remains true that profits tend to zero in the long run; and the only modification to be made is to include interest and dividends among the costs of production.

Neither definition of profit accords with that used by the businessman, who distinguishes between borrowed and equity capital and regards interest on the former as cost, earnings on the latter as profit. From the economist's point of view, however, this is seldom a useful distinction; and he usually regards all the earnings of capital as either cost or profit. To regard them as cost, and to define profit *net* of the earnings of capital is logically more correct and is the accepted usage of the literature of capital theory. The classical economists, however, included the earnings of capital in profit; and this usage is also followed by those modern writers who feel that the terminology of capital theory is so formal as to obscure the very questions that the theory sets out to solve. Personally, the present writer favors the terminology that includes he earnings of capital in profit, mainly because this conforms most closely to the terminology used by the man in the street. To avoid confusion, however, we shall distinguish, wherever necessary, between *gross* profit, which includes interest and dividends, and *net* profit, which excludes them.

We have now resolved the two problems with which we started out in this chapter; but, in doing so, we have raised a host of further problems. To begin with, if capital funds are a factor of production additional to the productive factors considered in previous chapters, that raises new problems of allocation. Under what conditions will this additional factor of production be efficiently allocated among different firms and industries; and under what conditions will it be efficiently combined with other factors of production? Furthermore, if interest and dividends are the remuneration of the factor capital, then we must ask ourselves whether they correspond to both the social cost of providing and the productive advantages of using capital in the same way in which the wages of a worker correspond to both the marginal effort of performing his services and the marginal advantages of using them. We cannot answer these and related questions fully in this chapter; but we shall at least indicate the nature of the answers that can be given. In this connection, it will be convenient to begin by investigating the question as to whether the firm's demand for and utilization of capital funds is comparable to its demand for and utilization of other factors of production.

4. THE INVESTMENT POLICY OF THE FIRM

We saw earlier that the possession of a capital fund is necessary and useful for the operation of the firm; but we must now express its usefulness in more definite terms. The usefulness of factors of production other than capital funds we expressed in terms of their marginal contribution to the firm's output and receipts. We showed how output can be raised by using more of one factor while keeping all others constant; and the increase in output due to using one additional unit of a factor we called the latter's marginal product. The value to the firm of this marginal product we called the producer's marginal valuation of the factor. We then showed that, under perfect competition, it is in the producer's interest to push the utilization of each of his factors to the point where its marginal value to him equals its price.

Can we and should we use the same kind of argument also in the case of capital funds? One difficulty arises immediately. To calculate his marginal valuation of a factor, the producer must be able to vary the quantity used of that factor while keeping the quantities of all other factors constant. But how can the firm vary the quantity of its capital funds without varying the quantity also of some other factor of production when the sole purpose of capital funds is to enable the firm to pay for the services of the other factors? The firm uses additional capital funds either to buy additional quantities of the other factors and so increase its output or to buy its other factors in different proportions and so produce its output in a different way. To use additional capital funds without an increased or otherwise changed utilization of other factors seems to make no sense and would certainly not increase output.

In fact, the very nature of this difficulty should warn us against expecting a close parallelism between the producer's demand for capital funds and his demand for other factors of production. But let us ignore this warning for the moment and consider a very special instance in which it is possible, in a sense, to change the quantity of capital funds used without changing the utilization of other factors of production. This is the case of a firm that produces timber, or wine, or any other product whose quantity or value increases with the mere passage of time. A winegrower, for example, can increase his annual receipts from the sale of wine without changing the quantity of grapes bought and processed annually, merely by aging his wine longer. To do this requires no additional labor or materials, only a larger capital fund, because it lengthens the gap between the time when the grapes are bought and paid for and the time when revenue is received for wine sold.

Let us consider, therefore, the wine producer's problem of how long to age his wine in order to maximize his profit. We could approach this problem in either of two ways. We could consider the problem of a producer who makes a once-and-for-all investment in a certain quantity of new wine and wants to know how long he should wait before selling this wine. Alternatively, we could consider the problem of a producer who wants to establish a going concern, which regularly lays down and sells equal quantities of wine every year. The first is the standard problem of most discussions of capital theory; [5] but we shall discuss only the second problem, since this is the more realistic of the two. This requires finding out how the producer's annual costs, annual receipts, and capital requirements change with the length of time for which he ages his wine. For simplicity's sake, we shall assume that his annual turnover is one barrel; in other words, we shall consider a firm whose annual input is one barrel of grape juice and whose annual output is one barrel of wine.

The firm's annual cost of production, other than interest cost, is the

---

[5] Cf. K. E. Boulding, *Economic Analysis* (rev. ed.; New York: Harper & Bros., 1948), Chap. xxxvi, for the best discussion of this problem.

price of one barrel of grape juice, that is, the cost of buying and process-ing the amount of grapes necessary to produce one barrel of grape juice. The annual receipts of this firm are equal to the price of a barrel of wine, which depends on the age of the wine. The firm's need for capital de-pends on the minimum stock of wine required to enable it to sell one barrel of wine per year; and this, in turn, depends on how long it wants to age its wine. For example, if the firm wants to sell 2-year-old wine, it must buy at the outset one barrel each of grape juice and of one-year-old wine, because this is the minimum stock which will enable it to sell one barrel of 2-year-old wine annually by buying one barrel of grape juice annually. Similarly, if the firm wants to sell one barrel of 3-year-old wine every year, it must invest at the outset in a minimum stock of one barrel each of grape juice and of one- and 2-year-old wine; and it must afterward buy one barrel of grape juice annually in order to maintain this stock. In general, if the firm wants to age its wine for n years, it must invest in a stock of n barrels, one each of grape juice and wine of 1, 2, . . . , $n - 1$ years of age. Hence, if we know the market prices of grape juice and wine at different ages, we can determine not only the firm's annual costs and receipts but also its capital requirements.

Assume, for example, that the market price of grape juice and wine at different ages is that shown in line 1 of Table I. These prices represent

TABLE I

	AGE OF WINE IN YEARS					
	0	1	2	3	4	5
1. Annual gross receipts (Market price of wine).	$27.00	$32.00	$41.00	$ 60.00	$ 75.00	$ 80.00
2. Capital fund needed (cumulative sum of line 1).	. . .	27.00	59.00	100.00	160.00	235.00
3. Annual material cost.	27.00	27.00	27.00	27.00	27.00	27.00
4. Annual gross profit (line 1 − line 3).	0	5.00	14.00	33.00	48.00	53.00
5. Annual interest cost (10 per cent of line 2).	0	2.70	5.90	10.00	16.00	23.50
6. Annual net profit (line 1 − [line 3 + line 5]).	0	2.30	8.10	23.00	32.00	29.50
7. Rate of (gross) profit per capital invested (line 4 ÷ line 2 × 100).	0	18.5%	23.7%	33.0%	30.0%	22.6%

the firm's annual gross receipts from selling wine of different ages; and we can also compute from them the firm's capital requirements, that is, the cost of the minimum stock of wine needed to enable the firm to sell wine of different ages. This is shown in the second line of Table I. The information contained in this table is also shown graphically in the

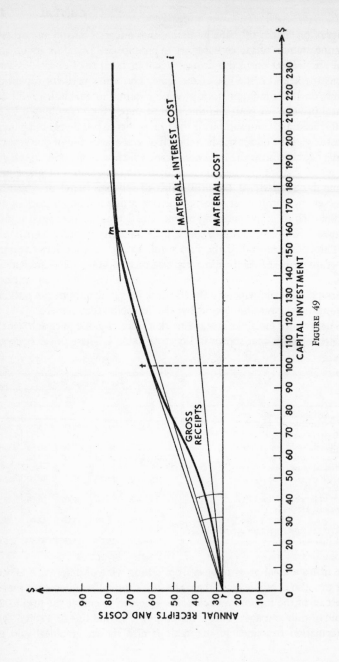

FIGURE 49

diagram of Figure 49, where capital funds required for the annual production of one barrel of wine are measured along the horizontal axis and the annual revenue from selling one barrel of wine is measured along the vertical axis. The curve in Figure 49 shows the firm's annual gross receipts as a function of its invested capital. For example, it shows that with a $100 investment the firm's annual gross receipts will be $60, because this investment enables the firm to sell 3-year-old wine, whose price is $60. It is apparent that this curve is a value-productivity curve, such as was discussed on page 141 in Chapter VII, because it shows the value of output produced with a fixed quantity of one factor, grape juice, and different quantities of the other factor, invested capital. The slope of the curve shows the marginal value of capital, that is, the addition to revenue obtainable by using one more unit of capital while keeping unchanged the quantity of the other factor, grape juice.

The producer's material cost is the $27 he pays annually for a barrel of grape juice; and this cost is independent of the length of time for which he ages his wine. This is shown in line 3 of Table I and is represented by a horizontal straight line in the diagram of Figure 49. The difference between gross receipts (l. 1) and material costs (l. 3) is the firm's gross profit, shown in line 4 of Table I and represented by the vertical distance between the productivity curve and the horizontal cost line in Figure 49. But part of this profit must be paid in interest on the capital invested; and it is apparent that the producer aims at maximizing net profit, or the excess of gross profit over the interest due on his capital. Interest payments rise in the same proportion as the capital funds invested; and line 5 of Table I shows the interest payable, on the assumption that the rate of interest is 10 per cent. The sum of material and interest costs is shown in Figure 49 by the ordinates of the upward-sloping straight line, which the reader will recognize as a price line, whose slope represents the 10 per cent rate of interest.

Line 6 in Table I, and the vertical distance between value-productivity curve and price line in Figure 49, show the firm's net profit for wine of different ages. This is greatest at point *m,* where the slope of the value-productivity curve equals the slope of the price line. In other words, net profit is maximized by equating the marginal value of capital funds to the interest payable on capital funds. In our example, this is an annual net profit of $32 (= $75 — $43), to attain which the wine producer must invest $160 and age his wine for 4 years. It appears, therefore, as though we had reached here a result closely parallel to that reached in Chapter VII, namely, that it is profitable for the producer to push his utilization of capital to the point where its marginal value equals its price, the rate of interest. A corollary of this result is that a fall in the rate of interest, the price of capital funds, would induce the producer to combine a greater quantity of capital funds with his other factors of production.

But the question now arises whether this really is the wine producer's best policy; and we shall show that, as a rule, it is not. Let us recall, to begin with, that our example relates to a firm whose annual turnover is one barrel; or, to interpret it more generally, it shows the firm's capital requirements, annual receipts, costs, and profit *per barrel of wine.* Hence, what we have proved so far is that an investment of $160 per barrel of wine would maximize the firm's net profit *per barrel of wine;* and it is by no means certain that this is what the firm aims at.

The producer aims at maximizing his total annual profit. If, in spite of this, economists generally express profit as a rate, dividing total annual profit by (the quantity of) total annual input or output or by the amount of capital invested, they do so only for the sake of convenience. It is much easier to derive and illustrate the conditions of maximizing a rate of profit than those of maximizing total profit. This, however, raises the question as to whether there is some rate of profit the maximizing of which would result in the maximizing of total profit. The answer is simple: The firm will maximize total profit if it maximizes that rate of profit which expresses profit per unit of some quantity or factor that is fixed to the firm, because this rate of profit will be maximized simultaneously with total profit. That this is so becomes obvious when we remember that the same conditions that maximize a given variable will also maximize any other variable that is obtained by dividing the first variable with a constant.

Hence, to maximize his total profit, the producer must maximize profit per unit of whichever of his factors is fixed or limited in quantity. If his annual input is limited, he must maximize profit per unit of input; if his capital funds are limited, he must maximize profit per capital invested; if his annual output is limited, he must maximize profit per unit of output; and each of these alternatives will generally lead to a different investment policy. The entrepreneur's investment policy depends, therefore, on what limits the size of his firm.

For example, a particular wine producer's input of grapes may be limited by his inability to raise the yield of his vineyard and by his unwillingness to buy an additional vineyard or to process and sell wine not grown by himself. To maximize his profit subject to these special limitations, he must maximize profit per barrel of wine processed. Hence, the result we reached above, that the wine producer should age his wine for four years, does hold good in this special case. We must bear in mind, however, that this is a very special case, and that the scale of the producer's enterprise is not usually determined by limitations on his rate of input.

In fact, we argued at the beginning of this chapter that, as a general rule, the size of the firm is limited by the amount of capital at the producer's disposal. It follows from this that, to maximize his total profit, the producer must aim at maximizing the rate of profit *per capital invested*. What investment policy will this rule lead to; and how will this policy compare to the policy discussed above, where the wine producer maximized profit per barrel of wine?

Let us begin by reconsidering that policy. The wine producer who ages his wine for 4 years makes an investment of $160 per barrel and gets a gross profit of ($75 — $27 =) $48. This represents a rate of profit of 30 per cent on the $160 capital invested. Geometrically, this rate is expressed by the slope of the line drawn from *r* to point *m* in Figure 49. Since this rate of profit is higher than the market rate of interest (line *rm* is steeper than the price line *ri*), which we assumed to be 10 per cent, the producer makes a net profit, in excess of the interest payable on his capital. It appears from Figure 49, however, that this is not the producer's best policy. For we saw that the rate of profit on a given production policy is shown by the slope of the line drawn from *r* to the point on the value-productivity curve which corresponds to this policy; and line *rm* is not the steepest of these lines. The steepest line is the tangent drawn from *r* to the value-productivity curve; and its point of tangency, *t*, must therefore represent the producer's most profitable policy. It appears from the diagram that this consists in investing $100, aging wine for 3 years, and selling it at a price of $60, with a gross profit of $33. Indeed, this profit represents a 33 per cent return on the $100 invested, a higher yield than the 30 per cent we got before.

That this is the best policy for the producer to adopt is also shown by the following numerical example, still based on Table I. If he has a capital of, say, $800, he will do best by setting up a firm that sells 8 barrels of 3-year-old wine per annum and makes a $33 profit on the barrel—a total profit of (8 × $33 =) $264. If, instead, he decided to sell 4-year-old wine, the same $800 capital investment would enable him to make an annual turnover of only 5 barrels; and although, in this way, he would make a profit of $48 per barrel, his total profit would

H

only be (5 × $48 =) $240. The interest payable on the $800 capital must be deducted, of course, to show the producer's net gain; but since this is the same whatever the way in which the $800 are invested, the aging of wine for 3 years remains the producer's most profitable policy.

The rate of profit per capital invested that the producer's most profitable policy yields has a special name in economic literature; it is called the marginal efficiency of investment.[6] In our example the marginal efficiency of investment in wine production is 33 per cent; and it is represented in Figure 49 by the slope of the tangent *rt*.

There are two significant points to note about the above result. The first is that the rate of interest has very little influence on the producer's investment policy. Whether or not he will produce wine at all depends on whether the rate of interest is lower or higher than 33 per cent, the marginal efficiency of investment in wine production in our example. But once the producer has decided to go into the wine-producing business, he will combine capital funds with grapes in the same proportion, age his wine for 3 years, and make a 33 per cent return on his capital *no matter what the rate of interest is.* This result follows from the fact that the slope and point of tangency of the tangent *rt* are independent of the market rate of interest and depend only on the shape of the value-productivity curve.

The second point, which is closely related to the first, is that the producer does not equate his marginal valuation of capital funds to the interest rate, although he pushes his demand for every other factor of production to the point where its marginal value to him equals its price.

These differences between capital funds on the one hand and all other factors of production on the other hand are due to the special function which capital funds fulfill in limiting the size of the firm. When, in Chapter VII, we discussed the way in which the firm combines its factors of production, we sought the cheapest way of producing *a given output.* When, later in the same chapter, we discussed the producer's demand for and marginal valuation of one factor, *we assumed the quantity of some other factor as given.* In short, when we discussed the producer's behavior with respect to any factor or factors other than

---

[6] It is also sometimes called the marginal efficiency of capital, or the rate of return over cost, or simply the rate of profit. We use the term "marginal efficiency of investment" because it is the one most often used; but the reader is well advised to bear in mind that this term is slightly confusing because, from the individual firm's point of view, at least, there is nothing "marginal" about it. This will become more apparent as we go along.

As here defined, the marginal efficiency of investment takes no account of the fact that expected returns on investment must be discounted for risk and uncertainty.

capital funds, we always assumed the size of his firm to be fixed; in other words, we always assumed that the scale of the producer's enterprise is limited by something else than the availability of the factor under discussion. This assumption necessarily set a limit to the amount of the factor which the firm could usefully employ and caused the producer's marginal valuation of the factor to diminish with its increased utilization. For on this assumption the increased utilization of a factor always meant an increase in its utilization *relative to the utilization of some other factor or factors;* and the combination of increased quantities of one factor with fixed quantities of other factors is bound to diminish its usefulness sooner or later.

In contrast, when we deal with the producer's use of capital funds, we must make exactly the opposite assumption. For we argued at the beginning of this chapter that the availability of capital funds is *the limit* that determines the size of the firm. Hence, when the producer decides on his investment policy, he knows that his capital funds are limited; but he *cannot* assume as given either the quantity of any other factor or his rate of output, since these are the very things that his investment policy must determine. In terms of our example, when the wine producer makes his investment decision, he knows in advance what capital funds he is able and willing to invest; and he determines how much wine to process and how long to age it when he decides on the policy that maximizes the return on his investment.

Let us now return to the two peculiarities of the producer's investment decision that we pointed out a little while ago. To deal with the second first, it should now be obvious why the producer fails to equate his marginal valuation of capital funds to the rate of interest. For the producer's investment decision determines *how* he invests his capital funds and not *how much* he invests. The scale of his investment is determined by the availability of funds and the producer's willingness to borrow— considerations we discussed in detail in section 2, above. If the increased use of capital funds would lower their marginal value to the producer, this would limit the size of his firm and his demand for funds; and there would be no need for the special limitations to the availability of capital discussed above. But it is now apparent that the increased utilization of capital funds cannot lower their marginal value to the firm. A producer whose enterprise yields an annual net profit which represents a return of *x* per cent on his invested capital can always earn the same *x* per cent return also on additional capital funds invested, by a simple expansion of his scale of operations, that is, by retaining his method of production, duplicating his productive facilities, and increasing his utilization of all his factors of production in the same proportion. This follows from the assumption of proportional returns. The assumption of proportional returns implies, therefore, that the return on capital funds cannot decline with their increased utilization. In terms of our example, if the wine producer had a capital not of $800 but of $8,000, he would age 80 instead of 8 barrels of wine for 3 years and still make the same 33 per cent profit on his investment.

It must be added here that the assumption of proportional returns does *not* exclude the possibility that the return on capital funds might *rise* with their increased utilization. For an expansion of the firm and its scale of operations may yield economies of scale and result in an increase in output more than proportional to the increase in costs. This was not illustrated in our example; but its possibility in the general case must be borne in mind.

We next come to the puzzling problem of why the rate of interest has no influence on the length of time for which the producer ages his wine. To answer this question, we must look at the wine producer's behavior in a different light from that in which we have looked at it so far. Until now, we have thought of wine as being produced with the aid of two factors of production: grape juice and capital funds, the latter being needed to enable the producer to maintain an adequate stock of wine in the process of aging. But we might also have said that to produce n-year-old wine requires a capital fund, an annual input of grape juice, *and* an initial investment in a number of other productive factors, namely, in wines one year through $n - 1$ years old. In fact, this way of looking at the wine producer's behavior makes his case look much less exceptional and much more like that of any other producer—quite apart from the fact that it is also more in keeping with our analysis of previous sections. Wines in the process of aging are, from the wine-grower's point of view, intermediate products or produced factors; and his initial investment in these wines is not significantly different from, say, the steel producer's initial investment in his plant and equipment. In other words, the wine producer's decision how long to age his wine can also be regarded as his decision in what proportions to combine such factors of production as grape juice and wines of different ages.

This problem, however, has already been discussed in general terms in section 1 of Chapter VII. We showed there, with the aid of isoquants and price lines, that the most profitable combination of the factors of production is determined by the firm's production function and the relative prices of the factors. It appears, therefore, that there is nothing surprising about the result that the wine producer's most profitable method of production depends solely on the shape of his value-productivity curve, which in turn depends on the prices of grape juice and wines of different ages. In fact, this result, while reached in an entirely different way, is identical with and confirms the result we arrived at in Chapter VII, although here we have paid special attention to the time-consuming nature of production, which was neglected in Chapter VII.

Having found that the wine producer's problem is not as exceptional as it looked at first sight, we may now proceed to draw what general conclusions we can from our analysis of his behavior. We saw at the beginning of this chapter that the one factor whose quantity is limited to the firm is its fund of capital. Accordingly, we can assume that the producer's capital fund is fixed and given. His investment decision, therefore, is concerned with only one problem: how best to invest a given capital fund. On the solution of this problem the rate of interest has only a very limited bearing: it keeps the producer from entering any industry in which the marginal efficiency of investment (i.e., the highest attainable rate of profit) is lower than the interest payable on his capital funds. But once the producer has settled on an industry in which the marginal efficiency of investment exceeds the rate of interest, the latter has no further influence on his investment decision. After this initial decision has been made, the producer's choice how to invest his capital and what method of production to adopt is guided, first of all, by the considerations discussed in the first section of Chapter VII. To express these in the geometrical terms of the isoquant map of Figure 32 (p. 123), he will choose a method of production represented by a point on the expansion path and determined by the shape of his production function and the prices of the productive factors he employs. Each point on the expansion path represents a different combination of factors, whose employment requires a different capital fund and yields a different level of output. The producer's choice from among these alternatives is determined by the size of his capital fund, which therefore can be said to determine his scale of operations.

The reader may still find it surprising that the rate of interest should have no influence on the producer's investment policy. For some methods of production require little equipment and a small investment, others require much machinery and hence a large investment per unit of output; and one might think that the choice between these alternatives would be influenced by the terms on which the producer obtains his capital funds. This line of reasoning would be correct if the producer aimed at producing *a given output* in the cheapest way and his choice lay between different ways of producing a given output.[7] We saw, however, that this is not his aim. As a rule, the producer aims at investing *a given capital fund* in the most profitable way; and his alternatives may be to produce either a larger output with simple equipment or a smaller output with the aid of more elaborate equipment. When the producer's alternatives are formulated in this way, it immediately becomes obvious why his choice between them is unaffected by the rate of interest. The method of production chosen by the producer would be independent also of the amount of funds available to him, were it not for the fact that in some industries the cheapest methods of production are mass-production methods, which become feasible only when the scale of the producer's enterprise is large.

5. THE ALLOCATION OF CAPITAL

Having discussed the individual producer's investment policy, we are now prepared to analyze the allocation of capital funds among different firms and different industries. The allocation of factors other than capital funds was discussed in Chapter VIII. We showed there that the allocation of a given factor is efficient if its marginal value is the same in all firms, provided that these firms are perfect competitors in the markets where they sell their products.[8] The same argument applies also to capital funds. It can be shown that the allocation of capital funds among different firms is efficient if the marginal efficiency of investment is the same in all firms, provided that these firms are perfect competitors in the markets where they sell their products.[9] The question is whether there is a tendency for capital funds to be so allocated.

We saw in the last section that the individual firm does not equate the marginal efficiency of its investment to the market rate of interest as it equates the marginal value of its other factors to their market prices. Nevertheless, the marginal efficiency of investment tends to equal the rate of interest in markets to which the entry of newcomers is free and

---

[7] Our first approach to the wine producer's problem was based on this assumption; but we subsequently discarded this assumption as incorrect.

[8] See pp. 153–54. The argument concerned the efficient allocation of a factor within one industry only; but it is easy to see that it also applies more generally to the efficient allocation of a factor among all firms and industries.

[9] The reader must accept this statement on trust, because it is beyond the scope of this book to prove it. For proof the reader is referred to the articles on capital theory listed in the Bibliographical Note at the end of this chapter.

unrestrained. That this is so has already been shown on page 202; but it will be worth our while to repeat the argument here. We saw that the size or rate of growth of each individual firm is circumscribed by limitations on its ability and willingness to borrow; but nothing limits the *number* of producers who can, within these limits, expand existing capacity or found new firms and thus create new capacity. There is an inducement for established producers to expand and for newcomers to establish themselves as long as profit per capital invested (the marginal efficiency of investment) exceeds the rate of interest. The resulting expansion of productive capacity tends, in its turn, to lower the prices of products and to raise the prices of factors, thereby lowering the rate of profit and making it more nearly equal to the rate of interest. If entry were free to all markets, the rate of profit in every market would tend to equal the rate of interest and hence also the rate of profit in all other markets. In the long run, therefore, capital funds would tend to be efficiently allocated among different industries in the perfectly competitive economy.

There remains the question as to what is meant by an efficient allocation of capital funds and what is accomplished by it. We saw at the beginning of this chapter that the producer needs a capital fund to obtain the services of any and all productive resources—those of his plant and equipment as well as those of his labor force. Accordingly, the allocation of capital funds among firms and industries determines the allocation of *all* productive services, that is, of productive capacity in general. It appears, therefore, that equal rates of profit in different firms and industries are just an additional condition (additional to the conditions discussed in Chap. VIII) of the efficient allocation of labor, materials, equipment, and all the other productive resources. When we discussed the efficiency of resource allocation in Chapter VIII, it was not apparent that such an additional condition would also have to be fulfilled; but this is explained by our having abstracted, at that stage, from the time-consuming nature of production and from the producer's need for capital funds.

This completes our discussion of that part of capital theory which is relevant to the main subject matter of this book. Less important from our point of view is the next section, which deals with the "real" interpretation of capital and contains a further discussion of the capitalist's share in income. This discussion will throw light on the nature of the sacrifice for which interest is the reward and show the connection between the real and the monetary explanations of interest. All this, however, is not essential for an understanding of what follows; and, since it also happens to be the most difficult part of this book, the reader is advised to omit it on first reading and proceed directly to Chapter X (p. 229).

6. THE SCARCITY OF CAPITAL AND ITS REMUNERATION

Until now, we have thought of capital as a sum of money, the total value of his assets, which the entrepreneur needs to operate his firm, and for whose use he pays interest. But a factor that is paid for must be a *scarce* factor of production, since only scarce resources are able to fetch a price in the market. It is impossible, however, to think of money as a scarce factor, since its quantity is, in a sense, more or less arbitrarily determined by the monetary authority or by historical accident. Hence the need for a "real" interpretation of the concept of capital.

We saw that, to establish a firm, the entrepreneur needs the services of labor, equipment, and other such factors of production; and he also needs a capital fund with which to hire or buy them. This capital fund is his command over the products of other firms; for the owners of factors want command over products in exchange for their services; and the entrepreneur needs command over the products of other firms to tide him over the initial period during which he has no products of his own to sell. In a real sense, therefore, the firm's capital consists of other firms' products. If we then add together the capital of all the firms in the economy, we obtain society's real capital, which appears as the sum of all products in the productive system.

The above interpretation of capital becomes clearer if we imagine for a moment that the economy consists of one giant firm. The only market transactions of this giant firm would be the sale of final consumers' goods to consumers and the purchase of personal services from employees. In such an economy, materials, parts, machinery, and equipment would all be regarded as goods in process; and all disposition of these goods in process would be matters of the internal administration of the giant firm.

This giant firm, just like any other firm, would have to pay for the services of its employees at the time when they render their services and hence before the time when these services have ripened into final consumers' goods. To tide itself over this period, the firm could pay its employees by issuing claims for consumers' goods against itself; *but it would have to be prepared to honor these claims.* To be so prepared, the firm would have to have in its possession a stock of goods—consumers' goods, as well as goods in process capable of being transformed into consumers' goods as the latter's stock is getting exhausted. This means that the firm's capital fund is determined by the stock of products in its possession. In other words, the firm cannot issue more claims against itself than it can meet with the aid of its stock of products; and the latter may therefore be regarded as the firm's capital in a real sense. But since we assumed this giant firm to comprise the entire productive system, we can say that society's capital consists of the total quantity of products stored up in the productive system in the form of inventories of consumers' goods, plant and equipment of all kinds, goods in the process of manufacture, inventories of parts and raw materials, and so forth.

The presence of all these products in the productive system facilitates or contributes to the production of final output; and they must therefore be regarded as produced factors. This is obvious in the case of plant and equipment; but it also holds true of inventories, since they facilitate the smooth and uninterrupted flow of output. The capital of society, therefore, can also be defined as the totality of all produced factors in existence —bearing in mind that inventories of consumers' goods in the hands of producers, wholesalers, and retailers (i.e., in the hands of anybody but consumers) are also produced factors of production. When an entrepreneur uses capital funds to build new productive capacity or expand existing capacity, he adds to society's real capital by adding to the stock of produced factors in existence. It is true that he uses his capital funds not only to construct plant and buy equipment but also to hire the services of labor; on the other hand, while his actions usually create new plant and equipment, they do not create additional labor and only divert part of the existing labor force from other firms.

It is apparent that the quantity of society's "real" capital is limited and that, therefore, the quantity of capital funds, the monetary counterpart of real capital, must also be limited. But in what sense is capital scarce, and why does its possession yield an income?

To answer this question, let us first of all express the usefulness of capital in terms of its marginal product. This is defined as the addition to the annual output of consumers' goods that would result from a small addition to the total stock of produced factors in the productive system, while the quantities of the original factors, labor and management, are kept constant. Since both capital and the output of consumers' goods are collections of heterogeneous objects, their quantities, and changes in their quantities, can only be expressed in terms of money. Accordingly, the marginal product of capital must be expressed as the ratio of two sums of money, or as a percentage. For example, if adding $100 worth of products to the already existing stock of capital raises the annual output of consumers' goods by $15 worth, the marginal product of capital is 15 per cent.

It is important to realize that the marginal product of capital, as here defined, is not the same as the marginal product of the capital goods in which it is embodied. Imagine, for example, that the above $100 worth of capital assumes the shape of an electric drill whose cost of production is $100 and whose lifetime is 5 years. Then, for the marginal product of the $100 invested in this drill to be $15, the annual marginal product of the drill itself must be worth around $35; for it must exceed $15 by a sum large enough fully to amortize and repay the cost of the drill during its lifetime. In general, the marginal product of capital invested in a particular produced factor is the excess of the annual marginal product of that factor over its annual amortization cost.

The reason why the marginal product of a produced factor exceeds its amortization cost is, of course, its scarcity. We saw in Chapter VI that the less of one factor is used in combination with given quantities of other factors, the higher its marginal product. Hence, if the marginal product of electric drills is high, this is due to their limited supply, which keeps their price high and thus causes producers to employ relatively few electric drills in combination with other factors. If more electric drills became available, their price would fall; and this would encourage their use and thus lower their marginal product—possibly to or even below their amortization cost. This is true of all produced factors. We can say, in general, that if the stock of produced factors increased relatively to the stock of original factors, or if the accumulation of capital (the stock of produced factors) proceeded faster than the rate of growth of the labor force (the original factors), the marginal productivity of capital would fall; and it might ultimately fall to zero or even below zero if capital accumulation proceeded far enough.[10]

This raises the question: What limits the quantity of capital, that is, the stock of produced factors in existence? It is profitable to invest in produced factors whose marginal product is worth more than their amortization cost, but only if this excess is not completely absorbed by the interest payable on the capital funds needed for making such an investment. In the market economy, therefore, the stock of capital is

---

[10] This is true only if the state of technical knowledge is given and fixed. Technical progress may raise the marginal productivity of capital and thus offset, or more than offset, the effect of the accumulation of capital.

limited by the interest payable on capital funds; for this stock to be increased, the market rate of interest must be lower than the marginal productivity of capital.

In "real" terms the limit to the stock of capital is the social sacrifice involved in the possession of capital; and we must now see how and when this is reflected by the market rate of interest. The stock of capital in existence can be augmented by diverting part of the current output from current consumption; and it can be depleted for the sake of temporarily raising current consumption over current output. Accordingly, the sacrifice involved in accumulating capital is that of not consuming the entire current output; and the sacrifice of keeping the existing stock of capital intact is that of not consuming it in addition to consuming the current output. This latter is the sacrifice made by an investor who holds capital already in existence.[11] The *marginal* sacrifice made by the individual investor in holding capital is expressed by that rate of interest which would cause him neither to add to his accumulated savings nor to consume them. This hypothetical interest rate is called his time preference. The rate of interest which would cause an entire community's net saving to be zero is called the community's or society's time preference. This expresses the social marginal sacrifice involved in holding society's accumulated stock of capital. To cause the community to add to its accumulated savings, the market rate of interest must exceed the community's time preference.

We are now ready to answer the question we asked on page 203, whether the market rate of interest reflects both the social cost of providing and the productive advantages of using capital in a way similar to that in which the earnings of labor express, under perfect competition, both the effort involved in performing work and the advantage derived from utilizing it. It is apparent that the answer is negative and that the rate of interest reflects neither the cost of providing capital nor the advantages of using it. For in our progressive economy, where the stock of capital is currently being added to out of current savings, the market rate of interest is higher than society's time preference (the marginal sacrifice of providing capital), since otherwise net saving would not be positive; but, at the same time, it is also lower than the marginal productivity of capital (the marginal advantage of utilizing capital), for otherwise the stock of capital goods would not be added to.

With the continued accumulation of capital, however, the market rate

---

[11] See, however, p. 225.

of interest might, at some future date, become equal both to the community's time preference and to the marginal productivity of capital. This would stop the further accumulation of capital and thus bring about long-run equilibrium; and in this hypothetical future situation the parallelism between capital and labor as factors of production would be complete, in the sense that the rate of remuneration of each would express both its marginal contribution to output and the marginal sacrifice involved. But in this situation, capital, unlike labor, need not have any remuneration at all. For the accumulation of capital can bring down to nothing both the marginal usefulness of capital and the marginal sacrifice which its ownership involves.

We saw that the accumulation of capital, if it proceeds faster than the rate of increase of the labor force, lowers the marginal productivity of capital. But capital accumulation is likely to lower the community's time preference, too. The more capital is combined with a given labor force, the larger is output; and the larger the output, the less anxious is the community to supplement its consumption of current output by drawing on its accumulated savings. Hence, as capital accumulates and output increases, the community's time preference may well fall to zero or even below it. In fact, it is very likely that this is already the case in the United States today. People in this country would not start consuming their accumulated savings if the rate of interest fell to zero. They might not even consume their entire current income and would probably need the inducement of a negative interest rate to do so. This probably remains true even if we take into account, as we must, the fact that a zero or negative rate of interest would bring about a very different income distribution from the one that obtains today.

This suggests that long-run equilibrium may never be reached. Capital may, indeed, become plentiful enough to bring down its marginal productivity to zero. At this stage the marginal product of capital goods (produced factors) would be just sufficient to cover their amortization cost, so that while the capital goods themselves would not become free resources, the capital funds invested in them would, because no addition to the existing stock of capital would be able to increase society's net output. At this stage, therefore, the capitalist's remuneration would be nil. But this in itself need not discourage the further accumulation of savings. For people might refrain from consuming all their income and want to add to their accumulated savings even if the rate of interest were zero. This would raise problems that belong in the realm of monetary and employment theory and with which we shall not be concerned here. On the solution of these problems would depend whether long-run equilibrium, in the above-defined sense, would ever be reached.

But let us return to the problems of a progressive economy like ours. As stated above, the marginal productivity of capital exceeds society's time preference in such an economy; and the market rate of interest is somewhere between the two. In other words, the capitalist's rate of remuneration in such an economy is lower than the marginal usefulness of his services but higher than the marginal sacrifice involved in rendering them. The question is: Where exactly does the interest rate lie between these two limits, and how is it determined?

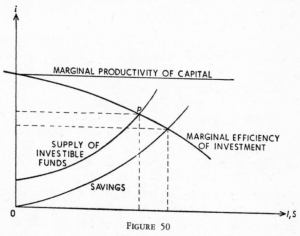

FIGURE 50

In trying to answer this question, it is natural to think of the interest rate as the price that equates the current demand for and the current supply of *additional* capital funds. We stated above that when the interest rate is below the marginal productivity of capital, entrepreneurs demand additional capital funds to build new productive capacity; and that when the interest rate is above society's time preference, a supply of net savings is forthcoming. It can further be shown that both the demand for additional capital funds and the supply of net savings rise, one with the gap between the marginal productivity of capital and the interest rate, the other with the gap between the interest rate and time preference. Hence, there must be some interest rate which equates the demand for additional capital funds to the supply of net savings.

This argument is illustrated in the diagram of Figure 50, in which percentages are measured along the vertical axis and the value of net investment and saving along the horizontal axis. We assume that the quantity of capital goods already in existence has rendered their marginal product such as to bring the marginal productivity of capital to the level shown by the horizontal straight line in the diagram, and that total output is such as to have brought society's time preference to zero —the level shown by the horizontal axis. We further assume that the current accumulation of capital is so small relative to the stock already in existence that it has no noticeable effect either on time preference or on the marginal product of capital goods.

Nevertheless, the rate of capital accumulation does affect the profitability of investment. The latter depends, it will be recalled, on the difference between the value of the marginal product of capital goods and their amortization cost. We just assumed that their marginal product is not affected by the current accumulation of capital goods; but their amortization cost is. Amortization cost depends on the cost of production; and the cost of production of capital goods depends on the rate of output of the industries producing capital goods. If firms in these industries have rising (short-run) marginal-cost curves, the cost of production of capital goods, and hence also their amortization cost, will rise with the rate at which capital goods are being produced. From this, it follows that the profitability of investment *falls* as the rate of investment rises.

It appears, therefore, that the profitability of investment depends on two factors. It depends, first of all, on the stock of capital in existence, since this determines the marginal product of capital goods; and it also depends on the rate at which the existing stock of capital is being added to, since this determines the amortization cost of capital goods. When we defined the marginal product of capital on page 217, we ignored the second factor, because the purpose of the marginal-product concept is to express and measure the importance of the first factor only. For marginal product is a static concept. It shows the difference between the total product of two alternative situations which differ from each other in the quantity of one of the factors used. The marginal-product concept, therefore, is used only in static analysis, where we are interested in comparing the relative merits of alternative situations. The so-called "dynamic" problems raised by the *transition* (or speed of transition) from one situation to another are of an entirely different nature; and experience has shown that, in the interests of clear thinking, it is essential to keep static and dynamic problems and analyses strictly apart.[12] Sometimes, it is even useful to have different names for what is essentially the same concept, depending on whether this is used in a static or dynamic framework.

Thus, we have two names for the usefulness and profitability of capital. Marginal product or marginal productivity of capital is the term used in static analysis, where we compare alternative situations with different quantities of capital and abstract from the problems raised by current investment, which effects the transition from one situation to the other. Accordingly, when we estimate the marginal product of capital, we must be careful to base this estimate not on the actual cost of production of capital goods but on what their cost of production would be if net investment were zero, that is, if the output of capital-goods industries were just sufficient to replace worn-out capital goods and maintain the existing stock unchanged. In other words, the marginal productivity of capital is a hypothetical figure and shows what the profitability of capital would be if net investment were zero.

The term used in dynamic analysis is marginal efficiency of investment. This expresses the actual profitability of capital; and, being based on the actual cost of producing capital goods, it varies with the rate of investment. The reader should have no difficulty in seeing that this is the same as the marginal efficiency of investment defined on page 210. In Figure 50 the marginal efficiency of investment is shown for each level of investment by the downward-sloping curve. This curve crosses the line that shows the marginal productivity of capital on the vertical axis, illustrating the fact that for zero net investment marginal productivity of capital and marginal efficiency of investment coincide.

We next come to the sacrifice that saving involves. This was already discussed and shown to consist in abstention from consuming the entire current net output. We also saw that the marginal sacrifice of providing existing savings can be expressed by the rate of interest that would render society's net saving zero. In exactly the same way, we can also express the marginal sacrifice involved in accumulating savings at any given rate by that rate of interest which would bring about that rate of savings.

The question arises, however, whether net saving would rise or fall with the rate of interest. We have no statistical evidence on this subject;

[12] For a more detailed discussion of the distinction between static and dynamic analysis, see sec. 1 of Chap. X and sec. 2 of Chap. XII.

but it is often taken for granted that savings rise with the rate of interest, on the argument that saving involves a sacrifice and that people are willing to make a greater sacrifice if the reward for it is greater. This argument, however, has several flaws. First of all, to save is not a sacrifice for everybody. Second, even people for whom saving is a sacrifice need not necessarily be induced to save more by a higher rate of interest. After all, work involves a sacrifice, too; and yet we saw in Chapter V that a higher wage rate may well cause people to work less. In fact, there is some reason to believe that most people's savings are either unaffected by the rate of interest or vary inversely with it.

To show that this is so, we shall distinguish between three sources of savings: (1) the small saver, (2) the large saver, and (3) the corporation.

1. The small saver saves in order to accumulate a fund out of which to provide for his old age, for his children, or for some emergency; and to accumulate a given fund, he must save the more the *lower* the rate of interest.

2. The large saver is a person whose accumulated savings are usually more than sufficient to provide for all emergencies; and he saves largely because his income happens to exceed his accustomed level of expenditure. It is very doubtful if he would change his consumption habits, and hence his rate of saving, in response to a change in interest rates.

3. Corporate savings are what is left of profits after dividends have been distributed. They would vary with the rate of interest only if dividends did. Dividend payments, however, are usually independent of the rate of interest. Corporate savings, therefore, are also usually independent of the rate of interest.

It appears, therefore, that the savings of none of these groups rise with the rate of interest.

The above conclusions notwithstanding, society's savings may still rise with the rate of interest. For an important, if not the most important, determinant of saving is the distribution of income. We know from statistical studies that the higher the income group a person belongs to, the greater percentage of his income he will save. This means that savings rise with the inequality of income distribution. The inequality of income distribution, in turn, is the greater the larger the capitalist's share, which in its turn depends on the rate of interest. It appears, therefore, that the rate of interest influences savings through its effect on income distribution; and, as far as this factor is concerned, a higher rate of interest leads to a higher rate of saving.

On the tentative assumption that this factor is more important than the tendency of small savings to fall when the rate of interest rises, let us draw the savings curve in Figure 50 with an upward slope. It makes little difference to the following argument whether this assumption is right or wrong. The point of intersection between this curve and the marginal-efficiency-of-investment curve shows the interest rate which would equate current savings to current investment in a fully employed economy; and it also shows what the level of savings and investment would be under these circumstances.

This point may be regarded, therefore, as the point of short-run, full-employment equilibrium. At this point the capitalist's rate of remuneration would equal not the marginal sacrifice of holding capital (time preference) but the marginal sacrifice involved in adding to the stock of capital. In other words, the capitalist's current income would be equal on the margin not to his current sacrifice of not consuming his accumulated savings but to the initial and once-and-for-all sacrifice involved in the initial act of saving.

In our society, however, the rate of interest is *not* determined by the point of intersection of the marginal-efficiency and savings curves. For, while the marginal-efficiency curve shows the demand of producers for investible funds, the savings curve does *not* show the supply of investible funds. The savings curve shows what full-employment savings would be at different rates of interest but not what part of these savings would be offered to producers for investment. To express the same point differently, the savings curve shows only the marginal sacrifice involved in adding to the accumulated stock of savings; whereas to make these additional savings available for investment would also involve the additional sacrifice of uncertainty and illiquidity, which was discussed on pages 198–99. The supply curve of investible funds, therefore, always lies above the savings curve and cuts the marginal-efficiency curve at a point that is always above (and usually to the left of) the latter's point of intersection with the savings curve. This is shown in Figure 50.[12A]*

What is the significance of this result? It appears, first of all, that the rate of interest, the capitalist's rate of remuneration, equals the sum of the marginal sacrifice of acquiring his funds *and* the marginal sacrifice of lending and investing them.[13] Of these two, only the first represents a social cost. The second does not; for while the individual investor sacrifices safety and liquidity when he invests his funds (and therefore feels that he deserves a reward for making this sacrifice), society as a

——————— *see page 228

[13] This statement is in seeming conflict with that made in the first paragraph of p. 219. For a detailed discussion and reconciliation of this apparent conflict, see my "Capital Accumulation, Employment and Price Rigidity," *Review of Economic Studies*, Vol. VIII (February, 1941), pp. 69–88.

whole makes no such sacrifice, because it has no choice between the productivity of investment and the safety of the cashbox.

From society's point of view, there is no way of holding capital in a safe and liquid form. Capital can only be held in real terms, in the form of products (produced factors); and it can only be added to by investment, that is, by adding to the stock of products in existence. But wealth held in the form of products is never safe and never liquid. Yet there is no other choice, because savings not invested are irretrievably lost to society. A person who saves can add his savings to society's total savings only by investing them. If he keeps his savings in cash, he merely causes other people's savings to fall by the same amount (through causing their incomes to fall by an even greater amount). This effect of one person's decision to hoard on other people's incomes and savings corresponds exactly to the effect that one person's decision to turn on his radio has on his neighbors' welfare—a case we discussed at length in the Note to Chapter VIII. Just as in that case we found the social marginal value of radios to be lower than their private marginal value, so also here we can say that the social advantage of liquidity is lower than its private advantage. As a matter of fact, here we can say a little more than we were able to say in the Note to Chapter VIII; for we know that the social advantage of liquidity is nil. This implies that the social cost of parting with liquidity is also nil.

As in all cases in which a discrepancy occurs between social and private marginal value or marginal cost, so here, too, the difference between the social and the private marginal cost of providing capital funds for investment interferes, or would interfere, with the efficiency of even the perfectly competitive economy and calls for corrective action. The nature of this inefficiency is, of course, the underemployment of scarce resources. That this will exist in the absence of corrective action can be seen from Figure 50. For the point of intersection, p, determines a rate of interest at which full-employment savings always exceed the amount of profitable investment, at least as long as the savings curve and the supply-of-investible-funds curve do not coincide. This problem, however, is the subject matter of monetary and employment theory and lies beyond the scope of this book.

BIBLIOGRAPHICAL NOTE

For a detailed discussion of the argument, in section 1, that the size of the firm is limited by entrepreneurship, see N. Kaldor, "The Equilibrium of the Firm," *Economic Journal*, Vol. XLIV (1934), pp. 60–76. In this connection, see also G. F. Shove,

"Increasing Returns and the Representative Firm," *Economic Journal*, Vol. XL (March, 1930), pp. 94–116.

For the discussion, in section 2, of capital and risk as the limiting factors, see M. W. Reder, "A Reconsideration of the Marginal Productivity Theory," *Journal of Political Economy*, Vol. LV (October, 1947), pp. 450–58; W. W. Cooper, "Theory of the Firm: Some Suggestions for Revision," *American Economic Review*, Vol. XXXIX (December, 1949), pp. 1204–22; and, perhaps most important, M. Kalecki, "The Principle of Increasing Risk," *Economica*, N.S., Vol. IV (1937), pp. 440–47, also contained in his *Essays in the Theory of Economic Fluctuations* (London: George Allen and Unwin, Ltd., 1939).

On the investment policy of the firm and other aspects of capital theory the best article is N. Kaldor's "Annual Survey of Economic Theory: The Recent Controversy on the Theory of Capital," *Econometrica*, Vol. V (1937), pp. 201–33. This was the main source and inspiration of sections 4–6 of this chapter. See also Knut Wicksell, *Lectures on Political Economy* (London: George Routledge & Sons, 1934), Vol. I, Part II, chap. ii, as well as the extensive bibliography given in Kaldor's article. A very simple and helpful (though not always entirely clear) presentation of the firm's investment policy is contained in K. E. Boulding, *Economic Analysis* (rev. ed.; New York: Harper & Bros., 1948), chaps. xxxv–xxxvii.

On section 6, see especially A. P. Lerner, *The Economics of Control* (New York: Macmillan Co., 1944), chap. xxv; and T. de Scitovszky, "A Study of Interest and Capital," *Economica*, N.S., Vol. VII (1940), pp. 293–317.

NOTE TO CHAPTER IX: LAND

This short Note aims not at dealing with the factor of production, *land*, but at explaining why we are not dealing with it. The analysis of land as a factor of production served, in the nineteenth century, the important historical function of leading to the development of the modern theories of income distribution and marginal productivity. Today, however, to regard land as a factor of production separate from and additional to personal services and capital would merely complicate the already complex and difficult theories of perfect competition and of income distribution under perfect competition, without adding anything to our understanding of the economy. Furthermore, there is no logical reason for treating land as a separate factor because, from the economist's point of view, it is similar in all essentials to produced factors. This is why we propose to regard land as a capital good.

Land, in the sense of mines, quarries, or oil fields, has a limited lifetime, just like a house or a piece of machinery; and even agricultural land is not an inexhaustible resource but needs maintenance and replacement of its minerals. As to the initial cost of production which we customarily associate with produced factors, we can, if we wish, regard the cost of opening up a mine or clearing a field for cultivation as its initial "construction" cost, although we must allow, as a limiting case, for the existence of some land whose initial cost of construction was zero. From the point of view of an individual firm or person, all land has to be bought; and its purchase price may be regarded as its initial cost. As to society's point of view, we usually assume the existence of a large stock of capital goods inherited from the past; and none of our arguments or results hinges on whether all these capital goods were produced at some distant past date or whether some of them have existed from time immemorial. From every point of view, therefore, land may be regarded as a capital good and the rent of land as similar in every respect to the gross earnings of a produced factor.

Note on page 225, line 29.

12A Mrs. Joan Robinson has since pointed out to me that in an inflationary situation part of the supply of investible funds curve could lie below and to the right of the savings curve.

CHAPTER X

THE STABILITY OF PERFECT COMPETITION

WE HAVE discussed in the foregoing chapters both the perfectly competitive behavior of the individual person and firm and the consequences for the economy as a whole of all its members being in a perfectly competitive position. This discussion, it will be recalled, was not meant to be a realistic description of any past or present economy but served merely to define the meaning and state the conditions of efficiency in economics. For we came to the conclusion that perfect competition on both sides of every market would lead to an efficient organization of all aspects of economic life, and that perfect competition can therefore be used as a standard of perfection by which to appraise the efficiency or inefficiency of real economic systems. But although this is the only purpose to which we shall put the theory of perfect competition, it will nevertheless be useful to ask ourselves the question: Would perfect competition, if somehow enforced or brought about, not only bring about but also *maintain* perfect efficiency?

There are two reasons why it is useful to ask and try to answer this question. First of all, while the problem of whether the perfect efficiency of the perfectly competitive economy would persist over time is not a practical problem, its discussion forms a very convenient and simple introduction to the subject of dynamic economics. Second, while no economy is or has ever been perfectly competitive, some markets in our economy *are* perfectly competitive. Let us recall from section 3 of Chapter II that the necessary conditions of perfect competition are large numbers and expertness on both the buyers' and the sellers' side; and, while these conditions have never been fulfilled for a whole economy, they have been and are fulfilled at least in a few markets. These few markets, then, are practical instances of pure competition; and in their case the problem of whether the perfect efficiency of pure competition would persist is of practical relevance.

1. THE SUBJECT MATTER OF DYNAMIC ECONOMICS

In view of the fact that the perfectly competitive economy is not and never has been a reality, we cannot test in the light of empirical evidence the theoretical conclusions of preceding chapters in their entirety. But since those few markets in which expert dealers trade in staple foods and raw materials are perfectly competitive, the question naturally arises whether the experience of these markets bears out those of our conclusions that apply to them.

It is true, of course, that most of our statements concerning the efficiency of perfect competition refer to an economy whose every market is perfect. But some forms of efficiency (e.g., the technological efficiency of an industry) were shown to be brought about even if perfect competition is confined to isolated markets. Is there empirical evidence that perfect competition in the markets for staple foods and materials causes their production to be more efficient than the manufacture of other products? The complaints of farmers about the extreme variability of the prices of staple agricultural products and the hardships that this imposes upon them suggest the contrary. Indeed, the belief is widely held that the farmer should be protected from the vagaries of the highly competitive markets for his produce; in fact, co-operative or governmental controls and regulations have been imposed in many countries on agricultural production and marketing, with the full approval of public opinion. How can this situation be reconciled with our theory of perfect competition?

Before we attempt to answer this question, we must first draw attention to the fact that so far, in all our discussion of perfectly competitive behavior and its consequences, we have hardly made any mention of *changes* in price. We have concentrated on the behavior of the price taker who faces a *given* price, and on the economic situation that would come about if every member of every market were a price taker, and if every price were such as to equate demand and supply in every market. In other words, until now, or at least up to and including Chapter VIII, we have been concerned with the static or equilibrium theory of perfect competition.

The word "equilibrium" means a state of rest. A person is in equilibrium when he regards his actual behavior as the best possible under the circumstances and feels no urge to change his behavior as long as circumstances remain unchanged. The same is true of the equilibrium of a firm. A market, or an economy, or any other group of persons and firms is in equilibrium when none of its members feels impelled to change his behavior. For a group to be in equilibrium, therefore, all its members must be in equilibrium; and the equilibrium behavior of each member must be compatible with the equilibrium behavior of all the other members.

This last assumption was never stated explicitly; but it was implied in our discussion of the perfectly competitive market, in which both the buyers and the sellers are price takers. For price takers are people who can transact all the business they want to at the market price; and this means that for all the buyers and all the sellers in the market to be price takers at the same time, the quantities that the buyers want to buy must add up exactly to the sum of the quantities that the sellers want to sell. If this condition is to be fulfilled, the market price must be such as to equate supply and demand. Hence, when we discussed the nature of economic organization on the assumption that everybody is a price taker, we implied also the further assumption that prices in every market equate supply and demand and thus render mutually compatible the equilibrium behavior of all the members of the economy. A theory based on this latter assumption is called a static or equilibrium theory. It is called an equilibrium theory because it shows what economic organization would be like *at the point of equilibrium;* and it is called static because an equilibrium situation remains unchanged if extraneous changes do not disturb it. What happens when a market or the economic system is in disequilibrium is an entirely different problem—and one that we have not yet touched upon. This is the problem of the dynamic theory of economics.

A group of persons and firms is in disequilibrium when some of its members are in disequilibrium and feel impelled to change their behavior. A disequilibrium situation, therefore, is one in which forces are present that tend to change the existing situation. Those members of the group who are in disequilibrium will undoubtedly move toward their equilibrium positions—or what seem to them their equilibrium positions in the light of the circumstances that obtain at the time when they decide to change their behavior. But, by changing their behavior, they change the circumstances faced by other members of the group, who may thus be thrown out of equilibrium and impelled to change their behavior, too. This, in turn, will change the circumstances faced by the people who first changed their behavior and may throw them out of the equilibrium they just reached. It may even happen that, in the light of these changed circumstances, they may find themselves still farther removed from equilibrium than they were in their initial position. But whether they are nearer or farther from equilibrium, they are likely, in a second attempt to reach equilibrium, to make further adjustments in their market behavior. This changes for a second time the circumstances faced by other members of the group and may impel them, too, to readjust their behavior. This chain of adjustments and readjustments may continue for a long time; and it may either bring the group progressively nearer equilibrium or make it shoot past its equilibrium position.

It appears, therefore, that the dynamic theory of economics has a number of tasks to fulfill. First of all, it must trace the path over time that the behavior of a group describes. Second, it must state the conditions under which this path approaches equilibrium and the conditions under which it does not. Third, when the behavior of a group approaches equilibrium, it must analyze the speed with which equilibrium is being approached. If a market or other group tends toward equilibrium and does so at a reasonably high speed, it is said to be dynamically efficient.

The first step toward accomplishing these tasks of dynamic theory is to analyze the behavior over time of a single person or firm. This is a relatively simple matter, because the individual person and firm always move toward equilibrium—that is, toward the position they consider most satisfactory from their own point of view. The only problem that this raises concerns the timing of change in the individual's behavior. The timing of the consumer's behavior was discussed in the last section of Chapter III; and the timing of the individual firm's behavior will be discussed in Chapter XII.

More interesting but also more difficult are the problems raised by the behavior over time of a *group* of persons and firms. To analyze these problems, it is necessary to trace the impact of each person's and firm's actions on all other members of the group. The simple analytical tools used in this book are inadequate for this purpose when the group considered is large and comprises the whole economy. They are inadequate to deal with even the much simpler problems raised by the behavior of a small group, like a market or an industry, except in especially simple cases. In the following, therefore, we shall confine ourselves to a discussion of the single market in such simple cases.

But, in discussing the behavior of a single market over time, one cannot neglect the impact of this market's behavior on all other markets just for simplicity's sake and without good cause. For this impact may, in certain cases, be important enough to vitiate or even reverse results arrived at by neglecting it. The standard and best-known example of such a case concerns the effect of a decision on the part of labor to accept a lower wage. By looking at the labor market in isolation, one would conclude that this will raise employment; but one may reach the opposite conclusion if one also takes into account the impact of this decision on product markets and the repercussions on the labor market of the resulting changes in product markets. A further and similar example will be given in footnote 1 on page 235.

The lesson to be drawn from such examples is that, in general, one cannot safely confine one's analysis to the behavior of a single market in isolation. One must always ascertain, first, whether to do so is justified; and it is justified only if the impact on other markets and the repercussions of this impact on the market under consideration are small enough to be negligible. It appears, therefore, that we must be doubly careful in our selection of the dynamic problems to be discussed here. Keeping these warnings in mind, let us now proceed to the analysis of a particular case.

2. STABILITY AND DYNAMIC EFFICIENCY

We saw in preceding chapters that in equilibrium, market prices reflect both the relative urgency of the buyers' demand and the relative cost of the sellers' supply. This fact renders prices a valuable source of information concerning the availability of supplies and the urgency of demands. In a market economy like ours, both buyers and sellers use this information as their main and sometimes only guide in their economic behavior; and we have seen that, at least under perfectly competitive conditions, the independent actions of every person and every firm, based on and co-ordinated by nothing more than a common knowledge of market prices, leads to an efficient organization of economic activity.

This conclusion of the theory of perfect competition is the basis of the belief in the economic advantages of free enterprise and the market economy. To achieve economic and technological efficiency by central economic planning seems, in a modern economy, a task of enormous complexity. By contrast, the market mechanism appears as a simple and efficient means of achieving the same aim. In the market economy, what would be the central plan is broken down into the small and separate production plans of individual firms; and the pricing system is relied upon to co-ordinate these plans automatically. For the pricing system to fulfill this function, however, prices must reflect faithfully the urgency of demands and the availability of supplies; and they must respond promptly and accurately to changes in demand and supply conditions. Let us therefore investigate to what extent they do this.

When a producer decides what products to produce and in what quantities and with what combination of factors to produce them, he is laying plans for the future. In order that his plans may maximize his profit and contribute to the efficient working of the economic system, they must fulfill the marginal conditions of maximum profit and maximum efficiency *at the time when they are being carried out*. In other words, he must plan to equate his marginal valuation of factors to what their market prices will be at the time when he buys them; and he must equate the marginal cost of his products to what their market prices will be when he sells them. Considering that production takes time and that plans must be made ahead of their execution, the producer, who cannot see into the future, will seldom be able to fulfill these conditions exactly. We must conclude, therefore, that a perfectly competitive economy would seldom be completely efficient. To some extent, this is unavoidable and due to man's inability to forecast future events. But, to some extent, it may also be due to the peculiarities of an economic system; and we must now try to answer the question as to whether the producer would have similar difficulties in predicting future conditions and planning his future actions in an economy that is not perfectly competitive.

Let us consider a perfectly competitive market for commodity A, whose price, p, equates supply and demand at a; and assume that this equilibrium situation is disturbed by a shift in consumers' demand from other goods to A. The resulting increase in the demand for A is represented in Figure 51 by a rightward shift of the demand curve from D to D'. The intersection of the new demand curve with the supply curve represents the new equilibrium position; and the question arises whether —and if so, when and how—this new equilibrium will be reached. To begin with, supply cannot be increased from one day to another; and the immediate effect of the rise in demand will be a rise in price to p_1, since it is only at this price that the existing supply can fill the new demand. If we now assume that a rise in price prompts producers to increase their output, then we can rest assured that the change in demand has set in motion forces that move supply toward equilibrium.

Before we go any further, it will be well to stop here for a moment and examine at least one of the implicit assumptions on which our result is based. Our main assumption, and one that was not stated explicitly, was that a rise in the price of A will prompt producers to increase their output of A. But, to increase its output of a product, the firm must either increase its demand for factors or diminish its output of other products. It will take the first course if the price of the product rises relative to the prices of factors; and it will take the second course if the price of the product rises relative to the prices of the firm's other products. This means that the rise in the price of A will raise its output only if the prices of factors and other products remain the same or at least do not rise in the same proportion in which the price of A has risen. Is this condition likely to be fulfilled?

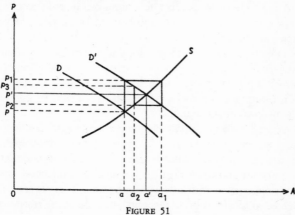

FIGURE 51

It is, if the increase in demand results from a change in tastes, as we postulated. For in such a case the higher price of A is matched by the lower price of another product the demand for which has fallen; and the additional output of A can be produced by lowering the output of the other product and with the aid of the factors released by the lowered output of this other product.[1]

---

[1] This is a good opportunity to cite a case with which our method of analysis cannot deal adequately. Assume for a moment that the increased demand for A results not from a change in tastes but from the desire of some people to consume more of A while keeping unchanged their consumption of all other goods. As before, the increased demand for A would raise its price; and this, in turn, would prompt the producers of A to lower their supply of their other products and raise their demand for factors. But now, with the demand for other products and the supply of factors unchanged, such behavior by the producers of A would raise the prices both of their other products and of the factors they use. In fact, it is conceivable that these prices might rise in the same proportion in which the price of A has risen; in this case the producers of A would have no inducement whatever to raise their output of A. To find out, therefore, whether the output of A responds at all to a rise in the demand for it—and, if so, how it responds—we would have to know how a rise in the price of A affects all other prices. This, however, is a problem for aggregate analysis and one to which our method of approach is inapplicable. (*Cont. p. 236.*)

Having shown that our assumption is likely to be fulfilled, we can now proceed to consider the effects of the increase in output. According to Figure 51, if the price p_1 is expected to persist, it will induce producers to lay plans for increasing their output to such an extent that the sum of the additional quantities of output planned by them will bring the market's total output to a_1. This, however, exceeds the equilibrium output a' and will, if brought about, lower price to p_2, causing producers to change their production plans again and reduce their output. If A is an industrial product, its output can be reduced instantaneously; and equilibrium will be established at a' soon after the unnecessary expansion of output to a_1. In the case of farm products, however, a reduction of output may take as long a time as an expansion; and the price p_2 may persist long enough to lead to a full reduction of output to a_2, which again overshoots the mark, this time in the opposite direction. With output down to a_2, price will rise again, to p_3, which in turn will again stimulate output.

The successive changes in production plans and resultant fluctuations in output are shown in Figure 52, where output is measured on the vertical axis and time on the horizontal axis. The corresponding fluctuations in price are shown in Figure 53, where the horizontal axis again measures time but the vertical axis shows price.[2] This argument is usually referred to as the "cobweb theorem," because of the resemblance of Figure 51 to a cobweb.

What is the cause of these fluctuations, and what are the chances of their coming about? It is apparent that the original price rise from p to p_1 will raise output to a_1 only if price is expected to remain at p_1, and actually remains at p_1, until every producer has completed his plans for increased production. Such price expectations are obviously incorrect and doomed to disappointment; but the market offers no help to enable its members to formulate correct expectations. Under perfect competition, each seller neglects the effect of his own expanded production plans on future price; and the market gives him no information about

---

For a discussion of this very important subject, see O. Lange, *Price Flexibility and Employment* (Bloomington, Ind.: Principia Press, 1944), especially chap. ii–v. The importance of Lange's discussion lies in the fact that it forms a link between partial analysis, such as is presented in this volume, and the aggregate analysis of employment theory.

[2] As drawn in Figs. 51, 52, and 53, the fluctuations diminish in amplitude and converge toward the equilibrium level; but this is due to the fact that the supply curve is drawn with a steeper slope than the demand curve. The amplitude of fluctuations would remain constant if the (positive) slope of the supply curve were equal to the (negative) slope of the demand curve; and they would increase in amplitude if the demand curve were steeper than the supply curve.

the production plans of his competitors. Such information may reach him, of course, through other channels; and this case will be considered at the beginning of the next section. For the time being, however, let us concentrate on the case in which the market is the only channel through which one producer learns about his competitors' actions. In this case the present price is all the information he has; and while

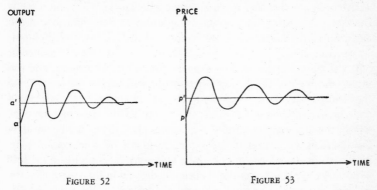

FIGURE 52   FIGURE 53

this tells him something about his competitors' present output as determined by their past production plans, it tells him nothing at all about their future output, *even when this is largely determined already by their present plans.* In this respect, perfect competition compares unfavorably with both monopoly and central planning. A monopolist, who controls most or all of the output of an industry, can estimate and allow for the effect of a planned change in his output on future price and lay his plans accordingly. The same is true of a public official in charge of planning an industry's output in a planned economy. The monopolist or public official may be wrong, of course, in his estimate of the effect of a planned expansion on future price. But he possesses information that competitive producers lack; and his decisions, therefore, are bound to bring output nearer the equilibrium level than the independent decisions of competing producers—assuming that his intelligence and ability are no greater and no less than the competitive producer's. The latter may, indeed, obtain information about his competitors' production plans and their foreseeable effect on future prices from trade journals or government publications; and this possibility will be discussed below. But the market itself gives him less information than is readily available to the monopolist or a planning authority. In the absence of additional information, therefore, the competitive producer cannot know and make allowance for his competitors' production plans and is likely to expect the price p_1 to persist.

However, as a result of frequent disappointments in their expectations, at least some producers may become cautious in forming their expectations and wait longer than others before they decide that the new, higher price has come to stay and is worth making adjustment to. Accordingly, the dates when different sellers make plans and commit themselves to expand output will be spread over time; and so will the dates when these plans come to fruition and result in expanded output. In general, those who first made up their minds to expand production will also be the first to sell an increased output in the market; and the important question now arises whether this will happen before or after the date by which even the most cautious producers have laid plans and committed themselves to expand output. If the span of time over which the different producers' expansion plans have been spread is shorter than the period required for the first seller's expansion plan to ripen into increased output, price will start falling only *after* full adjustment to price p_1 has already been made; and in this case the industry's total output can be expected to expand fully to a_1. But when the different sellers' decisions are so much spread out over time that some of them have not yet decided to expand at the time when the increased output of those who first made such decisions has already reached the market and had its effect on market price, then the market's total output may never rise to a_1 and will exceed the equilibrium point, a', either to a lesser extent or not at all. Hence, the fluctuations of price and output around their equilibrium values, as shown in Figures 51, 52, and 53, will occur mainly in markets and at occasions where special reasons account either for the concentration of production plans into a short span of time or for a long lag between the day when production plans are made and the day when these plans mature into output.

These special circumstances, which make for price and output fluctuations in the competitive market, are believed to occur primarily in agriculture, where nature imposes both a concentration of production plans into a short season and a long gap between the making of production plans and their fruition.[3] This does not mean, however, that in markets

---

[3] The standard example of fluctuations of this kind is the pig cycle. See R. H. Coase and R. F. Fowler, "The Pig Cycle in Great Britain," *Economica*, N.S., Vol. IV (1937), pp. 55–82. See also J. H. Lorie, *Causes of Annual Fluctuations in the Production of Livestock and Livestock Products* (Studies in Business Administration, Vol. XVII) (Chicago: University of Chicago Press, 1947).

for industrial products, where such fluctuations do not occur, perfect competition would insure perfect efficiency. For fluctuations in an industry's output are only one manifestation of dynamic inefficiency that can occur in the perfectly competitive market; and we must now proceed to consider some of its other forms and manifestations.

Let us consider a market where, in response to an initial rise in price to p_1, the producers prepare to expand output but their decisions to do so are spread over a long-enough period for additional output to reach the market and lower price in time to prevent overexpansion. In this case the industry's output will be a', and price will be p'; and economic efficiency, in the sense of the best allocation of output between this industry and other industries, will be achieved right away. Nevertheless, the industry will not yet be in equilibrium; and the allocation of output between the different firms constituting the industry will not yet be efficient. For efficiency in this latter sense requires that each firm plan its output and productive capacity on the basis of the same market price. In our example, however, the industry's total output is a' only because some firms have not yet adjusted their capacity to the rise in price from $\cdot p$ to p', whereas others have planned their capacity on the expectation that price would be p_1. This shows that the industry's organization is not yet efficient, since some firms have less and others more than their optimum share of its total output.

So far, we have been concerned with the allocation of output. But the same causes that interfere with the technologically efficient allocation of output between different firms may also prevent the economically efficient combination of factors by the firm and their efficient allocation among different firms. Each firm plans for the most economical combination and utilization of factors on the basis of what the prices of factors are at the time when its plans are laid. Efficiency depends, however, on how plans conform to factor prices at the time when these plans come to fruition. Hence, a change in factor prices between the time when plans are made and the time when they are put into effect may render a plan that seemed efficient when made inefficient by the time it is carried out. Some of the inefficiency that results from unforeseen changes in factor prices may again be regarded as unavoidable and imputed to man's inability to foresee the future; but we must again ask the question whether at least part of this inefficiency would not be avoided under a different economic organization.

Again, to take an example, let us assume an increase in demand for a commodity whose manufacture requires a certain type of highly skilled labor. Assume, further, that with the methods of production currently in use, the number of workers who possess this skill would be inadequate to meet the increased demand. This fact could be foreseen by a monopolist or a planning authority in control of the industry; and he might avoid the impending shortage of skilled workers by adopting new methods of production which spread thin the skill that is in short supply and thus produce a larger output with the same number of skilled workers. Whether he makes good use of his information or, for that matter, any use at all, depends, of course, on his ability and intelligence. But he at least has the requisite information on which to act; whereas the perfectly competitive producer has no such information made available to him by the market.

Under perfect competition, plans to increase output are made separately by each firm; and these plans are governed and co-ordinated by market prices alone. The rise in demand raises the price of the commodity, which in turn prompts manufacturers to expand capacity. The method of production adopted is determined by the relative prices of the factors of production; and new methods requiring fewer skilled workers would be adopted only if the wages of skilled workers rose. Their wages will be raised by the plans to increase production, *but only when these plans have already been put into effect.* At the planning stage, therefore, wages are unchanged; accordingly, each manufacturer, ignoring his competitors' plans and their future effect on the wages and availability of skilled workers, plans to increase his scale of operations while retaining his methods of production. Hence, competing manufacturers may make future production plans which are incompatible and could not be carried out simultaneously; and no amount of intelligence and ability on their part would prevent this.

The trouble will be realized, of course, as soon as the conflicting plans begin to be put into operation and raise the wages of skilled workers. If this happens with a long lag, the rise in wages may occur too late to prevent the building of more productive capacity than can be used with the available labor force—a flagrant case of inefficient resource allocation. But some harm will be done even if the lag is short. Assume, for example, that wages start rising in time to prevent the building of excess productive capacity. Even then, some manufacturers will have built additional capacity designed to use methods of production that have been rendered uneconomical in the meantime through the rise of skilled workers' wages; and this represents a social waste which could have been avoided by a closer co-ordination of the production plans of competing firms.

So far, we have been concerned with the behavior of firms and the efficiency of production. The above arguments, however, apply in the same way and with equal force also to the behavior of workers and to the efficiency of the labor market. Under perfect competition the urgency of society's demand for a skill is expressed through the wage it earns; and an increase in the demand for a skill is manifested by a rise in the wage offered for it. But here again, the rise in wages may be late in registering the rise in demand; and it may lead to an overadjustment of supply when it comes.

For example, an expanding industry needs additional workers of requisite skill as soon as its additional capacity is put into operation. This fact could easily be foreseen and acted upon at the time when the plans for expansion are laid. In fact, a monopolist or planning authority may start recruiting and training additional workers at the time when he starts expanding his plant capacity. In a competitive economy, however, it is the rise in wages which stimulates the recruitment and training of additional workers; and wages start rising only when the additional plant capacity has already been built and put into operation. This means that under perfect competition the recruitment and training of additional workers is unnecessarily delayed. At this belated stage, however, the impossibility of filling the additional demand for skilled workers immediately may cause wages to rise too much; and this, in turn, may induce more people to acquire the skill in question than are needed to man the additional plant capacity. The result of this may, in turn, be an undue lowering of wages at a later stage. In fact, this argument is an exact counterpart of that given on pages 234 ff. and can also be illustrated with the aid of Figures 51, 52, and 53.

All the above examples of maladjustment were instances of dynamic inefficiency and were due to the same cause: the failure of prices to register a change in conditions accurately and in time. Dynamic inefficiency, therefore, is likely to be small when changes in conditions are small or gradual; and it becomes serious only when changes in conditions are drastic and sudden. Hence the belief that the pricing system works satisfactorily only in normal times but breaks down under the stress of war and other major upheavals.

3. SPECULATION

Throughout the last section, we assumed that market prices are the only information on which members of the market base their economic behavior. This raises the question whether efficiency could be improved by supplementing the information contained in market prices by additional information made available through other channels. We saw that overadjustment and maladjustment are due to the individual producer's and worker's ignorance of other people's plans for future action. Hence, the publication of surveys or production plans, of estimates of present and planned productive capacity, and of estimates of future needs should improve the efficiency of a competitive economy. This, indeed, may often be the case. Unfortunately, however, additional information of this type is often in apparent conflict with the information conveyed through the market; and such conflict may cause people either to ignore the additional information or to have the wrong reaction to it. For example, if the market price is exceptionally high, producers may regard as alarmist and disbelieve information that planned output is already more than enough to meet future demand. On the other hand, if they believe this information, they may be induced to speed up (rather than drop) their expansion plans so as to make hay while the sun shines. Needless to say, when all producers react to it in this way, the additional information is of no avail. That this often is the case is suggested by the experience of the United States Department of Agriculture in trying to influence the production policies of farmers.

It therefore seems that, in order that the additional information may be acted upon, and acted upon correctly, it too would have to be imparted through the market mechanism. In other words, for competitive equilibrium to be reached quickly, present market prices would have to reflect not present market conditions but the present plans that determine future market conditions. This *may* happen when information about production plans and future needs leads to speculative buying or selling.

To illustrate this statement, let us return to the example of Figure 51, where demand for commodity A rises from D to D'. Supply would respond correctly, and the industry's output would be allocated efficiently among its members, if every firm planned its production on the assumption that price will be p'. We showed, of course, that price will at first rise to p_1, which may cause both overproduction and faulty allocation of the industry's output. But a speculator who correctly foresees that price will ultimately fall to p' can make a profit by selling at the present price, p_1, out of speculative stocks to be replenished later at the lower price, p'. If this speculator operates on a large-enough scale, or if there are many speculators operating on this assumption, then his or their actions will bring the price down to p' or near p' *already before the increase in output has had time to do so.* This is a useful result of speculation because, by bringing price to its equilibrium level sooner, it also causes producers to start making correct production plans sooner.

Unfortunately, however, there is no special reason to suppose that speculation will always be of this beneficial nature. To begin with, for speculation to bring about the equilibrium price, speculators would have to know in advance what the equilibrium price is going to be; and, for this, they would need the very information about production plans and future needs that is not usually available in a competitive market. Speculation alone, therefore, is unable to remedy this shortcoming of perfect competition. Speculation may be useful, however, in fields where surveys of production plans and estimates of future needs are being published. For such information, while often ignored or misinterpreted by producers, is quite likely to be fully considered, expertly interpreted, and correctly acted upon by the professional speculator.

Second, for speculators to profit from forecasting the equilibrium price and to hasten by their actions the establishment of the equilibrium price, it is essential that their influence should not be predominant in the market. In other words, speculators perform a useful function only if their influence is limited to the occasional diverting of price from what it would be in the absence of speculation. If speculators' financial resources and weight in the market are large, price becomes more dependent on speculators' actions than on nonspeculative demand and supply; and it may never reach, except by accident, the level that equates either current or estimated future nonspeculative demand and supply.

As the influence of nonspeculative demand and supply becomes less important as a determinant of price, speculators cease to estimate and speculate on the future equilibrium price. For when speculators' actions are the main determinant of market price, each speculator's profit depends on his correctly guessing not what the future equilibrium price will be but what future speculators will think it will be. In this case, market price becomes an index of speculators' opinions of what speculators' opinions will be in the future; and it ceases to provide information on the urgency of nonspeculative demand and the availability of nonspeculative supply. Therefore, speculation, which in moderation can improve the efficiency of the market mechanism, may destroy it altogether when carried to excess. This explains the paradoxical behavior of some experts' markets which happen to be also highly speculative.

We conclude, therefore, that perfect competition is a model of perfect efficiency *only in equilibrium*. We shall see later that when equilibrium has been disturbed, the forces that tend to re-establish equilibrium are likely to work better and faster under conditions in which competition is not perfect.

BIBLIOGRAPHICAL NOTE

On the cobweb theorem and the general problem of dynamic stability in an isolated market, see N. Kaldor, "A Classificatory Note on the Determinateness of Equilibrium," *Review of Economic Studies,* Vol. I (1934), pp. 122–36; Mordecai Ezekiel, "The Cobweb Theorem," *Quarterly Journal of Economics,* Vol. LII (1938), pp. 255–80 (reprinted in *Readings in Business Cycle Theory* [Philadelphia: Blakiston Co., 1944], pp. 422–42); N. S. Buchanah, "A Reconsideration of the Cobweb Theorem," *Journal of Political Economy,* Vol. XLVII (1939), pp. 100–10; F. G. Hooton, "Risk and the Cobweb Theorem," *Economic Journal,* Vol. LX (1950), pp. 69–80; P. N. Rosenstein-Rodan, "The Role of Time in Economic Theory," *Economica,* N.S., Vol. I (1934), pp. 77–97; M. Abramovitz, *An Approach to a Price Theory for a Changing Economy* (New York: Columbia University Press, 1939); and M. W. Reder, *Studies in the Theory of Welfare Economics* (New York: Columbia University Press, 1947), Part II.

On the problem of dynamic stability in the economy as a whole, see P. A. Samuelson, "The Stability of Equilibrium," *Econometrica,* Vol. IX (1941), pp. 97–120, and Vol. X (1942), pp. 1–25 (also contained in chaps. ix–x of Samuelson's *Foundations of Economic Analysis* [Cambridge, Mass.: Harvard University Press, 1947]); and O. Lange, *Price Flexibility and Employment* (Bloomington, Ind.: Principia Press, 1944), chaps. ii–v and Appendix.

On the subject of speculation, see J. M. Keynes, *The General Theory of Employment, Interest and Money* (London: Macmillan & Co., 1936), chap. xii; T. W. Schultz, "Spot and Future Prices as Production Guides," *American Economic Review (Proceedings),* Vol. XXXIX (1949), pp. 135–49; N. Kaldor, "Speculation and Economic Stability," *Review of Economic Studies,* Vol. VII (1939), pp. 1–27; and G. Blau, "Some Aspects of the Theory of Futures Trading," *Review of Economic Studies,* Vol. XII (1944–45), pp. 1–30.

PART III

The Price Maker's Behavior
and Free Competition

In the preceding part, we were concerned with the price taker's behavior and with an imaginary economy whose every member is a price taker. A realistic description and appraisal of our economy, however, requires that we investigate the market relation between price makers and price takers, and also the market relation which results from bargaining between persons and organizations. In this part, we shall limit ourselves to analyzing the individual price maker's behavior and discussing free competition, the simplest form of the relation between price makers and price takers.

The price maker is an important member of the economy not only numerically but also because he plays an active part in the market and takes the initiative in most economic decisions. Since he plays the active role in the market, there are many more facets to his market behavior than to the price taker's; furthermore, the price maker faces the problem of timing and co-ordinating his market behavior properly. For all these reasons the price maker's market behavior requires much more detailed discussion than did the price taker's. Accordingly, we shall discuss the general principles of the price maker's behavior in the next chapter (Chap. XI); the timing and stability of the price maker's market offer in Chapter XII; his price policy in Chapter XIII; and the estimation of the cost of producing his product in Chapter XIV. Chapters XI–XIV, therefore, contain a detailed discussion of the individual price maker's behavior.

This entire discussion, however, deals only with the firm and its profit-maximizing behavior; indeed, it may be regarded as the theory of the firm under monopolistic competition. It is conceivable, however, that persons as well as firms should be price makers in the market; and this raises the problem of whether there is need for a parallel discussion also of persons who aim at maximizing their satisfaction.

No such discussion will be presented here. In practice, relatively few persons are in the market position of price makers, able to set the price of their services on a take-it-or-leave-it basis; and most of these are professional people—architects, lawyers, doctors, dentists, and so forth. We argued in Chapter V that these people are likely to have a special type of psychology; and we showed in the Note to Chapter VII that a person with this type of psychology maximizes his satisfaction by maximizing his profit. In other words, a person with this type of psychology behaves just like a firm that aims at maximum profit. Accordingly, the main results of our discussion of the firm apply also to persons—at least to the extent that they have the psychology referred to above.

The last two chapters of this part are concerned with the economy as a whole. Chapter XV deals with the distinction between free and restricted competition and discusses the conditions of free competition. Chapter XVI contains an appraisal of the efficiency of free competition, that is, of an economy composed of price takers and price makers among whom competition is free.

CHAPTER XI

THE PRINCIPLES OF THE PRICE MAKER'S BEHAVIOR

THE price maker's problem is entirely different from that of the price taker. For the price maker is in no position to decide on the volume of his sales or purchases; he must let that be determined by the price takers who compose his market; and accordingly, he must expect his volume of transactions to vary with changing market conditions. But while he has no direct control over his rate of transactions, he sets the terms on which he offers to transact business; and he will try to set them in a way that will maximize his profit. In other words, while the price taker decides on the quantity he is going to buy or sell, the price maker offers to buy or sell undetermined quantities on his own terms.

In making his offer, the price maker determines not only the price but all other specifications of his offer as well. These include the terms on which he grants credit to his customers; the geographical location of his business; the conditions of work offered by the employer; the nature, quality, and appearance of the goods offered by the producer—in short, every detail and aspect of the price maker's offer that admits of variation. Moreover, the price maker must also be ready to meet the obligations that his offer entails. For instance, a producer offering goods for sale must plan his productive capacity in conformity with his anticipated rate of sales. Thus, as between price makers and price takers, the former determine all economic quantities save one, the rate of turnover, which they can only influence indirectly by the terms of their offers.

Firms often make a one-sided offer in the markets where they sell their products; but sometimes they also set the price at which they buy materials and the services of labor. Whether the sellers or the buyers are the price makers in a particular market depends on the relative numbers and the relative degree of expertness on the two sides of that market. In most markets in our society, it is the sellers who are the experts and whose number is the smaller, which explains why we usually think of the price maker as a seller and of price as being set by the seller. Accordingly, most of the discussion of the price maker's behavior will be centered on the seller; and it will often be left to the reader to extend results reached for the seller to the case of the buyer who is a price maker. In the present chapter, however, the principles of the price maker's behavior will be discussed in detail for both cases.

1. THE SELLER

The seller sets the terms at which he offers his product for sale in the market; but the quantity sold depends on the amount the market will buy from him on those terms. The goods he sells have a marginal cost to the seller, which depends on the total amount sold. Let us assume that a seller makes a tentative offer in the market and finds that his sales are such that his marginal cost is lower than price. He could then make a gain by selling more, *provided* that this gain is not offset by the cost of persuading the market to buy more from him. For, in order to raise his sales, the seller must improve the terms of his offer, which involves a cost. The cost of improving the seller's offer sufficiently to raise his sales by one unit will be called his variation cost. The price obtained for the additional unit sold less the variation cost incurred in persuading the market to buy it is the seller's marginal revenue. His net gain from selling an additional unit is the difference between marginal revenue and marginal cost; and the seller can therefore increase his gain by raising his sales as long as marginal revenue exceeds marginal cost.

It is possible, however, that the market's response to the seller's tentative offer is such that, while marginal cost is below price, the variation cost of persuading the market to buy more from him is higher than the gain to be had from selling more. In other words, price less variation cost may yield a marginal revenue which is lower than marginal cost. This provides the seller with no incentive to improve his offer and raise his sales; on the contrary, he will find it profitable to offer less favorable terms to the market and allow his sales to fall off. For, if improving one's offer involves a cost, making it less favorable yields a saving. Variation cost, therefore, may also be defined as the saving to be had by offering the market less attractive terms that lead to a one-unit fall in sales. It is reasonable to assume that the variation cost of raising and the variation cost of lowering sales by one unit are approximately the same. When the seller changes his offer so as to lower sales by one unit, the price of the unsold unit less the variation cost saved is his loss of marginal revenue. This loss must be set against the saving of the marginal cost of this unit in calculating the seller's net gain. He can add to his gain, therefore, as long as marginal revenue is below marginal cost, by offering less favorable terms to the market and selling less. The seller's profit is at a maximum when his sales have reached the point where marginal revenue and marginal cost are equal. At this point, he sells on his optimum terms and is in equilibrium in the sense of having no further inducement to change the terms of his offer.

This is the fundamental principle of the price maker's market behavior. It is so important that we shall repeat it in a slightly different form. To sell an additional unit in the market, the seller must incur two types of cost: the marginal cost of producing the additional unit and the variation cost of persuading the market to buy it. When the sum of marginal and variation costs is smaller than price, the seller can gain by selling more and will find it profitable to change his offer with a view to stimulating sales. If, on the other hand, the sum of marginal and variation costs exceeds price, the seller can gain by selling less. For, in this case, marginal cost is the seller's saving from producing one less unit; variation cost is the saving he makes by offering the market the less favorable terms which lead to a one-unit fall in his sales; and the seller makes a profit, because the sum of these savings is greater than the loss of revenue, which is the price of the unsold unit. Profit, therefore, is at its maximum when output is such as to equate the sum of marginal and variation costs to price.

To compare marginal cost with marginal revenue (defined as price minus variation cost) and to compare price with the sum of marginal and variation costs are merely two ways of looking at the same problem. Sometimes the one, sometimes the other is more convenient; and the reader will do well to familiarize himself with both methods of approach. In the literature of economics, it is more customary to compare marginal cost with marginal revenue; and, in order to conform to tradition, this way of looking at the price maker's problem will also be followed throughout most of this book. But the second line of approach is often more helpful when one compares the theory of the price maker with the businessman's actual behavior. Although businessmen think neither in terms of marginal revenue nor in terms of variation and marginal costs, it will appear as we go along that their way of thinking often conforms quite closely to the second method of approach.

At this point, it may be well briefly to contrast the price maker's behavior as outlined above with the price taker's conduct as discussed in Part II of this book. If the price taker wants to sell additional quantities of his product or services, he can go to the market and sell all he wants at the market's set price. His marginal revenue from selling one more unit is the price he receives for it. His profit, therefore, from selling an additional unit is the difference between price and marginal cost; and we saw how the price taker can maximize his profit by extending sales until marginal cost becomes equal to price.

The principle on which the price maker maximizes his profit is fundamentally the same. The only difference is that he, unlike the price taker, must persuade the market to buy more from him if he wants to extend his sales; and the variation cost incurred in persuading the market must be deducted from price to arrive at his marginal revenue. The price maker's marginal revenue, therefore, is always lower than his price; and when he maximizes profit by equating marginal revenue to marginal cost, the price he sets is always above marginal cost.

How can the price maker change his offer in order to raise the market's demand for his product? As a rule, he can do so in a variety of ways. He may reduce his price, grant easier terms of credit, improve the quality or appearance of his product, move to a better location, spend more on advertising,[1] and so forth. Each way of changing his offer has a variation cost; accordingly, we can speak of price variation cost, quality variation cost, location variation cost, advertising variation cost, and so on.

The seller's price variation cost consists in the loss of receipts due to the price reduction he makes in order to raise his sales by one unit. A producer, for example, who sells 1,000 units of his product at $20 each, and who could sell one more unit by making a one-cent price reduction, has a price variation cost:

$$VC_p = \$10 \ (= 1{,}000 \times 1\textcent) \ .[2]$$

Quality variation cost is the cost of improving quality sufficiently to raise sales by one unit. Hence, if our producer could sell one more unit by improving the quality of his product at an additional cost of two thirds of one cent per unit, but without altering his offer in other respects, his quality variation cost would be

$$VC_q = \$6.67 \ (= 1{,}000 \times \tfrac{2}{3}\textcent) \ .$$

---

[1] Strictly speaking, increased advertising does not change the seller's offer in the same sense in which a price reduction or any of the other improvements change his offer. To simplify the argument, however, it will be convenient to think of advertising as part of the seller's offer.

[2] The price variation cost, therefore, is not a proper cost at all but a loss of revenue. In this, it differs from all other variation costs, which are costs proper.

His advertising variation cost would be

$$VC_a = \$5$$

if that much more spent on advertising would raise his sales by one unit, again without any other change in his offer.

The price maker's variation cost depends on how responsive the market is to a change in his offer. The more readily the market responds to such a change, the less he need spend on persuading it to buy more from him, or, in other words, the smaller is the cost of effecting the change relative to the gross addition to receipts which results from it. The market's responsiveness, therefore, can be measured by the ratio between a small addition to gross receipts and the cost of effecting this addition. The addition to gross receipts which results from selling one more unit is the price of that unit, and the cost of effecting this addition is the variation cost. Accordingly, the ratio of price to variation cost measures the responsiveness of the market to a change in the seller's offer and will be called the market's elasticity of demand:

$$\eta = \frac{p}{VC} \ .$$

It follows from this definition of elasticity that variation cost can be expressed as the ratio of price to elasticity:

$$VC = \frac{p}{\eta} \ ;$$

and marginal revenue, defined as price less variation cost, can be shown in terms of price and elasticity by the expression:

$$MR = p - VC = p - \frac{p}{\eta} \ .$$

This expression makes apparent a simple but important relation between marginal revenue and the elasticity of demand. It shows that marginal revenue is positive when $\eta > 1$, zero when $\eta = 1$, and negative when $\eta < 1$.

Corresponding to different types of variation in the seller's offer, we can distinguish between different elasticities of demand, such as price elasticity, η_p; quality elasticity, η_q; advertising elasticity, η_a; and so forth. In the numerical example shown above, the producer's market has a price elasticity of demand, $\eta_p = \$20/\$10 = 2$; a quality elasticity of demand, $\eta_q = \$20/\$6.67 = 3$; and an advertising elasticity of demand, $\eta_a = \$20/\$5 = 4$. Similarly, we can distinguish between different types of marginal revenue, depending on the way in which the seller persuades the market to buy more from him. Thus, we can speak of marginal revenue from price variation, marginal revenue from quality variation, marginal revenue from advertising, and so on. In our numerical example, marginal revenue from price variation is $MR_p = \$20 - \$10 = \$10$;[3] marginal revenue from quality variation is $MR_q = \$20 - \$6.67 = \$13.33$; and marginal revenue from advertising is $MR_a = \$20 - \$5 = \$15$. The smaller the variation cost of a given aspect of the seller's offer, the larger the marginal revenue to be derived from it.

Needless to say, sellers usually find it impracticable to change the 'market's demand for their product by one unit only, or to estimate the cost of such a change. A shoe manufacturer may know what it would cost him to boost sales by 1,000 pairs of shoes without knowing the cost of boosting them by one pair. In such cases, variation cost must be calculated as the average per-unit cost of the smallest practicable change in the seller's offer; and the elasticity of demand and marginal revenue must be calculated accordingly. Usually it is easiest to estimate the elasticity of demand first and, from that, calculate variation cost and marginal revenue. For example, if spending $1,000 more on advertising would raise the shoe manufacturer's sales by $5,000, his advertising elasticity of demand is the ratio of additional gross receipts to the total cost of raising sales: $\eta_a = \$5,000/\$1,000 = 5$. If he sells his shoes at a price of $10, his advertising variation cost is $VC_a = p/\eta_a = \$10/5 = \$2$; and his marginal revenue from advertising is $MR_a = p - VC_a = \$10 - \$2 = \$8$.

The dependence of the price maker's sales on his market offer and the market's response to changes in his offer are easily illustrated geometrically with respect to only one aspect of his offer: price. The demand curve in Figure 54, for example, shows that at price p the seller can sell q units of his product; and, to raise his sales by Δq, he must lower the price by Δp. When price is p, the seller's total revenue is pq, shown in Figure 54 by the rectangle $0qap$. When he lowers price by Δp, his total revenue becomes $(p - \Delta p)(q + \Delta q) = pq + p\Delta q - \Delta p\Delta q - q\Delta p$, represented by the rectangle $0q_1bp_1$. The additional revenue due to the price change is $p\Delta q - \Delta p\Delta q - q\Delta p$, which in the diagram is the difference in area between the two shaded rectangles. The upright rectangle,

---

[3] To be exact, $MR_p = \$19.99 - \$10 = \$9.99$, because it is from the new, lower price that the $10 variation cost must be deducted. It is convenient, however, to neglect this slight difference.

whose area is $p\Delta q - \Delta p\Delta q = (p - \Delta p)\Delta q$, shows the addition to the seller's gross receipts earned on his additional sales. The recumbent rectangle, whose area is $q\Delta p$, shows the loss of receipts on his former volume of sales, which may be regarded as the cost of raising sales by the reduction of price from p to p_1. To represent the additional revenue graphically, we have drawn a line across the upright rectangle in such a way that it cuts off an area equal to that of the recumbent rectangle. The remaining rectangle, qq_1dc, represents the additional revenue. Proceed-

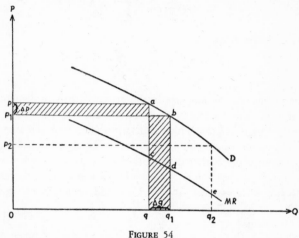

FIGURE 54

ing step by step in this way, the line cd can be extended into a curve such that the area under it between any two points shows the additional revenue to be gained by a price reduction which brings sales from one of these points to the other. For example, the additional revenue to be had by lowering price from p_1 to p_2 and thereby raising sales from q_1 to q_2 is shown by the area q_1q_2ed.

The additional revenue obtained from selling one unit more is the marginal revenue from price variation, which can be shown by the area of a strip under the curve whose width is unity. This area can be expressed as the product of width and height; and since the width is unity, it is numerically equal to the height (ordinate) of the curve. The ordinates of the curve, therefore, show the marginal revenue from price variation; and the curve itself is called a marginal-revenue curve.[4]

---

[4] For the geometrical relation between the marginal-revenue curve and the demand curve, and between marginal and average curves in general, see Joan Robinson, *The Economics of Imperfect Competition* (London: Macmillan & Co., 1933), pp. 37–42.

When the change in price, Δp, is small compared to price, p; and when the resulting change in sales, Δq, is small compared to total sales, q; then $\Delta p \Delta q$, the product of two small quantities, can be neglected, and the addition to the seller's gross receipts ($p\Delta q - \Delta p \Delta q$) becomes approximately equal to $p\Delta q$. The price elasticity of demand, which we defined above as the ratio of a small addition to gross receipts to the cost of effecting this addition, can then be expressed as

$$\eta_p = \frac{p\Delta q}{q\Delta p}.$$

This can also be written as

$$\eta_p = \frac{\Delta q}{q} \Big/ \frac{\Delta p}{p}.$$

To put this expression into words, the price elasticity of demand is the ratio of a relative (percentage) change in sales to the relative (percentage) change in price which brings it about. Here we have an alternative but equivalent definition of price elasticity of demand. That it is equivalent to our earlier definition becomes apparent when we consider a one-unit increase in sales, $\Delta q = 1$. The cost of bringing this about is the price variation cost: $q\Delta p = VC_p$; and we can write down the equality

$$\eta_p = \frac{p\Delta q}{q\Delta p} = \frac{p}{VC_p} \qquad\qquad \text{when } \Delta q = 1.$$

This shows the identity of the two definitions.[5]

To demonstrate the identity arithmetically, let us return to the example on pages 250–52, where we considered a producer who must lower his $20 price by one cent in order to sell a 1,001th unit of his product. The relative increase in his sales is $1/1000$, or one tenth of one percent; the relative change in his price is $1/2000$, or one twentieth of one per cent; and his price elasticity of demand, therefore, is

$$\eta_p = \frac{1}{1,000} \Big/ \frac{1}{2,000} = 2.$$

This is often a simpler way of expressing price elasticity of demand than to calculate price variation cost first ($1,000 \times 1\cancel{c} = \$10$ in the above

---

[5] The reader who has difficulty in following the argument of the last two paragraphs is advised to read at this stage the parallel argument for the buyer on pp. 262–63, which is similar to the above argument but easier in some respects.

example) and express price elasticity as the ratio of price to price variation cost:

$$\eta_p = \frac{\$20}{\$10} = 2 \ .$$

Unfortunately, there is no simple way of illustrating graphically the
market's response to changes in any other attribute of the price maker's
offer, because, unlike price, none of the other attributes of his offer is
measurable. For example, we cannot draw a demand curve showing sales
as a function of the seller's advertising policy, because we have no measure of advertising policy. The best we can do is to draw a curve that
shows how the variation cost of a particular attribute of the price maker's
offer depends on output. Usually, it is convenient either to add this curve
vertically to the marginal-cost curve or to subtract it vertically from the
price line. The first type of presentation is shown in Figure 55. Here, the

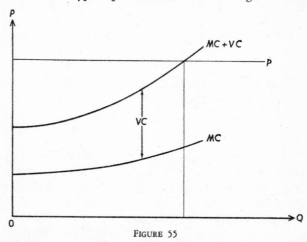

FIGURE 55

vertical distance between the two curves shows, for each level of output,
the variation cost of selling an additional unit of output; and the ordinate
of the upper curve shows, for each level of output, the sum of marginal
and variation costs. If we also draw a price line into this diagram, the
intersection of this price line with the upper curve shows the output that
will maximize profit, because it is at this point that the condition of
maximum profit,

$$MC + VC = p \ ,$$

is fulfilled.

The alternative form of presentation is shown in Figure 56. Here, the ordinates of the curve MR_a show, for each level of output, the marginal revenue from varying some attribute (other than price) of the price maker's offer, while the vertical distance between the MR_a curve and the price line shows the variation cost of this attribute. In this diagram the point of maximum profit is given by the intersection of the marginal-

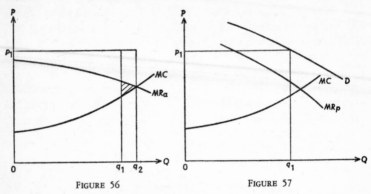

FIGURE 56   FIGURE 57

revenue (MR_a) and marginal-cost (MC) curves; for it is at this point that the condition of maximum profit,

$$MC = MR \,(\equiv p - VC) ,$$

is fulfilled.

We can now proceed to make use of these diagrams for a detailed discussion of the seller's market behavior. Let us take, for example, a seller who can vary his offer in two ways only, by changing his price and by changing his advertising policy. Let us assume that he starts out from an initial situation in which he sells the quantity q_1 at price p_1; and that, at this rate of sales, his marginal revenue from both advertising and price variation is higher than marginal cost. This situation is illustrated in Figures 56 and 57. The demand and marginal-revenue curves in Figure 57 show the market's responsiveness to changes in the seller's price; the marginal-revenue curve of Figure 56 shows the seller's marginal revenue from advertising. According to these diagrams, the seller can add to his rate of profit by stimulating the market's demand for his product both by lowering price and by spending more on advertising. In what order the price maker should adjust the various elements of his market offer is an important problem, which will be discussed in Chapter XIII. Let us assume, in the present example, that he starts to expand his sales by increased advertising. He can keep on increasing his profit in this way until his sales have risen to q_2, at which output marginal revenue from advertising is equal to marginal cost. The addition to profit so obtained is shown in Figure 56 by the shaded area.

At this stage the seller must ask himself what scope he has for raising his profit yet further—this time by a change in price. For in the meantime the demand curve of Figure 57 has shifted to the right, illustrating the fact that, thanks to increased advertising, the seller can now sell a larger quantity of output at the same old price. With the demand curve, the marginal-revenue curve shifts, too; and the new, shifted demand and marginal-revenue curves are shown in Figure 58. One cannot tell

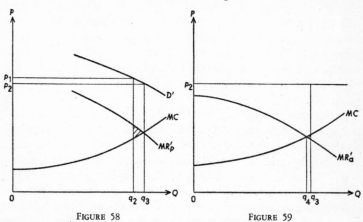

FIGURE 58   FIGURE 59

whether at q_2, in the new situation, the marginal revenue from price variation will be the same as it was at q_1, before the seller started on his new advertising campaign. But it is not likely to be very different; in any case, only by accident would it have become equal to marginal cost. So long as marginal cost and marginal revenue from price variation are not equal at q_2, the seller can raise his profit yet further by a suitable change in price. Figure 58 shows a situation in which marginal revenue from price variation exceeds marginal cost at q_2, so that the seller must lower his price to add to his profit. By lowering his price to p_2, he can raise his sales to q_3 and obtain the additional profit represented by the shaded triangle in Figure 58.

At this stage, however, the seller is not yet in equilibrium, because the price reduction has shifted the MR_a curve in Figure 56, showing his marginal revenue from advertising; and the latter is bound to be below marginal cost at q_3. This situation is shown in Figure 59 (p. 257), which indicates that now the seller is spending too much on advertising and could, by curtailing his advertising expenditures, save more on advertising and production costs than he would lose from the resulting diminution in sales. Now, therefore, the seller can make a further gain—additional to the gains already made and shown by the shaded areas in Figures 56 and 58—by scaling down advertising expenditures to the point where his sales reach q_4. At this point, he has added a further net gain to his profit, shown by the shaded area in Figure 59—a gain that is the saving in advertising expenditure made possible by the reduction in price. The reduction in sales again shifts the demand curve and the marginal-revenue-from-price-variation curve, and may thus call for a further readjustment of price. Successive readjustments of price and of advertising policy, however, will ultimately lead to a position of equilibrium, at which the seller has exhausted all possibilities of raising profit and has reached the point where both marginal revenue from advertising and marginal revenue from price variation are simultaneously equal to marginal cost.

In this example, we started out from an initial situation in which both marginal revenues were higher than marginal cost; but the argument would have been similar had we started from an initial situation in which both marginal revenues were *lower* than marginal cost. In such a situation the seller, to increase his gain, would change his offer in a way that would make it less attractive to his customers and so restrict his sales. Having adjusted one attribute of his offer in this way, he would turn around and recalculate the marginal revenue from varying the other attribute; and, if this were still different from marginal cost, he could further increase his gain by suitably adjusting also this attribute of his offer. These two adjustments might necessitate further readjustments; and equilibrium would be reached at the point where both marginal revenues are simultaneously equal to marginal cost. In the same way, when some marginal revenues are above and others below marginal cost in the initial situation, the seller must make some attributes of his offer more attractive and others less attractive to his customers in order to increase his gain; and, again, several adjustments and readjustments may be necessary in order to reach equilibrium. But the particular way and direction in which the seller approaches equilibrium is not important for us at this stage.[6] He reaches the same equilibrium however he approaches it, because the equilibrium conditions are always the same.

---

[6] It will be discussed in Chap. XIII.

Every attribute of the seller's offer must be such that its marginal revenue is equal to marginal cost; in other words, the variation cost of each attribute must be equal to the difference between price and marginal cost.[7]

What general conclusions can be drawn from the above example? First of all, we have seen that by adjusting one aspect of his offer only, the seller can increase his gain up to a point but does not exhaust all possibilities of raising his profit. Had we, in the above example, restricted the seller to advertising variation only, he would have reached equilibrium after raising his sales to q_2 and adding to his profit the gain shown by the shaded area in Figure 56. Only the possibility of changing price as well gave him the further profit represented by the shaded areas in Figure 58 (which shows the additional gain resulting from the increased sales caused by the price reduction) and in Figure 59 (which represents

---

[7] Mathematically, the seller's market behavior can be expressed as follows. His rate of sales, q, is a function of price, p, and of the attributes, $a_1, a_2, \ldots, a_n$, of his offer:

$$q = q(p, a_1, a_2, \cdots, a_n).$$

His total cost, C, is a function of the quantity produced and sold and the several attributes of his offer:

$$C = C(q, a_1, a_2, \cdots, a_n).$$

The seller's profit, P, is

$$P = pq - C;$$

and for this to be at a maximum, the following first-order maximum conditions must be fulfilled:

$$\frac{\partial P}{\partial p} = q + p\frac{\partial q}{\partial p} - \frac{\partial C}{\partial q}\frac{\partial q}{\partial p} = 0,$$

$$\frac{\partial P}{\partial a_i} = p\frac{\partial q}{\partial a_i} - \frac{\partial C}{\partial a_i} - \frac{\partial C}{\partial q}\frac{\partial q}{\partial a_i} = 0, \qquad \text{for } i = 1, 2, \ldots, n.$$

Rearranging and dividing through the first equation by $\partial q/\partial p$ and the ith of the set of equations by $\partial q/\partial a_i$, the above first-order maximum conditions can also be written as follows:

$$p = \frac{\partial C}{\partial q} + \left(- q\Big/\frac{\partial q}{\partial p}\right),$$

$$p = \frac{\partial C}{\partial q} + \left(\frac{\partial C}{\partial a_i}\Big/\frac{\partial q}{\partial a_i}\right), \qquad \text{for } i = 1, 2, \ldots, n.$$

In the above equations, $\partial C/\partial q$ is the seller's marginal cost, $- q/(\partial q/\partial p)$ is his price variation cost, and $(\partial C/\partial a_i)/(\partial q/\partial a_i)$ is the variation cost of the ith attribute of his offer. It will be noted that a_i need not be a *measure* but can also be an *index* of the ith attribute. For, if a_i is replaced by $f_i(a_i)$, any monotonic increasing function of a_i, the above results remain unaffected by the transformation.

the saving in advertising expenditure made possible by the increased sales due to the price reduction). In general, we can say that the more aspects of his offer the seller can vary, the greater is his scope for making a gain.

This implies that any restraint on the seller which prevents his adjusting some aspect of his offer as he sees fit may lower his profit. At first sight, this statement might appear to be incorrect. It could be argued, for example, that if a seller of chocolate bars maximizes his profit by selling one-ounce bars at 5 cents each, he could make the same profit by selling 2-ounce bars at 10 cents; and that, therefore, a government regulation fixing the size but not the price of chocolate bars would not restrict his profit. This, however, is not so. For making chocolate bars too large eliminates from the market the customers who do not want or cannot afford so large a size. Making them too small reduces the purchases of some customers without significantly enlarging the market. Hence, there is an optimum size of chocolate bar; and the seller can make a higher profit by selling the optimum size of chocolate bar at the appropriate optimum price than by selling any other size at any other price. If some regulation or other circumstance forces him to deviate from the optimum size, he can make an appropriate adjustment of price in an attempt to compensate himself for his loss of profit; but, as a rule, he cannot compensate himself fully. In the same way, when the government controls the price of a good or service, the seller can usually recoup himself for a part of his loss of profit by an appropriate adjustment of the quality of the good or service he sells at the prescribed price; but he can seldom recoup himself completely. In general, any limitation on the seller's freedom of making the offer he wants to make also limits his profit.

There are many examples of public restraint on the seller's freedom of action both in the United States and elsewhere. In this country the Pure Food and Drug Act regulates the quality of processed foodstuffs and prepared drugs; the Interstate Commerce Commission determines fares and freight rates in most commercial traffic across state frontiers; the Federal Communications Commission sets interstate telephone and telegraph rates; and during the war the Office of Price Administration controlled practically all prices and rents. In addition, price makers themselves often agree to impose restrictions on their own market behavior. The purpose of all such restrictions on the price maker's freedom of action will be discussed in detail—in Chapter XVII in connection with monopolistic restrictions, and in Chapter XXI in connection with trade and competition on terms prescribed by public authority.

2. THE BUYER

The preceding detailed discussion of the seller's behavior makes it possible to deal very quickly with the buyer, whose behavior in the market where he is a price maker is exactly parallel to the seller's. He offers to buy a certain factor of production on his own terms; but the quantity he gets depends on the amount that the market will sell to him at those terms.[8] The factors he buys have a marginal value to him, which depends on the amount he buys. When the marginal value of the factors bought is higher than the price paid for them, the buyer can add to his profit by buying more, provided that the addition to profit is not offset by the cost of inducing the market to sell more to him. The buyer can persuade the market to sell him more in a variety of ways: by raising his price, advertising more, promising prompter or advance payment for the factors bought, or offering more benefits and better working conditions to workers hired. The cost of persuading the market to sell him one more unit is the buyer's variation cost. The variation cost of a change in the buyer's offer is *added* to the price he pays; and the sum of price and variation cost is the buyer's marginal outlay, which he must incur in order to obtain an additional unit. The difference between marginal value and marginal outlay is a net gain to the buyer, which he can increase by stimulating turnover as long as marginal value exceeds marginal outlay. When marginal value is below marginal outlay, the buyer can gain by changing his offer in a way that will discourage the market from selling to him. Such a change in his offer is unfavorable to the market but favorable to him, because the variation cost of such a change is a saving to the buyer. He maximizes his profit and is in equilibrium when every variable aspect of his offer is at the point where marginal outlay with respect to that aspect is equal to marginal value.

The readiness with which the market responds to a change in the buyer's offer is measured by the market's elasticity of supply, which is defined, in exactly the same way as the elasticity of demand, as the ratio of price to variation cost:

$$\eta = \frac{p}{VC}.$$

Marginal outlay, defined as the sum of price and variation cost, can be expressed in terms of price and elasticity of supply by the formula:

---

[8] The only difference between a buyer and a seller is that there is a very definite upper limit to the quantity of the former's purchases, whereas the seller's rate of sales, though also limited, appears on the whole to be much more flexible.

$$MO = p + VC = p + \frac{p}{\eta}.$$

The close similarity between the buyer's marginal outlay and the seller's marginal revenue is apparent. Corresponding to changes in different aspects of the buyer's offer, and to the different variation costs of these changes, we can also distinguish, of course, between different elasticities of supply and between different marginal outlays.

There is a complete parallelism between these concepts and the corresponding concepts which we analyzed in detail for the seller's case; but it will nevertheless be useful to discuss, as an example, the geometrical derivation of the buyer's marginal outlay with respect to price variation and the price elasticity of supply confronting him. The market's response to a change in the buyer's price can be illustrated by a market supply curve, which shows the rate of turnover as a function of the buyer's price. The market supply curve in Figure 60 shows that at

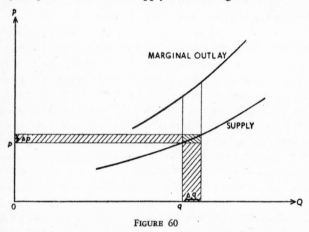

FIGURE 60

price p the buyer can buy q units, and that, to obtain Δq additional units, he must raise his price by Δp. His total outlay is pq when price is p; and it rises to $(p + \Delta p)(q + \Delta q) = pq + q\Delta p + \Delta q\Delta p + p\Delta q$ when he raises price by Δp. The additional outlay, therefore, is $q\Delta p + \Delta q\Delta p + p\Delta q$; and these three terms are represented in Figure 60 by the three shaded rectangles. By prolonging the upright rectangle upward so that the prolongation is equal in area to the other two shaded rectangles, we can derive a segment of the buyer's marginal-outlay curve.

The area of the recumbent rectangle, $q\Delta p$, represents the cost to the buyer of inducing the market by a change in price to sell him Δq more units. It represents the buyer's price variation cost when $\Delta q = 1$. When Δq and Δp are small compared to q and p, respectively, their product, $\Delta q \Delta p$ (represented by the small shaded rectangle), can be neglected; and the area of the upright rectangle, $p \Delta q$, can then be taken to represent the cost to the buyer of the additional units bought. The ratio of this cost to the cost of inducing the market to sell the additional units is defined as the price elasticity of supply,

$$\eta_p = \frac{p \Delta q}{q \Delta p},$$

when the change considered is small. As in the seller's case, this definition of elasticity is identical with the definition given above, because

$$\frac{p \Delta q}{q \Delta p} = \frac{p}{VC_p} \qquad \text{when } \Delta q = 1.$$

Since $p \Delta q / q \Delta p$ can also be written as $(\Delta q/q)/(\Delta p/p)$, the price elasticity of supply can be interpreted to mean the ratio of the percentage change in quantity bought to the percentage change in price.

To sum up the argument of this chapter, we discussed the market behavior of the price maker, both as a buyer and as a seller, on the assumption that he aims at maximizing his profit. We showed that the more attributes of his market offer he is free to vary, the better he can achieve this aim. To maximize his profit, he must not only set his optimum price but must also pursue his optimum advertising policy, choose his optimum location, give his product its optimum quality, and so forth. The optimum conditions are the same for each attribute of the price maker's offer. The seller maximizes his profit by adjusting every attribute of his offer in such a way as to render the variation cost of each attribute equal to the difference between price and marginal cost; the buyer achieves the same aim by equating the variation cost of each attribute of his offer to the difference between marginal value and price. If we call the difference between marginal value and price, and between price and marginal cost, the price maker's profit margin, we can consolidate the above two rules into one and say that to maximize his profit, the price maker must equate all variation costs to his profit margin.

BIBLIOGRAPHICAL NOTE

The modern analysis of the price maker's problems and market behavior is mainly the work of Professor Edward H. Chamberlin. See especially chapters vi–vii of his

Theory of Monopolistic Competition (Cambridge, Mass.: Harvard University Press, 1931). For a more detailed analysis of such special problems as sales promotion through advertising, see N. S. Buchanan, "Advertising Expenditures: A Suggested Treatment," *Journal of Political Economy,* Vol. L (1942), pp. 537–57; and H. Smith, "Advertising Costs and Equilibrium," *Review of Economic Studies,* Vol. II (1934), pp. 62–65.

For a detailed analysis of the price maker's behavior in the market where he buys factors of production, see Joan Robinson, *The Economics of Imperfect Competition* (London: Macmillan & Co., 1933), Bks. VII–VIII.

The approach presented in this chapter is somewhat different from the traditional one. It was first presented in a paper I read at the Chicago meeting of the Econometric Society in December, 1947, a summary of which appeared in the "Report of the Chicago Meeting, December 27–30, 1947," *Econometrica,* Vol. XVI (1948), pp. 214–15. For a very similar approach, see Joel Dean, "How Much to Spend on Advertising," *Harvard Business Review,* Vol. XXIX (1951), pp. 65–74.

CHAPTER XII

THE STABILITY OF THE PRICE MAKER'S BEHAVIOR

APART from a minor exception in Chapter X, our analysis of the firm's market behavior has been static until now. We showed what the firm's most profitable behavior is in a given situation; but we ignored all problems of change. In particular, we ignored the problem of transition from one market offer to another; and we ignored the problems raised by the impermanence of certain situations. These problems will have to be dealt with now. There are two reasons why this subject was not taken up in Part II. First of all, most of the problems to be dealt with here are peculiar to the price maker and are not raised at all by the price taker's passive market behavior. Second, although some of the problems to be discussed here are faced by price makers and price takers alike, we postponed their discussion for the sake of simplicity. Since the typical firm in our society is a price maker, it seemed preferable to present the detailed and more realistic analysis of the firm as part of our discussion of the price maker's behavior.

1. THE STABILIZING FACTORS

The price maker's offer to transact business on set terms but on any scale is based on definite expectations as to what his actual turnover will be. The market's response to his offer, however, may be different from what he expected it to be, either because he has misjudged the market situation or because the situation has changed. In such a case the price maker can change his plans and change the terms of his offer. But it is an essential feature of his offer that it must stand unchanged for some time.

Keeping a market offer unchanged for a while is, first of all, a matter of commercial usage and ethics. When a person makes a one-sided offer, he must stand by it for some time and give the market a chance to act upon it. Second, a market offer may be kept unchanged from sheer uncertainty when the price maker, while facing a changed situation, does not know how to interpret the change and how to react to it. Third, a

265

stable offer is called for also by the preferences of the market. Price takers, especially consumers, often put a premium on a certain brand of a commodity merely because its quality, appearance, and price have long remained the same. Merely by keeping his offer stable and thereby catering to his customers' preference for stability, the price maker can increase his turnover and profit. He will not change his offer, therefore, unless he expects the gain to be had from the change to surpass this premium on stability. Such preference for stability in market offers is part of the ordinary person's general desire for a certain amount of stability in the world around him; for he considers this essential for efficient and comfortable living. He disapproves of too many changes in price or quality in much the same spirit in which he resents the unstable character of a friend, the fickleness of a woman, the changing allegiance of a politician, or the frequent renaming of streets.

In addition to these general and somewhat intangible stabilizing factors, there are also specific economic considerations which keep stable the price maker's market offer as well as other elements of his behavior. One might think at first that, apart from the general considerations mentioned above, the price maker would maximize profits by adapting his behavior instantaneously to all changes in conditions, however impermanent and small these changes may be. There are, however, three stabilizing factors which will prevent his doing so. The first is the cost of change. This will keep him from making any change from which the gain would be insufficient to repay its cost. The second is the indivisibility of the services of certain productive resources, which must be hired and paid for a more or less extended length of time. A change in the price maker's behavior which requires additional productive resources is only worth making if it justifies the minimum expenditure involved in hiring these resources. The third factor is the turnover lag, that is, the time it takes for a change in the price maker's market offer to affect the behavior of his market and to have its full effect on his turnover. All elements of the price maker's plan—his decisions relating to price, quality, advertising, marketing, productive capacity, and so forth—are stabilized by one or more of these factors.

2. THE COST OF CHANGE

When a change in conditions or in their appraisal renders a new policy more profitable than his actual policy, the price maker faces a problem. By adopting this new policy, he would raise the flow of his profits above what it would be if he adhered to his previous policy; but the gain so achieved might be partly or wholly offset by the cost of changing his behavior. Hence, the cost of changing his behavior may keep him from adopting his most profitable market offer.

In the last chapter, we did not consider this problem at all. When we sought the seller's most profitable market offer, we always proceeded by comparing alternative market offers—and especially by comparing two offers one of which differed from the other just enough to result in the sale of one additional unit of output per unit of time. To determine which of two offers was preferable, we compared the difference between the gross receipts resulting from them to the difference between their respective costs. The difference in gross receipts was the price of the additional unit sold; the difference in cost was the sum of two components: the difference in cost due to the difference in output (marginal cost), and the difference in cost due to the difference in the nature of the two offers (variation cost). In short, we compared alternative modes of behavior each of which was static and gave rise to even flows of receipts and costs over time. Accordingly, the differences in receipts and costs which we compared were also even flows over time; and, on the basis of these comparisons, we determined what the price maker's most profitable offer was, *without regard to the cost involved in changing over to this offer.*

Analysis of this type is called comparative statics or static analysis. Such analysis can only show one thing, which is all we showed in the last chapter, namely, that the price maker would have no inducement to change his behavior if his actual offer happened to be also his most profitable offer. Static analysis cannot show whether the price maker would change his behavior if his actual offer were different from his most profitable offer; for this depends, among other things, on the cost that the mere changing of his offer would entail.

A manufacturer, for example, may believe that his annual profit would be higher if he produced a better quality of product than he actually produces, expecting that the resulting addition to annual sales and gross receipts would more than outweigh the addition to annual cost due to the higher output and to the better quality of his product. But against the estimated increase in annual profit must be weighed the initial cost of changing from the production of one type of product to that of the other; and if the increase in the flow of profit is small and the initial cost large, the manufacturer's best policy may well be to let matters alone and continue producing his present product.

The cost of change is an initial and once-and-for-all expenditure. It may consist of the cost of planning and designing new models, readjusting machinery or retooling if the change is to consist in altering the nature, quality, or appearance of a product; it includes the cost of lost time if the change necessitates the stoppage of a production process; or it may simply be the cost of publicizing a new price if only price is to be revised. The cost of change, therefore, is the cost of making a transition from one market offer to another; and, as such, it is entirely different from the variation cost, which is the difference between the costs entailed by two different offers. The once-and-for-all cost of change must be deducted from the addition to the flow of profit expected to result from a changed offer; and the change is worth making only if a net gain remains on balance. A changed situation, therefore, need not induce the price maker to adopt the policy best suited to that situation if so doing involves an initial cost of change. Whether or not he will change his behavior depends on the relative magnitude of the cost of change and of the addition to profit expected to accrue from it. These, in turn, depend on a variety of factors, which include the nature of the adjustment contemplated, the extent to which conditions have changed, the expected duration of the new situation (and hence of the gain to be had by adaptation to it), the uncertainty of expectations, and the market rate of interest.

2a. ADAPTATION TO A PERMANENTLY CHANGED SITUATION

When a changed situation is expected to persist indefinitely, the price maker would always find it profitable to adapt his behavior if the cost of change involved no interest cost and if he had absolute confidence in his expectations. For adaptation to a permanently changed situation holds out the promise of a gain persisting indefinitely; and an infinite flow of gain, however small the rate at which it flows, is always greater than the finite and once-and-for-all cost of change. In reality, however, the cost of change always involves an interest cost; and future expectations are always discounted for uncertainty. An automobile manufacturer, for example, may hope to raise his profit by launching on the market a new model of his car, with a redesigned body and a few technical improvements. Such a change will involve costs which include that of planning and designing the improvements, building a model of the new car and testing it, retooling the assembly line, interrupting production during the change-over, launching a new advertising campaign, and so forth. The new model would not be worth adopting if the additional profit expected to accrue from selling it instead of the old model were less than the interest on the cost of change. For either the price maker borrows the money to pay for the cost of change and has to pay interest on the loan, or he advances it himself and thus loses the interest he might have earned on it otherwise. Moreover, in order to render the change profitable, the expected additional profit must not only equal but exceed —and that by a considerable margin—the interest on the cost of change. For the cost of change is a certain expenditure, whereas the future gain expected to accrue from the change is uncertain and must be discounted for uncertainty. To discount for uncertainty, businessmen usually adopt the rule of thumb of making no change and undertaking no investment that cannot be amortized fully within a given period of time—say, within 5 or 10 years. Accordingly, a price maker will not change his market offer unless the additional profit he expects to gain from the change is large enough to repay the initial cost of change within, say, 5 years.

Such a policy on the price maker's part keeps him from adapting his market behavior to every minor change in market conditions and thus stabilizes his market offer. Moreover, since the cost of changing different attributes of the price maker's offer is generally different, the cost of change stabilizes different attributes of the price maker's offer to different degrees. The attribute that it probably stabilizes least is price. For the cost of changing price is relatively small, except in the few cases, like that of subway fares, where it involves the costly readjustment of slot machines. Usually, the cost of changing price consists only in the cost of printing and distributing the new price lists, catalogues, and advertisements which publicize the new price. This cost is small; but, being independent of the magnitude of the price change, it will prevent small price adjustments, whose effects on profit are also small. There is a lower limit, therefore, even to price adjustments; and the price maker will ignore changes in the market situation which would call for adjustments below this limit.[1]

2b. ADAPTATION TO TRANSITORY CHANGES

The cost of change prevents adaptation to a changed market situation not only when the change is small but also when the expected duration of the changed situation is short. For in this case the flow of the gain

---

[1] In markets where price is determined by agreement among competing firms, the difficulty and lengthiness of negotiating and reaching agreement on a new price is similar to a cost of change and has the same stabilizing effect on price. A further stabilizing factor, which occurs in markets where there is no formal restrictive agreement but where each price maker keeps a close watch over his competitors' actions, will be discussed in Chap. XVII.

expected to result from adaptation will also be of short duration and may, for this reason, be insufficient to repay the initial cost of making adaptation. Moreover, the temporary gain resulting from adaptation to a temporarily changed situation may have to pay not only for the cost of the initial change but for the cost of the back-to-normal change as well. For example, if a fashionable designer brings out a new model of a custom-made shoe, this may or may not be adopted for mass production, depending on how long shoe manufacturers expect the new fashion to last. They will not produce it at all if they expect the new fashion to be too fleeting to yield profits sufficient to repay the cost of adjusting machinery to producing the new model and afterward readjusting it again to the production of more stable models. The cost of change, therefore, prevents adjustment not only to minor but also to temporary changes; and there is a lower limit not only to the magnitude of change but also to the duration of a changed situation, which it must reach to render adjustment profitable.

3. THE INDIVISIBILITY OF PRODUCTIVE RESOURCES

The services of some productive resources cannot be secured in less than a certain minimum quantity. In most industries, for example, to obtain the services of plant and equipment, the producer must build his plant and buy his equipment. This means that he must buy a large quantity of their services all at once and pay (or pledge himself to pay) for them at the outset. This fact would create no problems if the producer could use up completely this minimum quantity of productive services during the period of time for which he can plan his production with full confidence. Problems arise only when, as is often the case, the quantity of productive services stored up in a piece of equipment is greater than the quantity the producer needs currently and expects with confidence that he can use. The purchase of such equipment is something of a gamble to the producer, because it implies the purchase of productive services a part of which he may never be able to use.

3a. ADAPTATION TO A PERMANENTLY CHANGED SITUATION

This consideration has almost exactly the same effect on the price maker's behavior as the cost of change. Take, for example, a manufacturer who expects a secular rise in the demand for his product and wants to profit from it by adding a new plant to his already existing manufacturing plants, with whose profitability he has firsthand experience. Nothing would keep him from building his new plant if he were certain in his expectations. But the lifetime of plant and equipment may be longer than the period for which he dares to plan ahead; and in such a case, he must weigh the certain expenditure on plant and equipment against the uncertain expectation of fully utilizing their services for the entire period of their lifetime. To discount for this uncertainty, the producer again uses the rule of thumb of investing in additional capacity only if he can amortize its cost out of the gain to be had from its use within some period shorter—sometimes considerably shorter—than its lifetime. Accordingly, the impossibility of obtaining the services of plant and equipment in small quantities and for short periods of time may prevent a producer from adopting the behavior that—from a static point of view—would yield him the highest profit.

The situation is similar and the argument the same when the price maker believes that his actual price is too high and that a lower price and consequent higher sales would give him a larger profit. If meeting the higher demand requires the building of additional plant or the purchase of additional equipment, the producer must again weigh the cost of such investment against the uncertainty of making full use of it throughout its entire lifetime; and his discounting for such uncertainty may easily keep him from expanding his capacity and adopting his most profitable price.

The above examples show that the parellelism between the effects of the cost of change and of the indivisibility of resources is very close. The only difference between them is that whereas the cost of change militates against any kind of adaptation or change in the price maker's market offer, the indivisibility of resources may prevent expansion (and changes that call for expansion) but not contraction, because only expansion necessitates the acquisition of additional productive resources.

Sometimes, the indivisibility of resources does not prevent but merely postpones the producer's response to a changed situation. Take, for example, a technical innovation or a change in factor prices which renders a new method of production, different from the producer's actual method, the most profitable. If adopting the new method requires the purchase of new equipment, a producer already equipped for producing with the old method will adopt the new method only if the total cost of operating *and amortizing* the new equipment is lower than the cost of operating his old equipment. This means that the new method of production must be considerably cheaper than the old for an established producer to scrap his old equipment and adopt the new method of production right away. But even if this is not the case and the producer decides to retain his old method of production, he will not retain it indefinitely. For, sooner or later, his existing equipment falls due for replacement or partial replacement; and as soon as this happens, he faces a new kind of choice. At this stage, he must choose between partly or wholly replacing his worn-out equipment with similar equipment and buying the new type of equipment; and, to make his choice, he must compare the cost of operating and amortizing the new type of equipment to the cost of operating the old type of equipment and amortizing the cost of replacement. It is apparent that if the needed replacement is at all substantial, the producer will at this stage adopt the new method of production.

3b. Adaptation to Transitory Changes

The indivisibility of resources may also prevent adjustment to a temporarily changed situation if this is not expected to last long enough to amortize the resources that would be bought if adjustment were made. The demand for munitions in time of war, for example, holds out the promise of proverbially high profits in war production; nevertheless, the prospect of these profits fails to induce manufacturers to expand their productive capacity if the war demand is expected to be of short duration only. Usually, wars and the resulting extraordinary demand for munitions are not expected to last long enough to render the building of additional war plants profitable. This fact prompted the British and American governments during the second World War not to rely exclusively on private initiative for the building of war plants but in many cases to build these plants themselves and rent such government-owned productive capacity to private firms for operation. The same fact, incidentally, also provides a partial explanation of why Nazi Germany— which in this respect relied largely on private initiative—failed to build up her war potential to its full extent. Similarly, a new invention or technical improvement will not be exploited commercially if it requires a large investment and if manufacturers expect it soon to be superseded and rendered obsolete by further developments in the same field.

4. THE TURNOVER LAG

A change in the price maker's offer affects, and is often designed to affect, his rate of turnover. But it takes time for a changed offer to have its full effect on turnover, because price takers need time to learn about the change and still more time to adapt their behavior to it; and it is on their behavior that the price maker's turnover depends. Strictly speaking, one can seldom assign a definite length of time to the turnover lag and say that it takes so many weeks or months before a change in the price maker's offer has its full effect on his rate of sales or purchases. For even if the majority of price takers did make adaptation within definite and not-too-wide time limits, there would always be some price takers who lag behind or form habits for a lifetime and never adapt their behavior. Hence, the dispersion over time of price takers' adjustments will often approach infinity—or what to the price maker would appear to be infinity. For practical purposes, however, the price maker ignores this tail end of adjustments. He is concerned with the bulk of price takers' adjustments and usually expects this to be accomplished within a definite period of time. It is this period that we shall refer to as the "turnover lag."

The factors that determine the price taker's reaction time were discussed in some detail in the last section of Chapter III. Since the price maker's turnover lag depends upon and is some average of his price takers' reaction times, it is obvious that the factors discussed in Chapter III from the price taker's point of view are, for the price maker, the determinants of his turnover lag. The reader is therefore referred to Chapter III for a detailed analysis of these factors. Here, we propose to discuss the relevance of the turnover lag to the price maker's decisions; and we shall take price setting as our example. It should be borne in mind, however, that the turnover lag affects all other aspects of the price maker's offer as well.

4a. ADAPTATION TO A PERMANENTLY CHANGED SITUATION

Consider, first, a price maker whose actual price has been the most profitable to him up to date but who is now confronted with a permanent change in conditions which renders a different price his optimum price. By adopting the new optimum price, he would raise his total profit over and above what it would be if he maintained his old price, which has ceased to be an optimum price. The gain would be the resultant of two effects: a change in per-unit profit and a change in turnover. These two effects are usually opposed to one another. That is, if the price change is such that it raises per-unit profit, turnover is likely to fall off; conversely, if it lowers per-unit profit, turnover is likely to increase as a result.[2] The net effect of these opposing changes, however, is always a gain. This is true by assumption; for we assumed the new price to be the most profitable price.

There is an important difference between these two effects both in

---

[2] This rule is not universal: "inferior goods" form an exception to it. But, for the purpose of the following discussion, we shall ignore this exception.

their timing and in the degree of certainty attached to them in the price maker's mind. The change in per-unit profit is instantaneous and certain; whereas the change in turnover comes about slowly and gradually, and its extent is a matter of conjecture. Hence, for a while, before the market has had time fully to adjust itself to the new price, the price maker's total profit will mainly be affected by the change in his per-unit profit. This may mean either that he will suffer a temporary loss of profit before the changed price has had its full effect of stimulating turnover, or that he will temporarily make an exceptionally high profit until the new price restricts his turnover. We can distinguish, therefore, between the initial and the long-run effects on profit of a change in price. The initial effect may either weaken or reinforce the long-run effect.

For example, if the price maker is a seller and he has raised his price, he will make an exceptionally large profit for the time during which he sells at the higher price to people who have formed their buying habits on the basis of his previous lower price. In the same way a buyer will make an exceptionally large profit during the period of transition immediately following the *lowering* of his price; for price takers need time to change their selling habits, to find other buyers, and to offer their wares or services to other buyers. The initial effect on profit of a seller lowering or a buyer raising his price is the exact opposite. He offers more favorable terms to price takers in the expectation that he will thereby increase his turnover. But before the new offer has had time to exercise its desired effect of expanding his market, the price maker will suffer a temporary loss of profit, doing business at the new price but not yet at the new rate of turnover.

This argument can be illustrated graphically on a diagram in which time is measured along the horizontal axis and profit per unit of time is measured on the vertical axis in terms of deviations from what profit would be if price had remained unchanged. In other words, a point on the horizontal axis shows not zero profit but the amount of profit the price maker would earn by keeping his price unchanged. A point above the horizontal axis shows the amount of additional profit due to a change in price; whereas a point below the axis represents a loss of profit due to a change in price. A curve in this diagram shows, for each moment of time, the price maker's differential profit (positive or negative) due to his having changed his price. If a seller raises or a buyer lowers his price in response to a changed market situation, his profit will rise very much at first and afterward gradually level off to a more modest gain, as the new price restricts his turnover. This is shown in Figure 61. The price maker's total gain due to the price change up to any point of time is shown by the area under the profit curve. When the seller lowers or the buyer raises his price, the initial effect on profit is a loss of profit, which changes into a gain gradually, as the new price stimulates turnover. This is illustrated in Figure 62, where the area under the horizontal axis shows the initial loss of profit and that above it shows the long-run gain. The difference between the two areas up to any point of time shows the net gain or net loss of profit due to the price change.

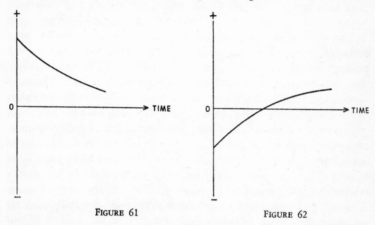

FIGURE 61   FIGURE 62

How does the magnitude of an initial gain due to a raise in the seller's price compare to that of an initial loss due to a price reduction? An inspection of Figure 61 and 62 suggests that the initial loss of profit would always be smaller than the initial gain if the turnover lag were the same in the two cases. But the turnover lag is not likely to be the same, because the market usually responds more slowly to a price reduction than to a price increase; and this difference tends to equalize the magnitudes of initial gain and initial loss. For the effect of a raise in the seller's price is to restrict his transactions with his actual market, which learns about the changed price in the course of normal business. By contrast, for a price reduction to have its full stimulating effect on sales, it must enlarge the seller's market and reach the ears not only of his actual but also of his potential customers; and this is bound to be a much slower process. The argument is almost exactly the same also in the buyer's case.

Unlike the cost of change and the indivisibility of resources, the turnover lag may not only impede but also promote changes in the price maker's market behavior. In particular, the turnover lag presents an obstacle only to changes aimed at expanding turnover; and it puts a premium on changes that would restrict turnover. For example, when changed conditions or their changed appraisal set the seller's most profitable price below his actual price, he will think twice before he lowers his price, having to weigh the initial loss of profit against the long-run gain. At the same time, when changed conditions call for a higher price, he will raise his price sooner and more easily, because the initial and long-run effects of the contemplated price increase are both stimuli. The same asymmetry exists also for the buyer; but in his case the turnover lag impedes the raising and stimulates the lowering of price.

This asymmetrical effect of the turnover lag on price raises and price reductions explains the price maker's bias in favor of restrictive price policies. Sellers, for example, tend to set their prices too high whenever they are uncertain as to what their most profitable price is. The same asymmetry explains also the resistance (stickiness) of the seller's price to downward pressure and of the buyer's price to upward pressure. Such resistance is the greater, the larger is the initial loss of profit, which in turn varies with the length of the turnover lag. Similar considerations apply even to bargained prices. Wages are the outstanding example of this case. The effect of a wage reduction on the demand for labor is remote and problematic, which partly explains the resistance of sellers (unions) to demands for lower wages in times of unemployment. By balancing the certain and immediate reduction in the incomes of employed wage earners against the doubtful and distant increase in employment, trade-union officials easily conclude that the certain loss outweighs the uncertain expectation of gain.

The initial loss of profit has exactly the same effect on the price maker's market behavior as the cost of change. The initial loss of profit is temporary but immediate and certain; and it is weighed against the long-run gain, which is permanent but distant and uncertain, and must be discounted for uncertainty. Accordingly, the seller will not lower (and the buyer will not raise) his price unless the long-run gain expected to result from such a price change is large enough to offset the initial loss of profit within a given period of time. Hence, the price maker may continue selling or buying at his established price, even if he knows that this is no longer his most profitable price.

As to the initial gain, we saw already that this provides an added incentive for the seller to raise (or the buyer to lower) his price when changed conditions or the changed appraisal of unchanged conditions makes a higher (lower) price appear more profitable. But unlike an initial loss of profit, which seems to follow a reduction in the seller's (or increase in the buyer's) price in every market whose response to price changes is not instantaneous, the initial gain is not nearly so general. For the gradual diminution of sales, which accounts for the initial gain, is only one of several possible results of the raising of the seller's price. An alternative behavior pattern of buyers is to lower their purchases at first in protest against and indignation over the price increase, and to return gradually to their old, established consumption habits as their indignation wears off. Yet another possibility is that they might try at first to substitute competing products, but, on finding these inferior, might gradually return to the original product. In all such cases the raising of the seller's price may cause an initial loss of profit rather than an initial gain.

There may be some markets, therefore, in which a price change in either direction results in an initial loss of profit. In such markets the turnover lag and resulting initial loss have exactly the same general stabilizing effect on the price maker's market behavior as the cost of change; and we can conclude right away that in such markets the turnover lag prevents both upward and downward price adjustments in response to minor and temporary changes in conditions.

It is likely, however, that the asymmetrical effect of the turnover lag is more common. This is especially true of the effect of the turnover lag on the other attributes of the price maker's market offer. For the above argument, which dealt with pricing policy, applies *pari passu* to most other aspects of the price maker's market policy as well. For example, the producer's problem of determining the quality of his product is very similar to that of determining price. By lowering quality, he can save on costs and so try to raise his profit; by improving quality, he may increase costs but can hope to raise profit if the improved quality attracts new customers and raises turnover. The change in costs is certain and immediate; the change in turnover expected to result from it is relatively distant and problematical. Hence, the first policy is always more readily adopted than the second; and in case of doubt the price maker is tempted to follow the first.

Similarly, an employer can try to lower costs either by economizing on measures needed to protect the safety and welfare of his workers or by introducing better working conditions designed to raise their morale and productivity. Here again, the contrast between the certainty of the immediate change in costs and the uncertainty of the resulting future change in productivity accounts for a natural bias in favor of the first policy. This bias in favor of higher prices and inferior quality on the seller's part and of lower prices and worse working conditions on the buyer's part is always unfavorable to the price taker, even though it does not always favor the price maker. That it is a powerful influence is strongly suggested by the great publicity given to each case in which a manufacturer has increased his profit by offering lower prices, better quality, higher wages, or better working conditions—the implication being that these cases are surprising and exceptional.

4b. Adaptation to Transitory Changes

Besides discouraging one type of adjustment to a permanently changed situation and encouraging another, the turnover lag also prevents adjustment to changes that are temporary. We mentioned already that this may be so in the special case of markets where the initial effect of both price reductions and price increases is an initial loss of profit. But the same holds true also in the asymmetrical case.

Let us consider a changed situation which is not expected to last long but which, if it were expected to persist indefinitely, would induce the price maker to change his price. Such a new situation may be expected to be followed either by a further change in the same direction or by a return to the old "normal" conditions. In the first case the turnover lag is no impediment to instantaneous price adjustment. In the second case, when conditions are expected to revert to the original situation after some time, the price maker's problem is whether he should change his price temporarily in response to the temporary change in conditions, or whether he should keep price unchanged at its actual "normal" level. The first of these alternatives would involve two price changes, opposite in sign but equal in magnitude: one away from the present price, and the other back to it. Their initial effects on profit would also be opposite in sign but approximately equal in magnitude; and in the absence of a discounting factor—which would give greater weight to the first than to the second—they would cancel each other out. In this case, therefore, adjustment would not be worth making if the new situation were expected to last no longer than for the duration of the turnover lag. For, whether the first price change would result in an initial loss of profit, or whether it would bring about exceptionally high profits, the initial effect of the second price change (i.e., the back-to-normal adjustment) would counterbalance it. The price maker may therefore just as well save himself the trouble of making adjustment and keep his price unchanged throughout the period.

The situation is different when the changed conditions outlast the turnover lag. In that case the price maker is able to maintain his new price long enough so that, in addition to its initial effect on profit, it also has a long-run effect, which is not offset by the initial effect of the back-to-normal price change. This long-run effect is a net gain to the price maker and is needed to make the price adjustment profitable. Hence, a temporary situation must be expected to outlast the turnover lag in order to prompt the price maker to make adjustment to it.

The argument can be illustrated graphically on the same kind of diagram that was used earlier in this chapter.[3] Figure 63 shows the effect

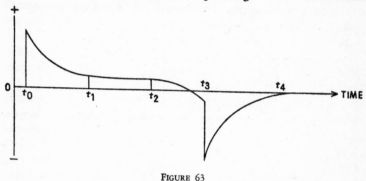

FIGURE 63

on profit of a seller's raising (or a buyer's lowering) his price at t_0 in response to a temporary change lasting for the period $t_0 t_2$, and lowering (respectively raising) it again at t_3 when conditions have reverted to the original situation. The initial gain lasts for the duration of the turnover lag $t_0 t_1$ and is given by the area enclosed by the differential profit curve between t_0 and t_1. It is approximately equal to and canceled out by the initial loss following the second (back-to-normal) price change at t_3, represented by the area above the profit curve between t_3 and t_4.

The long-run gain from the temporary price change is shown by the area under the curve between t_1 and t_2. It is obvious that a long-run gain arises only when the changed situation lasts longer than the turnover lag. When conditions revert to the original situation (in period $t_2 t_3$), the original price again becomes the optimum price, compared to which the new price yields a net loss, about as great as the net gain which it had yielded before. This is expressed in Figure 63 by the differential profit curve dipping below the horizontal axis by as much as it was above

[3] See p. 275 for Fig. 61 and its explanation.

it. This loss of profit will induce the seller to lower (or the buyer to raise) his price again (at t_3), which leads, for the duration of the turnover lag (t_3t_4), to a larger but temporary loss of profit, represented by the area under the curve between t_3 and t_4. This loss, called the initial loss, offsets the initial gain.

Figure 64 shows the effect on profit of a temporary lowering of the seller's price or a temporary raising of the buyer's price. Here, the initial loss of profit precedes the initial gain; but apart from this difference the argument is the same. As in the previous case, the initial loss and initial gain cancel out approximately; and the temporary situation must last long enough to exceed the turnover lag and so give rise to long-run gains.

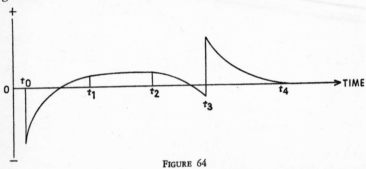

FIGURE 64

The above argument relates not only to price determination but applies *pari passu* to most of the price maker's other decisions as well. In fact, it applies to all decisions that affect his offer, since all such decisions affect the behavior of his price takers and therefore involve a turnover lag. When he contemplates introducing a new model, altering the quality of his product, or changing any other attribute of his offer, the price maker must always take into consideration the turnover lag; that is, the time his market requires to learn about a change and make adjustment to it. This will influence the price maker's other decisions in exactly the same way in which it influences his pricing policy. The same diagrams can be used to show the effect on profit of adapting any feature of the price maker's offer to a temporary change in conditions. Any such adaptation will give rise to an initial gain or initial loss of profit and will be worth making only if it also results in a long-run gain.

How large must the long-run gain be, and how long must it last, in order to render profitable a temporary change in the price maker's market offer? It must be sufficient, first of all, to repay the cost of change if changing the price maker's offer involves a cost. Second, it must be large enough and last long enough also to amortize the cost of any indivisible resources whose acquisition the change makes necessary. Third, the net gain which remains after deducting the cost of change and fully amortizing the additional resources must be sufficient to overcome the price maker's natural inertia and preference for a stable offer, which he knows to be preferred also by his market.

It seems, therefore, as though a changed situation would have to last considerably longer than the turnover lag in order to prompt the price maker to adjust his market offer to it. This, however, is not necessarily the case. For the above argument was based on the assumption that initial gain and initial loss are approximately equal in magnitude; and this assumption does not always hold true. To begin with, the back-to-normal change is a future and uncertain event, which, together with its initial effect, may be discounted for uncertainty. Such discounting of the second initial effect introduces the same kind of asymmetry which we discussed in the last section. In particular, it shortens the period of time for which the seller can make a temporary price increase; and it lengthens the period for which he can profitably make a temporary price reduction.

The second factor that may introduce an asymmetry between initial gain and initial loss is the possibility of reducing the initial loss of profit by shortening the turnover lag associated with it. When a price maker contemplates making his offer more favorable to the market with a view to expanding his turnover, he can usually reduce his initial loss of profit by advertising the contemplated change. Clearance sales at reduced prices, for example, are only worth making if the initial loss of profit can be substantially reduced by an advertising campaign. Without this, the lowering of per-unit profit would not raise turnover fast enough to make such sales profitable. The cost of advertising the temporary price reduction is, of course, a cost of change, which must be repaid out of the additional profit due to the change. But the large scale on which clearance sales are advertised is proof that the cost of such advertising is small compared to the saving in initial loss which it makes possible.

5. THE PLANNING PERIOD

We have seen above that the cost of change, the indivisibility of certain productive resources, and the turnover lag have varying effects on the price maker's behavior when he is faced with a permanent change in conditions. They impede adaptation to the new situation in some instances and encourage it in others. They are alike, however, in that they all tend to restrain the price maker from making adaptation to a temporarily changed situation. In other words, all these factors contribute to stabilizing the price maker's behavior and keeping it unchanged in the face of fleeting changes in the conditions confronting him. It is convenient to have a name for the minimum length of time for which the price maker must expect a changed situation to persist in order to adapt his behavior to it; and we shall call it the planning period.

The length of the planning period depends on a variety of factors. To begin with, it may be different for different aspects of the price maker's behavior. Thus, one might distinguish between a price-planning period, a quality-planning period, an advertising-planning period, a plant-planning period, and so forth. Differences in the lengths of these planning periods determine, first of all, the differences in the relative stability in time of the different aspects of the price maker's behavior. For example, if a producer's price-planning period is three months and his quality-planning period one year, he will change his price more often than the quality of his product. A three-month price-planning period does not mean, however, that intervals of three months must elapse between successive changes of the producer's price. It only means that changed conditions must be *expected* to persist for at least three months to prompt a change in price. The price maker may revise his price every week if he changes his mind weekly as to what the permanent (i.e., longer than three months) situation will be; conversely, he may keep his price unchanged over several years of violently changing market and cost conditions if, throughout that time, he never expects the new situation to persist for as long as three months and maintains an unshaken faith in the speedy return of "normal" times. Such cases of extreme behavior, however, are likely to be rare. As a rule, the frequency with which the price maker changes different aspects of his behavior tends to be closely correlated with their respective planning periods.

The planning periods associated with the different elements of the price maker's behavior also determine the type and degree of adaptation he will make to a given change in conditions. When a price maker faces a changed market situation which he expects to persist for, say, one year, he will adapt to it only those aspects of his behavior whose planning periods are one year or less; and he will leave unchanged the elements of his plan that have planning periods longer than one year. Hence, the longer a new situation is expected to last, the more complete will be the price maker's adaptation to it.

The producer's longest planning period is usually that associated with the planning of his plant capacity. As a rule, the producer's plant is the least divisible of his factors; and, for additional demand to prompt the building of additional plant, it must usually be expected to persist for several years. It is customary in the literature of economics to use the plant-planning period as the dividing line between the short and the long run. A long-run change in market or cost conditions, therefore, is a change to which the producer makes complete adaptation, including the adaptation of his plant capacity. To a short-run change in conditions he makes incomplete adaptation by keeping his plant capacity unchanged. This distinction will be discussed further in Chapter XIV.

Other determinants of the length of the planning period are the nature of the goods or services the price maker deals in, and the habits and psychology of the people he deals with. Accordingly, differences in planning periods explain not only why the same price maker adjusts some elements of his behavior sooner and more often than he adjusts others; they also explain why price makers in different markets behave differently under similar conditions. The main example of such differences is the different variability of prices in different markets.

Since the cost of changing price is negligibly small as a rule, the main factor determining the price-planning period is the turnover lag. Accordingly, differences between the lengths of price-planning periods in different markets correspond approximately to differences in turnover lags. But the price maker's turnover lag depends on the reaction times of his customers. Hence, to determine the price maker's price-planning period and the variability of his price, we must study the reaction times of the price takers to whom he sells or from whom he buys.

The factors that determine the reaction times of consumers—and hence also the turnover lags of price makers selling to consumers—were discussed in the last section of Chapter III; and it may be well to recall some of the results that we reached there. We argued, for example, that the reaction times of consumers increase with the durability of goods. Hence, we should expect durable goods to have long price-planning periods and relatively stable prices. This is borne out by experience. We also found that the unimportance of a good in the consumer's budget is likely to make for a long reaction time; therefore, we should also expect the prices of such goods to be relatively stable over time—an expectation that is also confirmed by experience. Another argument in Chapter III was that consumers' reaction times are likely to be short in informed and long in uninformed markets. Hence, price-planning periods will also be short in the first and long in the second type of market; accordingly, we should expect to find prices variable in the markets for simple goods, about whose nature the consumer is informed, and stable in the markets for technically complex products, whose quality the consumer cannot appraise unaided.[4] To cite just one more argument from Chapter III, we considered the availability of close substitutes a cause for short reaction times. Hence, when a consumers' good has close substitutes, the price-planning period associated with it is likely to be short; and its price is likely to be flexible. It will be seen later that the closeness of available substitutes for a good can be regarded as a measure of competition.[5] Accordingly, this factor explains in part why competitively produced goods have more flexible prices than goods produced under monopolistic conditions. This brief enumeration of the factors that influence the variability of market prices is far from complete; but it is beyond the scope of this book to present an exhaustive analysis of price variability.[6]

The foregoing discussion may have created the impression that in any given market a definite planning period can be associated with each aspect of the price maker's market offer and production policy. Unfortunately, however, this is not so. For the length of the planning period depends, in addition to the factors already mentioned, also on the nature and magnitude of the change in conditions to which adaptation is to be made. For example, to prompt an addition to productive capacity, a minor increase in demand must be expected to last longer than a major one. Strictly speaking, therefore, the price maker should determine the length of his planning periods separately for each change in market conditions. Sometimes, he actually does this. The investment-planning period, for example, is probably established separately for each individual investment. In other words, the producer probably makes a detailed calculation before every investment and every expansion of plant capacity in order to determine the number of months or years required

---

[4] In the experts' market, in which buyers react instantaneously to every change in price, the seller's price-planning period has zero length. This is only another way of saying that in the experts' market, everybody is a price taker; and no one can set his price. This subject will be discussed further in Chap. XV.

[5] See Chap. XVII, Sec. 4.

[6] For a more detailed treatment of this subject, see T. de Scitovszky, "Prices under Monopoly and Competition," *Journal of Political Economy*, Vol. XLIX (1941), pp. 663–85.

to make the additional capacity "pay for itself." At the same time, however, few producers would make a separate calculation before each price change to determine the length of time *this* would require to "pay for itself." With respect to price and other aspects of their market offer, most price makers probably establish conventional planning periods, presumably based on average past experience. Automobile manufacturers, for example, have established the convention of bringing out a new model once a year. On this aspect of market behavior, however, very little information is available.

The main importance of the planning period lies in the fact that it defines what we may call the price maker's horizon—that is, the length of time for which he plans his behavior and for which he must therefore look ahead when he makes his plans. He plans to keep his plant capacity unchanged for the duration of at least one plant-planning period, the quality of his product for at least one quality-planning period, his price for at least one price-planning period, and so forth. The different planning periods associated with his different decisions express the fact that he must look farther ahead when he decides whether to build or not to build a new factory than when he only sets his price. He plans to keep each aspect of his behavior unchanged for the duration of the planning period associated with it not only if conditions remain unchanged but despite temporary changes that are not expected to last for the length of the planning period. Temporary changes of this relatively fleeting character, therefore, are not relevant to the price maker when he makes his decision. A seller, for example, whose price-planning period is one month is not concerned with daily or weekly fluctuations in sales or costs when he determines his optimum price. To him the only data relevant for price determination are his expected volume of sales during one month and the marginal revenue and marginal cost associated with this volume of monthly sales. The planning period, therefore, is the unit of time for which the price maker must estimate his turnover, his marginal cost, and whatever other data he needs for making his decision.

We shall see in Chapter XIV that the cost estimate relevant to the producer's market decisions depends on the length of time for which he plans his behavior and makes his decisions. It would seem, therefore, that producers should base each of their decisions on a different cost estimate, depending on the planning period associated with each decision or type of decision. There is evidence that in some cases they do this. Investment decisions, for example, are based on a different cost estimate from that on which price is based. No information is available as to whether producers use different cost estimates also for determining different aspects of their market offer; but it is not likely that they would. The lengths of the planning periods associated with decisions relating to price, advertising, credit policy, and so forth, are not likely to differ greatly among themselves; and to base each of these decisions on a different cost estimate might well be a refinement that is not worth the trouble it would involve. Accordingly, we too shall make the simplifying assumption in Chapter XIV that the producer uses the same cost estimate as the basis for all attributes of his market offer, and that this cost estimate relates to one and the same period of time, which we shall simply call the planning period.

BIBLIOGRAPHICAL NOTE

The ideas and arguments contained in this chapter are simple and elementary; and many of them are to be found scattered here and there in the literature of economics. However, I know of no systematic discussion of the subject. My approach, as contained in this chapter, was first presented in a paper I read before a graduate seminar at Harvard University on February 12, 1942. Subsequently, this approach was applied to the problems of the labor market in J. T. Dunlop, *Wage Determination under Trade Unions* (New York: Macmillan Co., 1944), pp. 11–15.

For a detailed discussion of the special problem of price flexibility, see my "Prices under Monopoly and Competition," *Journal of Political Economy,* Vol. XLIX (1941), pp. 663–85.

CHAPTER XIII

THE PROFIT MARGIN

IN THE last two chapters, we discussed the general theory of the price maker's market behavior and stressed the fact that he has many competitive weapons, of which price is only one. In the present chapter, we shall concentrate on the firm's price policy and attempt to reconcile the formal theory of price determination with the firm's observed behavior.

There are two reasons for singling out price for special consideration. The first and main reason is the economist's special interest in prices. It must be remembered that our main concern is with the organization of the economic system and the co-ordination of its constituent parts. But in the market economy, prices determine the distribution of income; and the common knowledge of prices is the main co-ordinating link between the economic behavior of different people and of different firms. In the market economy, therefore, both the equity and the efficiency of economic organization depend largely on how prices are determined and how people react to them.

But not only to the economist are prices of special interest. Price determination is of prime concern also to the individual firm; and there is a very good reason for this. We saw, in Chapter XI, that in order to maximize his profit, the price maker must adopt not only an optimum price policy but also an optimum advertising policy, an optimum credit policy, and so forth; and we showed that reaching the point of maximum profit may necessitate repeated adjustments and readjustments of the several attributes of his market offer. At that stage, we were concerned only with the nature and conditions of the equilibrium position and not with the way in which it is reached. In the meantime, however, we saw that there exist stabilizing factors, which render uneconomical the making of minor and temporary adjustments. In particular, one of these stabilizing factors was the cost of change, which is a cost that the price maker must incur each time he changes his market offer. Hence, the number of steps in which he reaches his most profitable position is not immaterial to the price maker; and he will try to keep this number at a minimum. It can now be shown that to minimize the number of adjustments, the price maker must decide on his price policy first and determine all other attributes of his market offer afterward.

Let us recall that to maximize his profit, the price maker must equate the variation cost of every attribute of his offer to his profit margin.[1] Then imagine a price maker who starts out with a profit margin chosen at random and wants first to determine his advertising policy. He will find that the most profitable advertising policy for him to adopt is the one that renders his advertising variation cost equal to his profit margin. If, after having adopted this advertising policy, he discovers that his original profit margin was not a good one and needs revision, this will show him that he was too hasty also in the adoption of his advertising policy. For a revised profit margin will call for a change in advertising policy, since it will render profitable a new advertising policy that equates the advertising variation cost to the new, revised profit margin. In general, we can say that every change in the price maker's profit margin calls for a revision of every aspect of his market policy. This shows that to reach his most profitable market position in the smallest number of steps, the price maker must set his profit margin first and make all other adjustments afterward.

But to set one's profit margin is equivalent to establishing one's price policy. For the profit margin is the difference between price and the seller's marginal cost or the buyer's marginal value; and this difference is determined when the price maker sets his price. We showed in Chapter XI that to set his most profitable price, the price maker must add his price variation cost to marginal cost if he is a seller:

$$p = MC + VC_p ; \tag{1}$$

or subtract it from marginal value if he is a buyer:

$$p = PMV - VC_p . \tag{2}$$

The optimum price, therefore, differs from the seller's marginal cost or the buyer's marginal value by the price variation cost. This implies that the optimum profit margin is identical with the price variation cost. Hence, to minimize the number of steps in which he reaches his most profitable position, the price maker must first ascertain his price variation cost, on this basis set his profit margin and thus his price policy, and afterward decide on all the other attributes of his market offer.

---

[1] See p. 263.

Indeed, the behavior of businessmen in many markets is known to conform to this pattern. It is customary among sellers to calculate a per-unit cost base[2] and to set their price by adding to this base a profit margin which is traditionally and fairly permanently fixed, sometimes in absolute terms (as so many dollars and cents), but mostly in proportional terms (as a given percentage of the cost base to which it is added). Once the producer has determined his price policy in this way, he is likely to adhere to it. He usually keeps his price stable, changing it only in response to changes in the prices of his factors, and relies on other competitive weapons to deal with short-run changes in the market situation.

1. THE PRICE ELASTICITY OF THE MARKET

Let us now proceed to analyze the rationality of this type of market behavior in greater detail. Our first task in this connection is to discuss the factors that determine the price maker's optimum profit margin.

We recall that for the profit margin to yield the highest profit, it must equal the firm's price variation cost, which, in turn, depends on the market's responsiveness to a change in price. In fact, the price variation cost can be expressed as the ratio of price to the price elasticity of demand or supply:

$$VC_p = \frac{p}{\eta_p} .$$

Substituting from this into equations (1) and (2), above, we can express the price maker's optimum price by the equation

$$p = MC + \frac{p}{\eta_p} \tag{1.a}$$

for the seller, and by the equation

$$p = PMV - \frac{p}{\eta_p} \tag{2.a}$$

for the buyer; where p/η_p shows the optimum profit margin as a fraction of price. Sometimes, it is more convenient to express the optimum profit margin as a fraction not of price but of the seller's marginal cost to which it is added or the buyer's marginal value from which it is subtracted. Accordingly, the above equations can also be written in the equivalent forms

---

[2] The meaning and calculation of this cost base and its relation to marginal cost will be discussed in the next chapter. For the present, we shall assume that it is the same as marginal cost and that it is constant, i.e., independent of the rate of output.

$$p = MC\left(1 + \frac{1}{\eta_p - 1}\right)^3 \tag{1.b}$$

for the seller and

$$p = PMV\left(1 - \frac{1}{\eta_p + 1}\right) \tag{2.b}$$

for the buyer. The expressions $1/(\eta_p - 1)$ and $1/(\eta_p + 1)$, respectively, are the optimum profit margin which the seller adds to marginal cost and the buyer subtracts from marginal value. A seller, for example, whose market has a price elasticity of 3 will maximize his profit by adding a 50 per cent $[1/(3 - 1) = \frac{1}{2}]$ profit margin to marginal cost.

Having found that the price maker's optimum profit margin depends on the price elasticity of his market, we must next ask the question: What determines the market's price elasticity? To answer this question, we must bear in mind the fact that the market's response to a price change is the sum of the individual responses of the members of the market; and we recall that each individual's response to a change in price can be broken down into a substitution effect and an income effect. Hence, we can analyze the market's price elasticity by discussing the factors that determine the substitution and income effects.

Before we do this, however, let us recall that there is also a problem of timing here. For the market's response to a changed offer is not immediate. Days, weeks, or even months may elapse before a new price, or any other change in the price maker's market offer, has had its full effect on his turnover. Hence, to measure the elasticity of the market, dates must be assigned to the initial change in the price maker's offer and the resulting change in his turnover; and elasticity depends on the interval between the two dates or, in other words, on the length of time allowed to elapse after a change in offer before measuring the change in turnover to be imputed to it. The longer the span of time over which it is measured, the greater will be the elasticity of demand or supply. The problem arises, therefore, of determining what span of time gives the elasticity relevant to the price maker's decisions and, in particular, what price elasticity determines the price maker's optimum profit margin.

The solution of this problem was implicit in the analysis of section 4

---

[3] Because

$$p = MC\left(1 + \frac{1}{\eta_p - 1}\right) = MC\frac{\eta_p}{\eta_p - 1};$$

and hence,

$$MC = p\frac{\eta_p - 1}{\eta_p} = p\left(1 - \frac{1}{\eta_p}\right) = p - \frac{p}{\eta_p}.$$

of Chapter XII. For, as we showed there, the profit that prompts the price maker to change his offer is that which he hopes to earn after the initial effect of the change has subsided, that is, after turnover has fully adjusted itself to the new offer. This means that the elasticity relevant to the price maker, and the price elasticity which determines his optimum profit margin, is that which spans his turnover lag and shows the full effect of the change in the price or other features of his market offer. Hence, when we discuss the substitution and income effects of a price change, we shall always be concerned with the full effects of the change, as they appear after the turnover lag has fully elapsed.

The magnitude of the substitution effect depends, first of all, on the scope for substitution. The more substitutes there are to the price maker's offer, and the closer and more perfect are these substitutes, the greater will be the substitution effect of a change in price, and the greater, therefore, the price elasticity of the price maker's market.

But the availability and closeness of substitutes is not the only determinant of the substitution effect. For it is not enough that competing offers should exist and be substitutable for each other; it is also necessary for the members of the market to be aware of this fact. Given the existence and nature of competing offers, the response of the market to a change in price will be the greater, the better the existence and nature of the available alternatives are known. This means that the price elasticity of the market will be the greater, the better the members of the market are informed.

Furthermore, not even the existence of substitutes and knowledge of their existence will lead to substitution in response to a price change if the competitors who make the competing offers collude to prevent substitution. Such collusion may be implemented in a variety of ways, of which the most important is a common price policy. A rise in the price of a product will cause buyers to buy other products only if the prices of these other products have risen to a lesser extent or remained unchanged. The sellers of competing products, therefore, can prevent substitution among their products by agreeing always to change their prices together and in the same proportion. Agreements to prevent substitution will be discussed in detail later, when we deal with competitive restraints. For the time being, let us bear in mind that the presence or absence of such agreements is among the main factors which determine the market's price elasticity and the price maker's optimum profit margin.

Yet another determinant of the substitution effect of a price change is the existence and importance of complementarity between the good in question and other goods. Complementarity is, in a sense, the opposite of substitutability; and its effect on price elasticity is also the opposite. The more complementary a good is to other goods bought by the consumer, the less will his demand respond to a change in its price. For example, bread is complementary with butter and jam; and the consumer's demand for bread is little affected by a change in its price, because he thinks not so much of bread as of the combination bread-butter-and-jam as one commodity; and the price of this combination is but little affected by a change in the price of bread only. In a similar way the producer's demand far a factor is insensitive to changes in the latter's price if he uses this factor in close technical complementarity with other factors. An extreme case of technical complementarity is one in which the firm uses a factor in fixed proportions to output or to other factors. The producer's price elasticity of demand for such a factor is a fraction of the market's price elasticity of demand for his product; and it bears the same ratio to the latter elasticity that the cost of the factor bears to the producer's total cost of production.[4]

As to the income effect, its nature and magnitude depend, first of all, on the nature of the price maker's offer. This was amply discussed in Chapter III, where we distinguished between different types of consumers' goods (e.g., inferior goods and necessities) according to their income effects. But the income effect of a change in the price of a consumers' good also depends on the importance of that good in the consumer's budget. The greater the proportion of his income which a person spends on a given commodity, the more will his well-being be affected by a given change in the price of that commodity, and the greater, therefore, will be the income effect of the price change. Since the poor usually spend a larger proportion of their income than the rich on any given commodity, the market's response to a given price change tends to be greater if the market is composed mainly of people in the lower income groups than if it consists primarily of the rich.

These factors—the closeness of available substitutes, the market's information concerning these substitutes, the possible existence of agreements in restraint of competition, the importance of complementarity, and the market's composition by income groups—may be regarded as the main determinants of the market's price elasticity and hence of the price maker's optimum profit margin. But these factors in their turn

---

[4] The reader should be able to derive this simple result for himself. See, however, Joan Robinson, *The Economics of Imperfect Competition* (London: Macmillan & Co., 1933), pp. 255–56.

depend, at least partly, on the price maker's own market behavior. For example, by changing the quality of his product, the producer may render it a closer or less close substitute for competing products and so affect the price elasticity of the market's demand for it. Similarly, advertising may render the market more or less informed and so affect its price elasticity. Even a change in price may, if large enough, affect the market's price elasticity, since it may change the range of income groups represented in the market.

In short, the price elasticity of the market facing a producer is not independent of the nature of his market offer. This raises the problem how the price maker can estimate the price elasticity of his market and set his optimum profit margin *before* he has determined the other aspects of his market offer—considering that these other aspects are among the determinants of his market's price elasticity. It is apparent that any estimate of price elasticity which the price maker may make at this stage, before his offer is fully determined, is bound to be more or less inaccurate. But the crucial question is whether he could make a more accurate estimate at a later stage, when his market offer is fully determined. We shall argue in the following that the answer to this question is, in all probability, negative.

2. THE PROBLEM OF ESTIMATION

To begin with, the inaccuracy due to the price maker's estimating the price elasticity of his market before he knows the exact nature of his offer is probably very small. For one must bear in mind that when the price maker faces the problem of determining his market policy, he does not start from scratch, with a completely blank mind. He usually has a fairly definite notion of what kind of commodity he wants to produce, what type of market he wants to cater to, and on what scale he can operate. Hence, the problem of adopting his most profitable market policy is usually that of choosing the optimum price, optimum quality, optimum advertising policy, and so forth, within well-defined and fairly narrow limits. Variations in his offer within these limits may change the price elasticity of his market and hence also his optimum profit margin; but such changes are likely to be small and well within the margin of error with which elasticity and optimum profit margin are estimated at any stage.

For it must also be borne in mind that at no stage does the price maker have—or can he possibly have—a very definite notion of the market's responsiveness to changes in his price. To estimate the price elasticity of his market, the price maker must rely on past experience; and this is almost never in a form that would enable him to make an accurate calculation or, indeed, to do more than make an intelligent guess. A seller, for example, probably knows the price at which he sold his product during different past periods; and he also knows what quantities he sold during those periods. Differences in the quantities sold during different periods may partly be due to differences in his price; but they will also be partly due to differences in other factors. For the market's demand for one seller's product depends not only on the price he sets but also (1) on all the other characteristics of his market offer, (2) on all the characteristics (including price) of his competitors' market offers, and (3) on the incomes and preferences of his customers and potential customers. The price he sets is only one among a large number of factors that influence his sales; often, it is neither the most important nor the most variable factor. Hence, it is often impossible either to separate the effect of the price change from that of other changes, or to neglect the effect of other changes on demand, or to appraise the relative importance of price and other changes.

It may be helpful to repeat this argument in geometrical terms. To estimate the price elasticity of the seller's market amounts, in geometrical terms, to estimating the shape of his demand curve. His data, the price and sales of his product during a sequence of past periods, can be plotted in a price-quantity diagram, in which the price set and quantity sold during each period are represented by a point. This is shown in Figures 65 and 66. Each of these points may be thought of as the point of intersection of a supply curve and a demand curve. The supply curves are horizontal straight lines, which represent the price maker's offer to sell any quantity at a set price; and it is obvious that each price is represented by a different supply curve. As to the demand curve, its shape is what we want to determine. This would be easy if we could assume that there is only one demand curve. For, on this assumption, all the points in the diagram, being points of intersection between the one demand curve and the several supply curves, lie on or near this demand curve and thus determine its shape. This is illustrated in Figure 65. But to make this assumption is equivalent to assuming that changes in the seller's price were the only factor influencing his sales during the entire sequence of periods; for when we draw a demand curve, we imply that every factor influencing demand, except the seller's price, is held constant.

We know, however, that there are usually many changes other than changes in his price that also influence the seller's sales; and every change in demand due to these other changes must be represented by a shift of the demand curve. Usually, therefore, we must assume that a different demand curve goes through each of the points in the diagram; and when this is the case, our data do not, by themselves, enable us to determine the slope of these demand curves. This is illustrated in Figure 66, where the points are the same as those shown in Figure 65; but the demand curves drawn through them have a different and arbitrarily chosen slope.

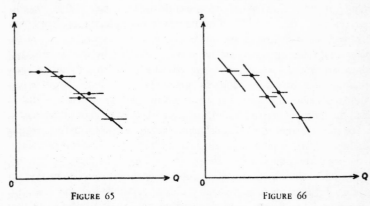

FIGURE 65   FIGURE 66

When the other factors influencing demand are small in number and statistical information on them is available, partial regression analysis makes it possible to separate the influence of these factors from that of price and to determine the market's price elasticity. This is what statistical demand studies try to do. But all these studies are concerned with demand, and with the price elasticity of demand, for the output of an industry as a whole; and this is relevant to the producer's market behavior only if he is a monopolist or a member of a collective monopoly or oligopolistic group in control of an industry's entire output. Statistical estimates of the price elasticity of demand faced by one of many sellers in a competitive market are seldom, if ever, feasible. For the competitive seller's sales vary not only with his price, his customers' income, and the secular changes in their tastes—the factors usually considered in statistical demand studies—but also with his competitors' prices and general market behavior; and to take account of this additional group of influences is usually beyond the powers of partial regression analysis.

The price maker may conceivably circumvent the above difficulties by making experiments. If his knowledge of past prices and turnover does not enable him to assess his market's response to price changes and determine his optimum profit margin, he can try to find them out by making experimental price changes during a period when other factors are relatively stable. This is feasible and has been done. The price maker may lower his profit margin in the hope that the resulting increase in turnover will more than offset the reduction in per-unit profit; or he may raise his profit margin, hoping that the consequent fall in turnover will fail to offset the gain in per-unit profit. But such experimental price changes may be rendered uneconomical by the same factors that prevent temporary and minor price adjustments. For example, the existence of a turnover lag discourages the price maker from experimenting with lower profit margins, because he will be deterred by the certain and immediate initial loss of profit, against which he can only set the expectation of a distant and doubtful gain. The importance of this factor would lead one to expect that actual profit margins, when they differ from the most profitable margin, are more likely to be above than below it. For the deterrent to the experimental *raising* of profit margins is not nearly so strong. It probably consists of nothing more than the premium that price takers put on price stability.

The importance of these stabilizing factors varies from one market to another. In some markets, they may rule out experimental price changes altogether. That they often are important we can only infer from the market behavior of price makers. It is known that profit margins are traditionally fixed in many markets. A certain percentage profit margin may be adhered to by a firm for many years; sometimes, the same percentage profit margin is considered best and adopted by every firm in a given market. This fact has occasionally been interpreted as proof that the members of such markets either are irrational or do not aim at maximizing profits. But a more reasonable interpretation would be that some time in the past, members of the market found one profit margin preferable to others and have retained it ever since. The market's price elasticity and hence the optimum profit margin may have changed in the meantime; but to ascertain the nature and magnitude of this change and revise profit margins accordingly might prove costly and something of a gamble, not worth undertaking for the sake of a doubtful and possibly insignificant gain.

Similarly, a newcomer to a market, with no past experience to rely on, may find it wisest to adopt the profit margins of his established competitors. When he enters the market, his best estimate of the price elasticity confronting him may well be that it is the same as that facing his competitors. His best policy, therefore, is to adopt his competitors' profit margins, assuming that their profit margins are equal to their price variation costs. Only when he has special reasons to think either that his price variation cost is different from theirs or that their profit margins are based on a mistaken estimate of their price variation costs will a new entrant to a market abandon the precedent set by established firms and adopt a profit margin different from theirs.

Let us stress once more that such reliance on one's own and on one's predecessors' and competitors' established profit margins need have nothing irrational about it. Probably it is the best way of setting price and maximizing profit whenever the price elasticity of the market cannot be determined statistically and experimental price changes are ruled out as unecenomical. This might very often be the case.

There is yet another reason, however, why price makers sometimes adopt or adhere to a traditional profit margin. In some cases the members of a market are reluctant to abandon a price policy generally accepted and sanctioned by long usage for fear of losing their competitors' good-will and disturbing the existing market situation. They feel bound to maintain the profit margin considered "fair" in their particular trade, either because loyalty to their group and observance of business ethics form part of their moral code, or because they suspect that by departing from traditional trade practices, they might precipitate a general adoption of "more exaggerated competition" which, on balance, would do them more harm than good. This type of market behavior will be discussed at length in Chapter XVII, which deals with the various forms of restricted competition. It is mentioned here only as a further explanation of the constancy of profit margins.

We tried above to explain the rationale of the practice common among price makers of setting price by adding to cost a fixed percentage profit margin. We showed that this practice may be perfectly rational and compatible with the desire to maximize profits, although we have no evidence to prove that it is, in fact, motivated by this desire. Our explanation, therefore, is necessarily tentative. But whether it is right or wrong makes comparatively little difference to the rest of the argument. For the economist's main aim is to observe the businessman's behavior and find out how it affects the efficiency of the economic system. If we try to rationalize the businessman's observed behavior and to explain it in terms of his motivation—such as his desire to maximize profit—we do so because in this way we can learn and say a little more about his behavior than we could otherwise. We could draw conclusions and make predictions on the basis of purely mechanical and uncritical observations of regularity in the price maker's behavior; but we can attach so much more confidence to these conclusions and predictions if we can explain the persistence of observed behavior as the logical consequence of rational motives.

The simple relation between the market's price elasticity and the price maker's optimum profit margin renders it relatively easy to analyze the latter's pricing policy and response to changes in cost and market conditions if we assume that he aims at maximizing his profit. It is obvious, for example, that a rise in the producer's costs—due, let us say, to a rise in wages—will raise prices by the same percentage by which marginal cost has risen, unless there is special reason to suppose that the wage raise has changed the market's price elasticity and hence also the producer's optimum percentage profit margin. In other words, we can generally expect producers not only to shift all changes in costs onto the consumer but to do more than that and change prices in the same proportion in which costs have changed.

Needless to say, this is not an exact rule but only a general tendency to which there are many exceptions. To begin with, the cost of change and other stabilizing factors will often induce the price maker to "absorb" minor or temporary changes in costs and so keep prices from following every fluctuation in cost conditions. Second, a change in costs may be absorbed and leave price unchanged if the price maker wants to make a contrary change in his profit margin. Third, a change in costs may, on occasion, result in a more than proportionate price adjustment, because it provides an excuse for carrying out price revisions which had previously been postponed for fear of their unfavorable effect on the firm's public relations, or not made earlier owing to the cost of change or some other stabilizing factor. Last but not least, we have definite information that, in some markets, producers tend to keep their profit margins unchanged in absolute terms.

Equally simple to appraise are the effects on price of a change in demand conditions. A rise in demand, for example, will not raise price unless it raises marginal cost or is accompanied by a fall in the price elasticity of demand. As will be shown in the next chapter, marginal cost tends to rise only if catering to the additional demand requires full-capacity production. As to the price elasticity of demand, it falls only if there are special reasons for it to fall. We know very little about these special reasons; but it is well to bear in mind the fact that a rise in demand need not, in itself, imply a fall in price elasticity and therefore need not lead to a rise in price.

One special case when it does is that in which the increased demand for a commodity is due to a rise in the incomes of its consumers. When a person's income rises, he is not only prompted to spend more on consumption but is also likely to become more negligent in planning his expenditures; for it is part of a higher standard of living that one can afford to be less calculating and less careful in shopping. Such a change in market behavior lowers the market's price elasticity and therefore raises the price maker's optimum profit margin. This reason for lower price elasticities and higher prices in times of high incomes and great prosperity is called the law of diminishing elasticity of demand.[5]

Another special reason for a change to occur in the price elasticity of demand and the seller's optimum profit margin is an organized buyers' strike. This consists not in a mere curtailment of expenditures, which in itself would not lower prices, but in a greater alertness in shopping, the withholding of expenditures coupled with a greater willingness to spend as soon as prices start falling. From the seller's point of view, this appears as an increase in the price elasticity of demand and provides an inducement to lower profit margins and prices.

It is worth noting here that this argument and the preceding ones concerning the producer's price policy hold true not only when his profit margin is at its optimum level and equals his price variation cost but also when he thinks that it is at that level, or at least thinks that it is sufficiently close to the optimum level for practical purposes.

3. THE OTHER ASPECTS OF THE PRICE MAKER'S MARKET OFFER

We saw above that for the price maker to choose his profit margin and set his price are one and the same thing. But the price maker's choice of a profit margin, besides determining his price, influences all other aspects of his market behavior as well. For when he chooses a profit margin and sets a price, whether or not they are his optimum profit margin and most profitable price, the price maker automatically determines what will be his most profitable advertising policy, credit policy, quality of product, and so forth. This follows from the fact that it is always profitable for the price maker to push his sales (or purchases) through advertising and through the offer of more credit, better

---

[5] Cf. R. F. Harrod, *The Trade Cycle* (Oxford: Oxford University Press, 1936), pp. 17–22.

quality, and other such methods, to the point where the variation cost of each of these attributes of his offer equals his profit margin. This is so, irrespective of whether or not his profit margin is the most profitable one. Hence, to every profit margin there corresponds a different advertising policy, credit policy, quality of product, and so on, which will maximize the firm's profit *for that profit margin.*

The above result is not nearly as surprising as it may appear at first sight. It is generally known, for example, that when a group of competitors make an agreement (express or tacit) to suspend price competition among themselves, nonprice competition among them tends to be intensified. This is exactly what the above analysis would lead us to expect. The price agreement raises the profit margins of the parties to the agreement; and it thereby encourages them to raise their expenditures on advertising and the offer of quality improvement, credit facilities, and other services to the point where the variation cost of each of these competitive weapons has become equal to the now higher profit margin. Needless to say, the effect on profit of one producer's increased competitive actions will be partly or wholly offset by the increased competitive actions of his rivals. This will not discourage them, however, unless they become fully conscious of the dependence of their profits on each other's actions. In this case, all producers may restrain their competitive actions for fear of retaliation; or they may extend their price agreement to cover and limit nonprice competition as well. This subject will be discussed further in Chapter XVI, where we shall deal with restricted competition in greater detail.

BIBLIOGRAPHICAL NOTE

On the subject matter of this chapter, there is no generally accepted and easily accessible theory. Such a theory is yet to be developed; and it will have to be based, of course, on studies of actual business behavior. Among such studies, perhaps the most important are the following: R. L. Hall and C. J. Hitch, "Price Theory and Business Behavior," *Oxford Economic Papers*, Vol. I (1939), pp. 12–45; National Bureau of Economic Research, *Cost Behavior and Price Policy* (New York, 1943); C. C. Saxton, *The Economics of Price Determination* (Oxford: Oxford University Press, 1942); and P. W. S. Andrews, *Manufacturing Business* (London: Macmillan & Co., 1949). See also E. A. G. Robinson, "The Pricing of Manufactured Products," *Economic Journal*, Vol. LX (1950), pp. 771–80, which is a review of the last-mentioned book.

CHAPTER XIV

THE COST OF PRODUCTION

UNTIL now, we have followed the economist's traditional approach and regarded marginal cost as the relevant cost concept, which serves as the basis of the producer's market policy. The concept of marginal cost, however, is the economist's invention; and businessmen are usually ignorant of it. They generally regard average variable cost as the basis for their market behavior. This fact has led some economists to accuse businessmen of irrational behavior; but simpler and more correct interpretations of it are (1) that the practical difficulties of calculating marginal cost may be insurmountable; (2) that average variable cost is in many cases a good approximation to marginal cost; and (3) that in some instances average variable cost, although different from marginal cost, may nevertheless properly be used as the basis for the firm's price policy. We shall see in section 2 of this chapter that there is need for all three interpretations.

In the following, we shall be concerned with the practical problems of calculating the firm's costs of production; and we shall try to reconcile the apparent contradiction between the economist's theory of the firm in terms of marginal cost and the businessman's habit of basing his price policy on average variable or average total cost. We have so far been able to ignore these problems because, in Part II, our analysis was admittedly and deliberately unrealistic, aimed merely at constructing a theoretical model of an efficient economy. Also, our analysis of the firm was static until Chapter XII; and it will be seen that many of the problems to be considered here are raised by the passage of time.

1. THE COST ELEMENTS

So far in our discussion of productive factors, we have paid little attention to differences in the divisibility of their services. From the price maker's point of view, however, such differences are important, because they affect the way in which he varies his rate of output; and this, in turn, has a bearing on his cost calculations and hence also on his market offer.

It is customary to distinguish between productive services which are freely divisible and those which are not. The services of a factor of production are freely divisible if they can be had and used in any quantity, however small. For example, raw materials, fuel, and electric power can usually be bought and used in any quantity. Similarly, production workers can usually be hired for any length of time and fired at an hour's notice. In contrast to these factors, there are others, whose services either cannot be had or are not worth having in less than a certain minimum quantity or for less than a minimum length of time. This minimum quantity in which, or length of time for which, a factor must be used will be called its service period; and the cost of obtaining the services of a factor for its service period may be called its acquisition cost.

For example, the services of industrial equipment—the use of a drill press, a machine lathe, or a steam hammer—can usually be obtained only by buying it. The service period of such equipment is its lifetime (sometimes expressed as so many machine-hours), and its acquisition cost is its purchase price. Similarly, the service period of a manufacturing plant is its useful lifetime; and its acquisition cost is the cost of building it plus the sum of those current expenses to which it gives rise during its lifetime independently of how much it is used. Examples of such expenses are real-estate taxes; fire insurance; and the cost of repainting, reroofing, and similar maintenance.

In a somewhat different category are the personal services of, say, a plant manager. His services might be obtained for any length of time, but usually they are not worth acquiring for too short a period. For, to be useful to his firm, a plant manager must first "learn the ropes," get to know the workings, and become acquainted with the special problems of his firm and his plant. All this takes time; and only after a more or less prolonged period of apprenticeship will he be able to prove his worth and become fully useful to the firm. For this reason also a plant manager can be thought of as having a service period, that is, a minimum length of time for less than which he will not be hired. This fact has found institutional expression in the custom of securing managerial services by contract that has a minimum term to run, during which minimum term it cannot be terminated. We can regard a person's term of contract as his service period and his salary for the term of his contract as the acquisition cost of his services. We shall say, for example, that a manager with a one-year contract has a service period of one year; and the acquisition cost of his services is one year's salary. It is well to bear in mind, however, that the manager' contract is the effect rather than the cause of the indivisibility of his services.

In a similar way, also the services of foremen, accountants, secretaries, and most administrative employees and salaried officials become useful only after a while; for this reason, it is customary to secure their services also for a minimum period, either by contract or by the stipulation of a minimum period of notice.

We can now proceed to classify the firm's factors of production into variable and fixed factors. The distinction is made from the point of view of the entrepreneur, who, in making his decisions, considers some factors variable and others fixed. Where he draws the line between variable and fixed factors depends on the period of time for which he makes his decisions; and, since he makes different decisions for different periods of time, he may well regard the same factor as fixed when he makes a short-run decision and as variable when he makes a long-run decision.

It is customary, however, to distinguish between fixed and variable factors from the point of view of those decisions of the entrepreneur which determine his market offer. We saw in Chapter XII that the entrepreneur makes his offer in the market with a view to eliciting a certain response to his offer and with production plans geared to meet the market's response. He stands ready to revise his offer if the market's response is not what he expected it to be; but he makes his offer, and plans to keep it unchanged, for the duration of a certain minimum period of time, which we called the planning period.[1] Hence, the entrepreneur's production plans associated with his market offer are also made for at least one planning period; and when he plans his production, he regards each factor as variable, or fixed, depending on whether its quantity can or cannot be adjusted within one planning period. Accordingly, we shall regard as variable all the freely divisible factors, like labor, materials, and fuel, and also those other factors whose service periods are no longer than the entrepreneur's planning period. The quantity of these factors employed depends on the producer's market offer; and it is determined as part of the production plan he makes to meet the market's response to his offer.

---

[1] The producer may, of course, associate different planning periods with different attributes of his market offer; but, for simplicity's sake, we shall neglect these differences throughout our discussion of costs and cost estimation. It is not likely that our results would be significantly affected by taking these differences into account.

By contrast, the factors whose service periods are longer than the producer's planning period we shall regard as fixed. Some of his fixed factors the producer inherits from the past; and the quantity of these is obviously given to him. He can add, of course, to the quantity of fixed factors already in his possession; but to do so requires a decision that is entirely separate from his market offer and from the production plan associated with his market offer.

Since the services of fixed factors become available to the firm for a minimum period which is longer than its planning period, the purchase or hire of fixed factors will be governed by expectations looking farther ahead than the expectations that govern the price maker's market offer. In other words, the decision as to how many additional fixed factors to obtain must be based on expected market conditions not only during the next planning period but during several future planning periods. For example, to decide whether or not to build a new manufacturing plant, the producer must appraise the profitability of the new plant over its entire lifetime, which usually extends far beyond the period for which he plans his market offer. Such a decision, which we shall call an investment decision, commits the producer more irrevocably and for a longer time than does his market offer; for this reason, he must make his investment decision first. Only after he has made his investment decision and determined the quantity of his fixed factors can he proceed to make his market offer; and when he formulates his market offer, he must regard the quantity of his fixed factors as given. Let us examine the implications of this statement more closely.

The price maker bases his market offer on his cost estimates; and, since he sets his offer for a planning period, he must also estimate his costs for a planning period, which he regards as the unit of time relevant to his market policy. Hence, when we speak of the cost of q units of output, we shall mean the cost of producing q units of output *per planning period;* and by current output, we shall mean the total output produced during the current planning period.

The price maker's costs of production consist of the cost of his variable and fixed factors of production. The cost of variable factors is the total cost of the services of all the variable factors utilized during one planning period. This constitutes the price maker's current cost and is usually an out-of-pocket expense. It varies directly with the rate of output he decides to produce, because the quantity of variable factors employed varies directly with his rate of output.

In contrast to variable factors, the quantity of fixed factors employed is independent of the price maker's market offer; therefore, the acquisition cost of his fixed factors is given. This does not mean, however, that the cost of fixed factors *imputed to the output of a planning period* is also given. Since the service periods of fixed factors are longer than the producer's planning period, he usually expects to use them during more than one planning period. He acquires a fixed factor as an investment and regards its acquisition cost as an investment cost, to be charged not against current output only but against the output of several planning periods. That part of a fixed factor's total acquisition cost which is charged against the output of one planning period is called its amortization cost for that planning period. The sum total of the amortization costs of all the fixed factors employed by the firm is called the firm's overhead cost.

How fast the producer amortizes a fixed factor, and how large a part of its acquisition cost he charges against current output, depends (1) on his estimate of its future usefulness and (2) sometimes also on its current utilization. For example, when a manufacturer buys a machine tool whose expected lifetime (service period) is 20 years, he may amortize its acquisition cost over 20 years; but if he believes that its usefulness to him will end sooner, he may decide to amortize its cost over 15 or 10 or only 5 years. It is apparent that the shorter the time for which he expects to use a fixed factor, the higher will be the latter's amortization cost charged against the output of any one planning period.

Whether the current amortization cost of a fixed factor varies also with its current utilization depends on whether its current utilization affects its future usefulness. For example, the future usefulness and lifetime of a manufacturing plant is usually independent of its current output; therefore, its amortization cost imputed to current output must also be independent of the rate of current output. Similarly, the future usefulness of a plant manager is independent of the amount of work he does in the current planning period; accordingly, the part of his salary imputed to current output must also be independent of the current rate of output. Such cost items, which are independent of the current rate of output, are called fixed costs or fixed overhead costs.

Consider, however, a piece of machinery, like a power tool or a delivery truck, whose useful life depends on the intensity of its utilization. The useful life of such equipment is sometimes expressed as so many thousand machine-hours, which can, within limits, be used up faster or more slowly, according to need. The more intensive the current utilization of such equipment, the less of its services will be left over for

L

future use. This is irrelevant to the producer who intends in any case to scrap his equipment before it wears out and expects its scrap value to be unaffected by its current use. But this may be an exceptional case. More often, the producer regards such machinery as an inventory of services, which he can exhaust sooner or later, and the unused part of which he can resell if necessary. Since the future usefulness or resale value of such equipment depends on its present utilization, its amortization cost charged against current output must also vary with the rate of current output. This variable part of a fixed factor's amortization cost is called variable overhead cost or prime user cost; and it is a payment for services that otherwise could and would be used at a later stage. The variable overhead cost of a piece of equipment, therefore, is the difference that current use makes to its future value to the producer. For example, a delivery truck which at the end of the year would be worth $1,000 if not used at all but only $800 if used currently at a given rate has a variable overhead cost of $200 for the current year.

The current cost of the producer's variable factors and the variable and fixed overhead cost of his fixed factors constitute the firm's total cost of production. Of these, current cost and variable overhead cost are usually bracketed together under the name of variable cost, because they—in contrast to fixed overhead cost—vary with the firm's rate of output.

It is well to bear in mind that since the distinction between variable and fixed factors is based on the producer's planning period, the relative importance of variable and fixed costs of production also depends on the producer's planning period. The longer the planning period, the fewer the factors considered fixed, and the smaller, therefore, the importance of fixed costs in the total cost of production.

In addition to its variable and fixed costs of production, the firm also has other costs, which we shall call marketing costs. We have seen in Chapters XI and XII that to sell its products and obtain its factors on the most profitable terms, the price maker takes the initiative in the market; and, in taking the initiative, he may incur expenses other than his costs of production. The cost of advertising, of offering customers credit facilities and delivery service, and of offering employees recreational facilities or low-cost housing are instances of marketing costs; but they are not the only forms of marketing costs. The initial cost to the price maker of changing his market offer with a view to raising or maintaining his profit is also a marketing cost, whether it is incurred in changing price or in designing, developing, and retooling for an improved version of his product. It is apparent from the above examples that the distinctions between marketing and production costs is rather arbitrary,[2] and that it does not correspond to a distinction between socially useless and socially useful costs.

Marketing costs, like production costs, can be divided into variable and fixed costs, according to whether or not they vary with the volume of output. For most decisions made by the firm, the distinction between marketing and production costs is irrelevant. Accordingly, it is best to lump them together and distinguish only between variable and fixed costs.

2. THE COST BASIS OF THE PRODUCER'S MARKET OFFER

The producer makes cost estimates for three purposes: first, for estimating his profit; second, as a basis for his market offer; and third, as a basis for his investment decisions. For estimating his profit, the producer needs an estimate of total cost, since profit is defined as the difference between total receipts and total costs. We defined total cost in the last section; and we have nothing to add here, except to stress once more that total cost is a flexible and subjective concept, since it depends on how fast the producer chooses to amortize the acquisition cost of his fixed factors, which in turn depends on his appraisal of their future usefulness to him.

In order to determine his most profitable market offer, the producer needs an estimate of marginal cost; and it is here that the distinction between variable and fixed costs becomes relevant, because marginal cost depends on variable cost alone. In symbols:

$$MC(q) \equiv TC(q + 1) - TC(q) \equiv [VC(q + 1) + FC]$$
$$- [VC(q) + FC] \equiv VC(q + 1) - VC(q).$$

This chain of identities shows that marginal cost, MC, is the increment in total cost, TC, due to a one-unit addition to output; and when total cost is expressed as the sum of variable cost, VC, and fixed cost, FC, it appears that marginal cost is the increment in variable cost alone. Hence, to estimate his marginal cost, the producer can ignore his fixed costs and concentrate on changes in variable costs only. The dependence of marginal on variable cost is most conveniently shown by expressing variable cost as an average, per unit of output; for the relation between

---

[2] For example, the elaborate bottles in which perfume is sold are definitely an integral part of the commodity, perfume; but they also have very much to do with sales appeal. Should their cost be considered part of production or marketing costs?

marginal and average variable costs and between marginal-cost and average variable-cost curves is the same as that between marginal and average revenue and between marginal-revenue and demand curves, respectively.[3]

The producer's average variable cost may conceivably fall, stay constant, or rise with increasing output; and to show that all three cases are conceivable, it is customary in elementary textbooks to draw the average variable-cost curve in U-shape, with a falling, a horizontal, and a rising segment. There is good reason to believe, however, that this way of drawing the average variable-cost curve is misleading.

Originally, the U-shape of the average variable-cost curve was supposed to emphasize the fact that when increasing quantities of the variable factors are combined with the fixed quantities of the fixed factors, it becomes increasingly difficult to produce additional quantities of the product, so that each additional unit of product requires the use of increasingly larger quantities of the variable factors. This argument, however, which we discussed in Chapter VI (pp. 116 ff.), is a purely formal argument. It is generally used at the high level of abstraction at which the theory of perfectly competitive behavior is held; but it must be modified for the more realistic theory of the price maker's behavior.

When the producer decides to change his rate of output and accordingly to change the number of his workers, he does not, as a rule, make his changed number of workers operate an unchanged number of machines. In most cases a reduction in the firm's labor force renders a proportionate number of machines idle; and an increase in its labor force is accompanied by putting into use previously idle machinery. In other words, short-run changes in the firm's rate of output do *not* change the proportions in which labor and equipment are combined; such changes, therefore, are likely to *leave unchanged* both the marginal input of the variable factors and their average input per unit of output. Accordingly, as long as the producer retains his method of production and stays within his normal operating range, we should expect his input of variable factors and—with given factor prices—also his variable costs to vary in proportion with output.[4]

The above theoretical result is also borne out by statistical cost studies.

---

[3] Cost as a basis for the producer's investment decisions will be discussed in the next section.

[4] For a more detailed discussion of this point, see George Stigler, "Production and Distribution in the Short Run," *Journal of Political Economy*, Vol. XLVII (1939), pp. 305–27.

Such studies have been made in a variety of industries; and they indicate, almost without exception, that average variable cost is constant throughout the firm's normal operating range and rises only in the range of full- (or more than full-) capacity production. Since marginal cost coincides with average variable cost whenever the latter is constant, this result shows that in these industries the producer can use average variable cost as his estimate of marginal cost as long as he stays within his normal operating range.[5] This is illustrated in Figure 67, which shows

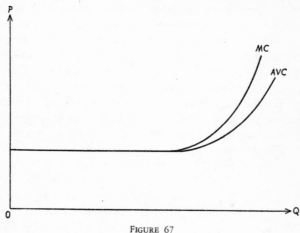

FIGURE 67

the typical shape of a statistically derived average variable-cost curve, together with its marginal-cost curve.

It is true, of course, that all statistical cost studies eliminate, by statistical correction, the effects of changes in factor prices. Their result, therefore, that average variable cost is constant, applies only to producers who are price takers in factor markets and who regard factor prices as given. Despite this qualification, which will be dealt with presently, the above result is an important one. For it has been found valid in such dissimilar industries as steel, women's hosiery, leather-belt manufacturing, and so forth; and it is for this reason a very strong confirmation of the logical argument stated on page 308.

In addition, however, to the logical argument and the statistical confirmation of this argument for expecting the firm's average variable

---

[5] Throughout this section, we shall only be concerned with the producer's cost estimate while he stays within his normal operating range. The problems he faces when he tries to expand output beyond this range will be discussed in the next section.

cost to be constant within its normal operating range, there is yet another argument for regarding the firm's average variable cost at least as though it were constant. This argument has to do with the practical difficulties of estimating the firm's variable costs.

Let us recall at this stage that we are interested not in the *true* value of the firm's costs and the *true* shape of its cost curves but in the best practical estimate which the producer or his accountant can make of the cost concept most useful as a basis for the firm's market policy. We saw above that, in some firms and industries, it is possible to derive statistically the firm's *true* average variable-cost curve, which, as we just saw, coincides with its marginal-cost curve in the normal operating range. There are many other industries, however (and they are probably in the majority), whose operations are far too complex to allow the derivation of statistical cost curves. Furthermore, these same complexities create problems also for the cost accountant; and we shall see presently that to meet these problems, the accountant usually has to *assume* that the output of products varies in proportion to the input of variable factors and that average variable cost is therefore constant.

It must be borne in mind that the producer's variable cost is as flexible and as subjective a concept as the total cost of production. To begin with, variable overhead cost is an imputed cost; and since there is no simple way of determining objectively how the depreciation of a piece of equipment depends on its utilization, it is usually determined conventionally, on the assumption that depreciation depends linearly on the rate of output. In other words, the accountant *assumes* average variable overhead cost to be constant.

The current cost of variable factors would seem easier to estimate; but the estimation of even this cost element raises two difficult problems. The first of these problems is due to the fact that production happens in time. Many commodities take days, weeks, or even months to produce; and the current cost of producing a particular unit of output is incurred over its entire period of processing, which precedes its date of completion. This implies that the current cost of producing the June output is incurred partly in June, partly in May, and sometimes partly in April. Hence, a changed June output will be correlated with changed costs in June, May, and April, which raises the problem of which cost to impute to which output.

The second and closely related problem of estimation arises from the fact that most firms in our economy produce not one but several commodities, or at least several variants of the same commodity. Costs of production are usually incurred in producing a whole array of commodities, which are produced jointly, and among which expenses must be allocated. How to allocate the firm's variable costs among its several products becomes a difficult problem when the same workers working in the same plant and using the same materials and the same machinery work on several products or on parts that go into several products.[6]

The accountant's customary way of solving these two problems is to study the average quantity of materials, fuel, labor time, machine-hours, and so forth, which goes into the production of each part and each product, and to allocate current costs (and also variable overhead costs) over time and among different products on the basis of these studies. This implies that the accountant calculates the current cost of each product *on the assumption* that the quantity of variable factors needed for producing one unit of any particular product is the same, irrespective of the firm's rate of output. In other words, he assumes that output varies in proportion to the input of variable factors. This seems a reasonable assumption to make; and—what is more important—it is very difficult to see what else the accountant could do. We conclude, therefore, that the inherent complexities of his task may compel the accountant to use a method of cost calculation which, together with the assumption of given factor prices, implies constant average variable costs. When the latter assumption is correct, therefore, the producer's average variable cost becomes his best estimate of marginal cost. Let us repeat that this may not be his *true* marginal cost; but it is the best estimate of marginal cost available to him; and, as such, it is the proper basis of his market policy.

The above result hinges on the assumption of given factor prices. In our economy, many firms are price takers in the markets where they buy their factors of production, because there is a general tendency for prices to be set by sellers rather than by buyers. The labor market is the main exception to this rule; but there, wages are usually determined by bargaining and, once agreed upon, are apt to be regarded as given by employers and workers alike. Factor prices, therefore, are given to many producers; and these producers are perfectly justified in using average variable costs as the relevant concept on which to base their market behavior and to which to add their profit margins.

There are also other producers, however, especially large producers, who are able to set the prices at which they buy raw materials and

---

[6] The allocation of the firm's *fixed* costs among its several products is an equally difficult problem; but we are not concerned with it here.

intermediate products. In the labor market, even the large producer settles wages by bargaining; but he usually feels that his bargaining advantage depends on his rate of operations and diminishes with increasing activity. Even if a wage rate has been agreed to and fixed in a wage contract, the employer may still feel that an increase in his output and consequent increase in his demand for labor would prompt the union to seek an early termination of the wage contract and ask for a higher wage. This type of situation in the labor market, together with the producer's ability to set his price in other factor markets, implies that he faces upward-sloping supply curves of his factors and expects factor prices to rise with his rate of output. In this case the producer's average variable-cost curve will also be rising, even if his output varies (or is assumed to vary) in proportion to the input of variable factors. What is the proper estimate of the firm's marginal cost in such a situation?

To answer this question, it is convenient to think of marginal cost as being composed of two parts. The first part is the market value of the additional factors needed to produce an additional unit of output. This is equal to average variable cost if output varies in proportion with the input of the variable factors—an assumption that we found justified and will adhere to throughout this discussion. The second part of marginal cost is the cost to the producer of persuading factor markets to sell him the additional factors. This part of marginal cost is in the nature of a variation cost; and it differs from variation cost as defined in Chapter XI only in that it is the cost of persuading the market to sell the producer not one additional factor but as many additional factors as are needed to produce an additional unit of output. In the labor market, where price is determined by bargaining, the variation cost may be defined as the rise in the wages bill occasioned by the producer's loss of bargaining power.[7] It appears, therefore, that when the producer is a price maker or bargainer in factor markets, the marginal cost of his output consists, in addition to average variable cost, of the sum total of the variation costs incurred in persuading factor markets to sell him additional factors.

How large is this second part of the firm's marginal cost; in other words, by how much does marginal cost exceed average variable cost? We have seen in Chapter XI that the ratio of price to variation cost measures the elasticity of the market. Hence, the ratio of the market value of all the additional factors needed to the sum total of all variation costs incurred in obtaining them must equal the weighted average elasticity of supply faced by the producer in all the factor markets of

---

[7] The same is true of other factor markets where price is settled by bargaining.

which he is a member. From this, it follows that to estimate his marginal cost, the producer must add to his average variable cost a margin that, expressed as a proportion of average variable cost, is the reciprocal of the weighted average elasticity of supply of his factors.[8]

Let us now summarize shortly the foregoing argument. The producer needs an estimate of the marginal cost of his product or products in order to determine his most profitable market behavior. As a rule, however, he cannot hope to estimate directly his marginal cost—let alone the entire shape of his marginal-cost curve—and must content himself with his accountant's computation of average variable cost as the only information available to him. Our problem was how to base an estimate of marginal cost on this information.

We have seen that average variable cost is equal to and the best estimate of marginal cost if output varies in proportion with the input of variable factors and if the prices of variable factors are given. The first condition is fulfilled in almost all the industries for which statistical cost studies are available; in many other industries it must be assumed if cost estimates are to be made at all. The second condition, given factor prices, obtains in some but not all industries and firms. Where it does not obtain, marginal cost exceeds average variable cost by a margin that depends on the weighted average elasticity of supply facing the firm in factor markets. A producer, therefore, who is a price maker in some or all factor markets must estimate the marginal cost of his product by adding an appropriate percentage margin to average variable cost. To the estimate of marginal cost so obtained, he must then add a further percentage margin in order to determine the most profitable price of his product.

This means, however, that we can express the producer's optimum price policy in terms not only of marginal cost but also of average variable cost. To do this, let us proceed as follows. To determine the price that will maximize his profit, the producer must equate receipts and costs on the margin. Every additional unit of product sold adds to his gross receipts the price of the product. To calculate the addition to his profit, he must deduct from this addition to gross receipts the addition to costs occasioned by the additional sale. These additional costs consist of three items. First, to produce the additional unit of product, the producer must buy additional quantities of his variable factors

---

[8] Strictly speaking, it is the margin expressed as a proportion of average *current* cost which is the reciprocal of the weighted average elasticity of supply. The version given in the text, however, is more convenient; and it can be rendered formally correct by assuming that the elasticity of supply of the services of the firm's fixed factors is infinite.

and pay for the faster depreciation of some of his fixed factors. This first cost item is the average variable cost of the firm's product. But if the producer is a price maker in factor markets, he cannot obtain additional factors merely by paying for them their market prices; he must persuade the owners of the factors to sell him the additional factors; and the cost of doing so is the producer's second cost item. Having obtained the additional factors and produced with their aid an additional unit of product, the producer faces yet another problem, that of persuading the market to buy from him the additional product. The cost of doing this is the producer's third cost item. The sum of these three cost items must be subtracted from the price of the additional product in order to obtain the addition to profit; and total profit will be highest at the point where the sum of additional costs equals price and the addition to profit is zero.

So far in our discussion, we have lumped together the first two cost items into marginal cost and discussed the price maker's market behavior in terms of marginal cost and variation cost or marginal cost and marginal revenue. We did so, and shall continue to do so, partly in order to simplify the analysis but mainly because this approach makes it easier to discuss the problems of efficiency, which are our main concern. However, if a realistic presentation of the producer's market behavior had been our primary aim, we could and should have discussed it in terms of the above three cost items, in which case average variable cost would have appeared as the basis of the producer's price policy. We have seen that the weighted average elasticity of supply in factor markets determines the percentage margin which must be added to average variable cost for a correct estimate of marginal cost, and that the elasticity of demand in the product market determines the further percentage margin to be superimposed on this in order to obtain the most profitable price. The estimation of marginal cost, therefore, is merely an intermediate step, which the price maker can easily leave out. Instead of adding first one margin to average variable cost and then superimposing another, the producer can combine the two margins into one, add this combined margin to average variable cost in order to obtain his most profitable price, and ignore or forget about marginal cost altogether.

3. THE COST BASIS OF THE PRODUCER'S EXPANSION POLICY

In the last section, we were concerned with the estimation of marginal cost within the producer's normal operating range, which is determined by the quantity and productive capacity of his fixed factors of production. Now, however, we must consider the problems faced by the producer when he contemplates expanding his output *beyond* the limits set by the fixed quantity of his fixed factors.

As a rule, the producer can raise his output above normal in several different ways. He can make his employees work overtime, he can introduce a night shift, he can crowd additional machinery and workers into his plant, or he can build additional plant. Generally, each way of expanding output involves a different cost; and the producer will always choose that way whose cost is lowest. The cost of any particular form of expansion, however, depends—among other things—on the period of time for which the producer expects to maintain his higher output and over which, therefore, he plans to amortize the acquisition cost of his additional fixed factors of production. Accordingly, the type of expansion that would be cheapest in the long run may be far from being the cheapest in the short run. The producer will therefore choose one way of expanding output if he expects to maintain his higher output indefinitely; but he may adopt quite a different way of expanding output if he only wants to cater to a temporarily increased demand. All this is obvious and mere common sense, but it is nevertheless worth discussing in a systematic fashion.

In a sense, this subject has been discussed already in Chapter XII. We showed there that one can associate a separate planning period with each element of the producer's plan, and that this planning period denotes the length of time for which a new situation must be expected to persist in order to render profitable the adjustment of that particular element of the producer's plan. In Chapter XII, however, we were concerned with the stability of different elements of his plan; whereas here we must look at the same problem from a different point of view and find out which of several alternative plans the producer will adopt in a given situation.

As an example, let us imagine a producer who customarily plans his market offer and makes his cost estimates for a planning period of one month and who is now faced with a substantially increased demand which he believes to be temporary but expects to persist for six months. Let us also assume that he can increase his output in any one of three ways: by overtime work, by introducing a night shift, or by expanding plant capacity. His problems in this case are (1) in what way to increase his output, (2) by how much to increase it, and (3) at what price to sell it.

No fully satisfactory analytical apparatus has as yet been developed for illustrating the nature of these problems and their solutions. For want of something better, therefore, we shall use an ordinary price-quantity diagram (see Fig. 68). In this diagram, we can draw, first of all, the demand curve (*D*) and its marginal-revenue curve (*MR*), which represent the producer's new and higher demand expectations.

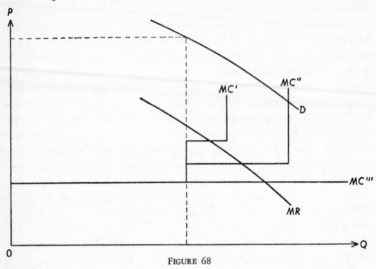

FIGURE 68

Facing these curves, we can draw, *for each way of increasing output,* the marginal-cost curve that would be applicable *after* that particular way of increasing output had been adopted. It should be noted, however, that such a marginal-cost curve does not show the *full* cost of increasing output when additional fixed factors must be purchased before a particular way of increasing output can be utilized. This complication will be considered a little later.

In Figure 68 the *MC′* curve shows the marginal-cost curve applicable if output is raised by requiring workers to work overtime. The *MC″* curve shows the marginal-cost curve applicable if output is raised by the introduction of a second shift. It shows that the scope for raising output is greater with a second shift than with overtime on a single shift, and that the labor cost of so raising output is lower, despite the somewhat higher wages and lower labor productivity customary on night shifts. The *MC‴* curve shows the marginal-cost curve applicable if output is raised by increasing plant capacity.

Once we know which way the entrepreneur will choose to raise his output, the diagram of Figure 68 can be used to determine his most profitable price and rate of output. For example, should the producer decide to introduce a second shift, his most profitable output would be shown by the abscissa of the intersection between the MR and MC'' curves; and his most profitable price would be shown by the ordinate of the demand curve for this abscissa.

As to the producer's choice between the three different ways of raising his output, he must clearly choose the one that promises him the highest additional profit. At first sight, one might think that the additional profit is represented in Figure 68 by the area enclosed by the marginal-revenue curve, the requisite marginal-cost curve, and the vertical line, which represents pre-expansion output. This, indeed, is correct as far as raising output through overtime work is concerned. It is not correct, however, as regards the two other ways of increasing output, because neither the MC'' nor the MC''' curve shows *all* the marginal cost of raising output. Whether he raises output by introducing a night shift or by increasing plant capacity, the producer must buy additional fixed factors,[9] whose amortization cost is part of the marginal cost of raising output in these ways. This amortization cost is not shown by the MC'' and MC''' curves; and it must be deducted, therefore, from the additional profit as shown in the diagram when comparing the relative profitability of the three ways of increasing output.

How is this additional element of marginal cost computed? If he introduces a night shift, for example, the producer must install additional lighting equipment, and sometimes also additional safety and recreational facilities prescribed by local ordinances or stipulated in his wage contract. To calculate the monthly amortization cost of this equipment, the producer must subtract from its acquisition cost the estimated value of having it six months later, when the night shift is no longer needed; and he must divide the remainder by six. If he is doubtful, as he often will be, whether the higher demand will persist for as long as six months, he may, for safety's sake, calculate his monthly amortization cost by amortizing the cost of the new facilities over, say, five months only. The monthly amortization cost so obtained forms part of the producer's marginal cost and must therefore be deducted from the profit represented in Figure 68 by the area between the MR and MC'' curves in order to calculate the true profitability of raising output by the introduction of a second shift.

---

[9] I.e., factors whose service periods are longer than the one month for which the producer makes his cost estimates.

In a similar way the cost of raising output by plant expansion includes, in addition to the marginal cost shown by the MC''' curve, also the monthly amortization cost of the additional plant equipment; and this amortization cost must be calculated in a way analogous to that described in the preceding paragraph.

The important thing to note about this part of the producer's marginal cost is its dependence on the period of time for which he expects the higher demand to persist. It is the greater, the shorter is the period over which the additional fixed factors have to be amortized.[10] Accordingly, the producer's choice between the three ways of raising output depends on the length of time for which he expects the higher demand to persist. If this period is very short, the amortization cost and hence marginal cost of either a night shift or plant expansion may be so high as to render overtime work the most (or the only) profitable way of raising output. If this period is very long, plant expansion is likely to become the most profitable; whereas the night shift will be the chosen policy somewhere between these two extremes.

BIBLIOGRAPHICAL NOTE

This chapter has presented a very simple—perhaps too simple—picture of the problems of cost calculation faced by the firm. For a further study of the problems discussed in section 1, see J. S. Bain, "Depression Pricing and the Depreciation Function," *Quarterly Journal of Economics,* Vol. LI (1937), pp. 705–15; Cann J. B. Canning, "A Certain Erratic Tendency in Accountants' Income Procedure," *Econometrica,* Vol. I (1933), pp. 52–62; J. M. Keynes, *The General Theory of Employment, Interest and Money* (London: Macmillan & Co., 1936), chaps. v–vi; A. P. Lerner, "User Cost and Prime User Cost," *American Economic Review,* Vol. XXXIII (1943), pp. 131–32; and A. C. Neal, "Marginal Cost and Dynamic Equilibrium of the Firm," *Journal of Political Economy,* Vol. L (1942), pp. 45–64.

As to section 2, the reader should be familiar with statistical cost studies and the problems they raise. See J. P. Dean, *Statistical Determination of Cost with Special Reference to Marginal Cost* (Chicago: University of Chicago Press, 1936); J. P. Dean, *Statistical Cost Functions of a Hosiery Mill* (Chicago: University of Chicago Press, 1941); J. P. Dean, *The Relation of Cost to Output for a Leather Belt Shop* (New York: National Bureau of Economic Research, 1941); and H. Staehle, "Statistical Cost Functions: Appraisal of Recent Contributions," *American Economic Review,* Vol. XXXII (1942), pp. 321–33.

---

[10] Yet another determining factor of monthly amortization cost is the degree of confidence the producer has in his own expectations.

CHAPTER XV

THE CONDITIONS OF FREE COMPETITION

AFTER our discussion in the last four chapters of the individual price maker's problems and market behavior, we can now proceed to consider in its entirety the market in which price makers compete among themselves and face the price takers on the other side of the market. We saw already in Chapter II that for such a market to come about, there must be a disparity in numbers between buyers and sellers; and the people on the side with the larger numbers must be inexpert in their market behavior. We shall now discuss the nature and condition of inexpertness in greater detail; and we shall begin by contrasting the market where price makers face price takers with the perfectly competitive market, in which both the buyers and the sellers are price takers.

It was shown in section 3 of Chapter II that for a market to be perfectly competitive, the average person on both sides of the market must be an expert, since it is the expert's constant vigilance and readiness to switch from one offer to another in response to the slightest change in their relative attractiveness which force the traders on the other side of the market to regard price and the other terms of trade as given to them. When people on one side of the market are not experts, their response to changes in price and market conditions is slow, incomplete, and subject to inertia. This inertia, which is typical of the nonexpert's market behavior, gives those on the other side of the market the opportunity to become price makers, that is, to set their market offers and keep them unchanged for a while.

To illustrate this statement, let us consider the consumers' market in our society. The average consumer is not an expert in the markets where he buys consumers' goods and services; and his market behavior is governed, to some extent, by habit. He does not compare competing offers incessantly, nor does he switch from one to another in response to each price change, either because he feels that the economies to be gained from such overcareful shopping would not be worth the expenditure of time and effort which this would involve or because he ignores the

319

relative merits of competing offers. The consumer's inertia, therefore, may be the result either of a rational economic choice or of ignorance. In the following, we shall distinguish very carefully between these two causes of inertia in the consumer's market behavior, because they will serve as the basis of our distinction between the informed and the uninformed market.

When it is the result of a rational choice, the consumer's inertia is limited. For in this case, he does compare available alternatives from time to time as a matter of routine; and major price changes do force him to abandon his accustomed consumption pattern soon after they occur. Hence, while consumers' inertia makes it possible for the prices of different makes and brands of the same product to differ, they cannot differ too much if the consumers are informed. We shall see later that, by contrast, the range of scatter of competing prices may be quite large when the consumers are uninformed and their inertia is due to ignorance.

Inertia in buying is shown also by buyers other than consumers. To begin with, retailers must respect and cater to the preferences of their customers; and in so doing, their own purchases echo, so to speak, the inertia of their customers' market behavior, even when they themselves happen to be experts in appraising the things they buy and sell. Second, even producers who employ expert buyers for buying their main productive factors are likely to be governed by habit in the purchase of minor items (e.g., office supplies), because the scope for economies in the purchase of these items is too small to repay the costs of expert shopping.

On the selling side, this same type of inertia characterizes the market behavior of unorganized workers and small farmers, owing largely to their lack of mobility and imperfect knowledge of the market they confront.

The inertia and inexpertness of price takers confer an apparent advantage on the price makers facing them; but this advantage is limited and may be rendered completely illusory by competition among the price makers themselves. For this reason, we shall not discuss competition among price makers in general but shall analyze free and restricted competition separately.[1] Before doing so, however, we must first analyze the conditions and institutional background which bring about the different types of competition. Since restraints on competition favor the established price maker, he always has an inducement to impose competitive restraints and will do so unless prevented by circumstances.

---

[1] For the definition of the two types of competition and of the difference between them, see sec. 5 of Chap. II.

The circumstances, therefore, that prevent or render difficult the imposition of competitive restraints are the factors that favor competition.

Restraints on competition, however, may not only be imposed by the deliberate action of the price maker or price makers who stand to profit by them; there also exist natural obstacles to entry, which restrain competition from newcomers. These natural obstacles to entry are the factors that restrain competition. Hence, for competition among price makers to be free from all restraints, some or all of the first set of factors —namely, the factors that favor competition—must be present; and *all* of the second set of factors—namely, the factors that restrain competition—must be absent. In the following pages, we shall discuss each set of factors separately.

1. FACTORS FAVORABLE TO COMPETITION

Competitive restraints may be imposed either by one firm upon the others or by a group of firms upon themselves; and for competition to be free, conditions must be unfavorable to both types of restraints. To keep the individual price maker from imposing restraints on his competitors, these must be stronger than he is. In order that every member of the group should find himself overpowered by his competitors, their strength must lie in numbers and not in size. In other words, there must be several (at least three) competing firms in the market; and their size and economic power must not be too dissimilar, so that none of them finds himself stronger than the others combined. When these two conditions are fulfilled, no member of the group can impose restraints upon the others.

Even when no individual price maker can impose restraints upon his competitors, the group as a whole may still impose restraints upon itself. It is true that from each individual competitor's point of view the ideal situation would be to have his rivals' competitive behavior curbed, while his own actions are free and unrestrained. But when the members of the group are about equal in size and power, and this ideal situation is therefore beyond the reach of any one of them, they may be willing to compromise. Any group of competitors—buyers or sellers—can always increase their combined profits by making common front in the market to block the entry of newcomers and to suspend or restrict competition among themselves. This implies that the individual competitor can always gain more by the restraints imposed upon his competitors' actions than he loses by the restraints imposed upon himself, so that, on balance, each member of the group can make a net gain. If he realizes this fact, which he is sure to do, each price maker will be willing to restrain his own competitive behavior on condition that his competitors restrain their competitive actions, too. In other words, we can expect every competitor to be willing to enter into an agreement restricting the entry of newcomers and the competitive actions of established firms. To prevent such agreement, therefore, and to keep competition free, conditions must be present that actively discourage or render impossible the conclusion of restrictive agreements. Our problem is to find out what these conditions are.

In seeking and discussing these conditions, however, we shall have to bear in mind that agreements in restraint of competition need not necessarily be explicit and formally entered into. Even in the absence of a formal agreement, each competitor may restrain his competitive actions voluntarily, either for fear lest the others retaliate, or in the hope that his competitors, realizing the common advantage of mutual restraints, will reciprocate. Such tacit agreements, however, cannot limit the entry of newcomers; and since limited entry is the prerequisite of reaping monopoly profits, self-imposed restraints by tacit agreement are likely to come about only in markets where potential competition from newcomers is already limited by the existence of natural obstacles to entry. But even in such markets, tacit agreement need not always come about; and we shall therefore have to find the conditions that militate against both express and tacit agreement. We shall see that these conditions are more or less the same.

1a. THE COMPETITIVE SPIRIT

The first and rather obvious condition necessary to prevent restrictive agreements is the presence of a competitive (or absence of a co-operative) spirit. A group of competitors usually realize the advantages to be gained from combination; and if they nevertheless prefer to remain independent and compete one with another, they do so largely because each one of them mistrusts the others' co-operative spirit and believes in his own superiority. This spirit of rugged individualism and competition has been peculiar to the last two centuries of Western civilization; and it is particularly strong and deliberately encouraged in the United States.[2] Its origins can probably be traced back to the fifteenth and sixteenth centuries of European history, to those early ancestors of capitalism who first revolted against the exclusiveness and excessive regulation of medi-

---

[2] Cf. Margaret Mead, *And Keep Your Powder Dry* (New York: W. Morrow & Co., 1942), chaps. vi, vii, and ix.

eval guilds and "made good" by themselves.[3] It is worth noting, in this connection, that Germany, where medieval collectivism survived until the nineteenth century and the spirit of individualism and competition never gained a proper footing, was also the originator of cartels, the earliest and perhaps most important form of collective monopoly, which in Germany were "far more general and more frankly accepted as part of a rational economic organization of society than among any other people."[4]

Even in the countries of rugged individualism, however, the competitive spirit alone has proved insufficient to prevent agreements in restraint of competition. The competitive spirit, therefore, needs buttressing. In the United States, it has received legal support in the form of antitrust legislation, which, while ineffective against tacit agreement, has had some success in preventing express agreements in restraint of competition. Another and perhaps more important support of the competitive spirit is the mere lack of opportunity to restrain competition. This is largely a matter of numbers and of the composition of the market.

1b. LARGE NUMBERS, SIMILARITY OF SIZE, AND CHANGING MEMBERSHIP

Formal agreement in restraint of competition must be negotiated and agreed to; and, once concluded, it must be supervised and enforced. All this requires organization and discipline, which are easier to impose when the group of competitors is small and its composition stable. Large numbers and a continuously changing membership in the group of competitors, therefore, are obstacles to restrictive agreements.

As to voluntary restraints by tacit agreement, they are usually adopted either among a small group of competitors, where the market behavior of each is closely watched by all the others, or among a group in which disparities in size and economic power are great enough for one firm to become the natural leader of the rest. This implies that large numbers and approximately equal size and power tend to prevent tacit agreement in restraint of competition.

It appears, therefore, that we could look upon these three factors— large numbers, similarity in size and power, and changing membership among price makers—as further prerequisites of free competition. For, as was just shown, these are the factors that render impossible, or at least

---

[3] Cf. Henri Pirenne, *Histoire de l'Europe* (Paris: Félix Alcan, 1939), Bk. IX, chap. i, par. 2.

[4] J. H. Clapham, *The Economic Development of France and Germany, 1815–1914* (Cambridge: Cambridge University Press, 1921), p. 309.

difficult, both express and tacit restrictive agreements; at the same time, they also render impossible the forcible imposition of competitive restraints by one firm upon its rivals.[5]

Not much is gained, however, by a mere listing of these factors as conditions of free competition. For our interest lies in the institutional conditions which favor free competition; and to find these, we must look behind factors like the above and seek the conditions that bring about large numbers, similarity in size, and changing membership within the group of competitors.

It is immediately obvious that one of these conditions is freedom of entry or, rather, the absence of natural obstacles to entry. For free entry is certainly necessary to permit the establishment of a large number of competitors; and it is also needed to render possible a changing membership within the group of price makers. This factor will be discussed further in the second section of this chapter, where we shall analyze in detail the various obstacles to entry. Suffice it to say here that obstacles to the entry of newcomers restrain competition in more ways than one. First of all, they limit potential competition from newcomers, which was shown in section 5 of Chapter II to be a necessary and sufficient condition for monopoly profits to arise. Second, we argued on page 322 that without natural obstacles to entry, tacit agreement among established competitors to impose voluntary restraints on their own competitive behavior is not likely to come about. Last, we just saw that obstacles to entry favor restrictive agreements—both tacit and formal—also in another way, by hindering the establishment of many competitors and by stabilizing the composition of the market.

The next condition necessary to insure free competition is the existence of a limit to the size of firms sufficient to keep the individual firm small relative to the size of the market of which it is a member. It is apparent that such a limit to size would both guarantee the existence of a large number of competitors and tend to equalize the size of competing firms. We conclude, therefore, that there are three conditions necessary to keep competition free from restraints: (1) the existence of a competitive spirit, (2) the existence of an adequate limit to the size of the individual firm, and (3) the absence of obstacles to the entry of newcomers to the market. Of these three the first has been discussed already, the last will be dealt with in the next section, and the second we shall proceed to discuss forthwith.

---

[5] See p. 321.

1c. LIMITS TO THE SIZE OF THE FIRM: CAPITAL

The problem of what limits the size of the firm was discussed at length in the first two sections of Chapter IX. Now, however, we must reopen the discussion, and this for two reasons. One is that, at this stage, we are concerned with competition among price makers; and this will necessitate reconsidering entrepreneurship as a limiting factor, which in Chapter IX we considered only from the point of view of perfect competition. The other reason is that while in the course of the more formal analysis of Chapter IX we merely showed that the need for capital funds limits the size of the firm, we must now see whether this limitation is sufficient to insure large numbers and thus maintain free competition.

To deal with the latter problem first, it is very likely that in the early days of capitalism, before the introduction of limited liability and the joint-stock company, the need for capital and its limited availability were a sufficient guaranty of large numbers and free competition. In eighteenth- and early nineteenth-century England and America the entrepreneur was usually his own capitalist, and the scale of his enterprise was limited by the amount of capital he possessed himself or could borrow within the circle of his relatives and friends. He could seldom expand his firm beyond the limits set by the funds thus obtainable; for the lack of an organized capital market induced owners of idle funds to enter the field as independent competitors rather than to lend to already established firms. Furthermore, with liability unlimited and extending to personal property, entrepreneurs themselves were none too eager to expand with borrowed capital. In England, another stabilizing factor, especially important in checking the growth of the largest and most successful enterprises, was the social and political ambition of businessmen. In a society in which social standards were set by a feudal aristocracy, this ambition led to the diversion of funds and energies from business to public life and country living, often already in the first generation but almost always by the second. These factors go a long way toward explaining the free and relatively unrestrained competition which we associate with the early days of industrial capitalism; and the existence, even today, of many small and independent firms in the oldest industries of Great Britain and this country bears witness to their importance.

Most of these limitations to the size of the firm were considerably weakened by two changes that occurred toward the middle of the nineteenth century. One was the enormous growth of commercial banking, which greatly increased the borrowing facilities available to entrepreneurs. The other was the passing of company laws and the introduction of limited liability, which increased both the ability and the willingness of entrepreneurs to expand on borrowed capital. That the introduction of joint-stock companies would very much increase the size of the individual firm and so endanger competition was clearly perceived by many people at the time when the company laws were being enacted. This explains the hostility to joint-stock companies of many economists and intellectuals of the time. "In these years, long before the era of trusts, ominous warnings were heard of the possibility of monopolies"[6] in the United States; and in England, at the same time, it was advocated that "all corporations for trading purposes should be prohibited. They [are] . . . injurious to ordinary traders, 'tending to introduce competition on an exaggerated scale.' "[7]

We saw in Chapter IX that the firm's willingness and ability to expand on borrowed capital are not unlimited even under present conditions; but present limitations on borrowing are not of a kind that would guarantee the large number of competitors necessary for free competition. On the contrary, the nature of today's capital market is such that the large firm can borrow more easily and at a lower cost than the small firm; and this tends actively to restrain competition. The risk of lending to small and newly established firms is usually considered greater than that of lending to large and long-established enterprises; and, since interest is the lender's remuneration for bearing risk, this renders the cost of borrowing higher to the small firm than to the large one. Moreover, the small firm is also discriminated against in the capital-issues market by the preponderance of overheads in the cost of floating a public securities issue, which is a further reason why capital is more expensive to the small than to the large borrower. Finally, large corporations have been accused of putting pressure on banks to make them deny credit facilities to newcomers, thus protecting their monopoly position.

1d. LIMITS TO THE SIZE OF THE FIRM: ENTREPRENEURSHIP IN THE INFORMED MARKET

In Chapter IX, we rejected entrepreneurship as a possible limitation to the size of the firm because, at that stage, we were concerned with the

---

[6] F. A. Shannon, *Economic History of the People of the United States* (New York: Macmillan Co., 1938), p. 251.

[7] B. C. Hunt, *The Development of the Business Corporation in England, 1800–1867* (Cambridge, Mass.: Harvard University Press, 1936), p. 132.

behavior of the price taker, who plays a purely passive role in the market and conforms as best he can to price and to the other terms of trade, which he regards as given to him. We expressed this at the time by saying that the price taker has no marketing problems and that all his problems are production problems, which are easily delegated and therefore unlikely to restrict the size of the firm.

Now, however, we are concerned with the price maker, who has not only production problems but marketing problems as well. He plays an active role in the market and must adopt an aggressive strategy to expand or a defensive strategy to hold his ground against the aggression of his opponents. To gain ground in the market, he must take the initiative in anticipating the market's wishes and sensing the possibilities of new technological developments. The firm's *rate of growth* depends, therefore, on the entrepreneur's ability and drive and is limited by his human limitations. But is the *size* of the firm also limited by the entrepreneur's human limitations? This depends on the nature of the market.

In some markets, sheer size and established goodwill are assets of great importance. Ground once gained in such a market is easily held, because the mere fact that a firm has once succeeded in establishing itself and making itself known creates a goodwill in its favor against which others find it difficult to compete. It is apparent that in such markets the entrepreneur's limitations do not restrict the size of his firm, but only its rate of growth. We shall call this type of market the uninformed market and discuss it in detail in the next section, which deals with obstacles to entry, since the same factors that enable the established firm to hold its ground easily also render difficult the establishment of new firms.

There are other markets, however, where the nature of competition is such that ground once gained is easily lost again by firms unable to maintain enough drive and flexibility to keep up with technological developments and the market's changing requirements. The premium put on flexibility and initiative in such markets renders entrepreneurship an essential factor not only for the growth of the firm but for its mere survival, which means that in such markets, the entrepreneur's limitations restrict also the size of his firm. This type of market we shall call the informed market.

The informed market is a market in which the average buyer knows enough about the quality of the goods and services offered to appraise them on their own merits, without relying on trade-marks, advertisements, and the reputation of the producers or sellers. The markets for furniture and other home furnishings, for clothes, and especially for women's dresses, handbags, and dress accessories, are examples of informed markets. In general, one might say that the market for any good whose appraisal requires little or no technical, chemical, medical, or other specialized knowledge, or requires knowledge that is easily and quickly acquired, is an informed market.

Buyers in the informed market usually display a variety of tastes and a taste for variety. This creates demand for a whole range of types and models of the same commodity; but, at the same time, it limits the demand for any particular type or model within that range. The producer of any one type of commodity often has a monopoly in producing that particular type; and his monopoly is usually insured by patent rights and buttressed by economies of scale. As a rule, however, the producer's monopoly in producing his particular model is of very limited advantage to him. First of all, he can never rely on an assured demand, since the demand for his model depends on what other models are like; and it is likely to fall off if other models are improved in design or quality. Hence, his competitors' desire to expand keeps each producer under constant pressure to improve his product on pain of losing sales and profits. Second, even if the producer keeps up with improvements, the market for his particular model is still likely to remain limited due to the variety of tastes, which characterizes the informed market.

To expand his business and extend his sales in the informed market, the producer must offer an additional model which caters to a different taste and serves a different need; and, in introducing a new model, he may have no special advantage over other producers or newcomers to his market. For if the producer must diversify his product in order to increase his sales, he will enjoy few, if any, economies of scale and may find even his patent rights of limited use only. He may still have certain advantages over a newcomer; but these are limited and therefore easily offset if the newcomer has more drive and ingenuity and brings a fresh mind and new ideas to his business. The new idea is often the main ingredient of the new model; and by discovering and catering to the needs and tastes that existing models leave unsatisfied, a newcomer can usually capture a sector of the informed market.

That the informed and varied tastes of buyers in the informed market are effective limits to economies of scale and the size of firms is strongly suggested by both European and American experience. In Europe the almost universal failure of manufacturers to develop or adopt mass-production methods has been explained in many ways; but among the most plausible and most important explanations are the average

European consumer's buying habits. Owing largely to the strength of the feudal tradition in Europe and to the tradition of a more leisurely way of life, the average European seems less concerned with maximizing his money income but more interested in how best to spend what income he has than is his American cousin. This explains the average European's greater insistence on craftsmanship and on the exact conformity of products to his individual tastes and requirements. These peculiarities of the European consumer are among the main factors accounting for the lesser standardization and greater variety of European products; and they have been cited to explain the lesser use of mass-production methods and consequent lower productivity of labor in European manufacturing industries.[8] We shall have to bear this in mind when, in Chapter XX, we appraise the relative efficiency of free and restricted competition; here, we must note how these factors have tended to keep competition free by limiting the scope for economies of scale and thereby minimizing the advantage of the large firm over the small one. The insistence on craftsmanship may even discriminate in favor of the small firm, which may also be favored by a snobbish preference for products that are out of the ordinary.[9]

In the United States, there probably are, in every industry, at least some firms that use mass-production methods. As long as the market is informed, however, the advantage of the large firm over the small one is not too great; and newcomers usually have a fair chance of establishing themselves on a small scale even when they have to meet the competition of established producers who enjoy the economies of mass production. For the informed buyer knows that the advantages of mass production are gained at the cost of less variety and inferior craftsmanship; and he takes account of this fact when he chooses between the mass-produced and custom-made varieties of a product. He is often willing to pay the higher price for which a newcomer, producing on a small

---

[8] Cf. E. Rothbarth, "Causes of the Superior Efficiency of U.S.A. Industry as Compared with British Industry," *Economic Journal*, Vol. LVI (1946), pp. 383–90.

[9] Snob value is usually attached to the uniqueness of a thing. Hence the special value of model dresses and of limited editions of books and etchings. Sometimes, however, snob value seems to be attached to labor-intensiveness per se. Before the development of large-scale manufacture the token of labor-intensiveness was perfect finish and the complete elimination of all traces of handiwork: Roger Fry's "luxury effect." (Cf. Roger Fry, *The Arts of Painting and Sculpture* [London: Victor Gollancz, 1932], p. 17; also his *Last Lectures* [Cambridge: Cambridge University Press, 1939], pp. xx–xxi and 34–35.) Today, in the machine age, a perfect finish, so far from being a proof of labor-intensiveness, has become a sign of capital-intensiveness. People therefore begin to attach a snob value to irregularities, which bear witness—sometimes false witness—to an object's being handmade.

scale, offers him novelty, more variety, better design, superior crafts-manship, or just something more to his taste. Such behavior on the consumer's part facilitates the entry of newcomers, encourages competi-tion and the establishment of a large number of firms, and explains the existence, side by side, of both mass-produced and custom- or handmade products in informed markets.

So far, we have shown that in the informed market the demand for any single model is limited, that the producer must introduce additional models if he wants to extend his sales, and that the introduction of new models is not more (or at any rate not much more) difficult for new and for small firms than for large and well-established enterprises. All this tends to promote free competition, provided that newcomers and small firms, in addition to being able to introduce new models, also have the incentive to do so; and it can easily be shown that they not only have the incentive but have a greater incentive than large and established firms. This is so because the introduction of a new model inevitably lowers the demand for its established competitors. This consideration leaves the newcomer's expected revenue unaffected; but it enters into the calculations of the established producer, whose additional revenue from introducing the new model is the difference between his revenue from selling the new model and the loss of revenue on his old model due to its diminished sales. Given equal costs of production, therefore, a new firm stands to make a higher profit by introducing a new product than an established firm. The newcomer might make a profit even where an established firm could make none or would suffer a loss, its revenue on the new model falling short of the loss of revenue on the old. The more important the old firm is in the market, the greater is this advan-tage of the new firm over the old. For the introduction of a new product will lower the sales of an established producer the more, the greater is the sector of the market to which he caters. The inducement to introduce a new product, therefore, is strongest for a newcomer to the market; less strong for an established, but small, firm; and least strong (or com-pletely absent) for the established, large producer.

One might think that the fear of losing sales and profits, which prompts the established producer to keep step with technical progress, would also prompt him to offer a greater variety of products. This, how-ever, is not so. He may indeed be afraid that competitors will introduce new products that will encroach upon his sales; but he can seldom protect himself against this danger by introducing additional models himself. For, in most markets, there is plenty of room for the introduction of new types and models; and no single producer can, by introducing his new model, forestall the introduction of new models by others. We conclude therefore that, in the informed market, there is pressure on all producers to improve existing products but a special inducement for newcomers and small producers to introduce additional products. Both these factors tend to limit and equalize the size of firms and to maintain high birth and mortality rates among them.

2. FACTORS RESTRAINING COMPETITION

In the preceding section, we were concerned with factors that favor competition by preventing or rendering difficult the deliberate imposition of competitive restrictions either by an individual price maker or by a group of price makers acting in concert. But there also exist natural restraints on competition; and it is to these natural restraints that we must now turn. We have already mentioned that these restraints are natural obstacles in the way of newcomers who may wish to enter the price maker's market. Free entry to a market means a person's ability to establish himself in that market and compete on equal terms with its already established members; and any factor that discriminates against a newcomer, merely because he is a newcomer, is an obstacle to entry. Such obstacles, needless to say, can be imposed by the deliberate action of a monopolist or collective monopoly; but they may also come about as the result of economies of scale and the uninformed nature of certain markets.

2a. THE ECONOMIES OF SCALE

In most industries, there is a certain size of plant or a certain range of sizes that is more efficient and therefore more economical to operate than either smaller or larger plants. We saw in Chapter IX that this fact need not set an *upper* limit to the size of the firm, since the firm can own and operate several optimum-sized plants; but it does set a *lower* limit to size, since the firm cannot consist of less than one plant

This lower limit, however, is not an absolute limit. Firms smaller than the optimum-sized plant may be able to exist; but their costs of production will be higher than those of firms with larger plants. The higher cost of production of small firms handicaps them in their competition with larger firms; and—unless the cost differential is very small, or unless they can offer something special for which consumers are willing to pay a higher price—it puts them in a precarious position. To begin with, they can be driven out of the market by their large competitors more or less at the latter's discretion; for when cost differentials exist, low-cost firms can inflict losses on high-cost firms without incurring any losses themselves. Second, even when not driven out, the smaller firms exist on sufferance; and, owing to their higher costs and lower profits, they tend to lose ground in the market. The economies of scale, therefore, either limit the number of firms in the market or perpetuate and enhance differences in size and economic power; and they facilitate agreement in restraint of competition in either case. Such agreements usually provide for limitations on the entry of newcomers; but the economies of scale create obstacles to the entry of newcomers even in the absence of agreement and restraints deliberately imposed by agreement. What is the nature of these obstacles?

A newcomer is induced to enter a market by the profits earned by already established firms. A person who wants to establish himself on a small scale in a large market will do so if he sees that established firms are making profits and if he feels that he can produce as good a product as they at a cost no higher than theirs. As long as his projected output is a small fraction of the market's total turnover, he can neglect the impact on profits made by his own entry and need not bother to consider whether there is room for him in that market. When economies of scale are present, however, small-scale production is more expensive than large-scale production; and this may render unprofitable and discourage the setting-up of small firms even in a market in which established firms, enjoying economies of scale, are reaping substantial profits. A newcomer can overcome this handicap by establishing himself on a large scale and using mass-production methods right from the outset; but there are two considerations that may prevent his doing so.

First of all, if his projected output is a substantial addition to the industry's total output, he must take into consideration the impact of his entry on profits. In such a case the fact that the established members of the industry are making a profit is no guaranty that he too can make a profit, because by adding his output to the industry's total output, he may lower the industry's profitability to such an extent as to inflict losses both on himself and on his competitors. This will happen whenever the market's total demand at cost price exceeds existing productive capacity by an amount that is less than the capacity of an optimum-sized plant (which is what a newcomer would have to build); and in such cases, established firms can reap a profit without fear of attracting additional competition from newcomers. The profits so gained tend to be the larger, the larger the capacity of the optimum-sized plant relatively to the market's total demand.

In an extreme case, economies of scale may create a so-called "natural monopoly" by calling for a plant so large that it can fill the market's total demand. The simplest case of natural monopoly is the general store of a small community. The owner of the store enjoys a monopoly position and can reap monopoly profits simply because he was the first to establish a store and because his potential competitors realize that the community's total demand is too small to be shared by two stores and yield a profit to both. Natural monopoly on a nationwide scale comes about in industries in which the full advantages of mass production can only be reaped in a plant whose capacity about equals the nation's total demand for that industry's product. Many instances of this occur in countries smaller than the United States. For example, the productive capacity of an optimum-sized plant in the automobile industry and in certain branches of the iron and steel industry is probably sufficient or more than sufficient to fill the total demand of almost any European or South American country. Natural monopoly of this kind, of course, is an extreme case; but economies of scale can give rise to substantial monopoly profits even when there is room in the market for several optimum-sized plants.

The second consideration which may keep a newcomer from establishing himself on a large scale is the risk factor. To establish a new firm always involves the risk of failure; and the cost of bearing this risk may be regarded as a cost of entry. The greater the initial investment in the firm, the greater is this cost; and it is to minimize this cost that businessmen prefer to start a new firm on a small scale and expand it gradually. The presence of economies of scale in a market renders such a cautious and gradual establishment of a new firm impossible and thereby raises the risk, and hence the cost, of entering the market. This may not prevent the entry of newcomers altogether; but it raises the cost of entry and with it the minimum level which expected profits must exceed in order to repay the cost of entry and render the establishment of a new firm profitable. This implies that as long as the profits of established firms are below this level, they are likely to remain protected from the additional competition of newcomers.

2b. THE UNINFORMED MARKET

The second factor that restrains competition by limiting the entry of newcomers is the uninformed nature of certain markets. A market is uninformed when the average buyer in the market has an incomplete idea of the nature of the goods or services he buys, and judges their quality not by his own standards but on the basis of advertising and indexes of quality. By indexes of quality, we mean trade-marks; the reputation, size, nationality, and age of the manufacturing or distributing firm; inessential but eye-catching features of the good itself; the price of the good— in short, anything by which the uninformed buyer is likely to judge quality.

The consumer is usually uninformed in the markets for all complex goods and services. The average buyer of an automobile, a radio, or a washing machine cannot appraise its quality in the way he would appraise the quality of a piece of furniture, a simple garden implement, or a suit of clothes. He lacks an independent and reliable judgment of the quality of complex goods through no fault of his own but as a result of the nature of such goods. Not so long ago the range of consumers' goods was confined to staple commodities; and housekeeping was a skilled craft requiring and imparting a thorough knowledge of its tools and raw materials. In those days, it was natural for the housewife, the typical consumer, to be an informed buyer in all the markets where she did her shopping. The uninformed market is the outcome of technical progress, which has so greatly expanded the range and variety of consumers' goods and increased the share of complex commodities in the consumer's budget. Housekeeping has been rendered simple by complicated machinery replacing the humble household implements of old and by processed foodstuffs and other ready-to-use articles taking the place of staple foods and materials. These changes have raised our standard of living, but at the cost of depriving the buyer of his independent judgment in the consumers' market. He is forced to rely on indexes of quality not only in buying a radio or an automobile but even for appraising many prime necessities. Few people can judge the quality of tooth paste or an electric iron; and the frequent introduction of new types and models tends to prevent reliance even on past experience. Recent discoveries in the field of nutrition have rendered the consumer chary even of relying entirely on his palate for judging the quality of food. To make matters worse, the consumer's bewilderment is often deliberately fostered by the partiality of advertisers for technical terms, exotic names of chemical ingredients, and impressive descriptions of awe-inspiring technical processes, about whose exact purpose and importance the consumer is usually left in the dark.

The nature of competition among firms that cater to an uninformed market will be discussed in Chapter XVIII as part of our discussion of restricted competition. Here, we are only concerned with the way in which the uninformed nature of certain markets creates obstacles to entry and so restrains potential competition from newcomers. We saw above that, in the informed market, newcomers are not handicapped by their lack of reputation and usually have a fair chance of entering the market if they can emulate established firms. Entirely different is the newcomer's position in the uninformed market. Here, it is not enough for him to make an offer equal or superior to competing offers, because the uninformed public is unable to appraise the true merits of a new offer and is likely to receive it with reserve and suspicion. The newcomer, therefore, must try to overcome this reserve and create confidence in his offer; but to do so involves a cost that is not incurred by his established competitors. For in the uninformed market, where the buyer judges quality by his familiarity with brands and the names and reputation of manufacturers, established firms and their products have an important advantage over newcomers and unknown brands, which consists in the goodwill attached to an established name and a familiar brand. The importance of goodwill is indicated by the high price which is sometimes asked and paid for the mere use of a name. This price, which a new firm has to pay for the use of an established name or well-known trade-mark and for the goodwill attached thereto, is a cost of entry for the new firm. A newcomer need not, of course, buy the established goodwill of an old firm; he can create his own goodwill for himself and his products; but this is a matter of advertising and time. It takes advertising to make the market familiar with a new name; and it takes time for the market to respond to advertising and take cognizance of the new product. The cost of such advertising is again a cost of entry; and so is the initial loss of profit which the firm suffers in the early weeks or months of its existence, during which its sales are low merely because it has not yet succeeded in overcoming the market's reserve. There are indications that these two factors are formidable obstacles in the way of newcomers to many markets in our economy.

2c. THE BUSINESSMAN'S OWNERSHIP OF CAPITAL

. So far in this section, we have been concerned with natural obstacles in the way of businessmen who want to enter a particular market or industry. But natural obstacles may inhibit entry also to occupations; and, in particular, they may inhibit entry to the occupation of the businessman. Such obstacles are financial and were mentioned already when we argued, in Chapter V (see p. 104), that free education, or at least equal opportunity to obtain free training for any skill or profession, is a prerequisite of free entry and the resulting efficiency of specialization.

Especial mention must be made, however, of the problem of free entry to business as a profession. We argued in Chapter IX (see pp. 194 ff.) that the institutional organization of our society is such that the entrepreneur needs a capital fund of his own if he wants to exercise his profession. There is some separation of the functions of ownership and management in large corporations, where it can and occasionally does happen that an outstanding employee rises to a top managerial position without having previously acquired an equity in the firm. Such cases, however, are the exception rather than the rule. By and large, a man needs not only talent but also capital to become a businessman; and this latter requirement must be regarded as an obstacle that impedes entry. Since business sense and managerial talent do not always go hand in hand with the ownership of capital, this obstacle to entry interferes with the efficiency of specialization; and it may raise the income of businessmen over and above their wages of management and the earnings of their investments.

The importance of this factor depends, of course, on how much capital is needed for setting up in business. Needless to say, the amount of capital needed varies from one market or industry to the next. This obstacle to entry, therefore, affects relative incomes and the efficiency of specialization not only between business and other occupations but also between different types of business. Furthermore, owing to the progressive mechanization of production and the consumer's ever increasing ignorance and bewilderment, the amount of capital needed for securing the economies of scale in production and for establishing goodwill in the market is constantly increasing.

In the days before the Industrial Revolution, and even during its early phases, capital requirements were so small that they were hardly effective as a restraint on entry. Ever since then, however, the need for capital for establishing an enterprise has been on the increase. It has been estimated that even over a period so recent and so short as that between 1890 and 1940, the initial investment required for establishing a viable enterprise in an average manufacturing industry has increased (in real terms) about tenfold.[10] It appears, therefore, that economies of scale and the uninformed nature of the consumer's demand are factors that

---

[10] This is one of the conclusions reached in an as yet unpublished research project undertaken by Professor Paul A. Baran.

restrict entry not only to particular industries but also to business as a profession.

BIBLIOGRAPHICAL NOTE

On the general subject of what factors favor and what factors restrain competition, see Corwin D. Edwards, *Maintaining Competition—Requisites of a Governmental Policy* (New York: McGraw-Hill Book Co., Inc., 1949), especially chaps. ii and vi.

M

CHAPTER XVI

THE EFFICIENCY OF FREE COMPETITION

AFTER our discussion in the last chapter of the conditions of free competition, we can now proceed to analyze its efficiency. As in Chapter VIII, where we discussed the efficiency of an imaginary economy under perfect competition, we shall again be concerned with the whole economy rather than with individual markets. The reason for this is, again, the close interdependence of the efficiency of different sectors of the economy, which makes it impossible to say much about the efficiency of an isolated market unless one knows something about the organization and efficiency of the rest of the economy. Hence, we shall deal with the freely competitive economy, even though there is probably no such economy in existence today. For let us recall that the distinguishing feature of free competition is free entry—the free entry of persons to occupations and of firms to markets and industries. A freely competitive economy, therefore, would be one in which there are no trusts, no cartels, no unions, no professional associations, or any other forms of monopoly; and in which, in addition, neither the need for capital, nor economies of scale, nor consumers' ignorance are important enough to create natural obstacles to entry.

Our economy obviously does not meet these specifications. Nevertheless, we shall find it useful to discuss the efficiency of a freely competitive economy, and this for two reasons. First of all, this discussion will prove a useful starting point for analyzing at a later stage the efficiency of our mixed economy, which, after all, does contain important sectors which are freely competitive. Second, the early days of industrial capitalism in England and the United States probably came fairly close to a freely competitive economy; and they seem to represent the ideal of an important group of economists who regard the fight against monopoly and monopolistic restriction as the main, if not the only legitimate function of economic policy. Hence the need of comparing the efficiency of our economy not only to that of perfect competition, our standard of perfec-

338

tion, but also to that of free competition, often regarded as the latter's practicable counterpart.

1. DISTRIBUTION AMONG CONSUMERS

In discussing the efficiency of free competition, we shall rely on comparisons with our model of the perfectly competitive economy; and to facilitate this comparison we shall follow as closely as we can the order in which we discussed the efficiency of perfect competition. We begin, therefore, with the efficiency of distribution among consumers. We have seen that under free competition, just as under perfect competition, consumers are price takers and are informed. It follows from this that the distribution among consumers of a given quantity of consumers' goods and services will be efficient. When we first discussed the efficiency of distribution among consumers, we did not mention explicitly that one condition of efficiency is that consumers be informed. But it obviously is a necessary condition and was implied in our earlier discussion when we assumed that consumers act rationally. For consumers can only act rationally if they are informed and able to appraise the relative merits of competing products.

A further consequence of consumers being informed and in the position of price takers is that it causes the prices of consumers' goods and services to reflect the (uniform) marginal preferences of the consuming public. Hence, also from this point of view, there is no difference between perfect and free competition.

2. SPECIALIZATION AMONG WORKERS

Like the distribution of consumers' goods among consumers, specialization among workers is also perfectly efficient under free competition. For the efficiency of specialization hinges on freedom of entry to professions and occupations; and freedom of entry, as shown earlier, is the distinguishing feature of free as against restricted competition. We might recall in this connection that efficient specialization implies that relative rates of earning in different occupations express the occupational preferences of marginal workers and hence also the relative cost to society of obtaining the services rendered in those occupations. This fact will be made use of below, in our discussion of productive efficiency.

In a changing world, of course, the efficiency of distribution among consumers and of specialization among workers would not be absolutely perfect even under free competition. For we have seen that even the informed consumer will not change his expenditure pattern in response to every minor price change; and workers, even if they wanted to, could hardly change occupations following every change in relative earnings. Moreover, the slow response of the consumer's and the worker's market behavior to changing prices enables the firms that set these prices to keep them unchanged for a while, even in the face of changing requirements and market conditions. Hence, when prices respond slowly to changing requirements, and when the market behavior of price takers responds slowly to changing prices, there will never be an instant of time when distribution and specialization are perfectly efficient but only a constant tendency toward greater efficiency, with prices and people's market behavior always moving in the right direction, though never quite catching up with changing events.

3. JOB ALLOCATION

The efficiency of job allocation depends, it will be remembered, on the offer of equal pay for equal work performed, and on the freedom of workers to decide how much work to perform. As a rule, neither condition is fulfilled under free competition. The first condition is not fulfilled because, when the employer has the power to set the terms of contract for his workers, he usually finds it both possible and profitable to pay different wages to different groups of workers for the same work, discriminating between men and women, white and colored, or juvenile and adult workers. The second condition is not fulfilled because employers are usually able to set not only the wage rate but also the length of the working day and the working week. When employers do this, the individual worker is not a price taker in the sense in which the consumer is; for the worker's freedom of action is more restricted than the consumer's, leaving him to choose only between the two alternatives of working a certain prescribed number of hours and not working at all. Both factors—the payment of discriminatory wages as well as the additional restraint on the worker's freedom of action—give the employer an added advantage in the labor market. This advantage will be discussed in Chapter XVIII, where we shall analyze the nature of price discrimination and of all-or-none offers. Suffice it to say here that under free competition the employer's ability to discriminate among workers and determine working hours renders job allocation inefficient. This means that under free competition the total amount of work performed and income earned by the members of any one profession or occupation are not distributed among them in the best and most efficient way.

A corollary of inefficient job allocation is that wage and salary rates do not express people's marginal valuation of leisure. Hence, when we discuss the problem of efficiency in production—while we shall be able to rely on the relative market prices of consumers' goods as an approximate indication of consumers' preferences,[1] and on the relative prices of productive services as an approximate index of their relative onerousness in the marginal worker's opinion—we shall not be able to look upon the relative prices of consumers' goods on the one hand and of productive services on the other hand as an index of workers' preferences between consumption and leisure.

4. THE TECHNOLOGICAL EFFICIENCY OF THE FIRM

We saw in section 1 of Chapter VIII that if the firm wants to maximize its profit, it must aim at technological efficiency; and we also stated that this holds true regardless of the firm's market position. Furthermore, in section 2b of the same chapter, we showed that under perfect competition the free entry of newcomers to an industry provides a special inducement for the members of that industry to maintain their technological efficiency, because it causes inefficiency to be punished by losses instead of by a mere lowering of profits.

The free entry of newcomers accomplishes much the same thing in much the same way also under free competition. The profits of established firms attract newcomers, whose entry to the industry increases competition in both product and factor markets. The increased competition in factor markets raises costs; the increased competition in the product market lowers the sales of the individual firm and may also lower its optimum profit margin by raising the elasticity of demand confronting it. Long-run equilibrium is achieved when the rise in costs, the fall in sales, and the possible lowering of profit margins have eliminated the profit of the most up-to-date and most profitable firm and, with it, have also eliminated the inducement for newcomers to enter the market. When the profit of the most profitable firm is zero, less profitable firms incur losses and are spurred to increase their technological efficiency. They either succeed in doing this or are eliminated from the market; and the industry's average technological efficiency is raised in either case.

4a. TECHNOLOGICAL PROGRESS

The above argument was almost word by word the same as the corresponding argument in Chapter VIII; but now we can go a little fur-

---

[1] Approximate because there is only a *tendency* toward efficient distribution.

ther. For, in Chapter VIII, our discussion was static and concerned with efficiency at a given moment of time; whereas now we can also say something about technological progress and prepare the ground for a comparison, in Chapter XX, of the relative influence of free and restricted competition on the increase in technological efficiency over time.

First of all, we must distinguish between the rate at which scientific progress is made and the rate at which new scientific knowledge is put to use and exploited. For the time being, we shall be concerned with the latter rate only; but let us bear in mind the fact that the speed with which new methods are introduced influences the rate at which they are discovered and developed.[2]

Technological progress may consist in the improvement of the methods of producing given products, in the improvement of the products themselves, and in the introduction of new products. We saw in the last chapter that in the informed market all producers are under pressure to improve existing products, whereas the introduction of new products is usually left to newcomers. Under free competition, therefore, where newcomers are free to enter, technological progress in both these senses is encouraged.

As to new methods of production, they are introduced when existing productive capacity is being either replaced or added to. We saw in Chapter XII that, extreme cases apart, it is not profitable to replace existing equipment with newer and more efficient equipment before the life span of the old equipment comes to an end. Similarly, it is seldom profitable for an established producer to add to his existing productive capacity if, to sell the output of his additional capacity, he would have to lower his price. For even if he produced the additional output with the new and cheaper method and thus made a profit on it, the price reduction would lower his profit on the output of his old equipment; and this loss of profit would, in many cases, more than offset the profit made on the additional output. Established producers, therefore, have little inducement to introduce new methods of production until the time when their existing capacity falls due for replacement. Not so the newcomer to an industry. If new and cheaper methods of production enable him to undersell his established competitors and yet make a profit, he will do so. It is not his concern if his action inflicts a loss of profit on his established competitors and causes them to write off the value (or part of the value) of their obsolete equipment. We conclude, therefore, that

---

[2] This latter subject will be dealt with in Chap. XX.

in industries to which entry is free, technological progress of all kinds will be exploited and utilized.

5. THE TECHNOLOGICAL EFFICIENCY OF THE INDUSTRY

In discussing the technological efficiency of an industry, we come up against a serious problem right away: What do we mean by an industry under free competition? Under perfect competition in the expert market, there is, as we have seen, a tendency to standardize; and it is easy to define an industry as a group of firms that produce an identical product or a set of identical products. It is true that, on this narrow definition, "industry" would mean something quite different from what we ordinarily understand by the term; and there would be an enormous number of separate "industries." On the high level of abstraction and artificiality, however, on which perfect competition is usually discussed, this is of no consequence.

Under free competition, there is no inducement to standardize; on the contrary, the variety of tastes in the informed market encourages competing firms to produce slightly different products whenever there is scope for product differentiation. This raises the problem of when to regard two goods as different variants of the same product and when to regard them as altogether different products. In fact, when the products of each firm differ from the products of all its competitors, the division of firms into industries is bound to be arbitrary, amounting at best to a grouping-together of the producers of goods that differ little and a separation of those whose products differ much. This difficulty and related ones have led some economists to abandon the concept of an industry altogether, to regard each firm as a separate entity, and to think of the economy as composed of firms, each of which produces products that are different from the products of all other firms. But, however loose and ill-defined the concept of an industry may be, it often is a useful concept and as such will be retained, at least for the purposes of the following section. The reader, however, who shares the doubts of the above-mentioned economists may skip the next four pages and proceed directly to section 5*b* on page 347. He will find that the analysis of section 5*b*, although concerned with an industry, applies to any group of firms whose products are competitive in the market.

5*a*. EFFICIENT ALLOCATION WITHIN THE INDUSTRY

Let us consider an industry in which the scope for product differentiation is limited, so that the products of competing firms are very similar.

In section 2*a* of Chapter VIII, we defined the technological efficiency of the organization of an industry as that allocation of the industry's total output among its members which assures the highest output with a given utilization of resources or, what amounts to the same thing, a given output with the smallest utilization of resources. The conditions that assure efficient allocation of this kind were stated in equations (1) of Chapter VIII, which we reproduce here for the sake of convenience:

$$\left.\begin{aligned}
MI_x{}^f &= MI_x{}^g = \cdots = MI_x{}^h\,, \\
MI_y{}^f &= MI_y{}^g = \cdots = MI_y{}^h\,, \\
&\quad\cdot\quad\cdot\quad\cdot\quad\cdot\quad\cdot\quad\cdot\,, \\
MI_z{}^f &= MI_z{}^g = \cdots = MI_z{}^h\,.
\end{aligned}\right\} \tag{1}$$

It will be recalled that under perfect competition these conditions are fulfilled, partly because each producer, facing the same market price and equating to it his marginal cost of production, equates the latter also to the marginal costs of all the other members of his industry, and partly because all producers calculate their marginal costs on the basis of the same factor prices. The question now arises whether, and if so, how and to what extent, equations (1) are fulfilled under a regime of free competition, where there is no single price for the market as a whole and where each competitor, being a price maker, sets his own price.

Let us consider the product market first. Each price maker sets the price of his product by adding a profit margin to his marginal cost; and since, at this stage, we have no reason to suppose that either the marginal costs or the profit margins of different producers are the same, we must assume that each firm sets a different price on its product.[3]

We have seen, however, that there are market forces which keep the dispersion of prices within bounds. We showed in our discussion of the informed market (Chap. XV, sec. 1*d*) that the scope for differences in the prices of different makes of the same product is limited. Most consumers feel that the price of a commodity is "normal" or "reasonable" if it is within a given range of its competitors' prices; and they pay little or no heed to price differences which fall within that range, because they do not consider minor price differences worth bothering about. At the same time, however, they will avoid buying a brand whose price

---

[3] Differences in the profit margins of different firms may, by sheer accident, offset differences in their marginal costs; but we ignore this case as an extremely unlikely one.

exceeds that of its cheapest competitor by an amount the saving of which *is* worth the extra effort of shopping around for a cheaper brand.[4] The minimum amount which buyers consider worth saving at the cost of such extra effort determines the range within which the prices of competing products must lie. The better informed the buyers in the market, the smaller this range will be, because the better the buyers' information, the lower are the cost and effort involved in comparing competing products.

Since the market must always be informed for competition to be free, we conclude that under free competition the market compels the members of the same industry to set the prices of their products within a given and not-too-wide range. This can also be expressed by saying that free competition causes the prices of different brands of the same product to be approximately equal:

$$p_1 \approx p_2 \approx \cdots \approx p_h .$$

The efficient organization of the industry, however, depends on the equality not of product prices but of marginal costs; our next task, therefore, is to investigate when and how the approximate equality of prices brings about the approximate equality also of the marginal costs of competing products. It is obvious, to begin with, that if all firms would set their prices by adding the same percentage profit margin to their respective marginal costs, the marginal costs of competing firms would lie within a range exactly as narrow—or as wide—as the range within which competing prices lie. The preceding argument, however, suggests that, far from encouraging the use of equal profit margins by different firms, the market may actually prevent this.

Assume, for example, that the *n* members of an industry operate with marginal costs ranging from $4 to $6, and that they all set their prices by adding a 50 per cent profit margin to their respective marginal costs, motivated by the belief that this is a "fair" profit margin and the one appropriate to their trade. Such a policy would cause the industry's prices to range from $6 to $9. But assume, next, that the discernment of buyers narrows the range of admissible prices to from $6 to $7.50, making it difficult for sellers to sell at prices above $7.50. For example, a producer whose marginal cost is $6 will be forced to reduce his profit margin at least to 25 percent and sell at $7.50. If such a reduction of his profit margin deprives him of all profit, he will probably make an effort to lower his costs. It may also happen, however, that he makes a

---

[4] Throughout this discussion, we assume that qualitative differences are negligible.

profit even with a 25 per cent profit margin; and as long as this is the case, he may adhere to his present policy indefinitely and make no attempt to lower his costs of production. In the short run, therefore, free competition, unlike perfect competition, may well do nothing or only very little to equalize or narrow the range of marginal costs within an industry.

In the long run, however, there is a tendency, even under free competition, toward the approximate equalization of different producers' marginal costs; and this tendency is due to the entry of newcomers to the market. Newcomers, attracted by the profits of established producers, are likely to follow the example set by the most successful ones, which are those whose costs are lowest and whose profit margins are nearest to the optimum. The entry of newcomers lowers the profits of all, but especially of the less successful producers, who are likely to suffer losses. Long-run equilibrium would be achieved, just as under perfect competition, at the point where the profits of the most successful firms have become zero and all other firms incur losses. The firms that incur losses will be spurred to improve both their productive efficiency and their market policy; and whether they succeed or (for lack of success) are eliminated from the industry, the costs of production *as well as the profit margins* of different members of the industry will be brought nearer to their respective optima in either case. The optimum profit margin is that which corresponds to the price elasticity of demand facing the individual producer in that market; and since the several producers of the same product are likely to face the same price elasticity of demand, the optimum profit margin is likely to be the same for all members of the industry. It appears, therefore, that the competitive pressure exerted by newcomers tends to compel producers to use the same percentage profit margin and to eliminate those whose unduly high marginal costs of production would force them to use lower profit margins. In other words, the competition of newcomers tends to keep different producers' marginal costs within the same relatively narrow range within which prices are kept by the market behavior of the buyers. Symbolically, this can be expressed by the chain of approximate equalities:

$$MC^f \approx MC^g \approx \cdots \approx MC^h , \qquad (2)$$

which corresponds to equations (2) of Chapter VIII.

To summarize the above argument, we saw that, just as perfect competition tends to equalize the marginal costs of different members of the same industry, so free competition tends, if not to equalize marginal costs, at least to bring them within a narrow range. The ways, however, in which free and perfect competition bring about these similar results are very different from each other. Whereas under perfect competition it is in the interest of each producer to equate his marginal cost of production to the marginal costs of all the other producers, under free competition each producer has a corresponding interest only in bringing his price to within close range of his competitors' prices; and it is only the indirect and long-run effect of the entry of newcomers to the market which causes also the marginal costs of different competitors to tend to be within the same close range of each other.

So far, we have been concerned with the relation of different firms' marginal costs; but let us recall that the equality (or approximate equality) of marginal costs throughout an industry insures the minimization only of the industry's *money* costs of production. To minimize the amount of resources needed to produce the industry's output or, in other words, to maximize the output produced with given resources, it is further necessary that the cost of each factor should be the same to all members of the industry. This second condition is always fulfilled when the members of the industry are price takers and face the same prices in each factor market. The question now arises, however, as to what happens when the members of the industry are price makers, able to set their own prices in the factor markets as well as in the product market. As may be expected, the answer to this question follows almost word by word the argument of the beginning of this section. Competing firms are forced to offer more or less the same price for any given factor by the informed and discerning market behavior of the owners of that factor; at the same time the competition of newcomers to the industry tends to equalize profit margins in any given factor market and thereby to equalize the marginal value of that factor to competing firms. The detailed analysis of the competitive process which brings the prices of factors and their marginal value to their users to approximate equality is left to the reader as an exercise.

5b. THE AVERAGE TECHNOLOGICAL EFFICIENCY OF THE INDUSTRY'S MEMBERS

We showed already in section 4 of this chapter that under free competition the entry of newcomers inflicts losses on all but the most efficient firms and thereby brings up to par those firms that can raise their efficiency and eliminates those that cannot. We have yet to see, however, whether free competition also insures the establishment of the optimum number of firms in the industry. This, it will be recalled from Chapter VIII, is equivalent to asking whether fixed and variable factors of production are utilized in the most efficient proportions.

We saw in section 4 that the entry of new firms to a market tends to raise the costs and lower the sales of existing firms, and that long-run equilibrium is approached as the most efficient firm's profit tends toward zero, because its average total cost tends to equal its price. This situation, the long-run equilibrium of the most efficient firm, is illustrated in Figure 69. This diagram corresponds to and should be com-

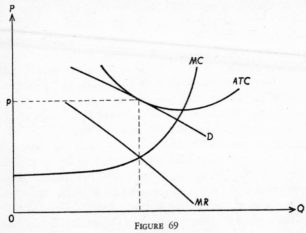

FIGURE 69

pared with Figure 45 of Chapter VIII (p. 157), which illustrates the long-run equilibrium of the firm under perfect competition. The average total cost curve is tangential to the demand curve at the point of equilibrium in both diagrams; and it follows from the geometry of the relation between average and marginal curves that this must always be so at any point where the two equalities

$$MC = MR \quad \text{and} \quad p = ATC$$

hold simultaneously.[5] In our discussion of perfect competition, this result served to show that the free entry of newcomers causes established firms to make the best possible use of their fixed resources by forcing them to produce at the point of lowest average total costs.[6] Under free competi-

---

[5] Cf. Joan Robinson, *The Economics of Imperfect Competition* (London: Macmillan & Co., 1933), p. 33.

[6] See pp. 169–70. The reader will notice that in Chap. VIII we regarded the combination of fixed and variable factors as a matter of economic efficiency; whereas here we are

tion, however, the demand curve facing the individual firm has a downward slope; and the cost curve, therefore, must also have a downward slope at its point of tangency with the demand curve. This means that under free competition the entry of new firms forces established firms to produce an output that is smaller than the output that would minimize average total cost. In other words, free competition tends, in the long run, to cause the individual firm to make insufficient use of its fixed resources and to operate with excess capacity.

This result is corroborated by the belief generally held by businessmen in competitive industries that they are operating under decreasing cost conditions, that is, that they could lower per-unit costs if only they could sell a larger output. It is apparent that this belief, if justified, is incompatible with perfect competition; but it fits in very well with the result we reached above concerning the utilization of fixed resources under free competition. As to examples of the excess capacity caused by free competition, they are not easy to point to; and the one we shall discuss is not, as will appear presently, an entirely correct example. In the United States today (1951), there seems to be an excessively large number of appliance dealers, each of whom could easily handle a much larger volume of business than comes his way. The economic loss caused by this form of inefficiency consists of the use in this trade of more manpower, equipment, and store space than is necessary. This is what is known in common parlance as competitive waste; and it is indeed due to the existence of free entry and the consequent influx of newcomers, who keep entering as long as the earnings of established firms are high enough to attract them.

Let us remember, however, that free entry creates competitive waste only under free competition and would not do so under perfect competition. To show that this is so, let us take an example. Assume that established appliance dealers are making profits, which cause additional appliance dealers to establish themselves. This would lower the sales of the individual storekeeper and might also raise the price elasticity of demand facing him, which would lower his optimum margin and thus put pressure on him to lower his price. If this process were

dealing with the same subject in a section concerned with technological efficiency. The reason for this seeming conflict is that while in Chap. VIII we made no special assumptions about the shape of the firm's production function, here we are utilizing the empirical finding that the firm's need of variable factors per unit of output is constant throughout its normal operating range (see pp. 308–9). The reader is invited to prove to himself that this fact renders a matter of technological efficiency what would, in the general case, be a matter of economic efficiency.

to render the market position of appliance stores perfectly competitive (i.e., if the price elasticity of demand facing them would approach infinity), they would be forced to sell at marginal cost; and a glance at Figure 45 (p. 157) shows that this would eliminate all excess capacity, at least for those firms that suffer no losses.[7]

This, however, is not what happens. To begin with, in the particular case of household appliances, the retail price is fixed—in some states by resale price-maintenance laws, in others by pressure exerted by manufacturers. The entry of newcomers, therefore, cannot lower prices and profit margins, although it will eliminate profits by lowering the individual firm's rate of sales. In this case, however, it takes a larger number of newcomers to eliminate profits; and this is why too many resources are drawn into the market and create excess capacity.

It now becomes apparent why we were hesitant to choose the market for household appliances as an example. Prices in this market are controlled; and this is the main reason for the existence of excess capacity and too many stores. Let us note that although the individual storekeeper may regard his guaranteed profit margin as an advantage, it does not make him significantly better off, because all that happens to him is that he earns about the same income on a small turnover with a large margin instead of on a large turnover with a small margin. The principal gainer is the manufacturer, whose products are displayed in more shopwindows; and the loser is society, part of whose resources are squandered on constructing, equipping, and manning too many retail outlets.

But let us see what happens in a market where the retail price is not controlled. In such a case an increase in the number of competitors is likely to raise elasticities of demand and so bring about a lowering of profit margins and prices; but as long as consumers' inertia is present, profit margins are bound to remain positive, and prices are bound to exceed marginal cost. Free competition proper, therefore, will also lead to excess capacity and a superfluity of firms, although to a lesser degree. In fact, the difficulty of finding examples of this case may be due to the lesser and therefore less conspicuous waste and inefficiency involved.[8] It is hardly necessary to add that competitive waste under free competi-

---

[7] We recall that full capacity is defined as that rate of output which minimizes average total costs.

[8] Perhaps the most conspicuous example of competitive waste under free competition is in Paris, where there is an enormous number of small shops that deal in scarves, handbags, belts, costume jewelry, etc. An example in this country might be the many small linen shops, with their perpetual sales, to be found in large cities.

tion is not confined to the distributive trades but exists in manufacturing and the service industries as well.

6. THE ECONOMIC EFFICIENCY OF THE FIRM AND OF THE PRODUCTIVE SYSTEM

In Chapter VIII, we stated the conditions of the economic efficiency of the individual firm first; and we showed afterward that these conditions, together with the conditions that cause a group of firms to behave like a single firm, constitute the conditions of the economic efficiency of the group also. In the present chapter, we shall simplify our analysis and deal with the economic efficiency of the individual firm, the industry, and the whole productive system, all at the same time. We shall be able to do this because under free competition the conditions for a group of firms to act like a single firm are fulfilled—at least approximately. These conditions, it will be recalled from sections 4 and 5 of Chapter VIII, were the equality of different producers' marginal costs of producing the same product and the equality of their marginal valuations of using the same factor. As was just shown, under free competition both these conditions tend to be approximated in the long run; therefore, all arguments and results concerning the economic efficiency of the firm under free competition apply, at least approximately, also to a group of firms, such as an industry or the productive system as a whole.

In the present section, we shall follow the sequence of section 3 in Chapter VIII and consider the problems of (1) the efficient combination of products, (2) the efficient combination of factors, and (3) the efficient rate of production. We shall again start out with the special case of a firm which (or of an economy or industry composed of firms each of which) produces only final consumers' goods and employs only original factors; and only afterward shall we consider the general case, where produced factors also are being produced and employed. For simplicity's sake, we shall often concentrate our attention on the individual firm; but the reader is asked to bear in mind the fact that all our statements will apply to firms, industries, and the productive system alike.

6a. THE EFFICIENT COMBINATION OF PRODUCTS

If different products are to be produced in the proportions that best conform to society's preferences, the marginal rate of transformation between any two products must equal the consumer's marginal rate of substitution between the same two products. This was shown in Chapter

VIII and expressed symbolically by equation (4) on page 161. We know that the marginal rate of transformation between two products is expressed by the ratio of their marginal costs; and we have also seen that under free (just as under perfect) competition the marginal rates of substitution of consumers are expressed by the ratio of the market prices of consumers' goods. Hence, for different products to be produced in economically efficient proportions, the ratio of market prices must equal the ratio of marginal costs for every pair of products:

$$\frac{p_a}{p_b} = \frac{MC_a}{MC_b} .$$

If we multiply both sides of this equation by p_b/MC_a, we can write this condition of efficiency in an equivalent but simpler form, which can immediately be generalized for n products and written as a chain of equations as follows:

$$\frac{p_a}{MC_a} = \frac{p_b}{MC_b} = \cdots = \frac{p_n}{MC_n} . \tag{3}$$

This chain of equations expresses the condition of efficient product combination by stating that the ratio of price to marginal cost must be equal for every product.

It is apparent that this condition is always fulfilled when the producers are price takers in the markets where they sell their products. For price takers equate marginal cost to price, which renders each member of chain (3) equal to unity. But is this efficiency condition fulfilled also under free competition, when the producers are price makers? Price makers set their prices by adding a profit margin to marginal cost. In symbols, the prices they set are given by the equations:

$$MC_a(1 + m_a) = p_a ,$$
$$MC_b(1 + m_b) = p_b ,$$
$$. \quad . \quad . \quad . \quad . ,$$
$$MC_n(1 + m_n) = p_n ,$$

or by the equivalent equations:

$$\left. \begin{aligned} 1 + m_a &= \frac{p_a}{MC_a} , \\ 1 + m_b &= \frac{p_b}{MC_b} , \\ . \quad . \quad . \quad &. , \\ 1 + m_n &= \frac{p_n}{MC_n} . \end{aligned} \right\} \tag{4}$$

It appears, therefore, that for the efficiency conditions (3) to be fulfilled, the chain of equations

$$1 + m_a = 1 + m_b = \cdots = 1 + m_n \qquad (5)$$

must hold; or, expressed in words, price makers must set the prices of their products by adding the same percentage profit margins to the marginal costs of each of their products.

To illustrate this result, let us consider an example. Take a firm that produces goods A and B at marginal costs of $4 and $6, respectively. This means that the firm's marginal rate of transformation between the two products is 4:6 or 1:1½. Assume, next, that the firm's pricing policy is to add a 50 per cent profit margin to the marginal cost of each of its products. This would be the producer's optimum profit margin if the market's price elasticity of demand were $\eta_p = 3$ for both his products— because $1/(3 - 1) = 0.5$; but he may also adopt this profit margin because he thinks that it is the best, or because it is his traditional profit margin and he cannot be bothered to experiment with other profit margins. Whatever the producer's reason for adopting this margin, it will cause him to sell A at $p_a = \$6$ and B at $p_b = \$9$. Facing these prices, each consumer will so adjust his purchases of the two goods as to render his marginal rate of substitution between them equal to 6:9 or 1:1½; and this equals the firm's marginal rate of transformation between the two goods. It is easy to see that we would reach the same result for any other profit margin as long as the percentage profit margins on the two goods are the same.

But assume for a moment that the firm's percentage profit margins on the two goods are not the same. Let us say that either because the market's price elasticity of demand for A and B is 5 and 2½, respectively, or for any other reason, the producer decides to sell A with a 25 per cent profit margin at $5 and B with a 66⅔ per cent profit margin at $10. Faced with these prices, the consumer would so adjust his purchases as to render his marginal rate of substitution between A and B 5:10 or 1:2. In this situation, therefore, the consumer would be willing to sacrifice two units of A for one additional unit of B at a time when the producer of the two goods would be able to produce additional units of B at a sacrifice of only 1½ units of A. This is clearly an unsatisfactory situation, in which the firm produces too much of A and too little of B.

We conclude, therefore, that price makers would produce their several products in the proportions that best conform to consumers' preferences only if they set their prices by adding the same percentage profit margin to the marginal cost of each of their products. If they use a different percentage profit margin on each product, the combination of their products will be inefficient; and they will be producing too much of products with low profit margins and too little of products with high profit margins. Furthermore, the greater the differences between the different profit margins, the greater will be such inefficiency.

Economic inefficiency of this kind is unavoidable in a market economy under any but perfect competition, because there is no economic force which would equalize the elasticity of demand in different markets or otherwise induce price makers to use the same percentage profit margin on different products. It is true that the free entry of newcomers to the informed market creates a wide variety and continuous range of products and that this tends to keep elasticities high and profit margins low; but it is unlikely to keep the price elasticities of demand for different products equally high and the corresponding profit margins equally low. All that free competition can accomplish is to narrow the range within which the different profit margins will lie. In other words, although free competition will not eliminate economic inefficiency in the combination of products, it will at least keep such inefficiency within bounds. This result, however, applies only to consumers' goods and will have to be modified when we take also intermediate products into account.

6b. The Efficient Combination of Factors

The condition for the efficient combination of factors is almost word by word the same as the condition derived above for the efficient combination of products. An efficient combination of factors is one that enables a firm or an industry to produce a given output at a minimum cost in terms of productive effort. We showed in Chapter VIII that this is conditional on the marginal rate of technical substitution between any two productive services being equal to the rate at which marginal workers are willing to substitute one of those services for the other. We saw that the latter rate is expressed by the ratio of the market prices of productive services whenever free entry to different occupations assures efficient specialization. We also know that the marginal rate of technical substitution of a firm or industry between two productive services is equal to the ratio of their marginal products. Hence, productive factors will be efficiently combined in production if the following condition is fulfilled:

$$\frac{p_x}{p_y} = \frac{MP_x}{MP_y},$$

or, in the equivalent but more general form:

$$\frac{p_x}{MP_x} = \frac{p_y}{MP_y} = \cdots = \frac{p_z}{MP_z}. \tag{6}$$

It was shown in Chapters VII and VIII that this condition is always fulfilled when producers are price takers in all factor markets. Under free competition, however, it can happen that producers are price makers not only in selling their products but also in buying their factors; and we must now see whether the conditions of efficiency are fulfilled in this case, too.

To set the prices of the factors they offer to buy, price makers subtract from the marginal value of each factor a profit margin.[9] In symbols:

$$p_x = PMV_x(1 - m_x),$$
$$p_y = PMV_y(1 - m_y),$$
$$\cdot \quad \cdot \quad \cdot \quad \cdot \quad \cdot \quad ,$$
$$p_z = PMV_z(1 - m_z).$$

Recalling that the marginal value of a factor is the marginal cost of its marginal product, $PMV = MC \cdot MP$, we can also write the above equations in the equivalent form:

$$\frac{p_x}{MP_x} = MC(1 - m_x),$$

$$\frac{p_y}{MP_y} = MC(1 - m_y),$$

$$\cdot \quad \cdot \quad \cdot \quad \cdot \quad \cdot \quad ,$$

$$\frac{p_z}{MP_z} = MC(1 - m_z).$$

From this, it immediately follows that for the efficiency conditions (6) to be fulfilled, the chain of equations:

$$MC(1 - m_x) = MC(1 - m_y) = \cdots = MC(1 - m_z);$$

or, dividing through by MC, the chain of equations:

$$1 - m_x = 1 - m_y = \cdots = 1 - m_z \tag{7}$$

must hold. Expressed in words, for the combination of factors to be efficient, producers must set the prices at which they offer to buy the services of the factors of production by subtracting the same percentage profit margin from the marginal value to them of every one of these services.

[9] See p. 290.

It appears, therefore, that equal percentage profit margins are the condition of economic efficiency not only in the combination of products but also in the combination of factors. Relying on the complete parallelism between the two cases, we can immediately state our results and say that free competition, while not insuring equal profit margins, tends at least to limit the range within which different profit margins lie and thereby tends to limit the scope for inefficiency in the combination of factors. Let us recall, however, that we are still concerned with the special case in which all factors are original factors, and that the above result therefore applies to original factors only. This fact greatly diminishes the importance of our result. For there are good reasons to believe that a much more important source of inefficiency lies in the wrong combination of original with produced factors. Let us proceed, therefore, to consider the general case, in which firms produce both final and intermediate products and employ both original and produced factors of production.

6c. THE GENERAL CASE

The Combination of Products. Let us first consider the conditions of the efficient combination of products. Assume, for example, that a producer of products A and B sells A to consumers and B to another firm, which utilizes B in the production of a consumers' good C. In this case, therefore, B is an intermediate product, which is useful to the consumer only indirectly, through its usefulness in the production of C. Accordingly, the consumer's marginal rate of substitution between A and B is given by the ratio of his marginal valuation of A to his marginal valuation of B's marginal product in the manufacture of C.[10] In symbols:

$$MS_{ab} = \frac{MV_a}{MV_c MP_b{}^c} .$$

Since consumers are price takers, their marginal valuation of consumers' goods is expressed by the latter's prices; and the above equation can also be written as

$$MS_{ab} = \frac{p_a}{p_c MP_b{}^c} ;$$

or, expressed in words, the consumer's marginal rate of substitution between A and B equals the ratio of the price of A to the market value of

---

[10] The reader will recall that the marginal product of B is defined as that quantity of C which can be produced with the aid of one unit of B.

the marginal product of B. From this, it immediately follows that the efficiency condition (3) must now be written as

$$\frac{p_a}{MC_a} = \frac{p_c MP_b^c}{MC_b} . \tag{3.a}$$

When is this condition fulfilled?

Assume, to begin with, that in transactions between the two firms the producer of B sets the price at which he sells B, and that the producer of C is a price taker when he buys B but a price maker in the consumers' market where he sells C. Under these conditions the producer of B will set the price of B by adding a profit margin to its marginal cost:

$$MC_b(1 + m_b) = p_b ;$$

whereas the producer of C will equate the price of B to its marginal value to him:

$$p_b = PMV_b = MC_c MP_b^c ,$$

and set the price of C by adding a profit margin to the marginal cost of C:

$$MC_c(1 + m_c) = p_c .$$

Combining these three equations and rearranging their terms, we get the equation

$$(1 + m_b)(1 + m_c) = \frac{p_c MP_b^c}{MC_b} . \tag{8}$$

It now follows from (8) and the first equation of (4) that the efficiency condition (3.a) can also be written as

$$(1 + m_a) = (1 + m_b)(1 + m_c) . \tag{5.a}$$

Expressed in words, equation (5.a) shows that for products A and B to be produced in the most efficient proportions, the profit margin on the consumer's good A would have to equal the combined profit margins on the intermediate product B, and on the consumer's good C, in whose production B is utilized.

This result can immediately be extended to the general case, in which the firm produces *n* products, some or all of which go through several hands or several stages of processing on their way to the consumer. In this case, we must compare the sequence of profit margins added at successive stages to the marginal cost of one product to the sequence of profit margins added to the marginal cost of each of the other products; and the firm will produce its different products in the correct proportions if the combined profit margins in each sequence are the same. Expressed in symbols, the condition of efficiency is:

$$(1 + m_a)(1 + m_i) \cdots (1 + m_z) = (1 + m_b)(1 + m_j) \cdots (1 + m_u)$$
$$= \cdots = (1 + m_d)(1 + m_l) \cdots (1 + m_z) , \tag{5.b}$$

where $a, b, \ldots, d$ are the products of the firm under consideration, and $i, j, \ldots, l, x, y, \ldots, z$ are those products of other firms in whose manufacture the intermediate products $a, b, \ldots, d$ are directly or indirectly utilized.

We obtained the above result on the assumption that in the markets for intermediate products, it is the sellers who set the prices and the buyers who regard them as given. We get almost exactly the same result, however, if we assume that the prices of intermediate products are set by the buyers and regarded as given by the sellers. To show that this is so, let us return to the producer of A and B and assume that while he still sells A to consumers at his own price, he now sells B at a price that he regards as given and that is set by the firm to which he sells it, the producer of C. In this case the producer of A and B, being a price taker with respect to B, equates the latter's marginal cost to its price:

$$MC_b = p_b ;$$

whereas the producer of C sets the price at which he offers to buy B by subtracting a profit margin from B's marginal value to him:

$$p_b = PMV_b(1 - m_b) \equiv MC_c MP_b{}^c (1 - m_b) ;$$

and he sets the price of C by adding a profit margin to the marginal cost of C:

$$MC_c(1 + m_c) = p_c .$$

Combining these three equations and rearranging their terms, we get the equation

$$\frac{1 + m_c}{1 - m_b} = \frac{p_c MP_b{}^c}{MC_b} , \tag{8.a}$$

which takes the place of equation (8), above. Substituting (8.a) for (8), the efficiency condition (5.a) becomes

$$1 + m_a = \frac{1 + m_c}{1 - m_b} . \tag{5.c}$$

The similarity of (5.a) and (5.c) becomes apparent when we recall that m_b is always smaller than unity and that, for small values of m_b, $1/(1 - m_b) \approx 1 + m_b$.

The Combination of Factors. Equations (5.a) and (5.c) express the conditions of the efficient combination of *products;* but the conditions of the efficient combination of *factors* are almost exactly the same. Assume, for example, that of factors X and Y employed by a given firm, X is an original factor, and Y is a factor produced by another firm with the aid of the original factor Z. In this case the factors X and Y will be efficiently combined by the firm using them if either of the following relations obtain among the profit margins set on factors X, Y and Z:

$$1 - m_x = (1 - m_y)(1 - m_z) \qquad (7.a)$$

if the price of Y is set by the buyer; or

$$1 - m_x = \frac{1 - m_z}{1 + m_y} \qquad (7.b)$$

if the price of Y is set by its producer. Since the derivation of these efficiency conditions follows exactly the argument used in deriving conditions (5.a) and (5.c), this is left to the reader as an exercise.

What conclusions can we draw from the formal efficiency conditions expressed in equations (5.a), (5.b), (5.c), (7.a), and (7.b)? They suggest, first of all, that the proportions in which different products are produced and in which different factors are employed under free competition are further removed from the optimum than we were led to expect in sections 6a and 6b. For it is likely (and generally believed by economists) that free competition, if it would not equalize profit margins in different markets, would at least keep them low and thus prevent their being too dissimilar. The results of this section have shown, however, that even equal percentage profit margins throughout the economy would *not* insure an efficient combination of products and of factors. In other words, we have *disproved* the statement sometimes made in textbooks that the existence of inefficiency in our economy is due not so much to market imperfection as to the lack of uniformity in the degree of imperfection in different markets, and that a uniform degree of imperfection (i.e., equal percentage profit margins) throughout the economy would lead to as high a degree of efficiency as would perfect competition.

Let us now investigate the form that inefficiency takes (or would take) under free competition; and to simplify the argument, let us imagine for a moment an economy in which all percentage profit margins are the same and in which there are only two stages of production.[11]

---

[11] The latter assumption implies that produced factors are not employed in the production of other produced factors.

It is easy to see that such an economy would be economically efficient as concerns (1) the proportions in which different consumers' goods are produced, (2) the proportions in which different intermediate products are produced, (3) the proportions in which the services of original factors are combined, and (4) the proportions in which the services of produced factors are combined. At the same time, however, the economy would be economically inefficient as concerns (1) the relative quantities in which consumers' goods and intermediate products are produced and (2) the proportions in which original factors are combined with produced factors. To see what this inefficiency consists in, let us return to the example of page 356. If m_a, m_b, and m_c, the profit margins on products A, B, and C, are equal, the efficiency condition (3.a) will not be fulfilled; instead, the inequality

$$\frac{p_a}{MC_a} < \frac{p_c MP_b{}^c}{MC_b}$$

will hold. This indicates that in our imaginary economy, too much would be produced of consumers' good A and too little of intermediate product B.

More generally, too many consumers' goods and too few intermediate products would be produced; and a similar bias would exist also in the utilization of productive services and lead to the combination of too many original factors with too few produced factors. If we now recall that intermediate product and produced factor are merely two names for one and the same thing, it appears that, in the kind of economy just considered, there would be a bias both against the production and against the use of produced factors.

This important result remains essentially unchanged when we drop our simplifying assumptions. When we drop the assumption of only two stages of production and admit the possibility of produced factors contributing to the production of other produced factors, the proportions in which different produced factors are produced and utilized cease to be economically efficient, because there is added to the bias against produced factors in general a further bias against the more roundabout methods of production and against those produced factors which are further removed from original resources and from final consumers. When we also drop the assumption of equal profit margins, it is the proportions in which consumers' goods are produced and in which original factors are utilized that cease to be efficient. The inefficiency, however, that is caused by the bias against produced factors remains present as long as the prices of these factors contain a profit margin greater than zero.[12] This is very likely to be the case under free competition.

What is the common-sense interpretation of the above result? When a producer decides how to combine his different factors and in what proportions to produce his different products, he is guided by the prices of his factors and his products; and we saw in Chapter VIII that under perfect competition these prices would be a reliable guide and would lead the producer to employ his factors and produce his products in the most efficient combinations. What the above analysis has shown is that the same is not true under free competition. Under free competition, a producer who combines, say, labor and materials in the proportions that minimize his (money) costs of production *fails* to minimize the productive effort involved, because the price he pays for the materials *overstates* the marginal effort embodied in them. This is so because the price of materials—a produced factor—exceeds the marginal cost of producing them by the manufacturer's profit margin. It could be countered to this argument that labor, too, might enjoy a monopoly position and also its price might contain a monopolistic profit margin; but in such a case the price of materials would contain two profit margins: that of the labor engaged in their manufacture and that of the firm manufacturing them. In either case, therefore, the price of materials overstates (as compared to the price of labor) the productive effort they represent and thereby unduly discourages their utilization. The argument is the same, of course, with respect to all other produced factors as well.

In a similar way, when a manufacturer produces his different products in the proportions that maximize his profit, he will fail, under free competition, to maximize the satisfaction consumers derive from his products if these include both consumers' goods and intermediate products. For the price of an intermediate product always *understates* consumers' marginal valuation of its marginal contribution to the output of consumers' goods by an amount equal to the profit margin of the firm that uses the intermediate product; and owing to this understatement, the production of intermediate products is unduly discouraged.[13]

---

[12] The reader should have no difficulty in seeing that if all the markets in which one firm buys another firm's products were perfectly competitive, so that the prices of all produced factors would equal both the producer's marginal cost and the user's marginal valuation, there would be no bias against produced factors and no consequent loss of economic efficiency. This case will be discussed at length in Chap. XX.

[13] The above argument has an important bearing on the valuation of the national product. We have seen in the Note to Chap. IV how the prices both of consumers' goods and of government services can be regarded as expressing their marginal valuation by

It is more difficult to assess the importance of this type of inefficiency. For example, it is likely that the scope for varying the proportions in which a manufacturer combines labor with materials and semimanufactures is very limited; if this is so, the inefficiency due to their being combined in the wrong proportions will also be very limited. On the other hand, there is plenty of scope for varying the proportions in which labor and capital equipment are combined, which leads one to seek the main source of inefficiency in the insufficient use of capital equipment and in the adoption of insufficiently capital-intensive methods of production.

That this factor can be an important source of inefficiency and economic loss is beyond doubt. For example, England's failure to maintain her leading position as an industrial producer is generally attributed to her insufficient use of capital-intensive methods of production; but it is another question to what extent this was due to the nature of competition in her markets. For the high price of equipment rendered high by the manufacturer's profit margin is only one deterrent to the use of equipment. Other and equally important deterrents are (1) the high price of equipment due to the use of costly methods in its manufacture, (2) the small firm's lack of scope for using much equipment, (3) the conservative temperament of manufacturers, and so forth. To assess the relative importance of these factors lies outside the scope of this book; but it is well to bear in mind that market imperfection is among these factors.[14]

In closing this section, a few words must be said about the relation between the type of economic inefficiency just discussed and the technological inefficiency analyzed in section 5*b* of this chapter. We have argued here that there is a bias under free competition against the production and use of produced factors, and especially against capital equipment; whereas, in section 5*b*, we showed that the free entry of newcomers to the market tends to make each firm operate with excess capacity. One might at first think that these two statements either are contradictory or offset each other and cancel out. In truth, however, they refer to altogether different things. For, in this section, we were concerned with the type of equipment and degree of mechanization the producer adopts when he sets up his plant and decides on his method of pro-

---

members of the community. It now appears that the same is not true of the prices of capital goods, which systematically understate consumers' marginal valuation of the marginal contribution of these goods to final output.

[14] See Chap. XX, however, for a further discussion of this subject.

duction; and we argued that under free competition he is likely to adopt less mechanized and less capital-intensive methods of production than would be called for by the requirements of economic efficiency. In section 5*b*, on the other hand, we took for granted the producer's method of production and only argued that under free competition there will be too many producers and that each will tend to make insufficient use of what equipment he has. To combine the two statements, therefore, we must say that under free competition the methods of production used will be insufficiently capital-intensive and that what capital equipment there is will be insufficiently utilized.

6d. THE EFFICIENT RATE OF PRODUCTION

The efficient rate of production was defined in Chapter VIII as that utilization of resources and output of products which render it impossible to increase anyone's welfare either by raising output at the cost of leisure or by increasing leisure at the cost of output. The formal condition of an efficient rate of production was shown to be the equality between people's marginal valuation of their productive efforts and their marginal valuation of the products of their productive efforts. This condition was expressed symbolically in equations (11) and (12) of Chapter VIII.

Unfortunately, it is impossible to appraise the efficiency of the rate of production under free competition, because with the length of the working week prescribed by employers, wages are no indication of people's marginal valuation of their productive effort; and we have no other way of ascertaining the latter. Nevertheless, it will be useful *to assume* for a moment that the prices of productive services do indicate their marginal valuation by their owners, and to see how efficient the rate of production would be on this assumption. We know that every price maker sets the price of his product higher than marginal cost:

$$p_a > MC_a ; \tag{9}$$

and we saw that when the firm is a price maker also in factor markets, he sets the price of a factor below its marginal value to him:

$$MC_a MP_x{}^a > p_x .^{15} \tag{10}$$

If we combine inequalities (9) and (10), we get the inequality

$$p_a MP_x{}^a > p_x , \tag{11}$$

---

[15] In the above two inequalities and throughout the following argument the suffix *a* represents *any* consumers' good and the suffix *x* stands for *any* original factor.

which shows that under free competition the price of a factor is always smaller than the price of its marginal product. If we then recall that the price of a consumers' good represents its marginal valuation by its consumers, and if we *assume* that the price of a factor shows its marginal valuation by its owner, we can write inequality (11) in the slightly different form:

$$MV_a MP_{x^a} = p_a MP_{x^a} > p_x = MV_x, \qquad (12)$$

which corresponds to the first of equations (12) in Chapter VIII (see p. 166). Inequality (12) shows that under free competition a person's marginal valuation of his productive services is always lower than his valuation of the marginal product of his services. He would gain, therefore, by making a greater productive effort *if* he would obtain the result of his additional effort. This implies that, on the assumption made above, we would have to conclude that production and the utilization of resources would, under free competition, always be below the economically efficient rate.

It is worth noting that the inequality

$$MV_a MP_{x^a} > MV_x \qquad (12.a)$$

remains true whether the firm is a price maker in both product and factor markets or only in one of them; and it remains true even if the firm is a price taker in both markets as long as either the consumers or the sellers of the factor are price makers. The proof of this statement is left to the reader as an exercise; and so is the generalization of our result for the case in which intermediate products and several stages of production separate the consumer from the owner of original services.

One is tempted to identify the above result with the popular belief that market imperfection and monopoly restrict production and cause unemployment. But, although inequality (12.a) does indicate that output is below the optimum, it does not imply unemployment. To begin with, let us recall that the entire analysis of this book is based on the assumption of the full employment of all resources. Second, we have only shown above that if a worker were to receive the entire value of the marginal product of his labor, he would want to work and produce more than he actually does under free competition. Production is kept below the optimum rate not by the employer's refusal to let his workers produce as much as they want to but by the insufficiency of their inducement to work. In other words, free competition would render the labor force smaller and the working week shorter than they should be. Inequality

(12) shows that under free competition the worker's wage rate, p_x, *understates* the value society puts on the marginal product of his services; whereas at the same time the price of consumers' goods, p_a, *overstates* the marginal cost of the effort required for their production. Free competition, therefore, keeps the rate of production below its optimum level by unduly discouraging workers from working and consumers from consuming. Whether, in addition, it also creates unemployment depends on its effect on the propensity to consume (e.g., via income distribution) and on the inducement to invest—subjects with which we are not concerned here.

Let us recall, however, that this entire argument was based on the assumption that the prices of productive services express their marginal valuation by their owners, and that this assumption is not justified when workers are not free to determine the amount of work they perform. For example, if employers were to make the working week longer than their employees preferred it, they might bring the rate of production to or near its optimum level; on the other hand, if employers were to shorten the working week below their workers' preferences, they would aggravate the inefficiency discussed above.

7. DYNAMIC EFFICIENCY

So far, we have been concerned with the efficiency of free competition in a static sense; our next task should be to appraise the stability of a freely competitive system and its responsiveness to changing conditions. Unfortunately, however, this important subject is largely unexplored; and we shall have to confine ourselves to a few general remarks. We saw in Chapter X that, as concerns dynamic efficiency, perfect competition is far from being a model of perfection; and that the response of a perfectly competitive industry to changing conditions compares unfavorably with that of an industry controlled by a monopolist, or a state official in charge of planning. Free competition is probably somewhere between these two extremes; but all we can offer in support of this statement is to show that overadjustment to changing conditions, while possible, is likely to be limited, and that the scope for speculation and the resultant price fluctuations are also limited.

Our discussion on pages 234–38 of Chapter X has shown that, under perfect competition, overadjustment may come about, because each price taker learns of the change in conditions through a change in price and thinks that he faces an unlimited market at the current price; and because he plans to adjust his behavior to the change in price without knowing of, and hence without taking into account, the similar plans made simultaneously by his competitors.

The price maker's position under free competition is similar in that he, too, ignores his competitors' plans and fails to take them into account when he makes his own plans; but he, unlike the price taker, is under no illusion of facing an unlimited market—a fact that lessens the danger of overadjustment. Furthermore, the price maker learns about a change in market conditions primarily through a change not in price but in the rate of his sales or of the orders he receives; and this, too, lessens the danger of overadjustment. As a matter of fact, there is no danger of overadjustment to a *fall* in demand which manifests itself only through a fall in sales or orders received. Nor can there be overadjustment to a *rise* in demand in markets where the buyers are firmly set in their buying habits and feel very loyal to the store or brand to which they are accustomed. For in such markets, each buyer would go to one seller only and, on learning that his demand cannot be filled or cannot be completely filled, would place his order with one seller and wait patiently for his turn. The danger of overadjustment arises only when the unsatisfied buyers make the rounds of several sellers and let their willingness to buy be known to each of them; or when, to play safe, they place orders with several sellers, intending to accept delivery only on the first order filled. Such behavior creates in each producer's mind an exaggerated idea of the extent to which the demand for his product exceeds his productive capacity; but only if the unsatisfied buyers made the rounds of *all* the competitors would the danger of overadjustment be as great as it is under perfect competition.

We conclude, therefore, that—while possible—overadjustment and consequent fluctuations in price and productive capacity are less likely occurrences under free competition than they are, or would be, under perfect competition. The implications of this result for the maintenance of equilibrium over time (dynamic efficiency) in the freely competitive market are left to the reader to develop.

Another factor that would prevent excessive price variability under free competition is the limited scope for speculation in the imperfect market. We argued in section 3 of Chapter X that speculation, when carried to excess, is likely to do more harm than good; and there is evidence that, in perfect markets, speculation is often carried to excess. Speculation consists in buying cheap in the hope of selling dear, or in selling dear in the hope of buying cheap; and the difference between the selling and the buying price is the speculator's profit. This profit is diminished by the cost involved in carrying out the two transactions, which in the perfect market is negligibly small and insufficient to discourage speculation.[16]

Not so in the imperfect market. We saw that the price maker must incur a cost to persuade the market to buy from him (or to sell to him); and this cost may substantially diminish speculative profits and discourage speculation in markets where price maker and price taker face each other. This is why speculation in such markets is usually confined to inventory accumulation and decumulation by producers, wholesalers, and retailers—in short, by firms that already have an established sales organization in the market. The destabilizing effects of inventory speculation are well known from business-cycle theory; but instability is greater in those few markets where the expertness of dealers and the consequent perfection of the market enable also the professional speculator to join the fray.

8. INCOME DISTRIBUTION

When, in Chapter II, we first discussed the market relation between price makers and price takers, we stated that the price maker has a bargaining advantage over the price takers with whom he deals, and that he exploits this advantage by taking the initiative in the market and in economic life in general. Under free competition, this favorable market position would be occupied by the businessman. He would be the person who assumes the role of the price maker in his dealings with the members of *all* the other groups in the economy, such as farmers, workers, and employees in general; and he would enjoy the price maker's favored market position not only when he buys the farmer's produce and his employees' services but also when he sells them his products. We must now investigate what advantages, if any, businessmen would derive from their favored market position as price makers; and to do so, we shall again take perfect competition as our standard of comparison.

Let us recall that under perfect competition the owner of each productive service would receive a rate of remuneration equal both to the value of the marginal product of his services and to the transfer price of the marginal owner of his type of services. The first equality is due to the fact that under perfect competition each entrepreneur, being a price taker in all markets, would equate the marginal costs of all his products and the marginal values of all his factors to their respective

---

[16] Except, of course, in the case of commodities whose storage costs and rate of deterioration are high.

prices. The second equality is insured by free entry to all occupations and all markets.

It is apparent that under free competition only the second equality would be insured. The first would not be, because the entrepreneur is a price maker, who sells his products at prices above their marginal costs and buys his factors at prices below their marginal value to him; and even if he did only one of these things (being a price maker in one and price taker in the other market), the owners of the factors he employs would receive a price for their services which is smaller than the market value of the marginal product of these services. This was expressed symbolically in inequality (11) on page 363 and is generally referred to in the literature of economics as the monopolistic (and/or monopsonistic) exploitation of these factors. Hence, if productive services were utilized in the same form and in the same quantities under free competition as they would be under perfect competition, the income of businessmen (and price makers in general) would be larger, and that of the other groups in the economy would be smaller than their respective incomes would be under perfect competition.

The utilization of productive services, however, would not be the same in the two situations. The main reason for this is that under free competition the higher income of businessmen and the lower income of others change the relative attractiveness of their economic positions; and, with freedom of entry assured under free competition, this would swell the ranks of businessmen and thin the ranks of the other groups in the economy.

That such a tendency exists under free competition we have already seen. We showed in section 5*b* of this chapter that free competition draws more firms and more businessmen into each industry than are necessary for the production of its output. At that stage, we discussed the inefficiency that this implies; now we are interested in it from the point of view of income distribution. We know that the establishment of more firms and more businessmen would lower the individual businessman's rate of income and would keep lowering it to the point where it ceases to attract additional businessmen. What the businessman's income would be at this point, it is impossible to say. One might be tempted to argue that at this point there are more people in business than there would be under perfect competition, and that to attract more people into any profession requires the attraction of a higher income in that profession. This argument, however, would be correct only if incomes in other occupations were the same as under perfect competition; whereas we have just seen that incomes in other occupations would probably be lower. Under free competition, therefore, the individual businessman might be no better off, or only a little better off, than he would be under perfect competition. In any case the businessman's income would contain no monopoly profit; and if his income were higher, this would correspond merely to the higher transfer price of the marginal entrepreneur in an economy that employs too many entrepreneurs. The only thing we can say with confidence about income distribution is that businessmen as a group would have a larger share in total national income than they would have under perfect competition; but this would be due mainly or solely to the larger number of businessmen.

The argument concerning the income of other economic groups is similar. We have already seen that the owners of other productive services would receive less than the market value of the marginal product of their services; on the other hand, their income would be raised by the diversion of people to business as a profession. On balance, their income might (though it is not likely to) be raised to the perfectly competitive level; but in any case the share of these other economic groups in the national income would be lower.

It should be added, in closing, that free competition would also confer advantages other than economic ones upon those who can assume the role of price maker in the market. To begin with, the price maker's ability to take the initiative in economic life gives him a sense of power and importance which he may value for its own sake. Furthermore, the price maker's training in organization and leadership often gives businessmen as a group special weight also in political life. These matters, however, are the concern of the sociologist and political scientist and lie outside the scope of this book.

To summarize the conclusions of this chapter, we might say that the economic situation brought about by free competition would, in many respects, approximate that which would obtain under the ideal conditions of pure competition. We have seen, in particular, that the distribution of goods and services among consumers and specialization among workers would be just about equally efficient under free and under pure competition, and so would the internal administration and technical organization of the firm. The allocation of resources and output among the members of an industry would, under free competition, only approximate the perfect efficiency of pure competition; and the same would be true also of the economic efficiency of the proportions in which different consumers' goods are produced and different types of labor (original factors) utilized. As to income distribution, there too, the difference between free and perfect competition would probably not be too great; but business would be favored and other economic groups discriminated against, compared to what their relative shares would be under perfect competition.

The main differences would occur in job allocation within occupations, in the utilization of fixed factors and of the businessman's services, and in the combination of produced with original factors of production. Job allocation would be generally inefficient; there would be more firms, businessmen, and business and manufacturing equipment than are needed to produce society's output economically; and there would be a tendency to use more labor- and less capital-intensive methods of production than are economically most efficient.

BIBLIOGRAPHICAL NOTE

On the general subject of this chapter, see R. F. Kahn, "Some Notes on Ideal Output," *Economic Journal*, Vol. XLV (1935), pp. 1–35. The theorem that free competition leads to excess capacity was first advanced by Professor Chamberlin, whose book (*The Theory of Monopolistic Competition* [Cambridge, Mass.: Harvard University Press, 1931]) has often been cited in these pages. For a further discussion of this subject, see N. Kaldor, "Market Imperfection and Excess Capacity," *Economica*, N.S., Vol. II (1935), pp. 33–50; R. F. Harrod, "Doctrines of Imperfect Competition," *Quarterly Journal of Economics*, Vol. XLVIII (1934), pp. 442–70; and J. M. Cassels, "Excess Capacity and Monopolistic Competition," *Quarterly Journal of Economics*, Vol. LI (1937), pp. 426–43.

PART IV

Restricted Competition

In this part, we shall be concerned with the nature and forms of restricted competition, with the price maker's behavior under restricted competition, and with the types of inefficiency brought about by competitive restriction. An exhaustive analysis of these topics, however, would require a volume by itself; and the following chapters, therefore, must be regarded as a mere summary of the subject.

In particular, Chapter XVII is a summary of the more formal analysis of the different types of monopolistic and oligopolistic behavior. Chapter XVIII deals with some of the more interesting special characteristics of restricted competition in markets in which competition is restrained by the buyer's lack of information. In this connection, Chapter XVIII also contains a general discussion of price discrimination, even though price discrimination, while most common in the uninformed market, occurs frequently also in other markets. Chapter XIX deals with the firm's market behavior and the effects of its behavior in markets where competition is restricted or absent on both sides of the market.

Following Chapter XIX, one might expect, on the pattern of Part III, to find a discussion of the conditions that bring about restricted competition. Of this, however, there is no need. For our detailed discussion, in Chapter XV, not only of the factors that favor free competition but also of those that restrain it, has rendered further consideration of this problem unnecessary. We said in Chapter XV that for competition to be free, some of the favorable factors must be present, and all the restraining factors must be absent. We may add here that for competition to be restricted, all the factors favoring competition would have to be weak or absent, and some of the restraining factors would have to be present.

The next chapter, therefore (Chap. XX), deals with the efficiency of restricted competition. This chapter parallels and should be read in conjunction with Chapters VIII and XVI, which deal with the efficiency of perfect and free competition, respectively. Finally, Chapter XXI concludes our discussion by raising the difficult problem of policy as it relates to the maintenance of competition and of the efficiency of the market mechanism.

CHAPTER XVII

THE FORMS AND NATURE OF RESTRICTED COMPETITION

RESTRICTED competition was defined in Chapter II as competition among price makers who are protected—partly or wholly—from the competition that the entry of newcomers to their market would entail. But the term "restricted competition" covers a large variety of market behavior, because established rivals, protected from the competition of newcomers, may not be restrained at all in their own competitive behavior; and when they are, they may be restrained in various forms and to varying degrees. To analyze the nature of restricted competition, therefore, we shall have to discuss separately the different forms which restricted competition may take.

1. SIMPLE RESTRICTED COMPETITION

The least severe form of restricted competition is simple restricted competition, which is competition among price makers whose competitive behavior is completely free and unrestrained but who enjoy protection from the threat of competition that the entry of newcomers to their market would entail. As was pointed out earlier, the entry of newcomers may be prevented or limited by natural obstacles, such as economies of scale and the uninformed nature of the market, or by the deliberate action of a group of established competitors. As an example of the latter type of simple restricted competition in the American economy, it is customary to cite the medical profession. Entry to this profession is said to be restricted by the very limited number of students existing medical schools are able and willing to admit, and by the reluctance of doctors' professional organizations to approve additional schools. At the same time, however, no restraints seem to be imposed on the market behavior of established members of the medical profession. As far as the individual price maker's market behavior is concerned, therefore, there is no difference between free competition and simple restricted competition. His behavior conforms in both cases to

373

the pattern described in Chapters XI–XIV. The only difference between the two cases is that under free competition the price maker's profit attracts to his market new competitors whose entry in turn tends to eliminate his profit; whereas under simple restricted competition the entry of newcomers is limited, which prevents the elimination of the price maker's profit.

2. MONOPOLY

At the other end of the scale from simple restricted competition is monopoly. This is the strongest restraint on competition and signifies the concentration of control over all or the most important market decisions in the hands either of one firm or of a group of firms acting in concert.

2a. THE ESTABLISHMENT OF MONOPOLY

Monopoly can come about naturally, as in the case of natural monopolies or when a group of competitors voluntarily fuse their interests to form a combination; but often—and perhaps more often—it is imposed, either by the state or by an exceptionally strong firm.

The state may create monopolies for a variety of reasons. The earliest state monopolies, such as the salt and iron monopolies of the Han Dynasty in China, and the salt and tobacco monopolies of France, Austria, and several other European countries, were established to secure monopoly profits for the state itself. In sixteenth- and seventeenth-century England the Crown created monopolies in favor of private persons, often as a reward for services rendered. State monopolies have also been established in fields where competition could not be expected to prevail and where it was therefore felt that the price maker's bargaining strength should be limited by public control. Hence the state monopolies of the telephone, telegraph, and public utilities in most European countries. State monopolies may also be imposed where, for one reason or another, private ownership is deemed incompatible with public welfare. This explains the state monopoly of broadcasting established in England in 1930 and most of the French and British nationalization measures of the recent past.

An individual price maker can establish a monopoly position for himself if he is strong enough to keep out newcomers and to drive out or restrain his established competitors. Such monopolies only occur, therefore, in markets where one price maker is in an exceptionally strong position. Once he has achieved this position—either through having been first in his field, or through superior efficiency, or in any other way

—the sheer weight of his economic power may secure him a monopoly position. For competition among price makers is not unlike the game of power politics among nations; and it is natural for small firms to expect their large competitor to make full use of his advantageous market position and put up a fight to prevent others from encroaching upon a market that he regards as his preserve. The mere threat of force may be sufficient to keep newcomers out and to cause already established firms both to curb their own desire to expand and to follow the dictates of their large competitor either by entering into a formal market agreement with him or by tacitly imitating and submitting to his market policy. If the mere threat of force is not enough to achieve these results, the large firm can make war on his competitors to bring them to heel or drive them out of the market. Such warfare, waged by a large firm against its smaller or weaker competitors, is called aggressive competition.[1]

It will be noted that the forms of competition we have discussed so far are peaceful in character, because they all accept the existence of competitors as a datum. Thus, the price taker takes for granted the terms on which he can transact business in the market; the price maker, under free competition and simple restricted competition, sets his own terms but regards as given the market offers of his competitors; and, as has been mentioned already and will presently be argued further, although under oligopoly the price maker influences his competitors' offers, he accepts as given their existence and the limitations that this imposes upon his market behavior. Within such limitations the peaceful competitor tries to make the best use of his market position by behaving in a way that will maximize his current profit. In his attempt to maximize his profit, he may encroach upon his competitors' markets if he happens to be more efficient or more energetic than they are; but as long as he accepts the fact of their existence, he will never make an offer that is unfair to his competitors.

Very different from this is the market behavior of the aggressive competitor. He tries to extend his market and increase his bargaining strength by eliminating his competitors or getting them under his control. In other words, he *aims* at encroaching upon his competitors' markets and will often do so even at the cost of temporary losses to himself. Often, his market offer is not made with a view to maximizing current profit; it may be a strategic move in his war on competitors. He is prepared to incur present losses for the sake of his future domination of the market; and his only economic calculation is the weighing of the cost of

---

[1] See below for a description of aggressive competition.

warfare against the chance of ultimate victory and its prize, monopoly profit. Hence, he will often engage in price war (cutthroat competition) and make an offer that, in the short run, inflicts losses upon himself as well as upon his competitors, hoping thereby to drive them into bankruptcy or subjugation, while his own greater financial strength enables him to prevail and to recoup himself for his temporary losses out of the monopoly profit to be earned after the defeat of his competitors.

Nor is aggressive competition confined in its methods to price war alone. It may extend to any other aspect of the price maker's market offer; it may consist in damaging the goodwill and reputation of competitors, in putting material and personal difficulties in their way, or in any other action calculated to sap their economic strength and induce them to sell out or come to terms. In short, aggressive competition is total war, which aims at more *Lebensraum,* and which may make use of every fair or unfair weapon.

Anyone who believes in competition as a beneficent economic force must be opposed to aggressive competition, which aims at undermining and destroying competition. Attempts have therefore been made, notably in the United States, to outlaw aggressive competition for the sake of maintaining peaceful competition. Unfortunately, while the aims of peaceful and aggressive competition are very different, their methods are not always easy to distinguish. It is very difficult to establish objective standards by which to distinguish between, say, peaceful and aggressive price competition. It is true that the setting of a seller's price below marginal cost would be a clear indication of aggressive intentions; but in view of the difficulties that beset the calculation of marginal cost, it is not easy to recognize, let alone to prove, the existence of such a situation. As a result, pressure groups have often taken advantage of the popular feeling against aggressive competition and brought about the enactment of legal and other measures ostensibly aimed at preventing aggressive competition but actually used for the imposition of monopolistic restraints. Resale price-maintenance laws are an obvious example and so are agreements within professional and occupational groups (such as barbers, lawyers, dry cleaners, etc.) providing for minimum fees.

Aggressive competition leads to the establishment of the victor as single monopolist if he succeeds in absorbing or driving out his competitors; it may lead to collective monopoly if the would-be monopolist is not wholly successful and has to admit his competitors as more or less equal partners in a combination designed to maintain monopoly prices and share monopoly profits; or it may lead to oligopoly if the defeated competitors accept the victor as their price leader and refrain from expanding and underselling him on pain of renewed warfare.

2b. SINGLE MONOPOLY

A single monopolist is defined as a firm or person who is all alone on his side of the market, or who, if not alone, controls the market behavior of his competitors. The monopolist sets his market offer in exactly the same way as any other price maker. In fact, we can regard the theory of the price maker's market behavior presented in Chapters XI–XIV as the theory of the monopolist's market behavior if we assume that he aims at maximizing his profit. The crucial question is, however, whether this assumption is justified.

To assume that the price maker aims at maximizing his profit seems perfectly realistic and reasonable when competition keeps his profits so small that every relaxation of the effort to maximize profits may wipe them out or lead to losses or even bankruptcy. But when the price maker is a monopolist, whose profit is large and protected from the encroachments of competitors, he may well relax his efforts. For to maximize profits implies a constant alertness and readiness to seize new opportunities and to adapt one's self to changed circumstances; and the strain that this entails may not appear worth while if all that it would achieve is to make already large profits even larger. There may come a point beyond which additional profits are less desirable than the relaxation of effort; and, in Professor Hicks's words, "it may well be that the best of all monopoly profits is a quiet life."[2]

Furthermore, not only does the monopolist's secure market position *enable* him to relax his efforts of maximizing profit, but his very position may *prevent* his aiming at maximum profit. He may regard his immunity from competition as precarious or be afraid of unfavorable publicity and public censure; and for either reason, he may judge it wiser to refrain from making full use of his monopoly position. We conclude, therefore, that although in some cases the monopolist will aim at maximizing his profit and behave in the way outlined in Chapters XI–XIV, in other cases—which may well be the important ones—he will refrain from maximizing profit.

When he does not aim at maximizing his profit, the monopolist has many alternative policies from which to choose; and it depends on his

[2] J. R. Hicks, "Annual Survey of Economic Theory: The Theory of Monopoly," *Econometrica*, Vol. III (1935), p. 8.

motives and disposition which he will adopt. For example, when the monopolist uses his monopoly position to relax his efforts and avoid the bother that profit maximizing would entail, he may reduce his entrepreneurial functions to mere routine and rely on rules of thumb for running his firm. Under such conditions, he may let the efficiency of his firm deteriorate; and he may fall behind the times through failure to keep up with technological progress and changing tastes and requirements. Indeed, inefficiency, the retention of antiquated productive methods, and failure to cater to consumers' changing requirements are all charges that are often leveled against monopoly. On the other hand, it can also happen that the monopolist will be interested in efficiency for its own sake and neglect to maximize profit only as far as his market policy is concerned. The monopolist may adopt a similar policy also in order to protect his monopoly position from public censure or government action. In such a case, he may set a price that does not exploit fully his monopoly position; and he may even show his public-spiritedness by maintaining a high level of efficiency and by spending more on scientific research and employees' welfare than would be called for by narrow mercenary considerations. In short, the assumption that the entrepreneur aims at maximum profit is subject to even more qualifications and exceptions in the monopolist's case than in that of the competitive producer; and when the assumption cannot be made, we have no alternative principle of comparable generality to put into its place.

2c. COLLECTIVE MONOPOLY

Collective monopoly is an agreement among a group of competing price makers to restrain competition among themselves. Such agreement may take a variety of forms, comprise any aspect or aspects of the price maker's market offer, and extend to any degree, ranging from informal rules of business ethics to the detailed regulation of all facets of market behavior. For what follows, it will be convenient to discuss, first, the tightest form of collective monopoly, whose members agree on a common market policy in all factor and product markets and suspend all competition among themselves.

What does it mean to suspend competition, and how does such behavior differ from competitive behavior? Let us consider, first, the difference between the two types of behavior as far as the individual firm's price policy is concerned. We saw in Chapter XIII that the price maker sets his price by adding to marginal cost (or subtracting from marginal value) a profit margin that depends on the price elasticity of the market facing him. The price elasticity measures the market's response to a change in the firm's price; and this response consists, as we know, of the income and substitution effects of the price change on the firm's customers. The larger these two effects, the higher the price elasticity of the market—and the smaller, therefore, the firm's optimum profit margin.

The magnitude of the substitution effect depends on the scope for substitution between the price maker's offer and the offers of his competitors. The less scope there is for substitution, the smaller is the substitution effect of a price change and, consequently, the lower the price elasticity

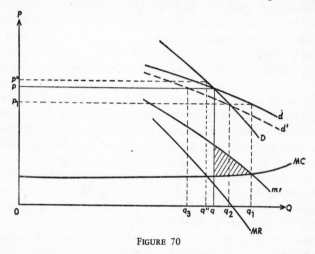

FIGURE 70

of demand facing the price maker and the higher his optimum profit margin. Collective monopoly, therefore, or agreement in restraint of competition, secures an advantage for its members by lessening or eliminating the scope for substitution among their products.

It is convenient to illustrate this argument in a diagram. In Figure 70, MC shows the marginal-cost curve of a seller who, let us assume, starts from an original situation where his price is set at p and his sales are at q. Curve d shows the demand curve facing him, drawn on the assumption that a change in his price would lead to some substitution between his product and those of his competitors. Curve mr is the marginal-revenue curve derived from d. Curve D shows the same seller's demand curve but drawn on the alternative assumption that there is no substitution between his product and those of his competitors; and

MR is the marginal-revenue curve derived from D. The two demand curves have different elasticities at price p; accordingly, they call for different profit margins and price policies. The question is: Which of the two curves is relevant to our seller for determining his price policy?

A seller who is a member of a large group of competing sellers among whom there is no market agreement will regard d as his demand curve and mr as his marginal-revenue curve; and he will feel that, to maximize his profit, he should lower his price to the level p_1, which renders $mr = MC$. For, being one seller among many, he knows that a change in his price will have so small an effect on the market situation of his competitors that it will not induce them to change their market behavior. Hence, he expects a reduction in his price to render his product cheaper in relation to his competitors' products and so encourage the substitution of his product for theirs, just as he would expect a raising of his price to cause some of his customers to switch from him to his competitors.

If lowering his price to p_1 would raise his sales to q_1, his profit would rise by an amount shown by the shaded triangle. But the lowering of his price need not necessarily raise his sales to q_1. For assume that his competitors are in exactly the same situation as he is; that also their positions can be represented by diagrams similar to Figure 70; and that also they decide, on the basis of similar reasoning, to lower their prices from p to p_1. In this case, each seller will be disappointed in his expectation that his lower price will attract some of his competitors' customers. His price and his competitors' prices having been lowered by the same amount, there will be no substitution between competing products, so that our seller's sales will rise only to q_2 and he will suffer a loss of profit.

Does this mean that our seller made a mistake in acting on the assumption that d, and not D, is the demand curve relevant to him? Not necessarily. For his competitors lowered their prices acting on the same basis as he *but independently of his action*. In other words, they would have lowered their prices even if he had not lowered his. If his competitors would have lowered their prices while he maintained his at p, his demand curve would have shifted to the left, as shown by curve d'; and his sales would have fallen to q_3, causing him an even greater fall of profit than he incurs with price at p_1, and sales at q_2. Hence, in the absence of an agreement with his competitors, selling q_2 output at price p_1 may well be the best that our seller can do.

It is only by concluding an agreement with his competitors that he could improve his position and raise his profit, because only by such an agreement could he rule out the possibility of substitution between his product and theirs. If there were no danger of losing customers to his competitors, he could move along the demand curve D and increase his profit by raising his price to p''.

There are several ways in which rival firms can, by agreement, rule out competition among themselves and substitution among their products. One is to divide the market into several parts and declare each part the preserve of one firm. An example would be if, say, there were an agreement between Montgomery Ward and Sears, Roebuck that one will not open a store in a town where the other already has one. A second way of restraining competition is to limit the total output of each party to the agreement. This was the system adopted, for example, by the European international sugar cartel in the interwar period. A third way, and the one with which we shall mainly be concerned, is by means of a price agreement.

If a group of price makers agree to pursue a common price policy and not to change their prices except together and by agreement, each of them can regard D as the demand curve relevant to his price policy, because he can rest assured that the others will not change their prices when he does not change his, and that each change in his price will be accompanied by a corresponding change in his competitors' prices and therefore will not lead to substitution between his product and those of his competitors.[3] If the several firms were identical in every respect and Figure 70 represented the cost and market conditions faced by each of them, p'' would become the most profitable common price from every producer's point of view; and they would soon agree to set this price, which would maximize the profits of every one of them. It is apparent that this price is identical with that which would come about if the parties to the agreement, instead of making the agreement, merged their identity, pooled their resources, and formed a single monopoly under one management.

The argument is almost word by word the same also with respect to other aspects of the price maker's market offer. For example, a seller's appraisal of the market's response to his advertising depends on whether or not he expects substitution to occur between his product and those

---

[3] Hence, one can also express the difference between the demand curves d and D by saying that d is drawn on the assumption that competitors' prices remain unchanged; whereas D shows the market's reaction to a price change which is matched by similar changes in competitors' prices.

of his competitors as a result of advertising. If he anticipates substitution, because he regards his competitors' advertising policies as given and uninfluenced by his own, he will expect the elasticity of the market's response to his advertising to be high and will accordingly spend much on advertising. This is usually the case when he is one of a large number of producers among whom there is no market agreement. If, on the other hand, he expects no substitution to take place—for example, because he expects his competitors to imitate his every move—then his estimate of the elasticity of the market's response to advertising will be relatively small. If the several firms were identical in every respect and faced the same market and cost conditions, they could easily agree on a common advertising policy advantageous to all of them; and it is again apparent that this policy would coincide with that which a single monopoly, composed of the same firms, would pursue.

The above conclusion, however—that a market agreement among independent firms leads to the same price, advertising, and other market policies as would be pursued by a single monopoly—holds true only in the very special and unlikely case when the parties to the market agreement are similar in every respect. Our next problem, therefore, is to find out what happens when, as is the rule, the parties to the restrictive agreement operate under different cost conditions, face slightly different markets, or appraise the market's responsiveness in different ways. Under such conditions, each producer has different ideas concerning the optimum market offer he would like to see agreed upon and adopted by the group; and the common market policy actually adopted will be the result of compromise.

This has two consequences. In the first place, since working out a compromise is a delicate, difficult, and lengthy process, the market offer adopted by a collective monopoly is likely to be more stable and longer adhered to than other market offers, simply because the parties to the agreement shirk the bother and difficulties that reaching a new compromise agreement would involve. In the second place—and this is the more important consequence—the monopoly profits yielded by a collective monopoly are likely to be smaller than they would be if the members to the monopolistic agreement gave up their independence, merged their interests, and formed a single monopoly. This difference between the profits of a single and of a collective monopoly arises from differences in their behavior, which are important from our point of view, because they bear on the relative efficiency of the two types of monopoly. In a collective monopoly, each member's profit depends on his sales; and since the members of a collective monopoly are anxious to receive what they regard as their fair share of the monopoly's total profit, their aim to maximize total profit is *subject to the restraint that each member maintains his share of the monopoly's total sales.* In a single monopoly the constituent firms pool their resources and lose their independence and identity; and their owners or stockholders share in the monopoly's profit in proportion to their contribution to the monopoly's total assets or according to some other principle, but independently of how the monopoly's total output is apportioned among its plants. Hence, a single monopoly can aim at maximum profits and adopt the most profitable market offer and the most profitable production policy without the restraints that hamper a collective monopoly, that is, without the necessity of keeping the relative output of different plants stable or of keeping prices in different sectors of the market equal or in some prearranged relation.

This means, first of all, that a single monopoly can make better use of its monopoly position in the market than collective monopoly can. Second, a single monopoly, unlike a collective monopoly, can increase its efficiency by concentrating production in its most efficient plants and shutting down the least efficient ones. Third, a single monopoly can further increase its efficiency by eliminating duplication in its administrative (and sometimes also in its distributive) machinery and by increased specialization as between its different plants—none of which a collective monopoly can do. It appears, therefore, that single monopoly can achieve both higher profit and higher efficiency than collective monopoly, provided that it has the incentive to achieve these aims.

Notwithstanding the higher profit attainable under single monopoly, a group of producers often prefer to form only a collective monopoly. The main reason for this is probably the high premium which they, together with most people, put on independence and all the advantages that this implies. The president of a corporation may prefer being master in his own house to earning the same or even a higher income as vice-president of a supercorporation in which he would only be second in command.

A further reason why a group of producers may have a preference for collective monopoly is their fear of taking the irrevocable step which a complete merger into a single monopoly involves. A collective monopoly can be dissolved and an agreement on market policies terminated if matters do not work out to the satisfaction of all the members; or the terms of the agreement can be revised if they are found to favor some members to the detriment of others—all of which is impossible under a single monopoly, which absorbs the identity of the constituent firms. Furthermore, producers may prefer a collective monopoly to a single monopoly, because the former leaves them some scope for improving their relative position within the monopoly itself. For agreements on a common market policy always leave some loopholes for competition among the parties to the agreement; in fact, the scope of such agreements is usually very limited owing to the difficulties both of reaching agreement on every aspect of market policy and of enforcing agreements once reached. In some·cases a restrictive agreement may go no further than to limit entry, prescribe a code of business ethics, and forbid certain competitive practices. More often, collective monopolies comprise a price agreement, presumably because this is the easiest to reach and enforce. In such cases the parties to the agreement continue to compete unrestricted as concerns all other aspects of their market offers. Sometimes, a collective monopoly will comprise, in addition to a price agreement, an agreement to keep advertising expenditure below a certain limit or not to introduce new models more often than, say, once a year. In any event, collective monopoly is a halfway house between single monopoly and simple restricted competition.

3. OLIGOPOLY

Oligopoly is restricted competition among price makers whose competitive behavior is restrained not by agreement but by their realization of the interdependence of their actions. In the majority of cases, this leads to a market behavior very similar to that of collective monopoly. In fact, the difference between the express agreement of collective monopoly and the tacit agreement of oligopoly is so slight as far as results are concerned that they are often bracketed together under the name of "oligopoly."

Oligopoly may come about when the number of competing price makers is small. Hence the name *oligopoly* ("few sellers") or, in English, competition among the few. When competitors are few, the actions of each competitor have a noticeable impact on market conditions; and each member of the market is aware both of the influence his competitors' actions have on his profit and of the influence his own actions have on his competitors' actions. His awareness of this interdependence restrains each price maker's competitive behavior, either because he fears reprisals or because he hopes that if he restrains his competition, the others will reciprocate.

This type of behavior may occur, however, even when the number of competitors is large. In a market, for example, where one large firm and many small firms are competing, the small firms, fearful lest their large competitor engage in aggressive competition against them, will often try to appease the large firm by restraining their competitive behavior; and the large firm, aware of this, will in turn be influenced in its competitive behavior. Similarly, in a market composed of a few large and many small firms, the large firms will often act as oligopolists, taking the interdependence of their actions into consideration and ignoring as unimportant the existence and behavior of the small firms.

What is the market behavior of the oligopolist, who is aware of the interdependence of his and his competitors' actions and takes this interdependence into account? Clearly, it depends on the particular assumptions he makes about his competitors' reaction patterns. Since there is a great variety of assumptions he can make, the theory of oligopoly is a collection of special cases and behavior patterns, each based on a different assumption or set of assumptions of varying importance and likelihood. To discuss all these in detail would go far beyond the scope of this book; and all we shall do in the following is to give an outline of the oligopolist's market behavior in some of the more common cases.

To begin with, let us return to the example we discussed and illustrated on page 379. Figure 70 depicted the situation of a seller who sets his price at p, and whose competitors also set their prices at p. The price p is intermediate between p_1, the price that would maximize the seller's profit if his competitors kept their prices unchanged when he changes his, and p'', the price that would maximize his profit if his competitors followed his every move. Starting from this initial situation, the oligopolist may adopt any one of three alternative price policies: he may lower, leave unchanged, or raise price. Similarly, his competitors also may adopt any one of these alternative policies. Hence, there are nine different combinations (3^2) of the price policies of the oligopolist and his competitors, and each combination has a different effect on his profit.

In Figure 71 (p. 386), this is illustrated in the form of a matrix whose rows refer to the three possible price policies which a given oligopolist might pursue, and whose columns refer to the three possible ways in which his rivals might change their price policies. The signs $\uparrow$, $=$, $\downarrow$, stand for the raising, leaving unchanged, and lowering of price, respectively. The symbols that appear in the boxes at the intersections of rows and columns show the effect upon the oligopolist's profit of each combination of his and his rivals' price policies.

It is obvious, to begin with, that if neither the oligopolist nor his rivals changed their prices, the oligopolist's profit would remain unchanged. This is denoted in the matrix by the letter O (meaning zero change) at the intersection of the row showing no change in the oligopolist's price and the column showing no change in his rivals' prices.

HIS COMPETITORS'
ALTERNATIVE
PRICE POLICIES

		↑	=	↓
THE PRICE MAKER'S ALTERNATIVE PRICE POLICIES	↑	G	L̲	L
	=	G	O̲	l
	↓	G	G	L̲

FIGURE 71

It is equally obvious that if the oligopolist kept his price unchanged while his rivals changed theirs, his profit would rise if they raised their prices and fall if they lowered them. This is denoted in the matrix by the letters G (gain) and L (loss of profit) to the left and right of the letter O, where the row showing no change in the oligopolist's price intersects the columns showing a raising and lowering, respectively, of his rivals' prices. If, on the other hand, our oligopolist were the only one to change his price while his competitors kept theirs fixed, he would lower his profit by raising his price and raise it by lowering his price.[4] This is denoted in the matrix by the letters L and G shown vertically above and below the letter O, where the row showing the raising and lowering, respectively, of the oligopolist's price intersects the column showing no change in his rivals' prices.

If the oligopolist can make a gain by lowering his price while his rivals' prices remain unchanged, he is bound to make an even greater gain if their prices are raised at the time when he lowers his. This is indicated by the letter G in the bottom left-hand square of the matrix. Conversely, if the oligopolist suffers a loss of profit by raising his price while the prices of his rivals remain unchanged, he is bound to incur

---

[4] Provided that he did not lower his price below p_1.

an even greater loss of profit if their prices are lowered at the time when he raises his. This accounts for the letter L in the top right-hand square of the matrix. This leaves two more squares yet to be filled in. The letter G in the upper left-hand corner and the letter L in the lower right-hand corner show that the simultaneous raising or lowering of the prices of the oligopolist and his rivals will raise or lower, respectively, the oligopolist's profit. This follows from our initial assumption that the initial price p is lower than p''.

The matrix of Figure 71 shows how the price maker's profit depends on both his actions and those of his competitors; and it also helps to explain how the price maker's behavior depends on what he believes his competitors' behavior to be. As mentioned earlier, we cannot discuss here all the forms that the oligopolist's behavior can take; and we shall deal only with three cases which are of special interest.

3a. PRICE LEADERSHIP

We mentioned earlier in this section that in markets where many small firms compete with one large producer, they often accept him as a price leader and fashion their market offers after his, in an effort to maintain good relations with him. Under such conditions the large producer can always assume that his every move will be matched by similar moves on the part of his competitors, which means that his alternatives are represented in Figure 71 by the squares of the diagonal extending from the top left to the bottom right-hand corner. It will be to his advantage, therefore, to raise his price; and, in terms of the diagram of Figure 70, he will raise it to p''. In other words, when one firm is a price leader and the others are price followers, they will act as though they had formed a collective monopoly and concluded an agreement to pursue a common price policy. It hardly needs to be added that this argument applies not only to price but also to all other aspects of market behavior with respect to which the small firms are willing to follow the example of their large competitor.

The above type of behavior is very common; it occurs not only within a group that consists of one large firm and many small ones but quite often also among competing firms of approximately the same size. This can happen because, in a competitive market, changing cost and demand conditions usually affect all firms in more or less the same way; consequently, all firms find it profitable to make the same kind of changes in their market offers at about the same time. There are always some firms, however, which respond more promptly to changing conditions than others; and if a group of competitors find at repeated occasions that one of their number is consistently ahead of them in all market actions, they gradually begin to look to him for leadership and may acquire the habit of automatically imitating his moves instead of making their own calculations for independent market actions. Once such a behavior pattern has become general and well established within a group, the leader of the group can take it for granted that his competitors will follow his behavior; and he will set his price (as well as other aspects of his market offer) accordingly. At this stage, therefore, the behavior of the group ceases to be competitive; and the prices set by the price leader and his followers begin to approach the monopolistic level denoted by p'' in Figure 70, even though the agreement to set price at this level is only a tacit one. As the price set by the group approaches this monopolistic level, the profits of members of the group rise; and this fact tends to strengthen the "follow-the-leader" relation between the price leader and his followers, since it convinces the latter that imitating the price leader's market actions is a more profitable policy than trying to formulate their market policies independently. We conclude, therefore, that price, and possibly also other aspects of the price maker's market offer, may be set at a monopolistic level by tacit agreement and without any monopolistic collusion if one member of a group of competitors assumes the initiative and the others accept his leadership, either because of a disparity in size between them or because of differences in their alertness and general temperament.

3b. THE CASE OF THE KINKED DEMAND CURVE

A second form of oligopoly occurs in markets where the number of competitors is small but where no single firm has enough power or initiative to assume the role of price leader. In such a situation, if any one of a group of competitors introduced a change in his market policy, the others might follow suit, but only if they felt compelled to retaliate in order to maintain their position. For example, if one seller lowered his price, the others might feel that they had to lower theirs, lest the first seller should encroach upon their markets and divert their customers. There would be no inducement, however, for them to follow if he raised his price, since by merely keeping their prices unchanged, they could capture some of his customers. When each seller expects his competitors to behave this way—that is, when he expects his competitors' prices to be lowered if he lowers his price but to remain unchanged if he raises his price or keeps it unchanged—then his profit expectations associated with his different alternative price policies are shown in our matrix by the three squares underlined in Figure 71. They show that both the lowering and the raising of his price would lower his profit; his best policy, therefore, would be to keep his price unchanged—provided it is somewhere between its competitive and monopolistic level.

The above argument is generally known as the theorem of the kinked demand curve because, in terms of the diagram of Figure 70, it can be represented by a kinked demand curve. This is shown in Figure 72,

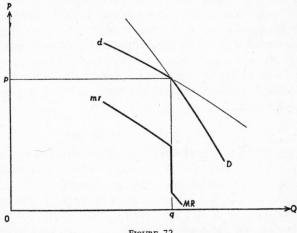

FIGURE 72

where the diagram of Figure 70 is reproduced. The seller's initial price is p; and his demand curve above p is the requisite portion of the curve d, which shows the market's response to a possible raising of his price on the assumption that all other prices remain unchanged; whereas, *below* p, his demand curve is the requisite portion of the curve D, which shows the market's response to a possible lowering of his price on the assumption that all his competitors would lower their prices, too.

The marginal-revenue curve derived from this kinked demand curve has a discontinuity at q, which explains the stabilizing effect of the type of thinking that the kinked demand curve illustrates. For the price maker has no inducement to change his price as long as his marginal-cost curve goes through the discontinuity (i.e., cuts the vertical segment) of his marginal-revenue curve. This implies that changes in cost or demand conditions must be substantial if they are to bring about a change in price.

Here again, it is worth stressing that the above argument applies to sellers and buyers alike, and that it applies not only to price but to all other aspects of the price maker's market offer as well. The reader will also notice the resemblance of this argument to one presented in the previous section. We argued there that a common market policy agreed upon by the members of a collective monopoly is likely to be stable, simply because the parties to the agreement shirk the bother and difficulties involved in negotiating and reaching a new agreement. The argument of the kinked demand curve is similar. In an oligopolistic situation, where market policies have settled down to routine and become stabilized, each price maker may be reluctant to change his market behavior for fear of disturbing what seems a stable and not unsatisfactory situation. He may not go through the explicit and elaborate reasoning implied by the kinked demand curve but may simply feel that he should sit still while he can, lest he should, by some untoward move, precipitate a competitive race.

3c. THE POLICY OF PLAYING SAFE

The two forms of oligopolistic behavior considered so far had one thing in common: they showed the market behavior of a group each member of which made definite assumptions concerning the behavior and reaction pattern of the other members of his group. The assumptions were different in each case, but they were always definite. We shall now discuss a case in which the individual price maker is uncertain as to how his competitors will act and hence can make only very limited assumptions about their behavior.

In particular, let us consider the case in which the price maker has the following general ideas about his competitors' reactions to his policies. He feels, first of all, that if he himself were to keep his price unchanged, it would be entirely unpredictable whether his rivals would raise, keep unchanged, or lower their prices. Second, he also thinks that if he were to raise his price, it would be uncertain whether his rivals would raise their prices or keep them unchanged, although it would be unlikely that they would lower their prices. Third, he believes that if he were to lower his price, his rivals would not raise their prices; but he could not predict whether they would lower them or keep them unchanged. This situation is represented in Figure 73, where the matrix of Figure 71 is reproduced except for its top-right and bottom-left squares, which represent the two unlikely occurrences. In this incomplete matrix the results of the price maker's alternative policies are represented not by individual squares but by the three rows. They show that whatever policy the price maker may adopt, he cannot foresee its effect on his profit, because this may rise or fall (or stay unchanged), depending on his rivals' policies, which he cannot predict.

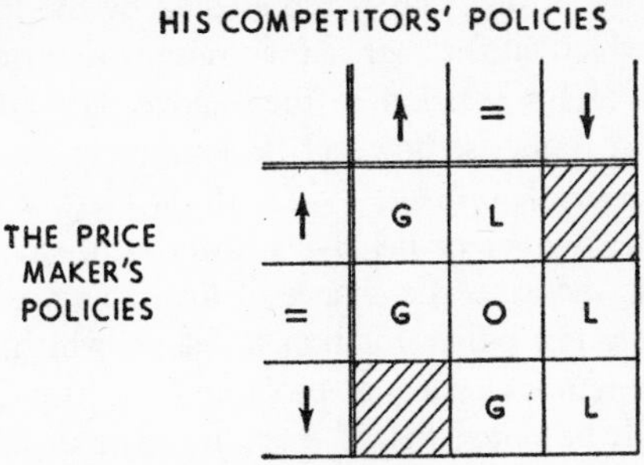

HIS COMPETITORS' POLICIES

		↑	=	↓
THE PRICE MAKER'S POLICIES	↑	G	L	//////
	=	G	O	L
	↓	//////	G	L

FIGURE 73

In such a situation, the price maker can find a guide to policy in the following consideration. He knows that whatever he does, he may suffer a loss of profit; but if the losses contingent on his three alternative policies are not equally great, he may find it desirable to play safe and adopt the policy that threatens the smallest loss of profit. Let us see what such a policy would lead to.

If the price maker were to keep his price unchanged, his profit would be reduced if his rivals lowered their prices; if this should happen, he could do nothing about it and would have to accept a permanent loss of profit. If he were to lower his price, his profit would be reduced if his rivals also lowered their prices; and although he might then try to rectify the situation by again raising his price, he would have no guaranty that this would cause his rivals to follow suit and raise their prices again, too. Hence, in this case, also, the price maker's loss of profit might be permanent and irremediable. The situation would be different only if the price maker raised his price. In this case, his profit would be reduced if his competitors kept their prices unchanged; but he could recover his old rate of profit by his own action, simply by bringing his price back to its previous lower level.

The above argument can also be put in a slightly different way by considering how the price maker's profit is affected by his rivals' price policies. In terms of Figure 73, this involves a comparison of the different *columns* of the matrix. It appears, to begin with, that what the price maker must try to ward off on all accounts is a reduction in his competitors' prices; for if they reduce their prices, he cannot avoid suffering a loss of profit, regardless of what action he takes. This is shown by the right-hand column of the matrix. On the other hand, it is also clear that the best thing which can happen to the price maker is a rise in his competitors' prices. This is represented by the left-hand column of the matrix, which shows that if they raise their prices, he stands to gain, regardless of his reaction to their move. His influence over his competitors' price policies, however, is extremely limited. According to the assumption made on page 390, nothing short of raising his price will ward off the danger of his rivals lowering theirs; and by raising his price, he also increases the chance of his rivals raising theirs. This, therefore, is the safest policy for him to adopt, which would at worst involve him in a temporary loss of profit and at best yield him a permanent gain. It will be noted that if every member of a market were to pursue this policy of playing safe, the outcome would be exactly the same as that of a price-leader–price-follower relationship. The prices set by the members of the market would, in both cases, approximate the monopolistic level, that is, the level where they would be set in case of a monopolistic price agreement concluded by the members of the group.

In conclusion, it must be emphasized again that price leadership, the case of the kinked demand curve, and the policy of playing safe are just three among many possible forms of oligopolistic behavior and are presented here as a representative sample and not as an exhaustive analysis.

4. MONOPOLY POWER AND BARGAINING STRENGTH

After our discussion of some of the *forms* that restricted competition may take, it would be desirable, next, to present a measure or index of the *degree* of competitive restriction. In fact, any discussion of the different forms of monopoly and competition gives one a vague feeling that it should be possible to arrange them along a scale. Unfortunately, however, none of the many attempts to develop such a measure or scale has been wholly successful; and all we can do here is to present the principles on which such a measure might be based and discuss some of the difficulties that have been encountered in attempts to construct such an index.

A common feature of all forms of restricted competition is that they favor the established price maker, by raising his bargaining strength in the market and enabling him to earn a monopoly profit. This is true not only of the price maker who can restrain the entry of newcomers and the actions of his rivals while his own actions remain unrestrained, but also of one who is party to an agreement—express or tacit—that calls for mutual competitive restraints. For we know that each competitor gains more by the restraints imposed on his competitors and potential competitors than he loses by the restraints imposed upon himself. This is the reason why it is often helpful to think of competitive restraints as the monopoly power of the price maker or group of price makers imposing them.

A price maker's monopoly power *extends* over his competitors. A seller has monopoly power over competing sellers, a buyer, over competing buyers; and his monopoly power *consists* in his control or influence over his actual and potential competitors' market behavior. A person's monopoly power over his competitors *results* in his enhanced bargaining strength in dealing with the people on the other side of the market. Thus, a monopolist seller has enhanced bargaining strength in dealing with the people to whom he sells; and a monopolist buyer, also called a monopsonist, has superior bargaining strength in dealing with the people or firms from whom he buys. This distinction between a person's monopoly power over his competitors and his consequent bargaining strength in dealing with his customers suggests that one should be able to express the degree of monopoly either directly by its extent or indirectly by its results.

A direct measure of monopoly power would establish a scale between the extremes of free competition, where no price maker has conscious influence over his competitors' actions, and of single monopoly, where one price maker stands alone or has absolute control on his side of the market. These are the simple and clear-cut terms in which most people think of competition and monopoly; and an attempt to express the intermediate stages between these two extremes is represented by the indexes of industrial concentration. They show the percentage of an industry's total output (or of a market's total turnover) controlled by some arbitrary number (usually 3 or 4) of its largest members. Such an index was used, for example, in *The Structure of the American Economy,* published by the National Resources Committee (Washington, D.C., 1939). All such indexes, however, are somewhat crude; and there is no possibility of refining them. For monopoly power depends both on the number of firms competing within a market and on inequalities in their size; and no single index could possibly express gradations in both these quantities.

Furthermore, even if a satisfactory direct measure of monopoly power could be developed, it would give no indication of what a certain monopoly position is worth in terms of the bargaining advantage it secures. For, to determine the advantages derived or derivable from a person's monopoly power, it is as important to know the size of the market over which his monopoly extends as the completeness of his monopoly. When told, for example, that a certain person has complete monopoly over all cinemas in a certain town, one learns that he has perfect control over the market behavior of all these cinemas; but to learn what advantages he can derive from his monopoly position, one needs information also on the size of the town, the availability and nature of other amusements, the accessibility of cinemas in the next town, and so forth. It is for this reason that it is often more useful to express the degree of monopoly in terms of the bargaining strength it secures or the monopoly profit it yields.

In many ways, monopoly profit is the most obvious and most logical measure of monopoly power. The main difficulty in using it as a measure is the problem of estimation. To begin with, the net income of a firm is a somewhat arbitrary figure and depends on how—and how fast—the firm amortizes the cost of its fixed resources. Second, to obtain the net profit, we must deduct from the firm's net income the interest on its capital and the owner-entrepreneur's wages of management; and this also creates some difficulties. Last, not all profit is monopoly profit, due to limitations on the entry of newcomers. In a changing world, changing demand and cost conditions often enable a firm to reap a temporary windfall profit, even if the entry of newcomers eliminates this in the end. Such temporary profits would arise even under free or perfect competition; and they must therefore be subtracted from total net profits to arrive at monopoly profits proper. These difficulties have not yet been surmounted; nevertheless, monopoly profit may yet turn out to be the most usable index of monopoly power. The main work in this field has been done by Professor J. S. Bain.

Less practical, but in some ways more interesting, is Professor A. P. Lerner's proposal to express monopoly power in terms of the bargaining strength it secures. The seller's bargaining strength consists of his ability to sell at a price above marginal cost. His interest would seem to be to sell at the highest possible price; but his ability to profit by a high price is checked by the loss of sales which results from the raising of his price. The more his sales respond to a change in price, the less scope he has for setting price above marginal cost with profit to himself. In fact, we saw in Chapter XIII that the most profitable profit margin by which the seller's price can exceed his marginal cost is a simple inverse function of the elasticity with which the market responds to a change in his price. The optimum profit margin, therefore, expressed as a fraction of price, is a convenient index of bargaining strength and hence also of the degree of monopoly. Since the optimum profit margin is equal to the price variation cost, it is apparent that this measure of bargaining strength and monopoly power is the reciprocal of the price elasticity of the market:

$$\text{Degree of monopoly} = \frac{\text{Optimum profit margin}}{\text{Price}} = \frac{VC_p}{p} = \frac{1}{\eta_p}.$$

In the same way the buyer's bargaining strength consists of his ability to buy services or goods at a price that is below their marginal value to him. His desire to buy at the lowest possible cost is checked by the loss of turnover which results from the lowering of his price; and the margin by which he can profitably lower his price below his marginal valuation of the goods or services bought is an inverse function of the price elasticity of his market. His bargaining strength and monopsony power are measured, just like the seller's, by the ratio of his optimum profit margin to price; and this ratio equals the reciprocal of the price elasticity of his market.

In terms of this index of the degree of monopoly (or monopsony), the only person who has no monopoly power at all is the price taker, who equates marginal cost (or marginal value) to price. This is why he is called a perfect competitor, and why a market whose every member is a price taker is called a perfectly competitive market.

More difficult to express in terms of this index is the other extreme: no competition and absolute monopoly power. In our discussion of the consumer's behavior, we showed that the raising of the seller's price may lower consumers' demand for his product in two ways. First, his higher price renders his customers poorer and less able to afford his product; and the consequent reduction in their purchases and his sales is the income effect of the price rise. Second, his higher price makes his product more expensive as compared to other products, which causes some of his customers to shift their custom from him to other sellers; and the resulting fall in his sales is the substitution effect of the price rise. Income and substitution effects together constitute the total effect of the price change on sales; and it is this total effect which the price elasticity of demand measures. Competition, however, affects only the substitution effect. The less competition a seller must contend with, the smaller is the substitution effect, which becomes zero when competition is completely absent. In this case the only effect of the price change is its income effect; and the price elasticity of demand measures the income effect only. The income effect, however, may have almost any value, positive or negative, which means that the above index of the degree of monopoly associates no definite numerical value with absolute monopoly.

To remedy this defect, Dr. R. Triffin has suggested an alternative measure of the degree of monopoly, which is the reciprocal not of price elasticity as defined above but of the so-called "price cross-elasticity." This measures the response of one firm's turnover to a change not in its own but in another firm's price and can therefore be regarded as an approximate measure of the degree of substitution between the two firms' offers.[5] If the sales of a firm are completely unaffected by changes in the prices of all other firms, the cross-elasticities of demand between this firm and all other firms are zero; and their reciprocals, tending to infinity, would denote absolute monopoly.

It is almost impossible, however, to imagine the complete absence of competition. For a rise in the price of, say, Ford cars may persuade consumers not only to substitute other makes of cars for Fords but also to buy, instead of a car, a new kitchen range, or an air-conditioning unit, or a trip to Europe. To prevent all competition, therefore, Ford would have to control not only all automobile production but the production of almost everything else as well. This example shows that absolute monopoly on this definition is not a particularly useful concept. In itself, however, this fact would not condemn the above measure of the degree of monopoly, whose main shortcoming is its unsuitability for statistical measurement.

BIBLIOGRAPHICAL NOTE

The subject matter of this chapter attracted the attention of economists at an early stage; and there was a voluminous and interesting literature on it already in the nineteenth century. For a critical discussion of this classical approach, see E. H. Chamberlin, *The Theory of Monopolistic Competition* (Cambridge, Mass.: Harvard University Press, 1931), chap. iii. Further important work on the subjects of oligopoly and duopoly has been done in Germany, especially by H. von Stackelberg in his *Marktform und Gleichgewicht* (Wien and Berlin, 1934). For the most complete and most up-to-date discussion of these problems, see W. Fellner, *Competi-*

---

[5] Only approximate, because a change in the price of one product has not only a substitution effect but also an income effect on the sales of other products. See p. 47.

tion among the Few (New York: Alfred A. Knopf, 1949), which also contains a complete bibliography.

For a modern and entirely different approach to these problems, see J. Von Neumann and O. Morgenstern, *Theory of Games and Economic Behavior* (Princeton: Princeton University Press, 1944).

As to detail, the argument of sections 2.*c* and 3 utilize a technique (that of Fig. 70) which is Professor Chamberlin's (*op. cit.*, chap. v). For the origin of the kinked demand curve (sec. 3*b*) see R. L. Hall and C. J. Hitch, "Price Theory and Business Behavior," *Oxford Economic Papers,* Vol. I (May, 1939), pp. 12–45; and P. M. Sweezy, "Demand under Conditions of Oligopoly," *Journal of Political Economy,* Vol. XLVII (1939), pp. 568–73.

On the degree of monopoly and its measurement, see A. P. Lerner, "The Concept of Monopoly and the Measurement of Monopoly Power," *Review of Economic Studies,* Vol. I (1934), pp. 157–75; R. Triffin, *Monopolistic Competition and General Equilibrium Theory* (Cambridge, Mass.: Harvard University Press, 1940), chap. iii; J. S. Bain, "The Profit Rate as a Measure of Monopoly Power," *Quarterly Journal of Economics,* Vol. LV (1941), pp. 271–93; K. W. Rothschild, "The Degree of Monopoly," *Economica,* N.S., Vol. IX (1942), pp. 24–39; and A. G. Papandreou, "Market Structure and Monopoly Power," *American Economic Review,* Vol. XXXIX (1949), pp. 883–97.

CHAPTER XVIII

COMPETITION IN THE UNINFORMED MARKET

IN THE last chapter, we discussed restricted competition and the price maker's behavior under restricted competition from a general point of view and without regard to the particular factor or factors which restrain the entry of newcomers and create the conditions of restricted competition. We were able to do so because the aspects of the price maker's behavior which we discussed there remain the same whatever the factor that restrains competition. When, however, competition is restricted by the uninformed nature of the market, the price maker's behavior and the nature of restricted competition assume additional aspects; and these will be discussed in the following. In particular, we shall show, first of all, that in the uninformed market there is a tendency for competing products to become similar to each other; second, that advertising assumes special importance in the uninformed market and contributes to keeping the market uninformed; and finally, that prices tend to become an index of quality in such markets, which in turn often leads to price discrimination. In this connection, we shall also present a general discussion of the principles of price discrimination.

1. LACK OF PRODUCT VARIATION

An important difference between the informed and the uninformed market is that while the variety of tastes in the former gives rise to a variety of products, each of which fills a special need and caters to a different taste, the lack of variety in the ignorant buyers' tastes accounts for the similarity of the products competing in the uninformed market. The buyer who is not familiar with the qualities and intrinsic nature of a product is most unlikely to develop a personal taste or set his own special requirements. Often, he is not even aware of his specific needs or of the particular qualities which would best serve his needs. He wants a product that serves its general purpose well, is reliable, durable, and up to date; but he is not aware of the possibility of a variety of standards.

He wants the best, or the best that a given sum of money will buy, but accepts the expert's opinion of what is best for him.

The expert's role in the uninformed market usually falls to the producer, who seldom finds it profitable to enlighten his customers about their special requirements and the possibility of catering to their special requirements. For, if he did so, he would confine the market for his product to that group of people to whose special requirements it best caters; and to expand his market beyond this group, he would have to offer other varieties of his product, catering to other special requirements. In a few cases the producer can do this without inconvenience or cost to himself. Insurance companies, for example, often find it profitable to differentiate their policies; and sometimes they take great pains to inform the public about the available alternatives and to sell everybody the policy best suited to his special needs. Usually, however, the producer can differentiate his product only at the sacrifice of economies of scale; in such cases, he finds it profitable not to enlighten his public and to cater to the average need and taste by offering a product of all-round usefulness. In markets where this situation prevails, competing products tend to be undifferentiated and to resemble each other, except as far as name, trade-marks, and other unessential features are concerned.

Let us recall, however, that the uninformed market is merely a convenient abstraction. An infinite gradation is possible between the completely informed and the completely uninformed market; and most actual markets fall somewhere between these two extremes. Most people are informed about some features of a product and uninformed about others; and the preceding argument applies only to the latter aspects. In the market for automobiles, for example, the buyer is informed and has his special personal preferences concerning body-type, color, styling, and similar superficial features; and with respect to all these the market does cater to the variety of tastes. The same holds true also of the markets for radios, kitchen equipment, household appliances, and the like; in all these markets, there is great emphasis on appearance, accessories, and special features. Furthermore, all consumers have a taste for a certain amount of variety, which creates an incentive to develop new models and new features. In the uninformed market the scope for the frequent changing of models is all the greater because the ignorant buyer is easily fooled by new models which are new in appearance and superficial features rather than in substance. Hence, the frequent introduction of new models, advertised as "completely new" and "totally different," is a feature characteristic of the uninformed market.

Curiously enough, however, the taste for variety and the superficial differences in taste which characterize the uninformed market lead to little differentiation as between competing products of different firms.[1] For the sales appeal of special features prompts each producer not only to develop new special features but also to copy the special features developed by his competitors. To expand his market, he must make his product more attractive to his competitors' customers without making it less attractive to his own customers. He imitates therefore the special features of competing products to attract the buyers of these products; but, at the same time, he retains the features peculiar to his original product in order to keep a hold on his own customers. Each competitor who adopts this policy may feel that he is extending his market. But when they all do this, the rival policies defeat each other; and their net result is that competing products become more uniform.

From society's point of view the tendency of competing products to resemble each other in the uninformed market is not necessarily a bad thing. The fact that basic differences in different consumers' needs are not catered to can hardly be regarded as a serious loss when the consumers themselves are not aware of these differences. One might think that the cost of the frequent introduction of new models, especially when they are new in name and superficial features only, could be regarded as a loss to society; on the other hand, the introduction of new models may be defended on the basis that it caters to the consumer's desire for variety. This conclusion, however, which goes counter to the common-sense view on this subject, suggests that our criterion of social usefulness, based on conformity to consumers' wishes, may break down in this instance. It does not seem right to accept conformity to consumers' wishes as the criterion of efficiency in a field in which the consumer is ignorant and in which his opinions are easily swayed. If it is true, as is often suggested, that the consumer's desire for new models and new features is an acquired taste, based on ignorance and created or enhanced by the advertising campaigns of producers catering to and profiting by this taste, then conformity to these artificially aroused wishes should not be accepted as a criterion of efficiency, even though we have no better criterion to put in its place. This important problem will be further discussed in section 6a of Chapter XX.

If price takers were aware of the basic similarity of competing products in the uninformed market, such awareness would result in easy

---

[1] Throughout this chapter the term "differentiation" will always mean differentiation of quality.

substitution and high price elasticities of demand, which in turn would limit the profit margins of price makers. In a monopolistic or oligopolistic situation, of course, ease of substitution does not prevent price makers from having high profit margins; but advertising and people's habit of judging quality by price may keep profit margins high even in the absence of monopoly or oligopoly.

2. ADVERTISING

The scope for advertising depends on the ignorance of the people to whom it is addressed. The more ignorant the buyer, the more he relies on advertising. In fact, the importance of advertising in a market could be used as a gauge of the degree of ignorance in that market; and the secular rise of advertising expenditure in our economy may be regarded as an indication of the increasing importance of the uninformed market.[2]

The aim of advertising is always the same, namely, to expand the advertiser's market. The effect of one firm's advertising, however, is largely offset by the advertising of its competitors; and the economist's interest lies in the net effect of advertising by all competitors. In the following, therefore, we shall try to answer the question as to whether advertising by all competitors renders their market more or less informed, more or less perfect.

To the extent that it provides information about the existence of available alternatives, advertising always renders the market more perfect. Beyond this, advertising may provide information that facilitates the comparison of available alternatives and thus may contribute yet further to rendering the market more perfect. If advertising is mainly suggestive and confined to emotional appeal, however, it is likely to impede rational comparison and choice, thus rendering the market *less* perfect. Which of these two forms advertising takes depends on the nature of the market to which it is addressed. In expert and informed markets, advertising is limited in scope; but what advertising there is tends to be factual and informative and thus contributes to keeping the market informed. This is so because expert and informed buyers insist on comparing several alternatives before making a purchase; and if a seller wants his product to be included among the alternatives considered, he must make it easily comparable to competing offers. We used

---

[2] The secular rise in advertising expenditure is a sign of the secular rise of profit margins and decline of price competition. (See sec. 3 of Chap. XIII on this subject.) The increasing importance of the uninformed market is only one of the reasons for the decline of price competition; but it probably is a very important one.

this argument in our discussion of expert markets to explain the geographical concentration of such markets and the standardization of their products;[3] and the same argument also shows that each seller has a motive to provide informative advertising. Examples of such advertising are classified advertisements, announcements of auction sales, manufacturers' catalogues, and most of the advertising in technical and trade journals, all of which are addressed to the expert or informed buyer.

In the uninformed market, the buyer is ill-equipped to make a rational comparison among competing offers; as a result, he is usually unable even to demand the right kind of information. The seller, therefore, has no incentive to supply information that would facilitate comparisons. In fact, in the uninformed market, it is in the seller's interest to prevent rather than to help buyers make rational comparisons, because such comparisons would make them realize the similarity of competing offers. This explains why advertising in the uninformed market concentrates on suggestion, repetition, and emotional appeal, which at best leave the buyer as uninformed as he was before and often tend to divert him from the important features of competing products, thus rendering him less informed rather than more so.

Examples of this type of advertising are such commonly used slogans as "It's different," "It's better," "The best," which quite openly make no attempt to tell the consumer anything concrete about the product advertised. Equally common are advertisements which, although apparently giving the consumer information about the products advertised, give him no helpful information and merely stress distinguishing features that are incidental, unimportant, unintelligible to the layman, or even meaningless. For instance, the information that Pepsodent tooth paste contains Irium or that Old Dutch Cleanser contains activated Seismotite is rather irrelevant, because the consumer knows neither what these ingredients are nor what they are good for, and even ignores whether competing products contain the same or similar ingredients. Further instances of this type of information are descriptions and illustrations of highly technical manufacturing processes and explanations or the spelling-out of the scientific name or formula of chemical ingredients which make little or no sense to the layman and are intended only to impress and overawe him.

The same intention to impress the buyer is also present in advertisements that stress the scientific research engaged in and the elaborate testing equipment used by the producer to maintain high standards of

---

[3] See pp. 17–18.

quality. Besides impressing the buyer, such advertising in effect also tells him that he, a mere layman, would be unwise to judge quality unaided, by mere inspection, and that he should rely instead on the guaranties offered by the manufacturer's reputation. The same idea is conveyed also by the stress on brands and trade-marks ("Look for the trade mark; only XYZ is genuine"; "Buy ABC beer; ask for it by name"; "Place your trust in these initials: XY"), and on the age or size of the manufacturing firm ("A hundred years' experience," "The world's largest producers of . . . ," "The first manufacturers of . . ."). Sometimes, the buyer is asked to accept the expert judgment not of the manufacturer but of other buyers whose discernment he presumably trusts—H.M. the King, "men of distinction," prominent socialities, stage and screen stars, famous sportsmen, and such groups as "millions of housewives" and "nearly everybody in Philadelphia." In a slightly different category are advertisements that appeal sometimes to the buyer's chauvinism, sometimes to his snobbery, by emphasizing national origin ("all-American," "imported," "genuine British").

An important characteristic common to all such noninformative advertising is that it does not restrict the advertiser's market. A real and relevant distinguishing feature of a product almost always limits the market for it. For example, if a certain brand of coffee is advertised as containing no caffein, it appeals only to those who do not want the stimulating effect of caffein and is avoided by all others. By contrast, few people are likely to refrain from buying a product because it is "worn by debutantes," because it is "to be found wherever important people congregate," or because it "made Milwaukee famous."

To sum up our main conclusions, all advertising in the uninformed market tends further to enhance the importance buyers attach to indexes of quality, which, to say the least, are of doubtful value to them. One result of this, the difficulty for newcomers to enter the uninformed market, has already been mentioned and discussed in Chapter XV. A second result is the buyer's increased loyalty to whatever brand he happens to be using, which impedes the substitution of one for another in response to price changes, thus lowers the price elasticity of demand in the market, and enables sellers to use high profit margins in setting price.

3. PRICE AS AN INDEX OF QUALITY

As we saw earlier, buyers in the uninformed market, lacking the requisite information and understanding of the nature of the products offered, appraise them as best they can by a variety of indexes of quality and reliability. Some of these—such as trade-marks and brand names, national origin, and the reputation and goodwill of the seller or manufacturing firm—we discussed in the previous section. In addition, however, there is yet another factor by which buyers judge quality; and that is price. In fact, price may well be a more important and more widely used index of quality than any of the others so far discussed.

The importance of price as an index of quality is strikingly attested by the fact that the word "cheap" has almost entirely lost its original meaning and become a synonym for "flimsy." Similarly, the word "expensive" has come to stand as much for high quality as for high cost. Even the expression "high priced" is sometimes used in this sense, as witness the advertisement of an American brewery which recommends its product as "America's highest-priced beer"!

To regard price as an index of quality is not necessarily irrational. It merely implies a belief that price is determined by the competitive interplay of the rational forces of supply and demand. Such a belief is true and perfectly justified when the majority of buyers are informed and able to judge what they buy. In such a case, differences in price can be trusted to reflect differences in quality. Hence, it is perfectly rational for a buyer to judge quality by price in an expert or informed market. He can assume that the prices and price differentials facing him are what they are because the majority of buyers have found them reasonable and justified; and they, unlike him, are expert or informed buyers. In the uninformed market, however, it is irrational to judge quality by price. For uninformed buyers tend to rely on indexes—often meaningless ones —for appraising quality. When the majority of buyers are uninformed and rely on such indexes, their opinion ceases to be trustworthy; prices, therefore, which reflect the untrustworthy opinion of buyers, also become unreliable indexes of quality.

If it is irrational to judge quality by price when price merely reflects the relatively meaningless indexes of quality discussed in the preceding section, the situation clearly becomes paradoxical when price itself is the index by which the majority of buyers judge quality.[4] In a market where this happens, price may cease altogether to be a competitive weapon and become instead an instrument wherewith the seller can influence his

---

[4] That price is an unreliable index of quality in markets where most buyers try to judge quality by price is a purely theoretical result, but one that is borne out by experience. The detailed studies of the relative quality of competing products published in *Consumer Reports* show that the correlation between the quality and the price of different brands of products is usually very low, in many cases absent, and in some cases negative. Unfor-

customers' opinions of the quality of his wares. A commodity offered at a lower price than competing commodities will be both more attractive to the buyer on account of its greater cheapness and less attractive on account of its suspected inferior quality. The two considerations tend to offset each other, with the result that price makers have little inducement, if any, to engage in price competition.

In fact, it seldom happens that a commodity is advertised as cheaper than but just as good as competing products. The usual advertisement in the uninformed market boasts of superior quality at the same price ("No more expensive but oh! so much better!") or, to reinforce the claim of superior quality, at a slightly higher price ("You pay very little more to get all these unique features").

When it occurs, price competition in the uninformed market usually takes the form of the seller's trying to introduce into the buyer's consciousness two distinct prices in connection with each commodity. One of them is the price to be paid for the commodity; the other is the price that is to indicate its worth. Sales of "50-cent jars" of shaving cream at 39 cents and of "dollar pens" at 89 cents are examples of this practice. Further examples are the granting of special discounts, and off-season, end-of-the-month, and other special sales at reduced prices, where both the "normal" and the reduced price are advertised or marked on the price tag, and the consumer judges the extent of the bargain by the difference between the two prices.

The uninformed buyer's habit of judging quality by price, although it seldom eliminates price competition completely, does have the effect of lowering the price elasticity of demand facing the sellers in the uninformed market and thus raising their optimum profit margins. This,

---

tunately, the results of the different studies are not always published in comparable form; and their scope is not yet large enough to warrant a statistical evaluation of their results. It may be worth our while, however, to summarize the results of a typical study.

One of these has evaluated the over-all quality of 14 different brands of thermostat-controlled electric irons. Altogether, 6 different grades of quality were distinguished, which we shall denote by the letters A ("best") through F ("not acceptable"); and below, we show the prices of the 14 brands, in order of decreasing price, together with their quality grades:

Price	Quality	Price	Quality
$17.65	E	$10.95	D
15.95	F	10.29	D
12.95	C	9.95	C
12.95	D	9.95	F
12.50	C	9.50	D
11.95	A	7.50	B
10.95	D	6.95	F

however, is the same result as that reached in the last section. We conclude, therefore, that both the importance of advertising and the buyer's habit of judging quality by price tend, in the uninformed market, to offset the effects of the lack of product differentiation in such markets and to enable sellers to keep their profit margins and prices high.

4. PRICE DISCRIMINATION

In our discussion of the price maker's market behavior, we have always assumed so far that he sets only one price for one commodity. In expert and informed markets, this is usually a realistic assumption to make; although, even there, price discrimination can be and is practiced in some cases. The greatest scope for price discrimination, however, is in the uninformed market; and that is why its discussion has been reserved for this chapter. The discussion will include, however, price discrimination in the informed market also.

It will be recalled that in order to maximize his profit, the seller sets his price by adding to marginal cost a profit margin which depends on the responsiveness of his customers to changes in his price. Generally, every person responds differently to a change in price, from which it follows that it would be profitable for the seller to use a different profit margin and set a different price for each of his customers, geared to the latter's price elasticity of demand. This is exactly what the seller does or tries to do when he is ready to bargain with his customers. In the course of bargaining, he tries to size up the financial position of each customer and to ascertain the urgency of his demand and its responsiveness to price changes; then, armed with this knowledge, he sets for each customer the price that he thinks will give him the greatest profit obtainable from that customer.[5] Bargaining, however, requires time and skill; and a seller who deals with many customers may be unable to do all the bargaining himself and may find prohibitive the cost of employing salesmen skilled in bargaining. Under such conditions, it is profitable for the seller to refuse bargaining and set his price on a take-it-or-leave-it basis, even though this is bound to lower his receipts, since a uniform price corresponds, at best, to the average price elasticity of demand of his customers and is thus too low for some of them and too high for others.

The question arises, however, whether at least some of the higher receipts due to price discrimination could not be obtained without bargaining and hence without incurring the cost of bargaining. It seems

---

[5] We assume that the price he faces determines the quantity of the customer's purchases.

obvious that only through bargaining can a seller set a different price and different profit margin to fit the price elasticity of demand of each of his customers separately. The machinery of bargaining is not necessary, however, for more limited forms of price discrimination, which involve the separation of the market into a few sectors and the setting of a different price for each sector. For this latter form of price discrimination to be profitable, it must be possible, first, to separate the market into sectors that have different price elasticities and, second, to keep these sectors isolated from each other.

The first condition is necessary because if the price elasticities were the same in the different sectors, the price maker would find it profitable to set the same price in every sector, in which case the separation of the market into different sectors would be pointless. The second condition is needed because, in its absence, speculators could profit by buying cheap in one sector and selling dear in another, thereby equalizing prices in the different sectors and rendering price discrimination impossible.

There is a variety of factors that may make price discrimination possible. The most obvious factor isolating different sectors of the price maker's market is their geographical separation. The price maker can sell his product at different prices in different localities if transportation costs and/or custom duties prevent others from reshipping his product and profiting from the price differential; and he will find it profitable to charge different prices if the price elasticity of demand for his product is different in the different localities. Price differentiation of this kind is called dumping. Producers whose domestic market is protected from foreign competition by tariffs often find it profitable to sell at a higher price in the domestic market than abroad, where the competition of foreign producers keeps the price elasticity of demand high. They are able to do this, in the absence of laws to prevent it, because tariffs and transportation costs keep others from reimporting their goods into the higher-priced domestic market. To give another example of dumping, there is some evidence that the California Orange Growers' Association finds it profitable to set a lower F.O.B. price on oranges in California than on those destined for the Eastern and Midwestern states—presumably because the competition of independent orange growers and the temptation of the Association's own members to circumvent their own sales organization in the case of retail sales in their own locality render the price elasticity of demand facing the Association higher in California than it is elsewhere.

Another field in which price discrimination is feasible is in the market for services, whose very nature precludes the possibility of resale. Examples are the practice of doctors, dentists, and some hospitals of graduating their fees according to the patient's income, and of lawyers to set their fees in proportion to the money value involved in a lawsuit. Price discrimination can be practiced not only by the seller but also by the buyer of services. In fact, the discriminatory wage rates employers pay to white and colored, male and female, or adult and juvenile workers are a very important instance of price discrimination in our economy.

So far, we have been concerned with price discrimination between sectors of the market isolated by the costliness or physical impossibility of transfer. An alternative and (in our economy) more important basis for price discrimination is the uninformed nature of certain markets, which renders it possible to sell identical or nearly identical goods at different prices, because the consumer is unaware of their identity. In the uninformed market, where the buyer appraises quality by indexes of quality, he is often willing to pay more for a good merely because it has a well-known trade-mark. Price discrimination is often based on this predilection of the uninformed buyer. Some manufacturers of widely known and advertised products try to get the custom of the lower-income groups by selling the identical product at a lower price but under a less well-known trade-mark or without one. Sometimes, one variant of a product is sold under the manufacturer's own name and another variant of the identical product is marketed under the name of a distributor. In this country, for example, mail-order houses often sell nationally advertised brands of merchandise under their own trade-mark and at a lower price. In France, some famous Parisian dress designers sell under their own name, and at a higher price, perfumes manufactured *and also marketed* by less famous perfume manufacturers.

The identity of differently priced variants of the same product is sometimes quietly admitted or even advertised. For example, Montgomery Ward customers are openly told that the pressure cooker sold by the firm under the Magic Seal trade-mark is identical with, and manufactured by the makers of, the more expensive Presto cooker. The imparting of this information undoubtedly stimulates the sales of Magic Seal cookers to Montgomery Ward customers; at the same time, it is unlikely to lower the sales of Presto cookers to others. In much the same way, most Parisians, but few others, seem to know that Lanvin perfumes are made by the Le Galion firm and are similar to and in at least one case identical with the somewhat cheaper perfumes sold under this firm's own name. Another example is that of Longines and Wittnauer watches.

The latter are advertised as "by the makers of Longines watches"; and although the advertisements do not say that the two watches, which differ in price, are identical in quality, watchmakers and other retail sellers will often voice the opinion that they are. But whether or not they are in fact identical is immaterial from our point of view. What matters is that they *could* be identical and that, if they were, this fact would probably not lower the sales of the more expensive but also more famous Longines watches enough to render such price discrimination unprofitable.

Price discrimination in the uninformed market is further facilitated by the uninformed buyer's habit of regarding price as an index of quality. We saw in the last section that when buyers judge quality by price, the latter ceases to be a competitive weapon and becomes instead a means whereby the seller indicates the quality of his product and addresses himself to a particular sector of the market. Under such conditions the seller can sell two or more variants of the same commodity at different prices even without the necessity of selling them through different retail outlets or under different names. Sometimes, it is sufficient for the differently priced models to look slightly different in order to fool the public and make it believe that the more expensive variants are better in quality; although in cases where buyers do not judge quality by price alone, the more expensive models must be slightly better, at least in design, in finish, or in some other visible feature. The buyer may not think that the differences he notices and can appraise are worth the difference in price; but he will frequently regard these noticeable differences, together with the price difference, as indications that there are also more essential differences in quality or durability which *do* justify the difference in price.

Even when the buyer knows or suspects that the difference in price is not justified by the difference in quality, he may nevertheless prefer the more expensive model for reasons of prestige. This often occurs in a society where people judge their fellow men, at least partly, by the scale on which they live. Some people may feel that they owe it to their social position always to stay at the most expensive hotels and drive the most expensive cars; others may regard conspicuous consumption as a means of raising or establishing their social position; and still others may consider it good business to inspire confidence through high living. In the eyes of all these groups the mere expensiveness of a good or service is a desirable characteristic, provided that it is conspicuous.

To trace the process through which price discrimination of this type may arise, let us analyze the problems of a businessman who wants to enter a market or introduce a new product. He usually decides at an early stage what income group he wants to reach, which means that he will often set his price before determining such other aspects of his offer as the quality and exact specifications of his product. If, at a later stage, after having launched his product, the producer wants to expand his market or thinks that he originally set his price too high, lowering his price may not be his best policy. For by then, he will have acquired regular customers; and even if a price reduction would not make him lose these customers,[6] it would probably reduce his receipts from them. To avoid this loss of receipts, he can either continue to sell his product at its old price and introduce an "economy" model at a lower price; or he can lower the price of his old model and introduce a new model at or around the old price, thus separating, and catering separately to, two sectors of his market, composed of people in different income groups. Experience shows that price discrimination in the uninformed market very often originates in this way.

When the differently priced models of a product differ also in quality, we no longer have price discrimination in the strict sense of the word; but we can use the term in a wider sense and shall speak of price discrimination whenever differences in price are out of proportion to differences in quality. We shall say, therefore, that a seller practices price discrimination if he offers similar goods at different prices and with different percentage profit margins. For example, he will be said to charge discriminatory prices if he adds, say, a 40 per cent markup to the cost of his better-quality model and only a 25 per cent markup to the cost of its cheaper variant.

5. QUANTITATIVE PRICE DISCRIMINATION

In the last section, we were concerned with price discrimination which consisted in setting different prices for different people or different groups of people. For the sake of completeness, we must also deal briefly with price discrimination which consists in setting a different per-unit price on different units or quantities of a commodity sold to or bought from the same person.

There are many examples of price discrimination of this type, which is equally common in informed and in uninformed markets. Many com-

---

[6] It might if they should interpret the price reduction as a sign of quality deterioration or if, owing to considerations of prestige, the price reduction per se renders the product less desirable to them.

modities can be obtained at a lower price if bought in larger quantities. An especially simple example of this is the custom of grocery stores to set the price of, say, grapes at 25 cents for 4 pounds, which implies a price of $6\frac{1}{4}$ cents per pound for 4 pounds, of $6\frac{1}{2}$ cents per pound for 2 pounds, and of 7 cents for one pound. Price reductions on return fares and monthly commuter tickets are further examples. Price discrimination of this type can also be practiced by the buyer, one of the main examples being the payment of higher wages for overtime.

When the price maker sets a price that depends on the quantity bought or sold by the individual price taker facing him, he does so to induce his price takers to buy from (or sell to) him a larger quantity than they would otherwise. In a limiting case the price maker, instead of merely encouraging the purchase (or sale) of larger quantities, may insist on it by making an all-for-none offer, thus depriving his price takers of their freedom to determine the quantity they buy (or sell). The main example of this is the employer's offer to employ workers for a working day or week of given length; further examples are the wholesaler's habit of selling in large quantities only and the practice of some restaurants of having minimum charges or of serving only complete meals.

It remains to be shown why such price discrimination is in the price maker's interest. This can best be done diagrammatically. Let us draw the indifference map of a buyer, B, together with his price-consumption curve; and superimpose on this the indifference map and price-offer curve of the seller, S, assuming for simplicity's sake that he is not a producer but sells his personal services. This is shown in Figure 74, where quantities of the seller's services, A, are measured along the horizontal axes, and income, expenditures, and receipts, expressed in terms of money, are measured along the vertical axes. It appears from the diagram that the buyer's price-consumption curve and the seller's price-offer curve intersect on the contract curve—an illustration of the fact that when both buyer and seller are price takers, trade between them is economically efficient. It also appears from Figure 74 that the transaction that brings the exchanging parties to point H is beneficial to both of them. This is shown by the fact that, at point H, both buyer and seller are on a higher indifference curve than at W, the point where they would be if no transaction had taken place between them.

If the seller is able to assume the role of price maker, he can, by setting a higher price, force the buyer back along his price-consumption curve; and the seller can force the buyer back the farther, the greater his (the seller's) bargaining strength. The price most advantageous to the seller is that which forces the buyer back to point *M*, because this point is on the highest of the seller's indifference curves with which the price-consumption curve comes into contact.

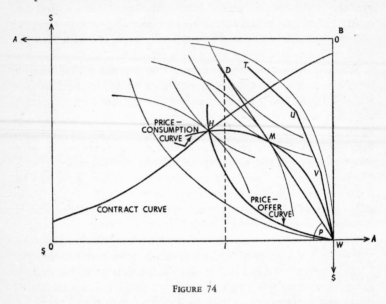

FIGURE 74

At this point, however, the buyer is still on a higher indifference curve and therefore better off than he would be at point *W*, in the absence of trade. This suggests that there might be still further scope for exploiting the buyer if only he could somehow be pushed off his price-consumption curve. This the seller can do by depriving the buyer of his freedom to buy the quantity he wants at a given price. For example, the seller may make an all-or-none offer and say that he is willing to sell at price *p* but only a minimum quantity of *lW*—thus hoping to get to point *D*. It appears from the diagram that the buyer would be better off buying less at price *p;* but if his only choice lay between staying at point *W* and going to point *D*, he would still prefer *D*, at which point his satisfaction would be higher than at *W*.

An alternative way in which the seller can push the buyer off the price-consumption curve in order to increase his (the seller's) gain is to let the buyer choose between different quantities but offer him each successive quantity at a lower price. In Figure 74, such an offer is represented geometrically by the curve *WVUT*.[7] It is apparent that such price discrimination is similar to an all-or-none offer in its effect of increasing the seller's gain at the buyer's cost. The reader is invited to repeat the above agrument to show how the buyer can exploit the seller, either by making him an all-or-none offer or by offering to buy from him successive quantities at successively *higher* prices.

BIBLIOGRAPHICAL NOTE

Very little has been published on the uninformed market and the nature of competition in the uninformed market. The argument of section 1, however, is a simple generalization of the theory of spatial competition—a subject with which the reader should be familiar. See H. Hotelling, "Stability in Competition," *Economic Journal*, Vol. XXXIX (1929), pp. 41–57; Edward H. Chamberlin, *The Theory of Monopolistic Competition* (Cambridge, Mass.: Harvard University Press, 1931), App. C; A. P. Lerner and H. W. Singer, "Some Notes on Duopoly and Spatial Competition," *Journal of Political Economy*, Vol. XLV (1937), pp. 145–86; and A. Smithies, "Optimum Location in Spatial Competition," *Journal of Political Economy*, Vol. XLIX (1941), pp. 423–39.

On advertising (sec. 2), see Nicholas Kaldor, "The Economic Aspects of Advertising," *Review of Economic Studies*, Vol. XVIII (1949–50), pp. 1–27.

On price discrimination (secs. 4–5), see Joan Robinson, *The Economics of Imperfect Competition* (London: Macmillan & Co., 1933), chap. xv; W. Leontief, "Theory of Limited and Unlimited Discrimination," *Quarterly Journal of Economics*, Vol. LIV (1940), pp. 490–501; C. G. F. Simkin, "Some Aspects and Generalisations of the Theory of Discrimination," *Review of Economic Studies*, Vol. XV (1947–48), pp. 1–13; and E. O. Edwards, "The Analysis of Output under Discrimination," *Econometrica*, Vol. XVIII (1950), pp. 163–72.

Consult also W. A. Lewis, "Competition in Retail Trade," *Economica*, Vol. XII (1945), pp. 202–34.

---

[7] In other words, the seller charges one price for the first batch of merchandise, a somewhat lower price for the next additional batch of merchandise, and so forth. Alternatively, the seller may tell the buyer that he must pay one price if he buys a small quantity, a somewhat lower price *on all he buys* if he buys a larger quantity, and so on. These are alternative ways of expressing the same conditions; both, therefore, can be illustrated by the *WVUT* curve.

CHAPTER XIX

BARGAINING AND BILATERAL MONOPOLY

AS WAS pointed out in Chapter II, bargaining comes about whenever the difference in numbers between the two sides of the market is not too great. This condition was generally fulfilled in bygone days; and it still is fulfilled in economies less highly developed than our own. Today, however, at least in industrial societies, the importance of large-scale enterprise has eliminated bargaining from practically all markets except those where two equally large firms or organizations face each other.

The theory of bargaining between two large firms or between a firm and a union is known in the literature of economics under the name of bilateral monopoly. It is well to bear in mind, however, that bargaining between two firms (or between a firm and a union) is similar in all essentials to bargaining between two persons; there is no difference, therefore, between the theory of bilateral monopoly and the theory of bargaining. Furthermore, most conclusions of the theory of bilateral monopoly (and *all* the conclusions with which we shall be concerned) hold true whether or not the two parties to the bargain are monopolists in the strict sense of the word. Accordingly, the theory of bilateral monopoly could just as well be called the theory of bilateral oligopoly or the theory of bilaterally restricted competition—or simply the theory of bargaining. But bilateral monopoly is the traditional and generally accepted term; and for this reason, we shall adhere to it. The reader is warned, however, that throughout this chapter the terms "monopoly" and "monopolist" must be interpreted in a wider sense than they were given in Chapter XVII; they will mean "restricted competition" and "a firm enjoying the advantages of restricted competition," respectively.

We saw earlier that monopoly (restricted competition) yields a profit due to the superior bargaining strength it secures over people and firms on the other side of the market. But this is so only if those on the other side of the market are in a competitive position. If the monopolist has the bad luck to encounter a monopolist on the other side of the market, he will find his monopoly power more or less offset by that of his opponent. This holds true of monopoly, oligopoly, or any other form of restricted competition.

Bilateral monopoly may arise when two firms that want to deal with each other both happen to be in a monopolistic or oligopolistic position on their own side of the market. Often, however, bilateral monopoly is established by the action of price takers who form a monopolistic combination on their side of the market in response to and as a defense against their monopolistic exploitation by the price makers on the other side of the market. Examples of such defensive combinations are labor unions and consumers' and farmers' co-operatives.

However it comes about, bilateral monopoly usually leads to the replacement of the price-maker–price-taker relation by bargaining. In a general way, two parties bargaining with each other are on a more equal footing than are price maker and price taker, which suggests—what indeed is obvious—that the gain from trade is more equally distributed under bilateral monopoly than it is under one-sided monopoly or oligopoly. One party, however, may have an advantage over the other party even in a bargaining situation. Thus, a defensive combination may have no more than partial success in eliminating the initial disadvantage of its members in the market; or, conversely, it may succeed in tipping the balance the other way and gaining the upper hand in the market. In an extreme case a defensive countermonopoly formed by the combination of price takers may succeed in reversing the roles of price maker and price taker and set the price for those on the other side of the market, who previously were price makers themselves. This has happened, on occasion, in the trade-union movement. The primary aim of trade-unionism was, and still is, to eliminate the worker's disadvantage of having to accept the employer's terms on a take-it-or-leave-it basis and to establish collective bargaining as the accepted machinery for determining wages. This aim of the labor movement achieved, unions usually are content to improve their bargaining position within the framework of collective bargaining. In a few isolated instances, however, unions have succeeded in setting wage rates and putting employers into the price taker's position. In the United States, for example, unions are able, in certain industries, to impose on the smaller firms the terms of contract agreed upon with the industry's largest firms.

Such cases, however, are exceptional. As a rule the terms of contract between two monopolies are settled by bargaining; and as far as the distribution of the gain from trade is concerned, bilateral monopoly usually comes nearer to the perfectly competitive situation than does the monopolistic restriction of competition on one side of the market only. This can· be an important argument in favor of bilateral monopoly, which is usually a more practicable alternative to one-sided monopoly than is free (let alone perfect) competition.[1]

Another important argument in favor of defensive combinations and of bilateral monopoly in general is that the latter comes nearer to perfect competition than one-sided restriction also as far as efficiency is concerned. In fact, bilateral monopoly is in many cases as efficient as perfect competition. This is by no means obvious, however; and its proof will require the rest of this chapter.

Let us start with the simple if not very important example of bargaining between two persons, one of whom buys the personal services of the other. This example will enable us to make use of individual indifference maps; and we shall show later that the results so reached apply *pari passu* also to bargaining between firms.

The problem of exchange between two people can be illustrated with the aid of superimposed indifference maps, such as were used in Chapters IV and XVIII. In fact, our present problem is essentially the same as the problem of Chapter IV. There, we dealt with the efficiency of distributing two consumers' goods between two consumers; here, we are concerned with the efficiency of distributing between two people the labor time of the one and the money income of the other. Accordingly, let us superimpose the buyer's indifference map on the seller's in such a way that the horizontal distance between the vertical axes shows the total labor time at the seller's disposal and the vertical distance between the horizontal axes shows the buyer's total money income. This is shown in Figure 75. If conditions were such as to put both people into the position of price takers and render trade between them perfectly competitive, they would exchange at H, the point of intersection between the seller's price-offer curve and the buyer's price-consumption curve; and trade between them would be efficient in the sense that, having arrived at this point, neither person could improve his position without detriment to the other. Geometrically, this is shown by H being on the contract curve.

Assume, next, that price is set by the seller, in which case trade will take place at the point of intersection between the buyer's price-consump-

---

[1] We do not mean to imply, however, that the income distribution which would obtain under perfect competition is necessarily the most desirable one from every point of view. See p. 180.

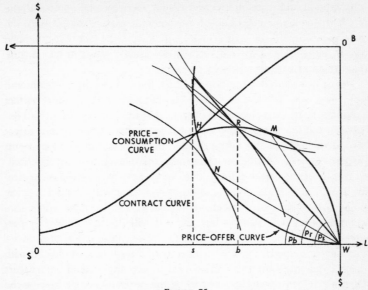

FIGURE 75

tion curve and the price line representing the seller's set price. It is in the seller's interest so to set his price as to arrive at or come as near as possible to point *M*, where the buyer's price-consumption curve touches his (the seller's) highest indifference curve.[2] In fact, if the seller is alone on his side of the market, he will set price p_s and get to *M*. Only the competition of rival sellers and the fear of losing his customer altogether will force him to set a lower price than this. In a limiting case, he may even be forced to set the perfectly competitive price; but, in general, he will reach some position on the buyer's price-consumption curve that lies between points *H* and *M*.

In a similar way, if the buyer is in the position of price maker, trade will come about at the point of intersection between the price line he sets and the seller's price-offer curve. The buyer will aim at reaching point *N*, where the price-offer curve reaches his highest indifference curve; but the competition of rival buyers may force him to offer a higher price and thus get to some point on the seller's price-offer curve that lies between the limiting points of *H* and *N*. Hence, if either the seller or the buyer sets the price, trade will take place at some point of the price-

---

[2] Highest, that is, of all the indifference curves with which the buyer's price-consumption curve comes in contact.

consumption and price-offer curves that lie between the points M and N. With the single exception of the point of perfect competition, all these points are off the contract curve, indicating the fact that price setting by either side of the market will not usually result in an efficient trade relation between the two parties.

Let us now consider the case in which buyer and seller bargain and agree on a price at which to do business, but make no agreement on the quantities to be exchanged. It is obvious that the price agreed to will lie between the limits p_s and p_b, since it is in neither party's interest to go beyond them. It is also very probable that a price agreed to by both parties will be nearer the perfectly competitive level than if it had been set by one of the parties acting alone. When they have agreed on a price for their future transactions, both buyer and seller will regard this price as given to them and will behave as price takers. In other words, the quantities they will want to buy and sell will be those shown by the intersections of the price line with the price-consumption and price-offer curves, respectively. The two points of intersection would coincide and the quantities the two parties want to exchange would be equal if the price agreed upon happened to be the perfectly competitive price. Apart from this special case, however, the quantities buyer and seller want to exchange will not be the same; and whichever quantity is the smaller of the two will be the quantity actually exchanged. For example, if the parties agree on the price p_r, the buyer will only buy bW of the seller's time, even though the latter would be willing to sell him sW of his services. Hence, if bargaining results in a price agreement only, the quantity bought and sold will be exactly equal to what it would have been had the same price been set unilaterally by one of the parties. However, since the price that is arrived at as a result of bargaining tends to be nearer the perfectly competitive level than it would be if set by one of the parties, and since trade at the perfectly competitive price is always efficient, we conclude that trade under a price agreement will usually be nearer to perfect efficiency than trade at a price set unilaterally.

Bargaining, however, is unlikely to lead to a price agreement alone. For, as we have just seen, unless it happens to hit upon the perfectly competitive price, it does not lead to an efficient relation between the two parties and leaves scope for the conclusion of a new and better agreement. In our above example, trade at the agreed price, p_r, leads to point R, which is off the contract curve, and from which a further move beneficial to both parties is therefore possible, in the sense that both parties can move simultaneously to higher indifference curves than those intersecting at point R. It is true that they cannot usually do this by negotiating a new price agreement, because any revision of price p_r would make one of the parties worse off than he is at point R. They can do it, however, and reach a new agreement acceptable to both parties, if the new agreement regulates not only price but also the quantities to be exchanged.

What will happen, then, is this: At price p_r, the seller is unable to sell as much as he would like to and may therefore be willing to make a price concession in return for a guaranty of higher sales. The buyer, in his turn, may be willing to pay for the advantage of a lower price by guaranteeing to buy more than he otherwise would. In this way the two parties can reach an agreement on both price *and quantity* that brings them into the area enclosed by the indifference curves intersecting at R and is therefore preferable to the previous price agreement from the points of view of both parties. Whether this new agreement is final depends on whether it brings the two parties onto their contract curve. If it does not, it leaves room for yet a new agreement on price and quantities exchanged which is preferred to the old by both parties. One might say, in general, that any agreement that fails to bring the two parties onto the contract curve is an unstable agreement, which can and probably will be replaced by a better one.

Hence, it appears that when bargaining between two persons is concerned with both price and the quantity exchanged, it will sooner or later lead to a stable agreement whose terms are represented geometrically by a point on the contract curve. Furthermore, since being on the contract curve is the condition not only of stable but also of efficient trade relations, we can also conclude that bargaining between two persons leads to efficient trade relations between them. As far as efficiency is concerned, therefore, bargaining between persons leads to the same result as perfect competition would; and the difference between bargaining and perfect competition is confined to income distribution. In geometrical terms, bargaining and perfect competition both lead to the contract curve, although they may lead to different points of the contract curve. It is true that bargaining leads to perfect efficiency only if it regulates both price and the quantity exchanged; but this is usually the case in bargaining agreements between persons.

To extend this result from persons to firms, we might, as is sometimes done, define indifference maps for firms and then apply the above geometrical reasoning to these reinterpreted indifference maps. Rather than perform this tour de force, however, we shall use a verbal argument which is both simpler and more satisfactory. When one firm sells its products to another firm, and when each has a monopoly position on its side of the market, the terms on which they will trade with each other are subject to bargaining and settled by agreement. Such agreement may or may not maximize the sum of two firms' profits; but we can easily prove that when it does not, there is always scope for so changing the terms of the agreement as to increase both firms' profits. Hence, final agreement is reached only when the sum of the two firms' profits attains its maximum.

To prove that this is so, let it first be observed that the sum of the two producers' profits depends solely on the quantity of the product sold by one producer to the other but not on the price at which a given quantity changes hands between them; for the price determines only the share of the two firms in their combined profits. Hence, if the agreement between the two firms regulates both the price and the quantity of the shipment between them, they can control the sum of their combined profit independently of its division between themselves. From this, our proof follows easily enough. Assume, for example, that a preliminary agreement between buyer and seller has fixed shipments at a rate that is not the optimum rate and does not maximize the sum of the two firms' profits. In this case, it will be in the interest of at least one of the firms to change the rate of shipments to the optimum rate. This firm may have to make a price concession in order to persuade the other firm to agree to the changed rate of shipments; but this is always possible, because there is always some price change which, when combined with the change in shipments, will raise both firms' profits. This follows from the fact that the optimum rate of shipments maximizes the sum of their profits independently of what price they happen to agree upon. It is hardly necessary to point out that this argument is the exact counterpart of the geometrical argument we used in the case of bargaining between two persons.

So far, we have shown that it is in the interest of both buyer and seller to reach an agreement that will maximize the sum of their profits, and that they can always reach such an agreement, provided it regulates quantity sold as well as price. It remains yet to be shown that the maximization of their profits also insures the efficiency of trade relations between the two firms. To prove that this is so, let us assume for a moment that the two firms form a combination and thus become the plants of one firm, whose profit is identical with the sum of the profits of its two plants. From the point of view of this firm the flow of products between the two plants which used to be two separate firms is now a matter of internal administrative decision and hence of internal technological efficiency. But we know that to maximize its profit, the firm must aim at internal technological efficiency, whatever its position and behavior in the markets where it buys and sells.[3] Hence, the most efficient flow of products between the two plants is at the same time also the one that maximizes the sum of their profits; and if this is true when they are parts of one firm, it must also be true when they are independent firms.

Hence, we can generally say that when buyer and seller settle their terms of contract by bargaining and agreement, and when this agreement deals with both price and quantity, their trade relations with each other will be efficient whether the two parties are persons or firms, and independently of how welfare or profits are distributed between them, as long as each party to the bargain aims at maximizing his welfare or profit.

The same, unfortunately, is not always true when one of the parties to the bargain (or both) is a collective monopoly, acting on behalf of its members. For we have just seen that bargaining leads to efficient trade relations between buyer and seller when each of them maximizes his profit; but we also saw, in Chapter XVII, that a collective monopoly is often prevented from adopting the policy that will maximize its (or rather the sum of its members') profits by the internal problem of distributing these profits satisfactorily among its members. Hence, when either the seller, or the buyer, or both, are prevented by internal problems from aiming at maximum profits, the efficiency of trade relations between the two parties is likely to suffer.

In particular, agreement between buyer and seller on the optimum rate of shipment may be prevented because the collective monopoly may be unable to agree on the optimum rate of shipment or on that division of a fixed rate of shipment among its members which will satisfy all of them. In fact, the existence of this problem is likely to force a collective monopoly to confine itself to a price agreement only, which —as was shown above—does not usually lead to efficient trade relations. Instances of yet another case are collective bargaining agreements between an employer and a trade-union. Such agreements usually specify both the wage rate and the length of the working week but leave the employer free to determine the number of workers he employs. In all such cases, trade relations between the two parties would be perfectly

---

[3] See p. 148.

efficient only in exceptional cases and by accident; and the only general statement we can make is that trade relations in these cases are likely to be more efficient than they would be if, instead of bargaining, one party were to set the terms of contract on a take-it-or-leave-it basis.

BIBLIOGRAPHICAL NOTE

The argument of this chapter is based on W. Fellner, "Prices and Wages under Bilateral Monopoly," *Quarterly Journal of Economics,* Vol. LXI (1947), pp. 503–32. See also Professor Fellner's *Competition among the Few* (New York: Alfred A. Knopf, 1949), chaps. ix–x. Since bilateral monopoly is usually discussed in conjunction with the theory of oligopoly and duopoly, the reader is referred for further reading to the Bibliographical Note at the end of Chapter XVII.

For a somewhat different approach, see J. F. Nash, "The Bargaining Problem," *Econometrica,* Vol. XVIII (1950), pp. 155–62. For a special instance of bilateral monopoly and bargaining, which often leads to quite different results from those discussed in this chapter, see my "A Reconsideration of the Theory of Tariffs," *Review of Economic Studies,* Vol. IX (1942), pp. 89–110.

CHAPTER XX

THE EFFICIENCY OF RESTRICTED COMPETITION

RESTRICTED competition is the rule in our economy; and the discussion of its efficiency should therefore be the most detailed and the most systematic. Unfortunately, however, little more than a sketch can be offered in the present chapter. There are two reasons for this. One is that restricted competition can take a great variety of forms; the other is that now at last we must aim at realism and discuss not a uniformly restricted economy but one in which all forms of competition and all degrees of monopoly and monopolistic restraint occur. Gone are the neat orderliness and uniformity of perfect and even of free competition. For greater realism, we must pay the price of a considerable loss in simplicity and generality. We saw and discussed the many forms that competitive restriction can assume; we must now consider an economy that is an agglomeration of all these forms, with many elements of free competition thrown in for good measure. Hence, our discussion of efficiency under restricted competition will largely take the form of amendments to results reached in Chapter XVI; and, to facilitate comparison with Chapter XVI, it will follow the order in which the different forms of efficiency were discussed there.

1. DISTRIBUTION AMONG CONSUMERS

The consumer remains a price taker even under restricted competition. Thus, the first condition of an efficient distribution of consumers' goods and services, perfect competition among consumers, still holds; but the second is no longer fulfilled: in many markets the consumer is not informed. The consumer's lack of information is, of course, a matter of degree. He is seldom completely ignorant—but to the extent that he is uninformed, he is unable to make a rational choice between the available alternatives and to plan his expenditures in a rational way. This, as we know, lowers the efficiency of the distribution of consumers' goods among consumers and also interferes with the efficient allocation of resources.

An inefficient distribution of consumers' goods means that some people buy goods they would not have bought had they known better, and they divert these goods from others who would have made better use of them. It is impossible to appraise the loss of welfare from the lowered efficiency of distribution caused by consumers' ignorance; but this loss may be offset, at least to some extent, by the effect of consumers' ignorance on the *equity* of distribution.

With the exception of Chapter IV, all discussion and mention of equity in this book has referred to the distribution of money income. What really matters, however, is the distribution of welfare and its equity. Income distribution is relevant only because it determines the distribution of consumers' goods and services, which in its turn is among the main determinants of the distribution of welfare. So far, we have always been concerned with income distribution, because this is the simpler and more familiar concept, and because economists naturally assume that the distribution of money incomes and that of consumers' goods go hand in hand, unless there is special reason to expect the contrary. We shall now proceed to show that consumers' ignorance is such a special reason to expect the contrary. In particular, we shall show that consumers' ignorance weakens the correspondence between income distribution and the distribution of consumers' goods and causes the latter to be distributed less unequally than incomes are.

To prove this, let us recall, first of all, that the consumer's lack of information, and especially the uninformed consumer's habit of judging quality by price, leads to price discrimination and the offer of essentially similar goods at different prices. This was shown in Chapter XVIII. It will also be recalled that the uninformed consumer's consumption pattern is easily influenced by advertising and propaganda, which tend to lead to a uniformity of tastes. Witness the surprising consensus on the ideal pattern of life in the United States of today, where people, under the influence of the press, the movies, and advertising in general, are more or less agreed on the list of commodities and services whose possession and enjoyment they regard as the main ingredients of a good life. Given such uniformity of tastes, and the sale of essentially identical commodities at discriminatory prices to an uninformed public, people with different incomes will often buy the same commodities at different prices under the illusion that they are buying qualitatively different goods. The Joneses, with an income double that of the Smiths, may spend twice as much as do the Smiths on what are essentially the same car, the same radio, the same clothes, and the same of many other amenities of life. The Joneses' belongings may come from more elegant stores, their car may be longer and have more chrome and accessories, Mrs. Jones may wear the same clothes as Mrs. Smith except that she has them half a year earlier, she may attend the first night of a play that Mrs. Smith sees at a matinee, and so forth.

The prestige and snob value of such differences are important; but by more material standards the difference in the standard of living of the two families is likely to be small—certainly much smaller than the difference in their expenditures would indicate. In a society like ours, therefore, where price discrimination in the consumers' market is widely practiced, and where consumers are concerned with prestige, have similar ideas about the ideal expenditure pattern, and are not too skillful in distinguishing good quality from bad, people will tend, above a certain limit, to buy themselves materially the same standard of living by spending varying money incomes. Hence, consumers' ignorance has a leveling effect on the distribution of consumers' welfare and thus tends to increase equity. This counteracts the effect of consumers' ignorance on the efficiency of distribution; but it is difficult to tell whether, on balance, it does more harm or good. It may be added here that price discrimination often has this same leveling effect on distribution also when it is not based on consumers' ignorance. The tendency of doctors to vary their fees with the patient's income is one example; the custom in some European countries of charging different public-utility rates in different residential districts is another.

As important as its effect on the efficiency and equity of distribution is the effect of consumers' ignorance on the utilization of resources. We saw in Chapter XVIII how the uninformed buyer's inability to distinguish good quality from bad inhibits quality competition, how his habit of judging quality by price discourages also price competition, and how his lack of self-reliance encourages the use of advertising as a competitive weapon. To the price maker, it makes no difference whether he uses advertising or price and quality competition as his main competitive weapon to attract customers and maximize profit; but, from society's point of view, there is the very important difference that the first method diverts resources from other uses, whereas the latter methods do not.

Advertising is a major industry in the market economy of today, and this fact renders very important the question whether or not the resources used in advertising fulfill a socially useful purpose. We argued in Chapter XVIII that some advertising is informative; and this part of advertising, of course, is useful. But by far the greater part of advertising is addressed to the uninformed buyer and neither aims at nor results in making him more informed. From this, however, it does not follow that the resources used in advertising of this kind are all wasted. For, incidental to swaying the consumer's preferences and spending habits, advertising also provides him with free services. Some of the radio and television programs financed by advertisers yield satisfaction to the consumer, for which he would be willing to pay directly if they were otherwise unobtainable. It is likely that the services paid for by advertisers would be much smaller in quantity and very different in character if the consumer paid for them directly; and it is only this difference that measures the social waste for which advertising is responsible.

2. SPECIALIZATION AMONG WORKERS

Freedom of entry to occupations was shown in Chapter V to be the condition of efficient specialization among workers. Under restricted competition, therefore, when entry to at least some occupations is blocked or rendered difficult, specialization will be inefficient. This means, first of all, that the number of people in different occupations will fail to correspond to society's need for the services rendered in those occupations. In occupations to which entry is restricted, there will not be enough people to render the services required by society; whereas in those occupations to which entry is free, there will be an excess of people and of services rendered. Second, restraints on entry to a given occupation may bar from it people whose preferences or special talents should have justified their admission and may keep in it submarginal people who under free entry would have been pushed out by the competition of newcomers. When this is the case, the quality of services rendered will suffer; and the rendering of a given quantity of services will require a greater sacrifice of effort than it would otherwise. This second type of loss, however, unlike the first type, is not a necessary consequence of restricted entry. It does not arise in occupations to which entry is limited by excessively high requirements of ability, and it comes about only where the principle on which entry is restrained is partly or wholly unconnected with the ability of newcomers.

3. JOB ALLOCATION

We argued in Chapter XVI that job allocation would often be inefficient under free competition, because employers would generally be able to practice price discrimination in the labor market both by paying different wages to different groups of workers for similar work performed and by depriving employees of their freedom to decide how long to work. Under restricted competition, where labor-management relations are determined by bargaining and agreement, the efficiency of job allocation is likely to be somewhat higher.

To begin with, many unions insist on equal wages for all workers in a given category; and, to the extent that they succeed in achieving this and in preventing discrimination on racial or other grounds, they raise efficiency. It should be noted, however, that since unions usually demand equal pay not for equal work but for every worker, independently of the quality and quantity of his work, nondiscrimination in the economist's sense of the word and complete efficiency of job allocation are not always achieved, even when unions attain their aims. Equal piece rates generally insure better job allocation than equal hourly wages; and union opposition to the former is an obstacle to perfectly efficient job allocation, however justified this policy may be on other grounds.

Furthermore, even equal hourly wages are not always attained. Sometimes, different groups of workers (e.g., white and colored) are represented by separate unions; and in such cases, of course, union action will do little or nothing to eliminate discrimination and improve efficiency. Occasionally, a union condones or acquiesces in discrimination. A union dominated by men, for example, may not insist on equal wages for its men and women members, even if its leaders know that this would benefit the membership as a whole.

As to the say of workers on the amount of work they want to do, here, too, the existence of unions improves matters compared to what they would be under free competition but fails to achieve perfect efficiency in job allocation. Unions will fight for working hours which best suit the majority of their members; and it seems obvious that this will lead to a better job allocation than if workers had no say on the matter at all. But unions do not stand up for each worker's freedom to decide the length of his individual working day or week—presumably because they realize the havoc such an arrangement might wreak with the productive efficiency of a modern factory or office. One might venture a guess that the loss of efficiency in job allocation due to the adoption of a uniform working week is offset or more than offset by the resulting gain in productive efficiency; but it is not impossible that a system could be worked out affording the individual worker a limited freedom of choice sufficient to yield a significant gain in job-allocating efficiency without causing a noticeable loss in productive efficiency.

4. THE TECHNOLOGICAL EFFICIENCY OF THE FIRM

We saw in Chapters VIII and XVI that if the entrepreneur aims at maximum profit, he must also aim at technological efficiency in his firm. The only question is whether he really aims at maximum profit. We argued earlier that when entry to a market is free, the whip hand of competition forces the policy of profit maximization upon every firm. But restricted competition puts little or no pressure on the entrepreneur to maximize his profit, since it is a state of affairs in which he can make a profit even if he does not try too hard. Under restricted competition, therefore, we cannot assume, without further investigation, that the firm is technologically efficient. Whether or not it is depends on the nature of its management and the aspirations of its managers. The latter's appetite for profit may be great enough for them to aim at maximum profit —and hence at maximum technological efficiency—even without the stimulus of free competition. It is also conceivable that the management should aim at maximum profit in some, but not in all, of its decisions. For example, the management may be guided by the principle of profit maximization in the internal organization and administration of the firm but exercise moderation or follow tradition in its market policy. Technological efficiency may be enforced and maintained also for other than economic reasons. The managers of the firm, or its engineers, may have an interest in efficiency per se, or the maintenance of efficiency may be regarded as a public service and an essential factor in advertising and in securing good public relations. On the other hand, it is also possible that the entrepreneur should let matters ride and efficiency deteriorate, relying on his protected market position to guarantee him a profit under almost any circumstances. In short, when competition is restricted, we can make no general statement about the individual firm's technological efficiency. One suspects that in the United States the almost passionate interest in efficiency for its own sake would insure the firm's technological efficiency in freely competitive and monopolistic industries alike; but we have no conclusive evidence on this score.

4a. TECHNOLOGICAL PROGRESS

In Chapter XVI, we distinguished between progress in scientific knowledge and progress in the industrial exploitation of existing scientific knowledge. At that stage, we were concerned with the latter type of progress only, which we discussed under three headings: the improvement of products, the improvement of methods of production, and the introduction of new products. We argued that every firm is under pressure to improve its existing products if it has competitors and if it faces an informed market. In the uninformed market and in markets controlled by a monopolist, this type of progress is likely to be impeded. We further argued that new products and new manufacturing processes are sooner introduced by newcomers than by established producers, because newcomers, unlike established producers, have no vested interest in maintaining the demand for existing products and the profitability of existing productive equipment. From this, we deduced that free entry under free competition would favor the introduction of new products and productive methods. Under restricted competition, however, where obstacles to entry bar or slow down the entry of new firms, technological progress is likely to be slow also in these two senses.

The above conclusions are accepted by most economists; but there exists also a contrary argument, which regards obstacles to entry not as impediments but as necessary conditions of technological progress. The industrial exploitation of an innovation usually requires a capital investment, which will only be made if the innovation is expected to have a sufficient market for a sufficient length of time to render the full amortization of the investment possible and yield a profit in addition. It is argued, however, that often such expectations would fail to arise in markets where free entry creates the danger that the innovation might soon be rendered obsolete by the introduction of further innovations. Hence, so the argument runs, free entry would in many instances deter established producers and newcomers alike from introducing innovations; and they would need the protection that restraints on entry afford to venture investments in new productive methods or in the manufacture of new products.

This argument is correct in the sense that there probably are *some* innovations that would be put into effect only under the protection of restraints on entry. There are many innovations, however, whose introduction is or would be profitable even in free markets. Businessmen often expect and find the production of a new product to be profitable even if the manufacturing plant they have to build is rendered (and is expected to be rendered) obsolete long before the end of its physical lifetime by the introduction of further improvements. The head start of the first man to introduce a new product and his strong position against later comers are often sufficient advantages to encourage innovation even in free markets. In such cases, restraints on entry would only slow down further progress and would clearly be undesirable.

As to those cases in which a new product or a new productive method would not be put into effect without the protection afforded by restraints on entry, it is by no means certain that the introduction of innovations in such cases would necessarily favor progress and be in the public interest. Restraints on entry might be needed to render profitable the introduction of a new product or a new productive method that would require a large investment and is still in the process of development. An established producer who holds some of the patents might be willing and anxious to start production, but only if he can secure guaranties that the exploitation of other and better patents will not render his own investment obsolete before it has been fully amortized. If restraints on entry provide the necessary protection and the firm goes ahead introducing the new product, the public will indeed benefit by the new product at an early date, but at the cost of inferior design and the slowing-down of the rate of further improvement; and these, from society's point of view, may well be too high a price to pay.

A possible example of the above case might be the recent attempt by an established firm to introduce and have generally accepted a method of colored television whose general adoption, according to its critics, would have slowed down scientific progress in this field and committed the industry—and, of course, the public—to a relatively primitive type of television for a long time. We are not qualified to assess the truth in this particular controversy; but it is clearly possible that the early exploitation of an innovation might not always be in society's interest. At a time when further laboratory work promises rapid progress in the further development of a new product or productive method, it is usually not in society's interest to divert many resources to the exploitation of an intermediate result that is likely soon to be rendered obsolete by further research. If such an investment is rendered profitable by restraints on entry designed to impede further research or the putting into effect of the results of further research in that particular field, then the early exploitation of that innovation is paid for by the slowing-down of further progress. No fully developed and generally accepted theory exists on this difficult subject; but the reader is reminded that there is a presumption at least that the profitability of an investment under freely competitive conditions is a test of its desirability from society's point of view.[1]

We can now proceed to a short discussion of technological progress in the sense of progress in scientific knowledge and discovery. How this

---

[1] Except in fields where social and private marginal value or marginal product differ. See the Note to Chap. VIII.

is affected by the nature of competition is not entirely clear; but it is widely believed to be furthered, rather than impeded, by monopoly and restraints on competition. Under modern conditions, scientific research in many fields requires elaborate and expensive laboratories and experiments; and this has led to the belief that only large firms, which often enjoy a monopoly or oligopoly position, can afford to engage in research. American experience shows that a very considerable part of scientific research is indeed carried on in the research departments of large corporations. This fact, however, need not necessarily imply that, in the absence of these firms, there would be less scientific research. Small firms may not be able to afford to conduct research under their own management; but they can and often do subsidize research at universities or jointly finance a research institute whose findings are made available to all members of the industry. Furthermore, firms producing on a small scale can often experiment without having a separate research department; and it is significant, for example, that so many of the latest features of the modern automobile were originally developed by small European motor-car manufacturers. It must be admitted, however, that large firms often have prestige and other noneconomic motives for spending on research much more than would be called for by economic considerations alone, although their lesser inducement to exploit the results of scientific progress may conceivably slow down scientific progress itself.[2]

5. THE TECHNOLOGICAL EFFICIENCY OF THE INDUSTRY

5a. EFFICIENT ALLOCATION WITHIN THE INDUSTRY

In our discussion of perfect and free competition, we analyzed in considerable detail the way in which the market allocates among the members of an industry the total output produced and the resources used by it. Under restricted competition, this problem is not always important. To begin with, in industries that are completely monopolized, the problem does not even arise, because the market performs no allocating function. The problem of efficiently allocating the monopolist's total resources and output among his different plants is still a real and important problem; but it is a problem of the internal administration of his

---

[2] We might add that patent rights seem to be essential to scientific progress in a free-enterprise economy, in order to guarantee the reward needed to make worth while the effort and expense that invention and innovation involve. This fact is sometimes adduced as proof that monopolistic restraints on competition are essential to scientific progress. It seems to us, however, that from the need for one limited restraint it does not necessarily follow that all restraints on competition favor technological progress.

firm, which the monopolist can and usually does solve without having recourse to the market mechanism. He is likely to make full use of cost calculations and price considerations in solving it; but the efficiency with which he solves this problem depends on and is part of the general administrative efficiency of his firm.

The same is true, to a lesser degree, also of industries that consist of a few large firms. In such industries, too, the major part of the allocation problem is each producer's internal administrative problem of allocating his resources and output among his several plants. Allocation as between firms is necessarily the lesser part of the problem in such industries, and it assumes full importance only in industries in which the number of firms is large.

The formal conditions of efficient resource and output allocation within an industry have been stated in detail in Chapters VIII and XVI, where it was also shown that for the market mechanism to bring about efficient allocation, it must equalize both the marginal costs of different firms and their marginal outlays on each factor of production.

The competitive forces which would bring the marginal costs of different firms to equality or approximate equality under perfect or free competition are not nearly so strong under conditions of restricted competition. This is especially true of industries that cater to uninformed markets. In such markets, there is no competitive force, such as we found in the informed market, to compel competing firms to sell similar products at similar prices; and when competing firms are able to sell similar goods at different prices, the marginal costs of these firms could be equal only by accident.

The situation is somewhat better in industries in which the prices charged by different firms are rendered equal (or approximately equal) either by the buyers' informed market behavior or by monopolistic agreement or oligopolistic behavior among the members of the industry themselves. Equality of prices, however, does not necessarily imply equality of marginal costs; and the forces that, under free competition, would tend to equate the ratio of marginal costs to the ratio of prices are not present when the entry of newcomers to the industry is inhibited. Nevertheless, there may be a tendency even under restricted competition for firms with low marginal costs of production to gain at the expense of firms with high marginal costs. When competing firms sell at the same price what they produce at different marginal costs, those with the lowest marginal costs and highest profit margins will find that they have the greatest scope for nonprice competition and the boosting of sales by advertising, and by the offer of better quality, more service, and hidden price concessions.[3] Such action may not equalize the marginal costs of different members of the industry; but it will tend to concentrate the industry's output in the firms with the lowest marginal costs. It should be added, however, that there will be no such tendency (1) if monopolistic agreement rules out all forms of competition within the industry; (2) if agreement determines the share of each firm in the industry's total output; or (3) if each producer deems it wiser, even in the absence of agreement, not to engage in competition, not to try to expand at his competitors' expense, and in general not to disturb a delicately balanced oligopolistic situation.[4]

We can now proceed to consider the second condition of efficient resource allocation by the market, the equality of marginal outlays on factors of production. In the labor market, where unions seek to obtain uniform wage rates and working conditions throughout an industry and to impose industry-wide bargaining, the price of labor tends to be equal for different firms. As far as the allocation of labor is concerned, therefore, this second condition of efficiency tends to be more nearly fulfilled under restricted than under free competition.[5] This improvement in efficiency, however, is frequently bought at the cost of competition. Small producers often complain that by requiring them to pay the same wages and provide the same working conditions as large firms, unions tend to force them out of the market. Such complaints are often well founded and usually indicate that, previous to the union's action, the small firms were able to compete with their large competitors, because their lesser technological efficiency was offset by the more favorable terms on which they obtained the services of labor. In such cases the union's action and the consequent elimination of the small firms clearly increases the technological efficiency of the industry taken as a whole; but competition does suffer in the process. Here, then, is an instance where efficiency and the maintenance of competition are in conflict.

As to marginal outlays on other factors of production, they are ren-

---

[3] See sec. 3 in Chap. XIII.

[4] See sec. 3*b* in Chap. XV.

[5] It should be noted, however, that even if a union succeeds in imposing a uniform wage schedule on all members of an industry, this need not always result in equal marginal outlays on labor in that industry. For the marginal outlay on labor is equivalent to the wage rate only in the case of firms that regard the wage rate as given to them. Firms that are large enough to exert a noticeable influence on the wage contract have a marginal outlay on labor which includes, in addition to the price of labor, also a variation cost. See pp. 261 and 312.

P

dered equal for all producers whenever the supplier is a price maker and sets a uniform price for all buyers, or when the buyers are members of a collective monopoly, which has an agreement with the supplier or suppliers calling for a uniform price. But when factor prices are set by the buyer or are subject to separate agreement between each buyer and seller, large buyers may well obtain more favorable terms than their small competitors. A large buyer or a group of large buyers may even put pressure on the supplier and force him to discriminate against smaller competitors.

It appears, therefore, that under restricted competition, no general statement can be made about the efficiency of resource and output allocation within an industry. Allocation is likely to be efficient in fully monopolized industries, provided that their management is efficient. The same is true, to a lesser degree, also of oligopolistic industries. In industries that consist of many firms, allocation is likely to be generally inefficient whenever the industry faces an uninformed market. In industries that cater to informed markets, or in which the prices of competing products are rendered equal by some other consideration, there is likely to be some tendency toward efficient allocation; but this tendency may not extend to all factors. As we have seen, union action may well improve the allocation of labor over what it would be in the absence of unions; but no general statement can be made about the allocation of other productive resources, and each case must be judged separately.

5b. THE AVERAGE TECHNOLOGICAL EFFICIENCY OF THE INDUSTRY'S MEMBERS

It will be recalled from Chapter XVI that we discussed two effects of free competition under this heading, one good and one bad. We argued that free entry, by limiting profits, would provide each firm with an inducement to maintain its technological efficiency; but we also showed that as a result of free entry, every firm would tend to operate with excess capacity. Under restricted competition the argument is exactly the reverse. As we have seen already, restraints on entry weaken the firm's economic inducement to maintain its technological efficiency; but the same restraints will also tend to prevent excess capacity from developing.

6. THE ECONOMIC EFFICIENCY OF THE FIRM AND OF THE PRODUCTIVE SYSTEM

Our analysis of economic efficiency under free competition applies, by and large, also to restricted competition; and little will be added here to what has already been said on the subject in Chapter XVI, except to point out that in most respects the economic efficiency of the productive system tends to be lower under restricted competition.

6a. THE EFFICIENT COMBINATION OF PRODUCTS

We showed in Chapter XVI that the relative quantities in which different consumers' goods are produced would conform to the community's preferences only if they would all be sold with the same percentage profit margin. We then proceeded to argue that free competition, although not insuring perfect conformity, would at least keep the lack of conformity within limits by limiting the range within which different profit margins would lie. No such limits exist under restricted competition. Profit margins may be large in one market and small in another; and the greater diversity of profit margins which restricted competition renders possible lowers the economic efficiency of the combination of products; in other words, it lowers the conformity between consumers' preferences and the composition of the consumers' good output. As we saw in Chapter XVI, too, too little will be produced of goods on which the percentage profit margin is higher than the average profit margin, and too much of goods sold at profit margins which are below the average.

Unfortunately, no measure or index has as yet been developed for expressing the magnitude of such inefficiency and the loss of consumers' satisfaction which results from it. Our inability to measure this loss is an important, though inadequate, reason why many economists regard this loss as negligible.

Another reason why many economists minimize the importance of this type of inefficiency is their realization that consumers' preferences are not immutable and not wholly rational. The ease with which advertising can sway consumers' preferences has raised doubts as to whether perfect conformity to these preferences is really such an important and desirable goal of economic organization. It seems to us, however, that consumers' preferences—even if they are not always informed and not wholly rational, and therefore cannot insure an efficient distribution of a given output of consumers' goods—are nevertheless the best standard we have by which to judge the composition of the consumers'-good output.

Yet another argument advanced by some economists against taking this type of inefficiency too seriously rests on the realization that the community's preferences as reflected by market prices are the weighted sum of the preferences of individual consumers, with each person's preferences weighted by his total expenditure. Anyone who regards the actual distribution of incomes and expenditures as inequitable or otherwise undesirable is bound to feel that the use of these expenditures as weights in deriving the community's preferences is also undesirable. Such a person, therefore, will not consider market prices a "true" expression of the community's preferences[6] and will not be overly concerned if the composition of output fails to conform to the community's preferences so expressed.

Unlike the first two arguments, this argument seems to me to be valid; but it does not condone any and every divergence between the composition of output and the community's preferences as expressed by market prices. Only if there is reason to believe that the composition of output comes nearer to conforming to the community's "true" preferences when it fails to conform to preferences as expressed by market prices is it justifiable to ignore or minimize the importance of this type of inefficiency. It so happens that this condition may well be fulfilled in our economy. We suggested in the first section of this chapter that consumers in the high-income brackets tend to pay prices that contain a higher percentage profit margin than the prices paid by consumers in the low-income brackets. At that stage, we were concerned with the leveling effect which such price discrimination has on the distribution of consumers' goods; but it has a leveling effect also on the relative *influence* of consumers in different income brackets on the composition of output. We have seen that goods sold with high profit margins tend to be produced in too small quantities; but if these goods are bought predominantly by consumers in high-income brackets, then this tendency causes the preferences of high-income recipients to be given less weight than their expenditures could call for.

In connection with the above discussion, two warnings are in order. First of all, it must not be supposed that restricted competition leads to lesser inequalities in distribution than free competition. What leveling effects differences in profit margins may have are probably very small as compared to the greater inequality in income distribution to which restricted competition gives rise. Second, it must also be recalled that the leveling effect is not the only effect of differences in profit margins. Under restricted competition, each consumer buys goods and services whose

---

[6] The community's "true" preferences would be correctly reflected by market prices if the distribution of expenditures were ideal. We leave open the question as to what constitutes an ideal distribution of expenditures.

prices contain widely divergent percentage profit margins; and as long as this is the case, the composition of the consumers'-good output will still fail to conform to the preferences of the consuming public, whatever the weight attached to each individual's tastes.

6b. The Efficient Combination of Factors

We showed in sections 6b and 6c of Chapter XVI that the efficiency with which different factors of production are combined diminishes with differences both in the percentage profit margins on different factors and in the number of markets and firms through which different factors go on their way to the final consumer. We then proceeded to argue that, under free competition, differences in profit margins would be kept within limits, and that the main cause of inefficiency would be differences in the number of independent productive stages, which would result in a chronic underutilization of produced factors in the productive process.

Under restricted competition the scope for differences between profit margins in different factor markets is unlimited; and on this score, therefore, the combination of factors is likely to be less efficient. Furthermore, the restrictions on entry to various occupations disrupt the correspondence between relative wage rates and the real cost to society of obtaining personal services in different occupations; and this consideration lowers yet further the economic efficiency with which different *original* factors are combined.

On the other hand, restricted competition probably gives less scope for the systematic bias against the utilization of produced factors, which we claimed would characterize free competition. This is so, first of all, because under restricted competition there are some industries in which the individual firm controls most, if not all, productive stages. Although the horizontal integration of former competitors is more frequent in our economy than the vertical integration of firms that have previously done business with each other, this latter is by no means rare. Large firms often find it profitable to absorb their suppliers or set up their own plants for manufacturing parts, materials, or even equipment that they had previously bought from other firms—and occasionally a large firm controls even the distribution of its products. The producer is prompted to assume control over the manufacture of his produced factors by his desire to obtain them cheaper; but when produced factors have become cheaper to him, he will tend to use them more intensively and thus improve the economic efficiency of the combination of produced with original factors.

Second, even in industries in which vertical integration does not take place, produced and original factors will often be combined efficiently if the firms dealing with each other are large. Business transactions between such firms are usually settled by bargaining, and bargaining between firms generally results in an agreement that determines both price and quantity. We saw in Chapter XIX that such an agreement, unlike trade at set prices, tends to bring about trade relations as efficient as those of perfect competition. This implies that there will be no bias against the use of those produced factors which change hands under the terms of an agreement that specifies both price and the quantity exchanged. Although such agreements would be rare under free competition, they are likely to be quite common under restricted competition, where a substantial part of trade is done by large firms.

It is impossible to tell whether the greater general inefficiency of restricted competition and its lesser bias against the use of produced factors lead, on balance, to a more or a less efficient combination of factors than would free competition. There can be serious economic inefficiency even in the absence of bias—as, for example, when the highly monopolistic production and pricing of some materials and types of equipment discourage their use as compared to that of materials and equipment produced and sold under more competitive conditions. It should also be recalled that we are concerned not with a uniformly restricted economy but with one in which there are many freely competitive markets and industries; and in these, of course, the bias against produced factors is likely to prevail. Furthermore, many markets and industries comprise both large and small firms; and in such cases the small firms often combine their factors differently, and usually less efficiently, than the large ones. It is well known that small firms usually employ more labor per unit of output and use less machinery and less capital-intensive methods of production than do large firms. This fact is partly explained by the lesser scope which small-scale production gives to mechanization; but a further explanation is that small firms are often unable to obtain equipment and even materials on as favorable terms as their large competitors.

6c. THE EFFICIENT RATE OF PRODUCTION

On this subject, there is hardly anything to add to the analysis contained in section 6d of Chapter XVI. We argued there that the rate of production and of resource utilization would fall short of the optimum if every worker were free to determine the length of his working week;

but we warned that this condition is not likely to be fulfilled under free competition. We might add here that, the condition comes nearer to being fulfilled under restricted competition, where organized labor does have a say in determining the length of the working week. It is hard to tell, however, whether this renders restricted competition less or more efficient than free competition.

7. DYNAMIC EFFICIENCY

The reader will recall that, in Chapter X, we found that perfect competition would not achieve dynamic efficiency; and we compared its inefficiency in this respect to the relative efficiency of monopoly and central planning. In section 7 of Chapter XVI, we argued that free competition would probably be a halfway house between the dynamic efficiency of monopoly and the dynamic inefficiency of perfect competition. When we recall the meaning of dynamic efficiency, however, these conclusions turn out to be not quite as favorable to monopoly and restricted competition as they might appear at first sight.

All the other forms of efficiency discussed in this book had to do with the degree to which the economic organization of a firm, a market, an industry, or a whole society conforms, *in equilibrium,* to the wishes of the members of that society. By contrast, dynamic efficiency merely denotes the speed with which economic organization tends toward and reaches equilibrium after the previous equilibrium situation has been disturbed. It might perhaps be argued that dynamic efficiency, that is, a speedy return to a position of equilibrium, is desirable under any circumstances. But it is not nearly so valuable when the technological and economic efficiency of the equilibrium situation leaves much to be desired as when the equilibrium situation is one that is technologically and economically efficient. All that the dynamic efficiency of restricted competition means, therefore, is that it is likely to return to equilibrium sooner than perfect or free competition; but there is no implication that the equilibrium situation itself is efficient.

8. INCOME DISTRIBUTION

There exists no theory of income distribution under restricted competition. Indeed, one might be tempted to argue that, in view of the great importance of bargaining power and artificial obstacles to entry in determining income distribution under restricted competition, no theory is possible if it were not for the observed fact that the share of labor in the national income has been remarkably stable over time in all the free-enterprise economies for which the relevant statistical data are available. This stability in labor's share has not yet received a satisfactory explanation, and none will be attempted here.[7] In the following, we shall confine ourselves to stating a few formal conclusions and making a few general remarks.

Under restricted competition a person's rate of earnings corresponds neither to the market value of his marginal product nor to the transfer price of the marginal owner of his type of services. To begin with, the members of any professional or occupational group to which entry is limited receive an income that is higher than the transfer income of the marginal member of that group. The extent to which their income is higher depends, of course, on the nature and degree of the limitations to entry.

Whether or not entry is limited, the rate of earnings of the members of a group exceed the marginal value of the marginal product of their services if they sell directly to the consumer and if, as is usual, they have the advantage of being price makers in their market relations with him. This is the case of members of the professions and of such groups as barbers, dry cleaners, and the like. As to the total income of individual members of these groups, it is probably higher than it would be under perfect competition as long as they limit entry and practice simple restricted competition. It is higher still if, in addition, they restrict competition among themselves.

Entirely different is the situation of labor and of employees in general. They, too, can raise their earnings above the marginal person's transfer price if they succeed in limiting entry to their occupation. Their rates of earnings, however, almost invariably remain below the market value of their marginal product. To prove that this is so, even in a case unfavorable to the argument, let us assume that a group of employees are organized into a union that is strong enough to set wage rates on a take-it-or-leave-it basis—as happens, for example, in the printing trades in this country. In such a case the employer is in the position of a price taker in the labor market and equates his marginal valuation of his employees' services to their wage rates. His marginal valuation of their services, however, is smaller than the market value of the marginal

---

[7] For the best and most interesting attempt at a theory of income distribution under restricted competition, see M. Kalecki, "The Distribution of the National Income," *Econometrica*, Vol. VI (1938), pp. 97–112, reprinted, with minor changes, as chap. i of his *Essays in the Theory of Economic Fluctuations* (London: George Allen and Unwin, Ltd., 1939). Strictly speaking, however, Kalecki's theory is not a proper distribution theory, because it only shows labor's share in the *gross* national product.

product of these services as long as he is a price maker in the market where he sells his product or as long as the consumers' good to whose manufacture his product contributes is sold to the consumer at a set price. Since one of these conditions is virtually always fulfilled, we can conclude that wage rates are virtually always below the market value of the marginal product of the services of labor, however strong may be labor's bargaining position in the labor market. This result has already been implied in section 2 of Chapter XIII (p. 298), where we showed that the price maker can always pass on to the consumer *more than* the increase in costs due, for example, to a rise in wage rates.

The argument is exactly the same if the wage rate is arrived at by bargaining and specified in a wage agreement, and if the employer regards this as given to him. The argument becomes even stronger, of course, if the employer feels that his own actions influence the wage level—in other words, if his bargaining position is strong in the labor market as well as in the market where he sells. Only in the exceptional case that the union is able to practice price discrimination by forcing the employer into accepting an all-or-none offer can it raise the wage rate to or above the market value of the marginal product of labor. The practice of the musicians' union in the United States of requiring the employment of "stand-in" musicians for recorded broadcasts and for recitals by nonunion members probably comes fairly close to such an all-or-none contract.

It follows from the above argument that labor incomes are lower under restricted competition than they would be under perfect competition if we assume that the number of workers and the number of hours worked are not significantly smaller under restricted competition than under the hypothetical conditions of perfect competition. This assumption is probably justified as regards labor as a whole. For the field of manual labor is still easier to enter than most other occupations, in spite of the restrictions on entry imposed by some unions. One can probably say, therefore, that average labor incomes, as well as the share of labor as a whole, are smaller than they would be under perfect competition. At the same time, however, incomes in some skilled occupations may be higher than they would be under perfect competition, owing to the ability of unions in these occupations to restrict membership and the quantity of services very drastically.[8]

The group that gains most under restricted competition is, of course,

---

[8] See the corresponding section in Chap. XVI for a more detailed exposition of the above type of argument.

business. This is so, first of all, because every businessman is a price maker or otherwise enjoys a favored bargaining position in at least *some* of the markets in which he deals; and, although we cannot prove as a general proposition that the businessman's rate of earnings is always higher than the market value of the marginal product of his services, this is often likely to be the case.

Second, the obstacles to entering a market or industry as an independent businessman are more numerous and often much greater than the obstacles to entering the professions or a skilled occupation. Obstacles to entering the latter consist partly of the cost of training and partly of excessively high and unreasonable entrance requirements imposed by some professional groups and unions. Both these obstacles, however, are kept within limits in our society, the one by the availability of free public education, the other by the scrutiny of public opinion. Obstacles to entry faced by the businessman include the above two and others in addition. He, too, needs training and is confronted in some markets by the "conspiracy" of established firms anxious to keep out newcomers. In our society, however, entry to the businessman's profession is further limited by the requirement that he own some of the capital invested in his firm. This restriction may not be very serious in fields where small-scale production is feasible and the buyers are informed; and this is why we felt justified in neglecting it altogether in our discussion of free competition. The restriction becomes highly effective, however, in industries where economies of scale and in markets where the importance of goodwill render the cost of entry very high. Such restraints on entry, being natural, not only are difficult to mitigate; but, by keeping the size of firms large and their numbers small, they facilitate the imposition of further restraints, both on the entry of newcomers and on competition among the established competitors themselves. It would appear, therefore, that the restraints that raise the profits of businessmen are greater and more effective than those that maintain earnings in other professions and occupations at a monopolistic level. Needless to say, not all businessmen are thus favored, but only those in sheltered markets and industries. The marginal businessman's earnings are probably no higher than they would be under perfect competition; but the range of businessmen's earnings is much greater than it would be under perfect competition and is not accounted for by differences in ability.

To summarize, we found restricted competition to be significantly different in its effects from free competition. We found, in particular, that the three main shortcomings of free competition are not shared by restricted competition. The latter is more efficient than free competition would be, as far as job allocation within occupations is concerned; it is less likely to lead to the development of excess capacity; and it introduces less bias against the use of produced factors and capital-intensive methods of production. As to its effect on technological progress, that is a matter of debate. In all other respects, however, restricted competition compares unfavorably with free competition and equally or even more unfavorably with perfect competition. It fails to lead to efficient distribution among consumers and efficient specialization among workers. It puts no pressure on the individual producer to maintain the technological efficiency of his firm. It is likely to fall short of free competition in insuring an efficient allocation of resources and output among the several members of an industry. It probably falls seriously short of free competition as regards the economic efficiency of the proportions in which final products are produced and in which resources—especially original resources—are utilized. Last, but not least, restricted competition gives rise to a much more unequal distribution of income than would either free or perfect competition.

BIBLIOGRAPHICAL NOTE

For a bibliography on the subject matter of this chapter the reader is referred to the Bibliographical Note at the end of Chapter XVI. See also Joseph A. Schumpeter, *Capitalism, Socialism, and Democracy* (New York: Harper & Bros., 1942), Part II.

CHAPTER XXI

THE ROLE OF THE STATE

THIS chapter is in the nature of a conclusion and summary. In our detailed discussion of the different forms of competition, we paid special attention to their shortcomings; and this naturally raises the question as to what can be and what has been done about these shortcomings. The main function of economic policy is considered by most economists to be the maintenance of employment and price stability; but the state has important functions to fulfill also in remedying the shortcomings with which we have been concerned. To attempt a full discussion of these functions would lie far beyond the scope of this book; but they must at least be stated and some of the related problems mentioned.

It is convenient to begin with a short discussion of the role of the state in remedying those shortcomings of the competitive system which would exist even under perfect competition. We pointed out in the Note to Chapter VIII that perfect competition would not insure perfect efficiency if there were differences between social and private marginal value and social and private marginal product; and we also discussed several forms of government action aimed at correcting such situations. It is well to bear in mind that, in the past, public policy in the economic sphere has largely been limited to such measures and similar ones. The imposition of protective tariffs, for example, was for a long time considered the only legitimate interference by the state with the free play of the market.

A second function of the state, closely related to the first, is the provision of services whose very nature is such that the whole community benefits by them collectively. National defense, police protection, public-health measures, and the provision of roads, public parks, are the main examples; and they, too, were discussed in the Note to Chapter VIII.

A shortcoming of the competitive system which arises especially under perfect or nearly perfect competition is the extreme variability and dynamic inefficiency of some markets. This was discussed in detail in Chapter X. The obvious examples are the markets for staple farm products; and almost the entire farm policy of the United States federal government may be said to be aimed at solving this problem.

Throughout the entire discussion of Part II, and especially in Chapters IV, V, VIII, and IX, we emphasized the fact that an equitable distribution of income would hardly be achieved even under perfect competition. Here again, most governments have assumed responsibility at least for mitigating extreme inequities. This has been done in various ways. Unemployment compensation and old-age and survivors' insurance try to even out fluctuations over time in the individual's income. Public assistance and work relief are designed to provide a minimum standard of living for all; whereas free education, free health services, and low-cost public housing aim at mitigating inequalities by assuring everybody of certain basic necessities. Progressive income taxation, although originally not aimed at mitigating inequalities of income, certainly has this effect; and in some countries, it has now become an important device used deliberately for this purpose.

The above summary classification covers the main policies aimed at mitigating the shortcomings of the competitive system that would occur even under perfect competition; and we can now proceed to a somewhat more detailed discussion of the policies that are designed to eliminate or offset the particular shortcomings due to the imperfectly competitive nature of our economy. These measures can be grouped into two broad classes. The first includes the measures that combat monopoly and try to remove the *conditions* that make for monopoly and restricted competition. The second comprises those measures that try to offset the undesirable *effects* of monopoly and restricted competition. Both types of measures exist side by side in the American economy as well as in all other free-enterprise economies. Nevertheless, the classification is a useful one, because it corresponds to two schools of thought, the differences between which are perhaps the main dividing line between economists today.

Of the measures that try to combat monopoly, the most obvious and best known is antitrust legislation. This aims primarily at preventing the formation of outright monopoly and the conclusion of restrictive agreements. The success of such legislation, however, has been relatively limited, owing to the difficulties encountered in its enforcement.

Other measures have tried to prevent aggressive competition, which aims at the establishment of monopoly. Safeguards against unfair competition and unfair trade practices belong in this category, but these are double-edged weapons which often favor monopoly. This was discussed in section 2a of Chapter XVII.

More successful in some respects have been measures designed to eliminate restraints on entry. It will be recalled that we made restraints on entry the basis of our definition of restricted competition; and the elimination of such restraints must be the basic aim of any economic policy which tries to combat monopoly. Indeed, one of the earliest measures of public policy in this group was the provision of free public education, one of whose aims is to give everybody equal opportunities to acquire the knowledge and training required for entry to many occupations. Another closely related institution in this country was the Fair Employment Practices Commission, which, for the duration of World War II, barred discrimination among employees on racial, religious, and other grounds.

Yet another measure aimed at or resulting in a greater equality of opportunity is the inheritance tax. John Stuart Mill proposed to set an upper limit to the total amount any one person could inherit; and, whereas inheritance taxes in force at present do not go nearly so far, they do have an equalizing influence, especially in the long run. Inheritance taxes are especially important in equalizing opportunities in business, where so much hinges on the ownership of funds.

Another measure aimed at giving businessmen greater equality of opportunity was the setting-up of the Reconstruction Finance Corporation in the United States and of the Industrial and Commercial Finance Corporation and the Finance Corporation for Industry in Great Britain. All these institutions have had as one of their purposes the removal or reduction of the small businessman's handicap in the capital market by enabling him to obtain loans on the same terms as those available to large corporations.

A measure that has not yet been widely used but that, if used on a large scale, could result in giving businessmen freer access to many markets, is grade labeling. The primary aim of grade labeling is to protect the uninformed consumer and to facilitate his task of making rational decisions in the market. While this aim is valuable in itself, grade labeling and other such measures have the further important result of facilitating entry to industries that cater to uninformed markets. Anything that helps the buyer compare the relative merits of competing goods makes him less dependent on brand names, advertising, and the producer's reputation; and this, in turn, lowers the value of the established firm's goodwill and the cost of entry which newcomers have to pay. Indeed, this last effect explains the strong opposition which such measures have encountered.

Many of the above measures have fallen short of their aim to maintain free competition—most often for political reasons, with which we shall not be concerned here. It will be useful, however, to ask ourselves the question: What could be accomplished by the above measures and similar ones under ideal circumstances, that is, under the conditions most favorable to their success?

Assuming that public policy were fully successful in eliminating all restraints on entry deliberately imposed by business, professional groups, and unions; and that it would succeed in providing consumers with enough information to render negligible the importance of goodwill and the protection it secures for the established firm; even then there would still remain one important restraint on entry which cannot be removed by any legislation: the economies of large-scale production. However successful the fight against monopoly might be, economies of scale would still call, in many industries, for firms that are large in size and small in number. Even if antitrust legislation succeeded in preventing restrictive agreements and in breaking up outright monopoly, it could hardly prevent an oligopoly situation in industries in which firms are large and few; and we saw in Chapter XVII that there is very little difference between oligopoly and monopoly from the point of view of income distribution; and what difference there is from the point of view of efficiency may well be in favor of monopoly. It seems, therefore, that the economies of mass production would keep even a full-fledged and otherwise successful fight against monopoly from establishing free competition throughout the economy.

Futhermore, let us also remember that even free competition, while it comes reasonably near the perfect efficiency of pure competition in many respects, does have some undesirable features. For one thing, as a comparison of sections 3 of Chapters XVI and XX will show, the efficiency of job allocation might well be lower under free competition than when labor is organized into unions. For another, free competition is likely to lead to the formation of excess productive capacity and to the establishment of too many business firms—a form of inefficiency which restraints on entry will prevent. This was explained in sections 5*b* of Chapters XVI and XX. Yet another respect in which free competition compares unfavorably with restricted competition is the underutilization of produced factors and capital-intensive methods of production, to which free competition gives rise. This was shown in section 6c of Chapter XVI and section 6b of Chapter XX. Furthermore, if it should be true, as is often maintained, that scientific progress in our time is largely the achievement of giant corporations, then this would be a further and very important argument in favor of restricted as against free competition. This was discussed in section 4a of Chapter XX. Finally, let us also remember that the monopolistic organization of labor into unions and of farmers and consumers into co-operatives is defensive in nature and tries to redress the balance that in its absence would be wholly in favor of the business community.[1]

It is quite possible that these shortcomings of free competition would be small compared to those of restricted competition. We must bear in mind, however, that free competition has its shortcomings, and that these shortcomings go beyond a mere divergence between the mathematical perfection of the perfectly competitive model and the inevitable imperfections of a practical approximation to it.

These considerations, as well as skepticism about the feasibility of the fight against monopoly, have led many economists to advocate that we accept monopoly as inevitable in our economy; and that public policy, instead of fighting a losing battle against it, should try to control what monopoly there is and to offset its inefficiencies and other undesirable consequences.

This brings us to a consideration of our second class of measures: those that are designed to offset the effects of monopoly and restricted competition. The school of thought which favors such measures is as old as the belief in competition itself. The early protagonists of the competitive system realized that there were some fields of activity in which competition could not be relied upon to regulate economic organization and income distribution; they believed, therefore, that in these fields either a state monopoly should be established or the market behavior of private monoplies should be subjected to regulation by the state. Such monopolies were regarded as natural monoplies and included the railways, public utilities, and means of public communication like the telephone and telegraph. In Belgium, the country that first built railways on the Continent of Europe, there was a long parliamentary debate in the 1830's on whether railway construction was a legitimate field for private enterprise; and the final decision was in favor of state action. In England, similar considerations led to the establishment of a Royal Commission to control the rate policy of private railway com-

---

[1] It might well be, however, that labor and farmers would gain on balance by the simultaneous abolition of monopoly on both sides of the fence.

panies—an example that was followed also in this country. In a similar way and for the same reasons, public utilities and means of public communications are, in most countries, either in public ownership or at least subject to public regulation.

Another form of public policy which belongs to this category is the establishment of publicly owned firms, which compete with private firms and through their competition force the latter to pursue a more competitive market policy than they would otherwise adopt. In this country, low-cost public housing and the power plants of the Tennessee Valley Authority are the main examples of this type of policy.

A further function for which the state has recently assumed responsibility in many countries in order to offset the undesirable effects of monopoly is mediation and arbitration (sometimes compulsory arbitration) between labor and management. We saw in our discussion of restricted competiton that one of its important characteristics is the predominance of large firms and of collective action by large groups, which in many markets has led to the establishment (or re-establishment) of bargaining—often isolated bargaining—as the normal form of settling trade relations. In Chapter XIX, we discussed in detail the favorable consequences of bargaining as a form of trade; but it also has an unfavorable consequence: it can embitter and render violent the trade relations between the bargaining parties. This was mentioned in Chapter II (sec. 2), where we pointed out that an important argument in favor of competition is its pacifying influence on trade relations. The decline of competition, therefore, calls for some other moderating influence; and in the labor market, where the need seems particularly great, many governments have found it necessary to step in to fill the void.

Of all the different forms of public policy, however, that aim at offsetting the effects of monopoly and restricted competition, public ownership and public price regulation are by far the most important. In nineteenth-century economic thinking the scope for public ownership and public price regulation was strictly limited to those narrowly defined natural monopolies mentioned above. In the meantime, however, thinking on these matters has changed, especially in Europe; and today, many economists and others favor a considerable extension of state ownership and public price regulation.

There are several reasons for this, not all of which are economic. For one thing, the development of mass-production methods has rendered the optimum size of the productive unit so large in some of the heavy industries as to turn them into natural monopolies, at least in smaller countries. For another, political and military considerations have, in some countries, led to the belief that private control of certain strategic industries is undesirable. In France, this was among the main reasons for the nationalization of air transport, the banking system, and the sources of power (coal, electricity, gas, and oil) under the De Gaulle government in the period immediately following the second World War. Yet another reason, already mentioned, is the belief that restricted competition has serious shortcomings as regards both efficiency and equity, and that the scope for improvement by antimonopoly legislation is very limited. Last, but not least, the rapid pace of industrialization in Soviet Russia and the wartime experience of Western countries with economic planning have persuaded many of the efficacy of central planning.

Whether such confidence is justified remains yet to be seen. The experience of Great Britain, for example, with postwar planning and the postwar continuation of wartime controls has not been an unqualified success and has received criticism from many quarters. Some of the shortcomings of restricted competition can probably be eliminated by the extension of state control; but this may well create more problems than it solves.

Furthermore, even if it would improve the efficiency of economic organization and the equity of distribution, the extension of state control over economic affairs might still be undesirable for political reasons. The nature of political institutions depends to a great extent on the nature and form of economic organization; and if it should be found that the extension of state control beyond a certain limit would endanger our political institutions, this could be sufficient reason against such extension of state control, even if purely economic considerations should favor it. The question of where exactly this limit lies and what forms of economic policy stay within it is one of the major problems of our time, and it is by no means settled. We have, however, reached the frontier between economic and political theory; and we shall not cross it.

BIBLIOGRAPHICAL NOTE

For the best and most complete discussion of the subject matter of this chapter, see Corwin D. Edwards, *Maintaining Competition—Requisites of a Governmental Policy* (New York: McGraw-Hill Book Co., Inc., 1949).

Index

GEORGE ALLEN & UNWIN LTD

London: 40 Museum Street, W.C.1.

Auckland: Box 36013, Northcote Central
Bombay: 15 Graham Road, Ballard Estate, Bombay 1
Bridgetown: P.O. Box 222
Buenos Aires: Escritorio 454-459, Florida 165
Calcutta: 17 Chittaranjan Avenue, Calcutta 13
Cape Town: 68 Shortmarket Street
Hong Kong: 44 Mody Road, Kowloon
Ibadan: P.O. Box 62
Karachi: Karachi Chambers, McLeod Road
Madras: Mohan Mansions, 38c Mount Road, Madras 6
Mexico: Villalongin 32-10, Piso, Mexico 5, D.F.
Nairobi: P.O. Box 4536
New Delhi: 13-14 Asaf Ali Road, New Delhi 1
Ontario: 81 Curlew Drive, Don Mills
Philippines: 7 Waling-Waling Street, Roxas District,
Quezon City
São Paulo: Caixa Postal 8675
Singapore: 36c Prinsep Street, Singapore 7
Sydney, N.S.W.: Bradbury House, 55 York Street
Tokyo: 10 Kanda-Ogawamachi, 3-Chome, Chiyoda-Ku

READINGS IN THE THEORY
OF INTERNATIONAL TRADE

38s. net

Compiled by Lord Keynes, Fritz Machlup, Joan Robinson and others, this volume brings together timely topics.

"Coupled with a comprehensive and systematic article bibliography, the papers here reproduced provide an indispensable survey of modern theory from 1923 *to* 1947."

THE ECONOMIST

READINGS IN BUSINESS
CYCLE THEORY

30s. net

An intimate analysis of the Business Cycle Theory by Professors D. H. Robertson and Joseph A. Schumpeter, R. G. Hawtrey and others in which the articles included give a comprehensive and well integrated study of subjects, such as Saving, Investments, Interest Rate Theory, Multiplier and Acceleration Principles, Fiscal Policy and other specific problems of importance. A classified, well-indexed bibliography is included.

READINGS IN THE THEORY
OF INCOME DISTRIBUTION

45s. net

The book is divided into six parts: Concept of Income and Distribution, Production Function and Marginal Productivity, Wages, Interest, Profit and Rent. There are many articles in each section and several writers of international fame are included—Lord Keynes, Dr. Lange, Professor Hayek and others.

READINGS IN MONETARY THEORY
Demy 8vo.   *35s. net*

This addition to the series of republished articles sponsored by the American Economic Association contains the most important articles on monetary theory and policy published since 1900. A complete bibliography adds to its value for students or for reference use.

The book is divided into four parts. 1. Integration of the Theory of Money and the Theory of Price. 2. The Demand For and the Supply of Money—The Value of Money. 3. Money, the Rate of Interest and Employment. 4. Monetary Policy.

Amongst the eminent contributors are J. R. Hicks, J. E. Meade, R. G. Hawtrey, D. H. Robertson, A. C. Pigou, and Gustav Cassel.

A STUDY IN THE THEORY OF INFLATION

by Dr. Bent Hansen

Demy 8vo.   *25s. net*

This is a study of some of the central economic problems of our post-war world, in particular of suppressed inflation. After his introductory chapters the author develops a monetary theory for suppressed inflation. He deals much more explicitly than is usual in ordinary "Keynesian" theory with the problem of disequilibrium in the labour market, i.e. *overfull employment*. He discusses the market effects of price and wage control, and surveys various measures for abolishing suppressed inflation. The results of changes in productivity are closely considered.

Dr. Hansen also deals with open inflation, with particular regard to scarcities of goods and labour, and an attempt is made to generalize the results obtained in the form of a Walrassian system of equations, without presupposing a static equilibrium. The author thus builds a bridge between ordinary static equilibrium theory and the theory of inflation. Finally he examines the problem of monetary equilibrium, i.e. that of full employment with a stable price-level.

APPLIED ECONOMICS

by Professor A. J. Brown

Demy 8vo.   *2nd impression 18s. net*

A study of the economic transformation of the Great Powers and some other countries, first in the period of rearmament and then in the war, supplemented by an analysis of the world-wide inflation resulting from the war.

AN OUTLINE OF THE SCIENCE
OF POLITICAL ECONOMY

by Nassau Senior

Demy 8vo.   *21s. net*

THE LONDON SCHOOL OF
ECONOMICS

by Lord Beveridge

Demy 8vo.   *21s. net*

"As always his writing is brilliant, and his story is marked by a generous appreciation of the helpful co-operation he enjoyed from both the Governors and the entire academic body of the school." SIR ARNOLD PLANT in *John O'Londons*

MONETARY THEORY AND PUBLIC POLICY

by Kenneth K. Kurihara

Demy 8vo.   30s. *net*

Monetary Theory and Public Policy treats systematically the important concepts of modern economic theory, particularly as these concepts apply to problems of money and banking and to related public policy, both national and international. The latest developments in monetary theory, Keynesian and non-Keynesian, are discussed.

Part One is concerned with money and general prices, with problems of inflation as well as those of depression. Inflation is discussed in terms of modern monetary theory rather than in terms of the traditional quantity theory, that is, as an integral part of the general theory of effective demand.

Part Two deals with interest, the consumption function, the savings-investment equilibrium, and related policy discussions. Here the Keynesian and non-Keynesian contributions to economic theory are examined in considerable detail to facilitate later policy consideration.

Part Three provides an application of the Keynesian "income-expenditure" approach to an "open system" economy with foreign economic relations. Various theories about the external value of money, the roles of the International Bank and the International Monetary Fund, the international aspects of depression, the problems of a chronic dollar shortage, and related problems of international currency and finance are considered against the background of the changing international setting.

ECONOMIC AND FINANCIAL ASPECTS OF SOCIAL SECURITY

by J. H. Richardson

Demy 8vo.   30s. *net*

This important book by an experienced authority on social security discusses a subject of vital interest to governments and people everywhere. In all countries social security is still experimental, its principles and methods are being actively reviewed, and nowhere has a final pattern evolved. In many countries the systems have grown piecemeal with numerous anomalies and gaps. Professor Richardson's survey is timely in directing attention to those basic principles and methods which are essential for sound progress.

Specially valuable is the chapter which considers what proportion of the national income can be afforded for social security, and also that on the alternatives of financing by accumulating large funds or by "pay-as-you-go" methods.

FINANCIAL ADMINISTRATION
IN LOCAL GOVERNMENT

by A. H. Marshall

Demy 8vo.   *32s. net*

The financial administration which Local Government demands is as complex as the services are varied and vital. But Dr. Marshall's book on this important subject is neither involved nor fragmentary. Deftly he explains the internal organization of local authorities, describes the responsibilities with which Councils generally charge their Finance Committees, and then analyses stage by stage the methods employed by Chief Financial Officers and their staffs to implement the Council's policies.

THE SOCIAL FOUNDATIONS OF WAGE POLICY

by Barbara Wootton

UNWIN UNVERSITY BOOKS   *Demy 8vo.*   *15s. net*

A STUDY OF CONTEMPORARY BRITISH WAGE AND SALARY STRUCTURE

". . . the pattern of income distribution is essentially a political question. . . . The place for the discussion of wage policy is on the agenda of the political conferences; and the responsibility for . . . action must lie on governments." In quoting the above from this book at the head of a First Leader, *The Times* went on: "It has taken eight years to do it. When . . . Professor Barbara Wootton wrote those words . . . she seemed a voice crying in the silence. Today a wages and income policy is news . . . As Professor Wootton said, the matter is essentially political."

Her message is now more urgent than when it was first written.

INDUSTRIAL CONCILIATION
AND ARBITRATION IN GREAT BRITAIN

by Ian G. Sharp

Demy 8vo.   *25s. net*

In this authoritative book Dr. Sharp traces the development and describes the present organization of conciliation and arbitration in seven major industries in Britain.

In the first part of the book one chapter is devoted to each of the following industries: coal, iron and steel, engineering and shipbuilding, cotton, building, the boot and shoe industry, and railways. Each is dealt with historically, beginning in the middle nineteenth century and going up to the present time, and the organizational development during that period is described. The seven chapters of the second part deal with the role of the State prior to the Act of 1896—under that Act—1914-18—Whitleyism—the Industrial Courts Act of 1919—the Minimum Wage—the effects of World War II.

Dr. Sharp's book is for everyone concerned with industrial relations, whether as a practical negotiator, official, trade union leader, employer, arbitrator, personnel manager, student or teacher.

FISCAL POLICY IN
UNDERDEVELOPED COUNTRIES

by Raja J. Chelliah

Demy 8vo.   25s. net

The central thesis of this important book is an application of recent advances
in the theory of fiscal policy to the promotion of economic development,
while at the same time diminishing inequalities. The author demonstrates
why advanced and underdeveloped countries need different policies, and
thereby makes a distinct contribution to fiscal theory.

The book will interest those concerned with the theory of public finance,
to those responsible for practical policy, and particularly to economists working in underdeveloped areas. What makes it very topical is the growing
awareness of economic problems in general, and in particular the desire to
employ taxation in the service of economic development.

TRADE UNION GROWTH,
STRUCTURE AND POLICY

by H. A. Turner

Demy 8vo.   45s. net

A COMPARATIVE STUDY OF THE COTTON UNIONS
Professor Turner starts with the long history of the textile unions and their
remarkable structures and techniques. By comparing these unions to each
other and to other key unions, he explores those major problems in the
development and present position of trade unionism which are of urgent
public interest.

The author is widely known for his work on arbitration and industrial
relations and this long-awaited study, with its depth of historical analysis
leading to some unexpected conclusions, will be of equal value to the student
of trade unionism and industrial relations and to the economic historian.

THE COMMERCE OF NATIONS

by J. B. Condliffe

Demy 8vo.   36s. net

In *The Commerce of Nations* the author traces the long and fascinating story of
the ebb and flow of world trade from the caravans of the ancient world to the
barter agreements and currency blocks of to-day. And paralleling this account
he presents in skilful summary the important contributions to economic thought
that have influenced policy and practice, such as mercantilism, the pioneering
philosophy of Adam Smith, the bold achievements of the classical economists
led by David Ricardo, the doctrines of the dissenters, and the ideas of John
Maynard Keynes and other modern economists.

THE BRITISH COAL INDUSTRY

by H. Townshend-Rose

Demy 8vo.   *15s. net*

This book is a straightforward account of the British nationalized coal industry. An introductory chapter gives sufficient of the history of the industry during the inter-war years to explain the problems and difficulties which beset it to-day. Then follows an account of the complex operations entailed in the transfer of the industry to public ownership. The author examines the constitutional position of the National Coal Board and explains in detail the new organization which has been set up at national level, in divisions and areas, and at the collieries. An explanation is given in simple terms of the way in which coal is mined, and of the processes by which coal products are extracted.

ECONOMIC SURVEY 1919—1939

by Professor W. Arthur Lewis

Demy 8vo.   UNWIN UNIVERSITY BOOK   *paper 15s. net*

Part I deals with the effects of the war, with the re-establishment of production and trade, and with the great depression of the thirties. Part II seeks the lessons of the great experiments in economic policy made by Britain, Germany, France, the U.S.A., Japan and the Soviet Union in the 1930's. And finally Part III is concerned with trends in world economic development, comparing the inter-war years with pre-war years in search of fundamental change.

"Any history or analysis of the economy events of the inter-war years is likely to be either ponderously unreadable or inaccurately sketchy. Professor Lewis has contrived with great skill to provide something which is neither; which, without pretending more than a 'starting point,' a first approximation, gives the reader both a perspective against which to set special knowledge or to verify speculations, and a guide to further learning. . . ."

THE ECONOMIST

ECONOMIC THEORY AND WESTERN EUROPEAN INTEGRATION

by Tibor Scitovsky

UNWIN UNIVERSITY BOOKS   *Demy 8vo.*   *12s. 6d. net*

Professor Scitovsky's book was written, to quote his own words, "at a time when Western European integration was little more than a hope and an idea—or rather a number of different ideas, competing, complementary, some even contradictory". His object was to analyse both the advantages and the difficulties at the same technical level, for although the gains seem obvious, both are in fact complex.

Today the E.E.C. has fulfilled many of its hopes and realized many of its ideas. Yet the underlying issues and problems remain, perhaps becoming more pressing than before. This book is a major contribution to their solution and has been reprinted with a new Introduction. As the *Economist* summed it up, "the insight into the realities of business life and the concern with its dynamic propensities that have given Professor Scitovsky a notable place in the study of competition are brought to bear with revealing effect on the potentialities of European integration . . ."

"This is a clearly written and most valuable study"—*International Relations*.

". . . a very good example of a first-class economist at work on a complicated problem."—*Gregorianum.*

GEORGE ALLEN AND UNWIN LTD